DEVELOPMENT AND INSTABILITY:

Political Change
in the Non-Western World

ROBERT P. CLARK, JR.

DEPARTMENT OF POLITICAL SCIENCE
UNIVERSITY OF TENNESSEE AT CHATTANOOGA

Copyright © 1974 by The Dryden Press, a division of
        Holt, Rinehart and Winston, Inc.
All Rights Reserved
Library of Congress Catalog Card Number 73-83343
ISBN: 03-0-85662-0
Printed in the United States of America
4567   090   98765432

To My Wife

Preface

The several score nations of the non-Western world—Asia, Africa, and Latin America—are today the scene of one of the most dramatic of contemporary political events: the development of political capacity. Where once the elites of these countries would have been content to preside over governmental structures, bureaucracies, and parties which are powerless, today the national leadership can settle for nothing less than a fundamental realignment of internal political forces, a transformation which has as its objective the creation of political power sufficient to deal with the enormous economic and social problems of these states.

This book is an attempt to describe this transformation, to analyze the reasons why such change may deteriorate into instability, and to suggest some ways in which this decline or stagnation may be avoided. We began our examination with a portrayal of some of the underlying dimensions of political development. In the course of the first four chapters, we were concerned with shaping the concept of "development" as a tool with which we can better analyze the politics of a developing state. Our concern with the personal, psychological dimension of political change led us to expand on this discussion by introducing some of the attitudinal adjustments which normally occur in a modernizing polity. Finally, we sought to put the development process into context by examining the historical experiences of the United States and the Soviet Union as developing countries, and by examining the ways in which the international system intrudes into the political process of a developing state.

Precisely because the process of political development involves the adjustment of personal attitudes and the reallocation of goods, resources, and values, developing countries seem especially prone to instability. This special susceptibility has led most observers to conclude that the development process is *inherently* destabilizing, but that after a brief period of disruption the developing state will emerge into the clarity and stability of the modern political order (assuming external forces do not exploit and exacerbate the temporary instability).

We proposed to examine in greater detail several questions dealing with the complex relationships between instability and development. We began in Chapter Five by setting forth our belief that development need not be destabilizing, given proper guidance and the correct setting. Two critical variables in the control of instability—the stress of change, and the propensity of development elites (and counter-elites) to take high risks—were the subjects of Chapters Six and Seven. We concluded this section by relating six case studies of incumbent development leaders coping with, or managing, violent threats to their regimes.

To bring our excursion into political development to a close, we looked at several other attempts to devise a suitable "strategy" of developmental change. Since we found that most strategic writing in this field tends to focus either at too high a level of abstraction (the cosmic), or at too low a level (the tactical), we sought a conclusion which would synthesize the various approaches, and yield a useful decision-making model for development leaders. This portion of our study was undertaken with no small amount of misgiving, since we have the greatest respect for the problem of translating the ideas of the academic world into guidelines for the world of action. Nevertheless, it is our conviction that we do not advance understanding of social problems much if we can not address ourselves squarely to the question of what to do to ameliorate them.

Most importantly, in this book we have taken as one of our base assumptions the idea that men *can* influence their political destiny. Leaders of developing states need not accept the verdict of Western behavioral scientists who condemn them to disruption and reversal. Political development, like all social processes, can be subjected to human intervention and guidance. While we cannot dictate with certainty the path a developing state can take, we may certainly throw the weight of human intelligence into the scales to insure that some paths will be more likely than others. The challenge to behavioral science is to demonstrate how this is done, and to show what the costs and benefits of certain strategies may be. It is to this challenge that this book is addressed.

It is customary at this point to express one's gratitude to all those who contributed to the shaping of the final product. In this case, I owe a special debt to three men—Howard Wriggins, Dean Mann, and William Gibbons— each of whom, in his own way, has shown me the benefit to be derived from blending the theoretical and the practical, to turn the knowledge of the academic world to an improvement of the human condition. While these three men may find many of their ideas expressed in these pages, of course it is I, not they, who must bear responsibility for the faithfulness with which I have interpreted their views. And, naturally, I thank my friends in Latin America and Southeast Asia who convinced me of the need to rethink many of the traditional assumptions about the developing world.

Acknowledgments would not be complete without an expression of thanks to Mrs. Dorothy Crisman, who not only typed the manuscript several times, but also saved me from numerous embarrassments of spelling, grammar, and so on. Finally, I wish to thank my wife, who not only has helped me to a better understanding of the political style of Latin America, but who also recognized my need to let my ego show through in this book.

Chattanooga, Tennessee   Robert P. Clark, Jr.
October, 1973

Table of Contents

Part 1

POLITICAL DEVELOPMENT

Chapter 1

THE DEVELOPMENT OF POLITICAL SYSTEMS

This book is concerned with the efforts of leaders of Latin America, Africa, and Asia to bring about substantial changes in the political institutions and processes of their nations in very brief time and under arduous conditions. Their goal, stated very broadly, is to foster the development of their polities in an atmosphere of relative calm, both for the individual and for the system in which he lives. Development is understood by most of these leaders to connote a process through which the political system expands its capabilities, or becomes more capable of performing certain key functions.

Regardless of the ideological bases on which their political system might be founded, citizens the world over look to their political institutions to perform certain tasks which they as individuals are incapable of performing. Each set of political leaders and institutions justifies itself to its people by the manner in which these tasks are performed. These tasks may range from regulating traffic in the capital to building schools in the remote interior of the country, from fielding an impressive army on maneuvers to curing a serious disease which plagues the country, or from harnessing hydroelectric power to administering justice.

We are only just beginning to acquire the knowledge and expertise necessary to trace, in broad outline, the style in which a given political order accomplishes its culturally assigned tasks; and we are even farther away from being able to measure the performance levels of political systems with any degree of

3

accuracy. But this we do know: to an increasing extent throughout the non-Western world, political leaders are committed to raising the capacity of their state to perform crucial tasks. They are seeking to *develop* their political systems.

The way in which economists approach the dual concepts of "growth" and "development" is instructive for the student of political development.[1] For the economist, economic growth implies an increase in the total wealth of the unit of concern (nation, village, firm, and so on) without any concomitant structural changes; an increase in gross national product, for example, would be due simply to an increase in the resources injected into the system. Economic development, on the other hand, is a process defined by the structural transformations which attend it; gross national product rises because the system devises new ways to use present resources more efficiently.

In the same way, analysts of political development must separate mere growth of the political order from those examples of changes which involve some degree of structural alteration. Simply by adding more men to the police force of the central political system, the government has not developed its regulative capability, even though in terms of sheer coercion the state has probably experienced a net increase in capacity. If, on the other hand, the polity redefines the legal relationships between certain individuals or sectors and the state so as to bring these groups within the regulative purview of the government, then we can say that some development of a political nature has occurred.

In approaching the problem of political development from the perspective of an expansion of the capabilities of the state, we recognize that we are suggesting a path which runs counter to the predilections of Western, liberal interpretations of the political order. While hardly anyone contests the idea that the sum total of national economic resources should not be maximized, most students of politics as practiced in Western representative democracies harbor quite substantial doubts about the same kind of expansion of capabilities in the political realm. As we shall explore in Chapter Three, the United States initiated its development sequence in an ideological atmosphere in which the paramount desire was to *limit* the powers of the state, not expand them.[2] This view continues to influence our analytical perspective in examining the performance levels of non-Western states in the mid-1970's.

In adopting the capabilities approach to understanding political development, however, we are not merely bowing to the exigencies of political reality in Asia, Africa, and Latin America, for which the United States Constitution provides little which is visibly transferable. We seek, rather, to provide the student of comparative political behavior with a set of analytical tools with which he can measure political systems as diverse as those of Mexico, Nigeria, and the Philippines, and arrive at some conclusions about the relative performance levels of these, and other, polities. This should by no means imply that we must be insensitive to normative details; the purpose for which a state seeks to expand its capabilities will, and should, continue to be a legitimate concern in the study of political development. We may even some day reach the position in what some call the science of *polimetrics* when we can extend our techniques to concepts of a normative character, such as "liberty," "justice," and so on.[3] As a precursor of these advances, however, we must deepen our understanding of what a political system is capable of doing, what the system's goals are, and how politicians who so desire manage to reduce the gap between the two.

Before introducing our inventory of political system capabilities which will guide us in this opening chapter, it would be well to describe the criteria we intend to use in judging whether a certain state has more or less of a certain capacity. First, in the statistical appendix at the end of the book, we employ several indicators of the order of magnitude of system performance of various capabilities; the *absolute level of performance,* then, is our easiest criterion to quantify using data readily available. In addition, however, we should also be sensitive to changes in the *relative level of performance* by comparing the current performance of State A with either State A at an earlier date, or with State B which is facing similar problems under similar circumstances. Third, we should endeavor to examine the extent to which a system has *institutionalized* the improved capability, meaning the degree to which the system is able to attain improved levels of performance repeatedly and consistently, under varying amounts of pressure. Finally, we are interested in the *flexibility* of state performance, or the system's capability to adjust performance to temporary, abnormally high requirements.

REGULATIVE CAPABILITY

Gabriel Almond and G. B. Powell describe the regulative capability of a political system as the ability of that system to exercise control over the behavior of individuals and groups.[4] Although, as subsequent discussion will make clear, the state's ability to regulate and to extract resources from the society are closely intertwined, we have selected to begin our analysis with the regulative capability, inasmuch as the distinctive character of the political system derives from its alleged legitimate monopoly of the coercive forces in a society. Further, without a firmly established regulative capability, a development leader soon will find that he is diverting precious resources away from the improvement of more productive capabilities and into the sector of pure coercion, simply to avoid being deposed.

A brief glance over the past two decades of development politics in Latin America, Asia, and Africa clearly shows that a leader's concern for his survival is not an idle caprice, nor does it derive from the fears of paranoia. As Howard Wriggins has pointed out, for most leaders in Africa and Asia today (and one could easily add Latin America), the foremost preoccupation has been how to survive in positions of authority while trying to reconcile bitter hatreds and establish a self-sustaining development process.[5] Other sectors of the state clamor for attention; and the reformer is prone to look to the expansion of capabilities of a distributive or symbolic character first. Were we to have the chance to talk with Juan Bosch of the Dominican Republic, Kwame Nkrumah of Ghana, Sukarno of Indonesia, or Fernando Belaunde Terry of Peru, however, surely one of their strongest messages would be that all the grand designs for advancing the society amount to nought if the development elite cannot even muster the power necessary to remain in control of the state's apparatus.

The evidence available indicates that most of the leaders in non-Western states have caught the essence of this fact, and have devoted major sums of resources to enhancing their regulative power, even at the cost of moving more slowly in other areas. A review of internal security forces in some 85 nations in Latin America, Africa, the Middle East, and Asia in 1970 reveals that every one has mobilized, for internal security purposes, some kind of paramilitary force, with the exceptions of the city-state of Singapore and the near-city-state of Uruguay.[6] The remainder report the capability to put into the field units ranging from Syria's Internal Security Camel Corps of 1,500 men and Ghana's worker's brigade of 3,000, up to at least seven states which boast of internal security forces of 100,000 troops or more—Egypt, the People's Republic of China, Taiwan, India, Indonesia, Pakistan, and Brazil. At the extreme end of the scale comes the Republic of Vietnam which, with a population of only some 18 million, claims a paramilitary force of more than 700,000 men!

The strengthening of the national police force of Japan during the first 35 years of the modernizing Meiji regime illustrates well the proposition that a high priority must be placed on improving the regulative capability of a rapidly developing state.[7] In 1874, seven years after the introduction of the Meiji constitution, the first police reform was undertaken, resulting in the removal of the police force from the jurisdiction of the Ministry of Justice to the Ministry of Home Affairs. There then followed a restructuring of the police which left the force a more unified, tightly organized unit under much closer national control and scrutiny. The entire operation was guided and inspired by one Kawaji Toshiyoshi, the first Chief of the Metropolitan Police Board of Tokyo, who had traveled throughout Europe in 1872 and 1873, and who attempted to put into practice the European standards which he had observed. As Kawaji reported upon his return, "The police are a daily cure and remedy to a state, as everyday hygiene is to an individual. The police are able to protect good citizens and nurture the active force of a country. For this reason, those who desired to make their imperial powers glorious and extend their territories paid attention to these facts. . . . the establishment of the police is an absolute necessity in strengthening the state and setting up relations with foreign nations."[8]

The nationalization and centralization of the police force was merely the first step in Japan's expansion of its regulative capabilities. In 1889, the police were granted substantial powers of control and regulation over public health and trade through the issuing of police ordinances, to cover areas of public policy not then administered by statute. In 1885 and again in 1908, the police were given additional power to adjudicate minor offenses in connection with these so-called "police ordinances," thereby making of the police chief in each prefecture an auxiliary of the nation's judicial system. Finally, in 1900, the police received sweeping powers of enforcement and adjudication of laws through the Law of Administrative Execution. Included in these provisions were the authority to imprison persons merely suspected of crimes ("preventive detention"), the right to enter private dwellings under specified circumstances, the right to seize weapons and retain them in custody under certain conditions, and the power to enforce compliance with certain laws through compulsory execution. All these laws were administered without recourse to warrants issued by judicial authorities.

During the first half century of the development of the Japanese political system, the centralized police force provided the cutting edge to control and disarm threats against the government in power. The Japanese were quite unabashed about admitting that the police force, recruited from unemployed ex-samurai, was used frequently to put down insurrections and disturbances from 1875 to 1925. With their enhanced powers and jurisdiction, the Japanese national police force became one of the major pillars supporting the system's rapid development effort.

So natural did the Japanese consider this state of affairs that, when the American Occupation Forces under General Douglas MacArthur attempted to "democratize" the police by decentralizing their control and stripping them of many of their judicial powers, the Japanese immediately sensed a vacuum in the regulative capability of the state. Local government officials protested that the Occupation reforms would leave the police weakened and alienated from the people, at a time when the Japanese government was under assault from subversive forces. In 1951, with the impact of the Korean War and the confrontation between the United States and the Soviet Union being felt on the Occupation, the police laws began to revert to their pre-1945 state. Finally, in 1954, the Japanese police system was returned to a condition somewhat resembling its traditional form, albeit with more strictly curtailed powers. Inasmuch as some 80 percent of the affected towns and villages had voted to yield up their local control over police in favor of coming under the jurisdiction of Tokyo, it is apparent that the bulk of the Japanese consider a nationalized police force to be a normal component of their state's regulative capabilities.

A political system does not increase its regulative capabilities simply by expanding its coercive power, although for most of our development elites that could quite properly be considered an essential prerequisite for such an increase. In addition to building the centralized structures of coercion, however, a developing polity must broaden its domain of authority by extending its regulative power into areas of the society previously beyond the control of the national government.

Certainly a key indicator of underdevelopment in a political sense is the existence of any substantial sectors in the country which hold a kind of residual sovereignty. Charles Anderson, in his discussion of economic policy-making in Latin America, describes at least three important economic groups—the subsistence farmer, the enormous agricultural estate (called *hacienda*), and the foreign extractive industry—which occupy enclaves within the national territory. They are isolated from the currents of national economic life; and they resist regulation directed from the national capital.[9] For Aristide Zolberg, the party-states of West Africa—Ghana, Ivory Coast, Senegal, Mali, and Guinea —suffer from the same affliction. Within their national societies exist dual political communities side by side—one is modern and governed from the capital, and the other tribal and traditional, governed by chieftains who owe little or no allegiance to the national development elite.[10] For any development leadership, one of their first priorities must be to erode the barriers which cut these residual political spaces off from the exercise of central governmental authority and regulation.

The physical process of expanding the effective realm of a developing polity across the entire surface of its national territory is apt to be highly uneven, as it is tied inevitably to the extension of lines of communication and other physical facilities. As a recent analysis of the spatial process of the spread of modernization in Tanzania illustrates, the basic pattern of the impact of modernization on the nation had already been formed by the infrastructural improvements made by the British during the colonial period.[11] In the first instance, these improvements consisted of roads and railway facilities; subsequently, they were broadened to include agricultural extension agents, police units, hospitals and clinics, and communications channels. Along these lines of communication, clusters or nodes of modernization began to spring up, indicating the discontinuous process by which regulation spread out from the capital, Dar es Salaam. Even after independence was granted to the nation in 1961, the "modern" political space of Tanzania was restricted almost entirely to the urban clusters to which the central authority had succeeded in extending its regulative capability. If the example of Tanzania is any guide, then, a developing polity concerned about broadening its domain must attend first to the basic infrastructure of the country; without these facilities, the regulative capability of the state will be condemned to being bottled up within the capital city and its tightly constricted hinterland.[12]

In addition to the spatial process of the growth of a political system's domain, however, we must also consider the conceptual or ideological expansion which has to accompany the process of political development. Briefly, what is at stake is the societal definition of precisely which aspects of human behavior may appropriately be encompassed within the jurisdiction of the state. As Zolberg has pointed out,[13] the governments of West Africa simply do not enjoy the power to regulate many of those features of human behavior —economic relations, social status, and others—which have been under the domain of the governments of industrial democracies for decades. Further, the boundaries placed around the legitimate exercise of state power may also originate in the international system as the relatively weak, developing state finds itself hemmed in by foreign enclaves—mining, petroleum, banking, electric power, transportation, and many others—which defy the regulatory authority of the host nation.

In reply to these restrictions, the developing states have turned to the dual ideologies of *socialism* and *nationalism* to expand the regulative capability of the state, and, in so doing, to define (perhaps for the first time) the nature of the nation-state. To be sure, doctrines of socialism and nationalism vary widely in their pronouncement and implementation throughout the non-Western world.[14] At one end of the spectrum (excluding the doctrinaire Marxist-Leninist states, such as North Korea), we would find the radical socialism of Ghana's Nkrumah or of Indonesia's Sukarno. Their intent clearly was to use state power to mobilize all the resources of the total society to fight the problems of economic underdevelopment, national weakness, and social maladjustment. Similar in character but varying in direction would be the socialist regimes in Cuba under Castro, Algeria under Ben Bella, and Mexico between 1920 and 1940. These movements, while they imply an enormous growth of central government regulative capability, directed much of their initial reform thrust toward the peasant sector of the society, inasmuch as it was that sector which provided the regime with much of its early support. Somewhat more conservative in nature would be the moderate reform socialist parties of the Democratic Left in Latin America—*Aprista* in Peru, Democratic Action in Venezuela, the Mexican revolutionary leaders after about 1940 —as well as several of the pragmatic socialist regimes in the Middle East and Asia, for example the Congress Party of India. These groups have argued that expansion of state power should be aimed at guiding the modern sector of the economy toward behavior which is more in keeping with the social welfare needs of the nation. For these development elites, taxation and administrative regulation are the tools of social reform, in contrast to the weapons of expropriation, nationalization, and state ownership of the economy's critical sectors, as they have been used in the more radical of the socialist states. Finally, there are certain regimes, such as those of El Salvador or Malaysia, which have eschewed all labels which connote socialism, yet which nevertheless have sought to expand state power to guide, regulate, and, in some cases, create portions of a modern, developed society. Whatever the ideology wielded to justify the actual expansion of a political system's authority, the fact remains that, for an overwhelming majority of nations in Latin America, Africa, and Asia, the first item on their agenda of reform has been, and will continue to be, a strengthening of their capability to regulate their nation.

EXTRACTIVE CAPABILITY

As the reader has probably already noted, the expansion of a state's regulative capability requires a simultaneous and parallel increase in the extraction of resources—human and economic—from the broader society. As Almond and Powell point out, the ability of a system to draw on its social environment for material resources and personnel constitutes a major limitation on the state's ability to perform other critical services.[15] Thus, we should want to consider the system's extractive capability as being simply one of the more important facets of the regulation of the society.

It seems that even the most simple example of regulation must involve some degree of resource extraction from the society. When a state expands its capacity to enforce laws and to maintain public order, for example, it is also committed to recruiting more police officers, to buying more equipment, to increasing the number of courts and judges and detention facilities to handle criminals, and so on. Regulation and resource extraction together, then, form the base from which a polity's development effort must be launched.

In many instances, developing elites in the non-Western world have seen their plans for system expansion fall short of the goal for want of resources. Helio Jaguaribe cites the case of Brazil in the early 1960's, where an impressive growth rate was allowed to deteriorate because the state's extractive pattern did not keep pace with government expenditures. Although the Brazilian economy had performed well through the latter half of the 1950's, by the end of the administration of President Juscelino Kubitschek (1955-1960), structural distortions had begun to appear, due principally to the inability of the central government to fund badly needed projects. While government expenditures grew from 12.4 percent of gross domestic product in 1960, to 18.5 percent in 1963, government *revenues* hovered steady at about 9.0 percent of GDP, producing thereby a rapidly expanding government deficit. During the same four-year period, the budget deficit grew from 13.7 percent of the GDP, to 105.1 percent, leading to a sharp expansion in the amount of currency in the system, galloping inflation, and systemic instability. The result was military intervention against the reform government of Joao Goulart in 1964.[16]

The place of resource extraction in defining the pace of economic and political development throughout the non-Western world is magnified by the fact that, in almost all cases, the state must assume the major role in mobilizing the funds needed for the development effort.[17] The reason for this lies in the enormous burden thrust upon the state to construct the requisite infrastructure, or social overhead facilities, in order to expand the society's general welfare. The responsibilities for social overhead capital improvements in a developing country go far beyond those more familiar investments in the public sector of an industrialized democracy, such as schools and roads. In all probability, the government of a developing nation in the 1970's will find itself called upon to finance the construction of such projects as communications networks, mass transportation facilities, industrial enterprises, minerals extraction operations, and many others. The government of a developed country has only to provide a favorable climate, and private investment is expected to flow into these sectors. The government of a state in Latin America, Africa, or Asia, on the contrary, finds that it must mobilize and direct the funds if these facilities are to be built at all. The vicious circle of the typical under-developed country—low income, high propensity to consume, low savings, and low investment—means that there usually exist few, if any, exploitable funds to invest in any but the most certain of business enterprises.

There are only a limited number of places from which a development elite can extract the needed resources. The major developed states of the international system can provide funds through foreign economic assistance programs; but these sources, discussed in greater detail in Chapter Four, attach substantial "strings" to their contributions, and the repayment of the loans quickly becomes an onerous burden which outweighs any receipt of new funds. Many non-Western states have sought financial salvation through the levying of an indirect tax on exports; these taxes are easy to collect, and they can yield a windfall profit if raw materials prices are driven up for a time on the world market. The flaw in relying too much on this source is that most of our countries have monocultural economies, dominated by only one or two crops or minerals. Whether the case is coffee in El Salvador, or oil in Venezuela, or copper in Chile, or cocoa in Ghana, the government which depends on one single export commodity stands to lose a great deal if the market fluctuates and fails to deliver a constant and predictable revenue for development purposes.

When the development leader turns to his domestic economy for resources, the alternatives do not appear to be very much brighter. He finds that he must either deprive certain sectors of some part of their consumption level, by taxing their wealth or income, or he must literally create the funds by expanding the money supply through the nation's banking system. As Albert O. Hirschman has discovered in the case of Chile, the latter solution—bringing with it the inevitable climbing inflation rate—has been necessary to avoid a head-on conflict between economic sectors who were not predisposed to compromise. In Chile, inflation has served as a substitute for governmental decisions involving the extraction of resources, when it appeared that the government simply did not have the authority necessary to implement any genuine extractive decisions.[18]

Thus, we are brought to consider the most critical of all extractive alternatives—the direct tax on personal and corporate income, and other classes of private wealth. For both economic and political reasons, the direct tax on income has received great attention from development leaders interested in expanding their extractive capabilities. The fact is, however, that the overall impact of direct taxation in the typical non-Western, developing country is considerably less than what it ideally should be. As measured against the typical Western industrialized democracy, which annually extracts 25–30 percent of its gross national product in taxation, the less developed states of Latin America, Africa, and Asia usually manage to take out 8–15 percent of GNP in this manner.[19]

Several factors combine to aggravate the developing country's inability to tax. First, income is distributed in a highly unequal fashion, with a very large percentage of the wealth concentrated in the hands of a very few persons. This fact, in itself, would not necessarily be damaging to a development effort, were it not also the case that the overall tax burdens in many less developed countries tends to be sharply *regressive.* That is, the net impact of taxation falls as the income level goes up, producing thereby a situation in which the lower classes pay more, proportionately, than do the wealthier members of the society. The result is that a great amount of personal wealth goes untaxed.

The tax structure in the Philippines offers a useful example of how a regressive tax can work in practice. In 1960, the tax structure provided for a *decline* in the percentage of tax imposed on income and property, as the income *rose* from 500 pesos to 6,999 pesos per year. Thereafter, the tax burden tended to increase along with income. This mild attempt at progressivity was negated, however, by a regressive sales tax, which took most of the money paid through taxes by the poorer classes. The overall thrust of the Philippines tax policy, then, was to place the greatest burden on those least able to pay.[20]

As the above cited article by Kaldor points out, the taxation capability of many underdeveloped countries suffers from not being able to reach most of the major sources of wealth in the nation's economy. Although highly progressive tax rates exist on paper, for example, they tend to cover only earned income; the wealthiest sectors of non-Western countries, however, derive large portions of their income from rents, profits, and land, sources which prove difficult to tax in actual practice. The land tax, in particular, while one of the most ancient sources of government revenue, has now become virtually useless in most cases, due to the myriad ways in which the landed gentry of a nation can avoid payment, the ambiguous nature of land ownership, and the admitted difficulty in adjusting the tax rate to keep pace with the increase in land values. While the land tax may have some limited value as a device to force land owners to put their idle land into agricultural production,[21] it has not proved to be of great significance as a technique for extracting more financial resources from the economy.

Because of the many difficulties which attend the expansion of a political system's ability to tax its citizens, we should be especially careful to note those few cases where a development elite has been able to increase its extractive capabilities. One such important case has been that of Japan, apparently the first non-Western state to create and administer effectively a tax on personal and corporate income.[22] Japan's first income tax law was put into effect in 1887, as a close copy of a proposal made by a German financial adviser to the Japanese government some 13 years previously. The law seems fairly primitive by modern standards; but it was significant for that period in that it contained the principle of progressive taxation, and it was a tax system administered by the central political authority. By comparison, the United States was not to enact a system of this sort until 1913. While the income tax and corporate tax combined (the two were treated as similar for collection purposes) provided

only about 1.5 percent of Japan's governmenta
established the base from which the government's
funds could be increased.

From 1899 to World War II, the Japanese income
depth and breadth of coverage. The tax impact becan
sive as a result of emergency tax increases to finance tı
1904–1905, and the Sino-Japanese War, 1937–1938. As
taxes levied to finance these wars were calculated to affec
most adversely, and the tax instruments which enacted t.
in effect after the wars had terminated. The taxes of 190·   levied to
finance the Russo-Japanese War, for example, lasted untıl 1913, when they
were replaced by a fundamental reform of the entire tax system, which retained
the steep progressive rates of the war emergency laws. In this way, the Japanese government expanded sharply its extractive capability through a modern
and far-reaching income and corporate tax which laid the basis for its substantial progress in other fields.[23] By 1939, personal and corporate income taxes
provided the Japanese government with 30.59 percent of total revenue.

The occupation of Japan by United States forces had the effect of modernizing the tax codes even more by lessening the burden of taxation on those
sectors with lower incomes, and spreading the burden more evenly throughout
the upper income classes. Personal income was separated from corporate, and
differential rates were applied to extract the necessary funds while not inhibit-
ing capital investment. The withholding device was introduced for certain
categories of income, thereby making the entire system more efficient. Finally,
the overall impact of the tax structure was broadened to the point where the
two income taxes together—personal and corporate—accounted for more than
half of all Japanese government revenue. In 1951, for example, these taxes
contributed some 56.54 percent of all central government income, quite an
expansion from the tax's early days when it was barely noticeable in the
government's overall income structure. Without the broad-scale extraction of
resources by the Japanese government on an ever-increasing scale from 1889
to 1955, it is difficult indeed to visualize how Japan could have sustained its
remarkable political development effort.

DISTRIBUTIVE CAPABILITY

Although regulation and extraction are the capabilities which form the base
for launching the development effort, the broad configurations of the "developed" political system—the end product, as it were—will be defined by the
way in which the polity increases its other capabilities—distributive, symbolic,
and responsive. State actions undertaken to distribute resources, create symbols, and respond to public needs will be determined by the development elite's
answers to these questions: For whose benefit is development sought? Who is
being asked to pay for development? In what terms should we justify the steps

velop the political system? Thus, it is at this level of political
ment that ideological predilections and local power considerations
n to weigh heavily in molding and directing policy outputs; and it is at this
point that we can begin to discern more clearly some important differences in
styles of development policy.

In general terms, the distributive capability of the state refers to the system's
ability to make discriminating choices about which sectors of the society will
receive which benefits, as well as which sectors will bear the burdens of
state-imposed sacrifices.[24] It is clear that the distribution of goods, services,
and status by the political system follows as an inherent feature of the extractive process described earlier. Resources extracted, in the shape of taxes, say,
must eventually "go" somewhere; that is, the government must make some
kind of distributive decision about what to do with these resources.

Distributive decisions may vary, however, in the degree to which they are
intended to alter fundamentally the prevailing pattern of resource allocation
in the society. Conservative or nondevelopmental decisions would result in
little disturbance in the societal status quo, and thus would require little
distributive *capability.* An example of such a distributive decision would be
the raising of taxes for the sole purpose of increasing the size of the nation's
armed forces to meet the threat of an external attack. At the other end of the
spectrum one finds distributive decisions of a most radical nature, in that they
seek fundamental changes in the manner by which society had previously
allocated its costs and benefits; these choices obviously require greatly enhanced distributive powers. The expropriation of private farms and redistribution of the land to peasants is such a policy.

The history of political development in the non-Western world is littered
with the names of radical leaders who were ousted from power (usually by
their own army) when they attempted to carry out an overly ambitious program of distribution of society's resources. While public dissatisfaction with
radical reallocation programs has generally not been the only cause for the
demise of these governments, it frequently has provided the preconditions on
which the *coup* or foreign intervention has been based. The radical Marxist
leader of Mali, Mobido Keita, was overthrown by the army in November,
1968, after his attempts to impose an orthodox Marxian-Leninism on his
still-traditional country stirred popular opposition while failing to solve some
of Mali's pressing economic problems.[25] While Keita intervened in many
different sectors of the Malian economy in an effort to redirect the allocation
of resources, it was in the agricultural sector that he sowed the seeds of his
downfall. In brief, Keita sought to convert private farm holdings into collectives by means of the traditional rural village cooperative, which little by little
would absorb all private farm property. These collectives would then be linked
to the state through governmental trading agencies. Keita's moves angered
certain key sectors in the private economy, and they were able to rally the army
against his regime. The government's failure to foster the growth of local

leadership cells meant that the farmers were in no position to oppose the army; Keita's experiment in radical distribution of land was brought to an unceremonious end.

A similar situation to that of Keita in Mali obtained some years earlier in Guatemala, where the revolutionary government of Jacobo Arbenz was overthrown in 1954 by a combination of an exile invasion from neighboring Honduras, covert assistance from the United States government, and a lack of desire on the part of the regular Guatemalan army to defend their legal government.[26] The Arbenz government was in the midst of a far-reaching agrarian reform program which would have not only stripped the traditional agricultural elite of much of their power in national politics, but which also would have catapulted the Guatemalan peasant into the nation's economic and political circles. Unlike Keita, Arbenz did succeed in establishing flourishing peasant unions in many local villages; but he was not able to arm them rapidly enough to provide a counterweight against the power of the army. As a result, the army, feeling itself threatened by Arbenz's intentions to redistribute military power to a peasant, paramilitary force, refused to engage in battle against the rebel exiles; and the Arbenz government fell in a matter of days.

There appear to be two general styles of public policy which have been adopted by those development elites who manage successfully to expand their distributive capability. In the first style, power and/or resources are extracted (either by means of coercion, or voluntarily), and then reallocated to an agency within the public sector—a government bureau, for example—which then proceeds to administer or deploy the resources *in the name of* a recipient sector. This example would seem more prevalent in those cases where the state wishes to have direct control over the economic and social decisions of the country. In the second style, the resources or power which are extracted from one group are distributed by the government to another group in the private sector of the society—the government seeks only to channel the reallocation. This scheme seems more appropriate to those systems where the state is limited merely to guiding and stimulating the development effort.

As an illustration of the first style, we shall consider the policies of the Cuban government under Fidel Castro regarding the rights and problems of organized labor.[27] Castro's approach to the management of labor-state relations was determined early in his regime's history by the Cuban government's decision to absorb progressively most of the private enterprise of the country. By means of successive steps, beginning with confiscation of property belonging to persons who had profited from corruption under Batista, and ranging through full nationalization of certain key domestic and foreign properties, the Cuban government came to enjoy virtually complete control over the means of production throughout the nation. As of the end of 1964, one report indicates that the only sectors to escape more than 50 percent control by the government were mechanical repair shops and small retail shops in the smaller cities. A few small manufacturing industries, and the nation's cattle, farming, and fishing industries were controlled by the government to a somewhat larger extent; all other sectors had been more than 90 percent nationalized.[28]

As we observed earlier, all these extracted powers and resources must eventually be assigned to a recipient; in the Cuban case, the recipient as far as labor relations were concerned was the Ministry of Labor of the Cuban government. Beginning in January, 1960, the Ministry set out to create Labor Control Offices whose job it was to regulate all facets of labor's contribution to the Cuban economy. As a consequence, many aspects of a working man's life style which ordinarily are determined by individual initiative or by organized unions passed under the control of the Cuban state.

At first, the Cuban Ministry of Labor extended its power only into the area of job selection, transfer, and hiring. All workers were required to obtain and carry with them the worker's identity card, a document of some 14 pages which records a worker's full employment history, as well as his adaptability to the Castro regime. This card is vital to the laborer in acquiring a job, and thereby it serves as a strong control by the state over a worker's political reliability. Further, in order to change jobs, a worker must secure permission from the government's Central Planning Board (JUCEPLAN); workers are also restricted in their movement by giving them food and housing cards which are valid only in certain locations. Finally, the Labor Ministry may transfer a worker from one location to another, and from one job to another, even against his will.

Also in 1960, the Ministry of Labor entered into the field of setting work standards, wages, and salaries. The Ministry at first attempted to stimulate high work performance through honorary awards; these proved to be unworkable, however, and financial incentives have been introduced. In a series of decrees from 1960 to 1962, the Minister of Labor was given the power to approve wage rates, determine the work day, and establish leisure and other labor conditions.

In 1961, the Cuban government also moved to restructure completely the trade unions of Cuba, leaving them tied tightly to the governmental apparatus. Unions were reorganized along shop or factory lines; and each union was given monopoly power to represent the workers of each industry. Inasmuch as the right to strike and bargain collectively have been curtailed so severely in Cuba, however, the unions have changed their organizational functions. Instead of representing the workers against management, they act as an arm of the state to mobilize the workers, and to control their behavior to avoid labor disruption.

It is important to recognize that the Cuban leadership has argued that the transfer of power and resources from private business to the state was done in the interests of the working man; and the final word on how these interests have been represented simply cannot be written at this time. We do not mean to imply that the average laborer in Cuba is materially any better or worse off than before 1959. But it should be evident from our discussion that the redistribution of the power to make economic decisions from the private sector to the state has left the worker significantly less able to control his own life style.

The second style of redistribution, in which the extracted resources are returned to another group in the private sector for management, is best exemplified by the agrarian reform program in Egypt.[29] One of the first acts of the revolutionary government which ousted King Farouk from power in 1952 was to issue a land reform decree which, among other things, made it illegal for a family to possess more than 200 *feddans* (300 if the family had children).[30] The land expropriated in this manner was to be distributed to families who were propertyless. In addition to destroying the power of a few representatives of the landed aristocracy, the law was intended to establish a more equitable pattern of land ownership. The 1952 law, broadened and amplified by subsequent decrees in 1957, 1961, and 1962, has resulted in the expropriation of approximately one million *feddans;* and it is estimated that, by the end of the program, between 250,000 and 350,000 families will have received their plots of three *feddans* each.

By comparison with other countries which have introduced vigorous agrarian reform laws, the Egyptian experiment is relatively conservative. Original owners were compensated in 3 percent nonnegotiable bonds which were redeemable in 30 years. New owners, moreover, had to pay the government a sum equal to the compensation price plus 15 percent for expenses, plus interest. In essence, the Egyptian program, then, was self-supporting; and one may wonder about the extent to which substantial amounts of resources were actually redistributed.

Of greater concern to us, however, is the mechanism by which the new owners took control over the land. Rather than nationalize the land, and turn the newly expropriated farms into state-run or collectivized facilities, as was done in Cuba, the Egyptians have attempted to maintain the principle of private ownership of the parcel, while, at the same time, trying to improve the efficiency with which the new lands are utilized. To accomplish this objective, the Egyptian government requires that each new recipient of land join a farmers cooperative, which is nominally autonomous, but which is closely supervised by a representative from the Ministry of Agrarian Reform. The purpose of this style of organization is to insure rational exploitation of the land. The cooperatives are charged with several responsibilities, including the extension of agricultural loans; the supply of inputs such as seeds, fertilizer, livestock, and agricultural machinery; the marketing of crops in the name of the farmer; and the provision of important social services to the farm families.

The relationship between each cooperative and the Ministry apparently varies according to time and circumstance. On occasion, the strength of control of the supervisor borders on state dictation; other times, the supervisor views his role as purely advisory. An exact and comprehensive conclusion is not possible. But it is significant that, in an atmosphere of emotion and opinion favoring state direction of development throughout the non-Western world, the Egyptians have made a concerted effort to retain not only the facade but the substance of private initiative in the agricultural sector, while tempering this commitment with programs to secure increased agricultural production.

SYMBOLIC CAPABILITY

One of the many dilemmas facing leaders of developing countries concerns their inability to fulfill popular demands for the increased distribution of material goods without, at the same time, extracting additional resources from the society. Limitations on coercive power may make it impossible either to ignore the demands of the masses, or to impose an austerity program on the economic elites, or—in the most unfortunate cases—both. In this situation, a regime's capability to create symbols—to distribute symbols instead of real goods, as it were—may be critical to its own survival.

Political symbols are more than merely the simplistic reproduction of a complex real object or policy, although they may be that, too. Symbols have their greatest value in politics as media to bestow the psychic benefit of a given policy on those sectors or individuals who do not receive any material benefit from the policy, and who did not have the opportunity to participate in its formulation.[31] In any political system, the creation of public policy goes on some distance away from the vast majority of the population; a comparatively small group of citizens reap material benefits from any specific policy decision, and an even smaller circle can intervene significantly in the decision-making process. In spite of this, if the system is to survive and flourish, a much larger percentage of the citizenry—probably approaching 90 percent of the population in a modern industrialized democracy—must feel that the whole process is not remote from him, but immediate and susceptible to his influence and will. Such are the myths by which societies are held together.[32]

Political symbols have taken on heightened importance in developing states today, for two reasons. First, the sum total of material benefits available for distribution by the political system remains quite small, when balanced against the heightened demands of a newly mobilized population. Second, since many of the governments in power today lack the air of legitimacy, and many key groups in the nation deny their very right to speak authoritatively for the social aggregate, these regimes find it correspondingly more difficult to extract the meager resources at their disposal. Time and public restiveness do not permit a breathing space, however; hence the tendency to rely on symbols to tide a threatened regime over hard times.

Symbols may perform a variety of crucial functions in non-Western polities. Herbert Feith has pointed to several different ways in which symbols were used by Indonesian President Sukarno, and other members of the national elite, to extend the reach of their government.[33] Apparently, the constant posturing and strutting of Sukarno across the national and international stage was very dysfunctional to the economic development of the nation, in that it impeded the rational solution of technical problems. In terms of political control, however, the vivid imagery of Sukarno's pronouncements and ideological formulations undoubtedly served the cause of stability, albeit a stability bought by postponing the hard decisions regarding resource allocation. For instance, the government's announcement of planning goals, or Sukarno's active participation in international affairs or his extensive travels around the interior of the country all served to make the government legitimate for much of the population. Symbol manipulation made the Sukarno regime appear larger than life, and gave it the facade of actively searching for solutions to Indonesia's chronic problems. In view of the Sukarno regime's inability to get on with the business of reforming the country's economy and social structure, and given their inability to coerce the population through material deprivation, symbol wielding quickly became literally the only means Sukarno had to stay in power.

For developmental regimes that have somewhat more radical goals, however, symbolism in politics may serve not only to retain power, but also to mold a new political culture and community ethic as well. In Cuba, the Castro regime has employed the dual symbol of nationalism and anti-Americanism to shape the "new Cuban man," as well as to shore up its power base.[34] Thus, certain aspects of Cuba's burgeoning political symbolism may be construed as intended to secure the legitimacy of the Castro regime, either by tracing its history back to the "true" Cuban nationalists, such as Jose Marti, or by identifying its solid anti-imperialism policies in opposition to the United States. In addition, Castro has undertaken to provide symbols which will drive his workers on toward ever-rising goals of production, which will involve ever more Cuban citizens in his mobilization regime, and which, eventually, will define an entirely new modal behavior for the exemplary Cuban citizen.[35]

There are obviously as many different varieties of symbol patterns in developing states as there are development elites to wield them. For purposes of illustration, we may review some of the more important and frequently observed styles of symbol creation in the non-Western world.

In the late 1950's and early 1960's, there appeared to be a great upsurge of charismatic leaders throughout Latin America, Africa, and Asia. In the context of rapid decolonization, the destruction of empires, and the heady thrills of independence, the charismatic leader such as Kwame Nkrumah of Ghana, or Sukarno of Indonesia appeared as the Great Leader destined to guide his people to a higher form of politics. Thus, as Howard Wriggins puts it, the primordial style of governance during this period lay in "projecting the personality."[36] Murray Edelman has remarked that men everywhere who are aware of their political structure need desperately to believe that their leaders are capable of solving the myriad problems which confront their society, and that, above all, these leaders accept the responsibility for leading the nation in times of stress.[37] The charismatic leader is one who can convince his people that, under his guidance, they (the leader and his followers working together) are capable of overcoming tremendous obstacles, obstacles which would defeat lesser men and societies.[38] We should also note that perfection in the solution of problems is not demanded by the populace; what citizens require is the acknowledgement by the leader that he accepts personal responsibility for solving the problem, even though at the same time he may admit that he is inadequate to do so. How else is one to interpret the surge in popular support for Nasser after Egypt's defeat at the hand of Israel in the 1967 war, when he offered to step down from leadership of the Egyptian state? How else should we understand the gains in popularity enjoyed by President Kennedy after the Bay of Pigs debacle? Given the fact that most developing countries will probably be faced with insurmountable problems during first years of the development drive, a charismatic symbol wielder will surely find fertile ground in which to sow his symbolic messages.

In addition to simply projecting his personality, however, the development leader will probably want to use symbols to define the nature of his regime, and, quite likely, of the nation as well. Put briefly, the development elite will wish to put their regime into some kind of historical context, in order to increase its claim to legitimacy, and the right to speak in the name of the state. The first way to do this is to emphasize the historical break with the past, to stress that the current regime is new, modern, and dedicated to social change in contrast to all the old regimes, which were sluggish, incredibly corrupt, and interested only in their own welfare. This was the essence of the modernization decisions of the great revolutionary leader of Turkey, Mustafa Kemal (Ataturk), who came to full power in 1923 as the founder of the Turkish Republic. Kemal rarely lost an opportunity to demonstrate to the Turkish people that his regime represented a complete break with the corrupt Ottoman government, typified by the autocratic rule of the Sultan, and the weakening of Turkey as a world power after World War I. In policy decisions covering such varied subjects as education, public works, even the location of the new national capital (to be discussed later), Kemal built a set of symbols clearly expressing a sharp break with the corrupt ways of the past. In similar ways, such regimes as that of Castro in Cuba, Ben Bella in Algeria, and Ho Chi Minh in the Democratic Republic of Vietnam all relied heavily on creating the revolutionary symbolism of a new beginning, a fresh attack on the nation's problems.[39]

In certain cases, however, the development leader has chosen to emphasize his ties with the past, the extent to which he has borrowed from the nation's classical tradition, and seeks to return the country to some "Golden Age" before the corruption introduced from abroad by the imperial power. Sukarno followed this route, for example, when he denounced the practice of parliamentary democracy in Indonesia in 1959, and exhorted his countrymen to return to the age-old Indonesian political customs of endless communal debate, consultation at the village level, *mufakat* (deciding issues according to some ill-defined consensus or sense of agreement resulting from debate), and *gotong rojong* (mutual assistance).[40] In much the same way, Julius Nyerere of Tanzania has argued for a return to the principles of *ujamaa* socialism, whereby land would be held along traditional communal lines and private exploitation of land would be discouraged. In advocating the traditional communal approach to organizing rural economic power, Nyerere is avowedly opposing that aspect of modernization which would place maximum emphasis on individual accomplishment, but which instead would return to a classless organization of the rural economy to eliminate exploitation of one group by another.[41]

Another symbolic device frequently employed by development regimes concerns the rapid opening and exploitation of the interior of the country. In many instances, the effective authority of the governments of non-Western countries has been strictly limited to the national capital, and a few other smaller cities, or "nodes" of development (see the preceding discussion of Tanzanian spatial development). Modernizing elites have seen, therefore, the possibility of opening up the unexploited interior of their nations to development, thereby symbolizing their new departures, as well as the depth of their commitment. As we have seen, one of the most significant acts of Ataturk was to move the national capital of Turkey away from the old site of Istanbul, where the Sultan's court had reigned, and into the new, underdeveloped area of central Anatolia, to the rough, mud-hut village of Ankara. In making this radical change, Ataturk meant not only to symbolize his break with the Ottoman regime, and what that regime had meant as exemplified by the city of Istanbul; Ataturk also intended to symbolize the desire of his government to make Turkey one nation, to extend the fruits of society to the poverty-stricken and backward interior, and to create a unified nation as a result.[42] In Brazil, the government of Juscelino Kubitschek attempted the same feat in the late 1950's, by making the construction of the new capital of Brasilia one of the government's six major goals. Other development elites have tried to introduce forgotten interior regions into the national society through massive industrial projects, such as the integrated steel-iron ore-aluminum complex at Ciudad Guayana in Eastern Venezuela, the Aswan High Dam in Egypt, or the Volta River hydroelectric project in Ghana.

In accord with a realization that the *setting* of a political act is an important component of the symbolic value of that act,[43] modernizing leaders have sought to construct physical symbols of their regime throughout their country, as if to reassure the populace that their government had the same solidity as the statues, cultural exhibits, sports stadia, and public offices it was building. Here again, Ataturk was at the forefront of modernization of Turkey as he traveled throughout the country exhorting local communities to build up their public meeting places, to beautify their villages, and, in short, to take civic pride in their surroundings. He also saw to it that statues in his likeness were erected in almost every village in the country, as well as providing numerous municipal buildings, sports fields, water works, paved streets, electricity, hospitals, and others. In addition to facilitating the exercise of other complementary capabilities—regulative and distributive—the construction of these important facilities was instrumental in Ataturk's policy of increasing his government's symbolic capability, and using that capability to mobilize the people to support his government and its plan to westernize the country.

RESPONSIVE CAPABILITY

When we extend our analysis to a consideration of a state's ability to respond to demands, we begin to touch for the first time on the values which support a government's development effort; the concept of responsive capability is the analytical link between normative evaluations of democracy, on the one hand, and empirical evaluations of development, on the other. While certainly we are not arguing that a highly developed political system must inevitably adopt the forms of representative democracy, we have assumed (following Almond and Powell) that the more developed a political system is, the better able it is to respond to the articulated needs of more citizens, and the better able it is to process more demands from more disparate centers of power.[44] Thus, our notion of political development *ultimately* must provide for explicit linkages between a pluralistic society and a government concerned with the welfare of the overwhelming majority of the members of that society.

The above comments reflect, however, an understanding of political development as exemplified by modern governments of the Western, liberal, parliamentary tradition. When we turn to the responsive capabilities of developing states in the non-Western world, our task of analysis is greatly complicated by the lack of "fit" between these ideas and the pragmatic exigencies of responsive government in backward countries.

For one thing, the very use of the word "response" implies something approaching a "stimulus-response" analogy drawn from psychology, which, in turn, implies that the "stimulus" (in our case, the popular demand) is a "given" in the equation. That is to say, we often presume that the stimuli of popular input into the political system are already in existence in our developing state, and all the government need do is improve its capacity to sense these stimuli, and process them into satisfactory policy outputs. In actual fact, however, in many non-Western countries, the stimuli of popular demands and supports do not exist, even in latent form, and the government may have to undertake the arduous and precarious task of creating the stimulus. In other words, the government, or the development elite, must endeavor to mobilize the citizenry, and shape them into a potential political power before the masses can initiate any demands to be processed.

In addition, the mere ability to know what people are saying and thinking in society in general is not sufficient to qualify a regime as possessing responsive capability. As Howard Wiarda has pointed out, Rafael Trujillo bolstered his oppressive dictatorship in the Dominican Republic with an extensive network of information-gathering devices which enabled him to know his people intimately. What he did with this information, of course, was quite a different matter.[45]

In the large majority of our cases, then, the political elite of the country must proceed on two fronts simultaneously. First, they must mobilize formerly inert citizens, and thrust them into the political process as active participants, either creating demands, or assisting the state in implementation of its policies. Second, they must develop the capacity to sense mass demands, and to process them in a way satisfying to the originators. Since these two objectives are being pursued simultaneously, it is not surprising that we should find them housed within the same general kind of structure—the mass, national political party (also sometimes known as the mobilization party).

Certainly the mass national party has become one of the most distinctive characteristics of non-Western development politics. In virtually every polity which is attempting successfully to meet the dual problem outlined above, the mass national party, with its overwhelming share of the vote, its local sections highly organized down to the block or township level and its counterpart organizations at every level of the formal government, has been a prominent feature of the political process. Examples of these parties are found in Mexico, with the PRI (Institutional Revolutionary Party), in Cuba, with the PCC (Cuban Communist Party), in Tunisia, with its Neo-Destour Party, and in North Vietnam, with its Dong Lao-Dong (Vietnam Workers Party). Some critics of these parties allege that the mass national party is only used to manipulate the masses; others praise the party for opening channels of access to the government, and institutionalizing popular participation in politics.[46] In reality, most such parties probably perform both functions. Only the "mix" changes from time to time, as circumstances change. If we attept to separate these two functions, however, we would run the risk of distorting the true roles these important non-Western political innovations play in political development.

To compound the confusion, the techniques devised by many non-Western elites to solve the dual problem of mobilization and response discussed above often have a corporatist flavor about them. That is, in states which have adopted the mass national party, it often appears as if the government and the party have fused into one organization, with the same individuals occupying equivalent positions in both organizations. Further, the state-party combination has expanded to include within its boundaries such institutions as labor unions, peasant associations, student unions, youth groups, women's leagues, and many other institutions which have usually enjoyed an autonomous, voluntary existence in Western, liberal democracies. Tunisia's Neo-Destour Party is a good example. At the top, the country's President, Habib Bourguiba, is also the effective leader of the party, which stands alone to dominate Tunisian politics. The nation's cabinet is paralleled by the party's Political Bureau; and the system of parallel hierarchies[47] extends down to the lowest precinct level, where the party has organized more than 1,000 *cells* with an average of

100–400 members in each cell. In addition, the party has formed a coalition with the country's only labor union, an artisans and shopkeepers association, a farmers union, a student group, a youth section, a scout organization for younger boys, and a women's organization. The combined state-party thus appears to have penetrated into, and gained control of, sectors of society which some Western observers feel should be independent and unregulated; hence the charge that the mass national party is an authoritarian solution to the problem of responding to popular demands.[48]

In further seeking to unravel the confusion about democratic politics in a non-Western context, we should also realize that most, if not all, non-Western leaders tend to interpret "democracy" as essentially a government output— social justice, economic prosperity, security, and so on, rather than a description of how the machinery of government must operate—representative parliaments, competing political parties, freedom of the press, and so on. Goverment *for* the people is many times more important than government *by* the people. Further, any of the mere *mechanics* of Western liberal democracy, such as majority rule in parliament, must be dispensed with if they ever interfere with the granting of social justice and economic well-being to the masses.[49]

With all these caveats in mind, let us look, then, at the example of Mexico, where the revolutionary government has built an impressive mass national party and an enhanced responsive capability. Historically and organizationally, the Institutional Revolutionary Party of Mexico can be traced back to the year 1929, when the country's incumbent president, Plutarco Elias Calles, created a personalistic political machine to allow him to retain informal control over Mexican politics in violation of the spirit of the constitutional provision that presidents could not seek reelection.[50] This organization, called the National Revolutionary Party (PNR) was described as merely a cartel, holding together in loose alliance all the regional chieftains who paid allegiance to Calles. Nevertheless, the PNR served as the vehicle for the mobilization of the Mexican people when the revolution entered into its radical phase in 1934.

When Lazaro Cardenas assumed the presidency in that year, it was taken for granted that he would continue to behave as a puppet for Calles, in the style of his predecessors. Once in office, however, Cardenas moved quickly to broaden his base of power in order to radicalize the revolution, and to spread its fruits. To accomplish this, he reorganized the PNR to include four "sectors"—peasant-farmer, labor, popular (middle class), and the army. To bolster the newly organized party, renamed the Party of the Mexican Revolution (PRM) in 1937, Cardenas created a strong national labor union in 1936 and an active and aggressive peasant coalition in 1938. Both of these organizations were trained as paramilitary formations, and both could be armed as a counterweight to the army.[51] Several aspects of Cardenas' reorganization of the revolutionary party stand out. First, it destroyed the old regional alliances and established a national party, based on functional representation. Second, it laid the base for extension of the party framework into the state and local levels, by creating local equivalents to all four sectors in all villages. Finally, it provided the basis for mass integration into the political process of Mexico. When, in 1945, the party was again reorganized to eliminate the army as one of its constituent sectors, and the name was changed to the present one, PRI, Mexico had established a truly national mass mobilization party.

The organizational structure of the PRI today illustrates the workings of a mass national party as both mobilizer of, and channel of access for, popular demands.[52] The farm sector, based on the National Peasant Federation and various smaller peasant unions, accounts for about 40 percent of the party's membership. The labor sector, which holds about 30 percent of the party's affiliates, is divided between the pro-government CTM (Mexican Workers Federation) and its lesser associates, and smaller dissident left-wing labor group, called the Revolutionary Federation of Workers and Peasants (CROC). It is quite significant that the latter group has oscillated between support for the PRI and efforts to create its own political party, but in the absence of any great success in the latter enterprise, it has had to return to limited participation with the official party as circumstances require. Finally, the popular sector, with slightly less than 30 percent of the party's membership, consists of an amazing variety of groups—civil servants, teachers, cooperatives of various types, small farmers who cannot see themselves represented in the peasant sector, small merchants, small industrialists, professionals, intellectuals, youth groups, artisans, and women. There is even a category called "diversos," to organize all those individuals who do not fit into any of the above sectors.

Each of the major and subordinate sectors is organized from the national capital down to the smallest and most remote village community. The national party headquarters machinery, financed by, and closely linked to the government's Minister of Interior, is an integral piece of the national policy-making process. In addition, the national party controls tightly the local party cells, even to the point of ruling on the acceptability of party candidates for municipal and state elections. The party's organizations extend into every conceivable corner of the country and seek to mobilize every possible functional sector. There is a price, however. Radical dissent from the official party views is not tolerated; if a dissenting agency cannot be swayed to change its position and allow itself to be absorbed into the PRI, it will very likely be hounded and coerced out of existence. The democratic achievements of the PRI are impressive, nevertheless. In what are acknowledged (even by opponents) to be fair contests, the PRI has won Mexico's last eight presidential elections, its last 14 congressional elections, and virtually all of its last 200 gubernatorial elections. The PRI has now become so firmly entrenched in Mexico's political system that its leaders have taken the unusual step of rewriting the nation's constitution so as to guarantee congressional seats for minority parties, no matter how poorly they do at the polls.

As is always the case with this type of national mobilization party, the observers differ on just how responsive it is to the popular will. Robert Scott, cited above, argues that, for a nation like Mexico with a highly fragmented and antagonistic political culture, a mass party with sectoral representation is the only possible answer if the system is to reconcile economic divisions. Anderson and Cockroft, although referring to the Mexican experiment as "tutelary democracy," seem to feel that, given the often contradictory goals of Mexican politics—political stability, substantial economic development, social welfare, *and* the encouragement of social and political pluralism—the mass national party is an appropriate solution, even if it does result in the stifling of extreme dissent.[53] John Womack argues, on the other hand, that the economic boom in Mexico since 1940 has covered up the autocratic way in which the PRI has manipulated the nation's economic and political process for the gain of a handful of top revolutionary leaders and their heirs. Government by PRI control is, in his words, "a licensed democracy" and "an exercise in schizophrenia, and in tragedy."[54] As we intimated earlier, the truth probably contains a mixture of both of these observations; a final evaluation depends on one's estimate of the worth of dissent and government response in an environment of rapid development.

It would be a mistake, however, to regard political development as occurring solely at the level of institutional or structural behavior. As we shall see in the following chapter, changes such as those introduced in the party structure in Mexico or in the tax policy in Japan, can not endure for long without supportive changes in the attitudinal orientations of the involved citizenry. It is to these changes in the political culture which we must now turn for a more complete picture of the transformation of a political order.

CHAPTER NOTES

1. See Warren F. Ilchman and Norman Thomas Uphoff, *The Political Economy of Change* (Berkeley: University of California Press, 1969). Also, Karl de Schweinitz, Jr., "Growth, Development, and Political Modernization," *World Politics,* XXII, 4 (July, 1970): 518-40. Also, Samuel P. Huntington, "The Change to Change: Modernization, Development and Politics," *Comparative Politics,* 3, 3 (April, 1971): 283-322.

2. John D. Montgomery, "The Quest for Development," *Comparative Politics,* 1, 2 (January, 1969): 285-95.

3. Gabriel A. Almond, "Political Development: Analytical and Normative Perspectives," *Comparative Political Studies,* I, 4 (January, 1969): 447-69.

4. Gabriel Almond and G. B. Powell, *Comparative Politics: A Developmental Approach* (Boston: Little, Brown & Company, 1966), p. 196.

5. W. Howard Wriggins, *The Ruler's Imperative: Strategies for Political Survival in Asia and Africa* (New York: Columbia University Press, 1969), esp. Chap. Two.

6. Data for this survey taken from Institute for Strategic Studies, *The Military Balance: 1970–1971* (London: ISS, 1970). Also from Richard Booth, *The Armed Forces of African States, 1970.* Adelphi Papers No. 67. (London: ISS, May, 1970).

7. Shuichi Sugai, "The Japanese Police System," in Robert E. Ward, ed., *Five Studies in Japanese Politics* (Ann Arbor: University of Michigan Press, 1957). University of Michigan Center for Japanese Studies, Occasional Papers No. 7 (pp. 1-14).
8. Cited in Sugai, p. 2.
9. Charles W. Anderson, *Politics and Economic Change in Latin America: The Governing of Restless Nations* (Princeton, N.J.: D. Van Nostrand Company, Inc., 1967), esp. Chap. Two.
10. Aristide R. Zolberg, *Creating Political Order: The Party-States of West Africa* (Chicago: Rand McNally & Company, 1966), esp. Chap. Five.
11. Peter R. Gould, "Tanzania 1920–63: The Spatial Impress of the Modernization Process," *World Politics,* XXII, 2 (January, 1970): 149-70.
12. For a full discussion of how the modernizing government of Kemal Ataturk spread the power of Turkey's political system outward from Istanbul, see Malcolm D. Rivkin, *Area Development for National Growth: The Turkish Precedent* (New York: Frederick A. Praeger, Inc., 1965).
13. In Zolberg, pp. 131-33.
14. For an excellent summary of possible meanings of these doctrines, see Charles W. Anderson, Fred R. von der Mehden and Crawford Young, *Issues of Political Development* (Englewood Cliffs, N.J.: Prentice-Hall, Inc., 1967), esp. Chaps. Ten and Eleven.
15. Almond and Powell, p. 195.
16. Helio Jaguaribe, "Political Strategies of National Development in Brazil," *Studies in Comparative International Development,* III, 2 (1967–68), number 028, esp. pp. 38-39.
17. Walter W. Heller, "Fiscal Policies for Under-developed Countries," in Richard M. Bird and Oliver Oldman, eds., *Readings on Taxation in Developing Countries,* rev. ed., (Baltimore: The Johns Hopkins Press, 1967), pp. 5-32.
18. Albert O. Hirschman, *Journeys Toward Progress* (New York: The Twentieth Century Fund, Inc., 1963), Chap. Three.
19. Nicholas Kaldor, "Will Underdeveloped Countries Learn to Tax?," *Foreign Affairs,* 41, 2 (January, 1963): 410-19.
20. Angel Q. Yoingco and Ruben F. Trinidad, *Fiscal Systems and Practices in Asian Countries* (New York: Praeger, 1968), Chap. Twelve.
21. For a balanced view of the advantages and disadvantages of the use of a land tax as a land reform measure in Columbia, see Hirschman, Chap. Two.
22. The bulk of this discussion is derived from Saburo Shiomi, *Japan's Finance and Taxation, 1940–1956,* trans. by Shotaro Hasegawa (New York: Columbia University Press, 1957). Chapter Seven gives a complete summary of Japanese tax developments from 1887 to 1955.
23. Albert O. Hirschman has commented that "External war, or threat of war, is frequently the condition for achieving a *peaceful* redistribution of income within the country." Hirschman, p. 137. This certainly seems to be borne out by the experience of Japan.
24. Almond and Powell, pp. 198-99.
25. John N. Hazard, "Marxian Socialism in Africa: The Case of Mali," *Comparative Politics,* 2, 1 (October, 1969): 1-16.
26. Richard N. Adams, *Crucifixion by Power: Essays on Guatemalan National Social Structure, 1944–1966* (Austin: University of Texas Press, 1970), esp. pp. 184-94.

28 POLITICAL DEVELOPMENT

27. For a full discussion of these points, see Cuban Economic Research Project, *Labor Conditions in Communist Cuba* (Miami, Fla.: University of Miami Press, 1963). Also, Carmelo Meso-Lago, *The Labor Sector and Socialist Distribution in Cuba* (New York: Praeger, 1968).
28. Cuban Economic Research Project, *A Study on Cuba* (Coral Gables, Fla.: University of Miami Press, 1965), pp. 683-84.
29. Magdi M. El-Kammash, *Economic Development and Planning in Egypt* (New York: Praeger, 1968), pp. 258-61, 267-70. Also, Charles Issawi, *Egypt in Revolution: An Economic Analysis* (London: Oxford University Press, 1963), pp. 158-66. Also, Patrick O'Brien, *The Revolution in Egypt's Economic System* (London: Oxford University Press, 1966), pp. 76-78, 136-46, 204-5.
30. A *feddan* is equal to 1.038 acres.
31. Murray Edelman, *The Symbolic Uses of Politics* (Urbana: University of Illinois Press, 1964), esp. Chap. One.
32. For a discussion of the role of parliaments as legitimating devices in a developing situation, see Jay E. Hakes, "The Weakness of Parliamentary Institutions as a Prelude to Military Coups in Africa: A Study of Regime Instability." Paper presented to the Southern Political Science Association meeting, November 11-13, 1971.
33. Herbert Feith, "Indonesia's Political Symbols and Their Wielders," *World Politics,* XVI, 1 (October, 1963): 79-97. Reprinted in Jason Finkle and Richard W. Gable, eds., *Political Development and Social Change* (New York: John Wiley & Sons, Inc., 1966), pp. 365-77.
34. Richard R. Fagen, "Mass Mobilization in Cuba: The Symbolism of Struggle," *Journal of International Affairs,* XX, 2 (1966): 254-71.
35. For a discussion of Castro's attempts to reshape the Cuban political culture, see Jose Yglesias, "Cuban Report: Their Hippies, Their Squares," *New York Times,* January 12, 1969.
36. Wriggins, Chap. Five.
37. Edelman, Chap. Four. See also Theodore McNelly, "The Role of the Monarchy in the Political Modernization of Japan," *Comparative Politics,* 1, 3 (April, 1969): pp. 366-81, esp. 370-71.
38. David McClelland, "The Two Faces of Power," *Journal of International Affairs,* XXIV, 1 (1970): 29-47.
39. For a discussion of the meaning of "revolution" in the developing world, see Charles W. Anderson, Fred R. von der Mehden, and Crawford Young, esp. Chap. Nine.
40. Feith, p. 367.
41. David Feldman, "The Economics of Ideology: Some Problems of Achieving Rural Socialism in Tanzania," in Colin Leys, ed., *Politics and Change in Developing Countries* (Cambridge, England: Cambridge University Press, 1969), pp. 85-111.
42. Malcolm D. Rivkin, pp. 28-77.
43. Edelman, Chap. Five.
44. Almond and Powell, pp. 201-3. For a good discussion of the relationships between development and democracy, see Arthur K. Smith, Jr., "Socio-Economic Development and Political Democracy: A Causal Analysis," *Midwest Journal of Political Science,* VIII, 1 (Feb., 1969): 95-125. Smith has developed a rank order of 110 nations according to their democratic features (see pp. 104-5), and it is interesting

to note that his rank order correlates only moderately positively with the rank order of states according to development as listed in our Appendix, Table A.11. (Spearman's rho = 0.66).

45. Howard J. Wiarda, *Dictatorship and Development: The Methods of Control in Trujillo's Dominican Republic* (Gainesville: University of Florida Press, 1968), pp. 78-79.

46. Samuel P. Huntington, *Political Order in Changing Societies* (New Haven: Yale University Press, 1968).

47. The term is from the North Vietnamese version of the mass national party. See Bernard Fall, *The Two Viet-Nams* (New York: Praeger, 1967), esp. Chap. Eight.

48. Clement Henry Moore, "The Neo-Destour Party of Tunisia: A Structure for Democracy?" *World Politics,* XXIV, 1 (October, 1961): 461-82. Reprinted in Finkle and Gable, pp. 535-50. See also Charles A. Micaud, "Leadership and Development: The Case of Tunisia," *Comparative Politics,* 1, 4 (July, 1969): 468-84.

49. Jose Arsenio Torres, "The Political Ideology of Guided Democracy," *Review of Politics,* XXV, 1 (January, 1963): 34-63. Reprinted in Claude E. Welch, Jr., *Political Modernization: A Reader in Comparative Political Change* (Belmont, Cal.: Wadsworth Publishing Company, 1969), pp. 346-63.

50. Howard F. Cline, *Mexico: Revolution to Evolution, 1940–1960* (London: Oxford University Press, 1962), esp. Chap. Fifteen.

51. Gerrit Huizer, "Peasant Organization in the Process of Agrarian Reform in Mexico," *Studies in Comparative International Development,* IV, 6 (1968–69), No. 044: 115-45.

52. Robert E. Scott, *Mexican Government in Transition* (Urbana: University of Illinois Press, 1959), pp. 162-76. Reprinted as "Mexico's Party System" in Robert D. Tomasek, ed., *Latin American Politics: 24 Studies of the Contemporary Scene* (Garden City, N. Y.: Doubleday & Company, Inc., Anchor Books, 1966), pp. 274-90.

53. Bo Anderson and James D. Cockroft, "Control and Co-optation in Mexican Politics," in K. Ishwaran, ed., *Politics and Social Change, Vol. IV, International Studies in Sociology and Social Anthropology* (Leiden, Netherlands: E. J. Brill, 1966), pp. 11-28.

54. John Womack, Jr., "The Spoils of the Mexican Revolution," *Foreign Affairs,* 48, 4 (July, 1970): 677-87.

Chapter 2

POLITICAL DEVELOPMENT AND ATTITUDINAL CHANGE

One of the basic tenets of this inquiry into political change in the non-Western world is that development involves transformation of human behavior at two closely connected levels—the expansion of systemic capabilities through institutional and processual modifications, on the one hand; and the modification of politically relevant attitudes and predispositions held by the population, on the other. Certainly the changes in state power discussed in Chapter One are impressive; but it is doubtful that they could have been introduced, and certain that they cannot endure, without concomitant changes in the mental attitudes of those whose lives are affected by such development. For this reason, a discussion of political development is incomplete without an examination of the attitudinal changes which must occur in the society if the political culture is to keep pace with the growth of institutional capabilities.

Once one has entered into such an inquiry, however, he finds himself in the midst of an incredible thicket of hypotheses which seek to enumerate those attitudes, values, beliefs, and predispositions which must undergo change in order for modernization to proceed apace. Some students of attitudinal change focus on one, or at most, several key beliefs which, if changed, will stimulate repercussions in other areas, and thus bring about self-sustaining psychological modernization. Daniel Lerner, for example, stresses the ability of modern man to empathize with others, to put himself in another's place and to imagine the problems faced by people in other circumstances and other times.[1] David

McClelland, on the other hand, finds the key to stable political and economic development to lie in achievement motivation, a complex attitude composed of a heightened drive to achieve or attain material goals, a willingness to compete with an internalized set of standards, and an ability to survive emotionally under conditions of psychological autonomy or independence.[2] Gabriel Almond and Sidney Verba have argued, in a slightly different context, that the psychological preconditions for the development of a stable democracy are based, apparently, on the widely held belief that man can influence the political process, plus a predisposition to associate with others to achieve this influence (as opposed to "going it alone").[3]

Other observers of political modernization have sought to demonstrate that the attitudinal changes which underlie development constitute an integral, coherent set of values and beliefs, all of which change more or less together. These social scientists see the psychological infrastructure of political development as forming a full syndrome of attitudes; since no single belief can be isolated as more important than the others, all presumably must change in the same direction, and at the same velocity.

One of the most powerful arguments in this vein has come from Alex Inkeles and his associates who have been engaged in a lengthy, six-nation study of the psychological impact of modernization. According to Inkeles, the modern man is characterized by at least nine attitudes or behavioral predispositions: (1) openness to innovation and change; (2) ability to formulate and articulate a large number of opinions about matters which are outside his immediate environment; (3) a time orientation which is directed more at the present and the future, than at the past; (4) a belief that man should plan and organize his life; (5) a sense of efficacy, or capability to control his environment; (6) confidence that he can calculate and predict on questions of environmental behavior; (7) respect for the opinions and feelings of others; (8) faith in science and technology; and (9) a belief in distributive justice. In addition to stressing the unified nature of the "modern man syndrome," Inkeles goes on to argue that these changes occur, for the most part, simultaneously, and that a special sequence of changes can not be described with any great degree of clarity.[4]

Another writer who has stressed the holistic character of the modernization process has been Joseph A. Kahl, who buttresses his hypotheses with empirical data drawn from Brazil and Mexico.[5] For Kahl, the "empirical syndrome of modernism" consists of seven attitudes, beliefs, or behavioral predelictions, as follows: (1) activism; (2) low magnitude of relationships with relatives; (3) a preference for living in an urban setting; (4) individualism; (5) trust; (6) sensitivity to the mass media; and (7) a belief in achievement as the proper way to earn a reward. As was the case with Inkeles, Kahl has argued that these seven attributes seem to occur in a cluster in men who have a modern outlook on life.

As a third illustration of the syndrome approach, we may cite the work of Leonard Doob who, on the basis of his comparative work in Africa and

Jamaica, has located eight distinguishing features of modern attitudes: (1) a temporal orientation toward the future; (2) a belief in the legitimacy of the current government; (3) a feeling of optimism in the future, as well as a sense that men can control their destiny to some degree; (4) a strong feeling of patriotism or national loyalty; (5) a deterministic conviction that the environment is intelligible, not irrational; (6) trust in other people; (7) approval of the nation's political leaders; and (8) a tendency to discredit tribal practices.[6] Doob breaks from our other two analysts, however, in one important respect, as he argues in another study that the process of becoming modern is most definitely a sequential and fragmented experience, not a unified one in which all values are changing simultaneously. We shall have occasion to return to this problem below in greater detail, when we examine the question about the sequence in which political elites try to change politically relevant attitudes.[7]

In an effort to summarize the findings of Inkeles, Kahl, and Doob, we present them in chart form (See Table 2.1), along with similar efforts made by two other observers—David McClelland and Kenneth Sherrill—who likewise have endeavored to catalogue the various components of a suggested "modernization syndrome." The reader will note that, although there is a considerable amount of duplication among the various authors, the overall picture is one of massive attitudinal change associated with political development. Small wonder that one often hears the suggestion that political modernization is a highly unsettling experience. If this much psychological change is required for an individual to become "modern," only the most durable of personalities will be able to achieve that goal. As we shall argue below, however, at least in the realm of *political* modernization, attitudinal change tends to be much more piecemeal and fragmented than suggested by Table 2.1.

Table 2.1 A Comparative Summary of the Modernization Syndromes of Five Behavioral Scientists. (An "X" indicates the author believes that the attitude in question is part of the overall process of psychological modernization.)

Attitudes	Inkeles	Doob	Kahl	McClelland	Sherrill
1. Identity with and loyalty to the nation-state.		X			X
2. Distinction between personal and political relationships.				X	X
3. Strong ego.			X	X	X
4. Has many opinions.	X				X
5. Can empathize with others.				X	X
6. Well-informed; high exposure to mass media.		X			

Table 2.1 (cont.)

Attitudes	Inkeles	Doob	Kahl	McClelland	Sherrill
7. Basically optimistic about life and future.		X		X	X
8. Has faith, confidence in people.		X	X		X
9. Needs to associate with others.			X	X	X
10. Participates in political activities.					X
11. Concerned with, but not obsessed by, political events.					X
12. Mildly partisan; respect for opinions of others.	X	X		X	X
13. Sense of political efficacy.			X		X
14. General faith in government.		X			X
15. Feels traditional, institutional pressures less frequently; less tied to family tribe.		X	X	X	
16. Places more emphasis on achievement, less on ascription.			X	X	
17. Able to control impulses.				X	
18. Believes that man can triumph over nature; activist.	X	X	X	X	
19. Material needs dominate over psychic.				X	
20. Future-oriented; able to deny immediate needs for long-term gain.	X	X	X		
21. Faith in science and technology; world not irrational.	X	X	X		
22. Openness to innovation.	X				
23. Belief that man should plan and organize his life.	X				
24. Belief in distributive justice.	X				

Table 2.1   (cont.)

Sources:

a. Inkeles: Footnote 4.
b. Doob: Footnote 6.
c. Kahl: Footnote 5.
d. McClelland: Footnote 2.
e. Sherrill: Kenneth S. Sherrill, "The Attitudes of Modernity," *Comparative Politics*, 1, 2 (January, 1969): pp 184-210.

One major difficulty which is often encountered in an analysis of psychological modernization arises from a lack of discussion of explicitly *political* attitudes. The authors we have met to this point are intrigued by the changes which a person must undergo to become modern in a global, or holistic sense; rarely, if ever, do they address themselves to the question of which attitudes must be altered for the individual to change his orientation to objects in his environment which are expressly political. In the remainder of this chapter, then, we propose to reduce the above list of attitudinal variables to a more manageable grouping by focusing directly on the way(s) in which such changes impinge on the political perceptions and orientations of the modal personality in a developing polity. In doing this, we shall employ as a guideline the five basic orientations toward the political world as described by Robert Ward, in a recent article on Japanese political culture: orientation toward the nation, orientation toward the political process, orientation toward political output, orientation toward the self as a political actor, and orientation toward other political actors.[8]

ORIENTATION TOWARD THE NATION-STATE

Although the argument is heard frequently that the nation-state is no longer a relevant or functional type of political organization, it is striking to note the degree to which political modernization seems to rest on national loyalty, pride, and commitment. As Ward puts it, in the above-cited article, "one of the most operationally crucial aspects of any political culture is the manner and degree of popular identification with the nation."[9]

Rupert Emerson has discussed at least two ways in which a growth of national spirit prepares the groundwork for a vigorous policy of national development.[10] The most significant contribution of nationalism to political change occurs when the development elite invokes the symbol of the nation to redefine, as it were, the horizons of interpersonal trust and confidence, as well as the parameters of personal loyalty and commitment, of the citizenry. As Emerson points out, in only a few unusual cases, such as that of Burma or Japan, the sense of communal ("national" would be overstating the case) identity existed prior to the creation of the modern state. In the vast majority of instances, however, the political order has defined the national arena, rather than vice versa. Such would appear to be the rule in virtually all Latin American and Sub-Saharan African states. By so doing, the political leadership have recast for their constituents the question of whom they could trust, and to whose welfare they must commit themselves. This redefinition has almost always meant the acceptance of new and strange criteria for identifying the "we" of the political community; but, without this transformation, the stable basis of national development could never have been laid down. In addition, Emerson goes on, the symbolism of national unity provides what he calls "the emotional cement" which holds the newly formed community together when subjected to the stresses of developmental change. Finally, we may suggest a third important function for national loyalty, that of smoothing the transition from a religious to a secular state, a transition which is as crucial to the stability of the development process as it is difficult to carry out. To illustrate, one of the most important functions of Arab nationalism has been to facilitate the secularization of politics in the Arab states, as the political elites of that area have moved away from Islam as a unifying ideology and a justifying rationale for their development process.[11]

Aside from the functions of nationalism at the level of the system, it appears as if there are some important psychological ramifications connected with national pride which are subtle, but nonetheless critical. For one thing, the open pronouncement of one's national independence is tantamount to claiming individual responsibility for one's actions. If modern man is supposed to possess a strong ego, and is to become an activist in his own behalf, then it stands to reason that he will also insist on personal responsibility for his success or failure. At the personal level, this change is reflected in a growing reluctance to blame mysterious and unseen forces for one's misfortunes, and an increased willingness to focus on one's own abilities and shortcomings as the source of his individual difficulties. When translated to the national level, this phenomenon is seen in the demands of the colonial polities that they be allowed to determine their own destiny, even if that destiny is not necessarily a comfortable or fruitful one. Emerson cites one of the oft-encountered nationalistic phrases in this context: "We would rather be governed like hell by ourselves than well by someone else."[12] While unsympathetic observers are apt to see in this expression a childish rebellion against parental authority, the above analysis would suggest that the statement is a natural outgrowth of the psychological transition from tradition to modernity. Empirical support for this allegation comes from a recent study of personality types and political opinions in four former British colonies in the Caribbean.[13] In this inquiry, the analysts found a strong correlation between nationalism and a belief that man has the ability to govern himself. Conversely, it was also discovered that those in the survey who did not hold to this belief, and were cynical about their nation's capacity for self-governance, favored by an overwhelming margin the retention of some kind of neocolonial relationship with Britain. On the basis of this and other evidence, it seems clear that there is a strong relationship between the psychological attributes of modern man and a proclivity to stress one's pride in his national community.[14]

Juan Bosch, the ardent nationalist leader of the Dominican Republic, has written eloquently of the sensitivity and pride with which he viewed the independence of his country, a country which had been delivered into the hands of foreigners so often in the past hundred years.

> [For the American Ambassador], dealing with me was no easy matter. . . . I was sensitive to anything that might affect Dominican sovereignty. My poor country had had, from the first breath of its life as a republic, a string of political leaders who had dedicated all their skills and resources to looking for any foreign power on which to unload our independence. . . .
>
> I felt wounded, as if it were a personal affront, at the spectacle of so many men without faith in the destiny of their own country. In my childhood, I had seen the Dominican flag coming down from the public buildings to give way to the U.S. banner. No one will ever know what my seven-year-old soul suffered at the sight. . . .
>
> Perhaps I love my little Antilles country so passionately because when I became aware of it as a nation, I realized that it was not that at all, but a dominion. This caused me indescribable pain, and often kept me awake a long time after I had been sent to bed . . . By the time I was ten, I was ashamed that Santana, who annexed the country to Spain in 1863, and Baez, who wanted to turn Samana [Bay] over to the United States, were Dominicans. As the years passed, that pain and that shame became transformed into passionate patriotism.[15]

For a man like Bosch, the cry of anguish over political independence is, at the same time, a proclamation of psychological independence and modernization.

ORIENTATION TOWARD THE POLITICAL PROCESS

Apart from a citizen's allegiance to the nation as an abstract symbol, one must also consider the legitimacy accorded by the populace generally to the specific machinery of decision-making. Political observers have usually found it useful to divide this commitment into two distinguishable (if only analytically) orientations: the first toward the *input* side of the process, to be discussed in this section; and the second toward the output or outcome of the policy-making sequence, to be dealt with below.

The attitudes, values, and beliefs held by the citizens which impinge upon the input side of the political process are among the least amenable to change, for reasons which will become clear subsequently. We are concerned here with what the citizen actually knows about the upward flow of policy proposals, what he feels about the leaders and structures that control this flow, and how he regards his ability to have some impact on the entire process. In short, is he satisfied with the way in which resources are allocated and rules made in his political system? Perhaps more importantly, does he feel capable of participating effectively in the decisions which affect him?

The acquisition of these, and similar, attitudes marks the emergence of what Almond and Verba call civic competence; and a considerable part of their ground-breaking study, *The Civic Culture,* is devoted to a discussion of those factors which facilitate or hinder development of this characteristic.[16] This inquiry presents substantial evidence to attest to the fact that civic competence is a very elusive set of orientations, arising as it does out of family, peer group, work group, educational and other learning experiences of the citizen. Of the five nations in the Almond and Verba study, only two—the United States and the United Kingdom—could be said to enjoy unequivocally a political culture characterized by high levels of civic competence. The other polities—Germany, Italy, and Mexico—seem quite far away from achieving this attitudinal change in their societies.

If many politically developed states have difficulty in engendering the change, one wonders how more traditional cultures will manage the task. Ward reports that Japanese political actors seem to be fairly well developed in this regard, in spite of the fact that their present constitution was imposed on them by an alien, conquering army. Working in their favor, however, has been the close congruence between the way decisions are actually made in the political system and the typical Japanese cultural image of how decisions should be made generally; that is, through consensus and unanimity, rather than through the Western adversary process.

In most other non-Western states, however, the active and effective participation of the average citizen in politics is still tightly restricted. To be sure, we are all accustomed to seeing and hearing reports of mobs of angry citizens marching or rioting in a Latin American, Asian, or Middle East national capital. As Myron Weiner quite rightly points out, however, this is not the kind of active participation envisioned by the Almond and Verba concept of civic competence, since, more often than not, the rioters are not expressing a political demand on their own initiative, but have been goaded into action by an activist elite. Furthermore, many of the citizens thus engaged are undoubtedly doing so out of anger and rage, and not out of any deep-seated belief that what they are about will accomplish any changes in the decision-making process. The mobilization of citizens in the typical non-Western setting does not generally connote for them an adventure into the input side of the political system, but rather an opportunity for them to displace their aggression against symbolic targets.[17]

While we cannot isolate all the factors which accompany the achievement of civic competence in a traditional state, the shift in attitude from fatalism to activism must certainly be regarded as central to the development of a more specific belief in the efficacy of one's political actions. Virtually every observer of traditional societies manages sooner or later to comment about the attitude found in these countries that the average human being has little or no ability to influence his environment, or to affect his destiny.[18] Further, Kahl found, in his study of Mexico and Brazil, that a fatalistic orientation toward nature was strongly correlated with a belief that politics was controlled by a small elite, and the average citizen had little or no chance to become involved in the political process.

Inasmuch as the fatalism-activism dichotomy lies at the very core of the problem of psychological modernization, it is understandable that development elites would find great difficulty in changing this attitude. In most, if not all, cases, a fatalistic orientation probably stems from lessons learned as a small child within the family, and is continually reinforced by subsequent learning experiences in school, village, and factory. Once a citizen has become socialized in this manner, only the most forceful programs of participant mobilization on the part of the mass party or the government can overcome this basically negative orientation toward activist behavior on one's own behalf.

ORIENTATION TOWARD POLITICAL OUTPUT

In contrast to the difficulty with which orientations toward political system inputs are changed, it would appear as if orientations toward the ouput side of policy-making can be altered somewhat more easily. Learning to view government as an instrument for securing one's personal or group welfare is, as Ward remarks, increasingly the "hallmark of a modern society."[19] As we pointed out in Chapter One, political systems are developing today in an atmosphere of high expectations about the quantity and quality of their outputs, the sum total of the goods and services which government dispenses to the populace, or to sectors of it. While these expectations may, and often are, sources of instability, they nevertheless constitute an indispensable part of the psychological baggage which modern political man carries with him on journeys into the political arena.

We saw earlier that the emergence of civic, or political, competence had been identified by Almond and Verba as crucial to the development of responsive political systems. In relation to political outputs, the attitude in question is called *subject,* or *administrative,* competence, reflecting the idea that the citizen believes that he can secure a satisfactory treatment of his interests and welfare by the executive or administrative arm of the political system. Although the development of subject competence also involves the shift from fatalism to activism, as described above, it appears that this change is easier to initiate and stimulate in the case of governmental outputs, than is the case with inputs.

Almond and Verba argue that, midway in the process of cultural change between the traditional, parochial culture and the modernized, civic culture, one finds the transitional, or subject, culture. If the politically modern individual is characterized by an awareness of both political inputs and outputs, and his parochial counterpart is aware of neither, the subject political actor falls in the middle, as he is aware of outputs but not inputs. Put another way, the subject political man believes himself capable of influencing the policy decisions of government *as they are administered or implemented,* but he does not hold this same belief about being able to influence the decision *before it is made.*

The reason for this difference lies in the relative ease with which a political actor can perceive the results of his actions in trying to influence the implementation of policy. If his goal is to secure favorable treatment from a district tax collector, for example, or to obtain a favor for his cousin who wishes to purchase more foreign currency than the law allows, our subject citizen can see immediately whether or not he has been successful in his efforts. On the other hand, the act of voting, as an example of an input device, is very difficult to understand for the subject citizen, in that the results of his act are aggregated with the same act undertaken by countless other citizens, nearly all of whom are unknown to him, filtered through some mysterious, distant process of tally and record, and emerge only much later in the conferring of legitimacy on the elected official. The cause-and-effect sequence here is most difficult to grasp, in contrast to the clear sequence which is perceived when the citizen acts to influence the bureaucracy's performance on the output side.

Lucian Pye, in his treatment of Burmese politics, suggests, in addition, that citizen orientation toward the administrative, or output, side of politics may be much more appropriate in a polity governed by an authoritarian or colonial regime. As citizens become more and more aware of their ability to affect change in their surroundings, they also note that they can make the most of these opportunities in the political sphere by concentrating on the bureaucracies of the state, rather than on the agencies which gather in and aggregate interests and demands. Hence their tendency to see politics as essentially a process by which they seek to defend themselves against unfavorable state decisions, as those decisions are implemented. As Pye puts it, "Where the [interest] associations are autonomous, the tendency is for them not to apply pressure openly on the government in order to influence the formation of public policy but to act as protective associations, shielding their members from the consequences of governmental decisions and the political power of others."[20] This being the case, as the traditional attitude of fatalism begins to give way to the more modern ideas of activism, the first area of the political arena to which the changes will be applied will be that devoted to the implementation of governmental decisions.

ORIENTATION TOWARD THE SELF AS
POLITICAL ACTOR

In addition to acquiring new attitudes and orientations about the ways in which policies are made and enforced, and about the institutions and organizations available for influencing the upward and downward flow of political information, our politically modern man also begins to change the manner in which he regards himself vis-à-vis the political order. Stated in general terms, the modernized political actor recognizes not only his capability to influence either the input or the output side of government, but his inherent *right* to do so as well. The two most obvious ways in which this development is manifested is in the rising number of citizens who demand the right to vote, and the rapid increase in individuals who claim the right to dissent from established policy, either through associational interest groups, opposition political parties, the press or other media, or through less well organized modes of expression.

Traditional political man, the typical component of Almond and Verba's parochial or subject political cultures, is dubious of exerting any inherent right of expression of opinion toward the state. Government, for him, is a "given" in his environment; he can try to adjust his life to it as best he can, but he does not enjoy the innate privilege of attempting to change the policies in question, or of dissenting from them once placed into operation. Even if constitutionally he may have access to legal mechanisms for affecting change in policy, through popular elections for example, and even if he is aware of the existence of these devices, traditional man will continue to be skeptical of either the value of such behavior, or of his right as a dutiful citizen to engage in disrespectful challenge of authority. Such appears to be the case in Ethiopia, for instance, where the deference toward authority shown by the typical citizen has actually made it very difficult for the government to encourage citizens to register to vote. Since participation in political inputs in Ethiopia has always been restricted to the highly deferential submission of petitions to the Emperor, which he was perfectly free to accept or not, as he willed, the modal personality of the Amhara resists the inducements of the state to participate actively in electoral politics.[21] Similarly, in the premodern states of West Africa prior to the arrival of the European colonists, there were few organizations formally constituted to affect politics; and those that did exist performed their tasks primarily through the application of sanctions *internally* against their own members for alleged transgressions. The idea of utilizing these guilds and other economic associations as a device to influence the political system seems not to have been widespread.[22]

If we take as our indicators of a more positive orientation of the citizen to the state an increase in either voter participation and/or political dissent, we can point to at least two characteristics of development politics which would inhibit the growth of this more positive orientation. First, however, a *caveat* must be lodged against interpreting mass voting as an indication of a politicized and self-aware citizenry. As Ward argues in the case of Japan, even though the Japanese consistently turn out on the order of 70 percent of elegible voters for national elections, many citizens do so not out of political convictions, but, rather, as a result of peer group and other social pressures.[23] While accepting increased voter turnout as superficially indicative of a more positive self-concept of the citizen, we must always be prepared to look beneath the surface to determine the actual motivational determinants of a heightened interest in such an abstract political act as casting one's ballot. The same note of caution holds true, essentially, for other indicators of politicization, such as the growth of an opposition party.

Given these restraints on our analysis, however, two factors seem of importance in slowing down the change in citizen orientation toward the state. The first such factor has to do with the idea often encountered in studies of traditional culture which portrays man as basically evil and not capable of self-governance. This characteristically negative concept of human nature will redound to the benefit of authoritarian rule, since the typical citizens will be reluctant to argue for increased grants of power. They will always fear that such power, once granted, will be misused by their fellow citizens. Such appears to be an important factor at work in Ethiopia to prevent the emergence of a civic, or participant culture; levels of distrust are so high in the society that individual citizens seem unwilling to press for more civil liberties and enlarged access to the decision-making process.[24] Similar findings were reported in the study of the British Caribbean, cited above, in which the authors argued that leaders of Jamaica, Trinidad-Tobago, British Guiana, and the so-called "Little Eight" Islands reveal a very close correlation between authoritarian tendencies and a professed lack of confidence in human nature.[25]

A second factor which works against the emergence of a more self-assured orientation toward government is the shaky position occupied by opposition parties in most new nations. David Apter has pointed out that in nearly every new state in Africa and Asia the political party structure either contains very many parties or only a single dominant party.[26] Sooner or later, the stresses and exigencies of rapid economic change will place great pressure on the multi-party systems to consolidate, while the one-party dominant state begins to redefine the political arena so as to exclude the concept of "the loyal opposition." When this occurs, whatever momentum built up in support of citizen mobilization is likely to fade away rapidly (if it does not escalate into violent conflict).[27] Only a very secure and successful regime, such as that of the PRI in Mexico, can afford to encourage the growth of opposition parties by guaranteeing them a place in the national legislative branch regardless of the low vote they obtain. In most other developing systems, the stimulation of a self-confident citizen orientation toward the state must usually await considerable economic progress, progress so great that the system will not be destabilized by the rapid influx of new participants into its ranks.

ORIENTATION TOWARD OTHER POLITICAL ACTORS

In order for our typical political man to emerge as a more nearly modernized actor, a more positive self-conception as an agent of political change is not sufficient; to be an effective actor in a modern state, our subject must be prepared to extend his positive orientation beyond his own personality and embrace others as coequals and potential sources of organizational support. As Ward puts it, does the typical political actor view his fellows with a reasonable amount of trust and confidence, or is he highly distrustful of others who seek to participate in the political arena? The answer to that question will weigh heavily in determining whether or not the system will produce a responsible electorate, mature and moderate political parties, and, in general, the human raw material necessary to participate effectively in politics.

For those polities fortunate enough to possess a political culture which stresses mutual trust and confidence, there is apt to be a significant level of joint, or group, activities in the political realm. Because people trust one another, they are prone to seek the organizational support of others in trying to achieve certain political goals. Where this is not the case, where the political culture teaches that people are not to be trusted unless they are blood relations, or from the same village or kin-group. then common interests are less easy to demonstrate, and large-scale group projects in politics more difficult to mount and maintain. It seems clear, then, that the ability of a polity to develop the extra-political supportive structures—associational interest groups, for instance—so necessary for the growth of a modern state will be heavily dependent on the degree to which the popular culture sanctions group cooperation for common goals.

Almond and Verba, in their five-nation study of political cultures, sought to compare the United States, Great Britain, Mexico, Italy, and Germany along this axis of group actions in politics. In response to a question regarding what an individual would do to oppose the passage of a certain undesirable law, they found that the percentage of respondents who said they would "organize an informal group, arouse friends and neighbors, get them to write letters of protest, or to sign a petition," was significantly higher in the United States than in any of the other four countries.[28] The authors felt that the results for the United States (32 percent), when contrasted with the Italian figures (10 percent) indicate clearly the difference between a political culture based on mutual trust, and one rooted in suspicion and lack of confidence in others.

The other side of the coin is more frequently seen in rapidly developing countries of the non-Western world. In most instances where the political culture has not made major strides toward modernization, the resultant sense of distrust which pervades the political arena inhibits the formation of solid and lasting bonds of organizational unity. In West Africa, for instance, the forces of ethnicity or tribalism have carried over into the postcolonial period to foster divisiveness and even separatism in the new states of that region. While some observers sought the solution to the problem in the mass national party in the late 1950's and early 1960's, that experiment has usually failed as the party became more and more closely tied to one specific ethnic or tribal unit.[29] In several states of South and Southeast Asia, such as Ceylon, Burma, and Thailand, the effect of certain forms of Buddhism has been felt in the growth of what Philip Hauser has called "atomistic social structure," characterized by—among other things—a tendency to ignore one's obligations to others or to society, and "a general lack of national or organizational consciousness or imagery."[30] In Ceylon and Lebanon, especially, religious divisions have reinforced already existing cultural chasms to yield societies so dominated by class fear and suspicion that they cannot mobilize the state effort necessary to get on with the jobs of development.[31]

It would be a mistake to assume, however, that mutual interpersonal fear and distrust are either (1) based on superficial acculturation events, (2) that they can be wiped out easily, or (3) that states in Western Europe and North America are immune from these afflictions. Frank Pinner has hypothesized that political distrust can actually be traced back to an overprotective parent-child relationship, in which the parents sought to keep the children close to home by depicting the outside world as bad or capricious.[32] In this kind of home life, children are discouraged from spontaneous experimentation, their contacts with nonfamily persons are kept to a bare minimum, and they are generally instructed that the world beyond the warmth of the home is a threatening place. The outcome, according to Pinner, is a syndrome of beliefs including the ideas that politics is threatening and conflictual, that politicians are immoral and do not have the general welfare at heart, and that the average citizen cannot trust people active in politics. As if to emphasize one of our earlier points, Pinner tested his hypothesis with high school and college students in Belgium, France, and the Netherlands, finding a perfect "fit" between family protectiveness and political distrust, (Belgian students were most protected and least trustful; Dutch students, the least protected and most trustful; and French students were in the middle.) In addition to stressing our point that distrust in a political culture is a deep-rooted psychological phenomenon, the Pinner study also makes it clear that psychological modernity is a relative concept, that some cultures possess greater degrees of modern orientations and attitudes than do others, but that no national culture can ever call itself completely modernized.

SEQUENCES OF ATTITUDINAL CHANGE

Having now taken an inventory of those orientations and attitudes which must undergo change during the process of attitudinal modernization, we are ready to examine the much more challenging questions concerning the possible *sequences* or *combinations* in which these orientations are altered.

It is possible, in theory, to imagine a case of massive political change in which the development elite tries to change attitudes simultaneously in all five categories described above. Perhaps when the dust has settled in Cuba, and behavioral scientists have had an opportunity to examine that regime's results, we shall discover striking changes in Cuban political culture across all the relevant attitudinal areas. Certainly, if any revolutionary leader can be identified as attempting total psychological change, Fidel Castro would be that leader.[33]

A more probable scenario of guided attitudinal change, however, is that exhibited by the development elite of Japan, as described by Robert Ward. During the early years of Japan's drive to development, the latter third of the nineteenth century, the nation's leaders clearly emphasized change in some aspects of political culture, while other facets of the traditional culture were left untouched or were actually reinforced. On the one hand, the Japanese placed great emphasis on the fostering of popular identification with the nation, and its symbols. Through the exhaltation of the emperor, the establishment of an imperial base, and the creation of compulsory public education, the Japanese elite sought to create a deeply rooted sentimental attachment to the national polity. Other aspects of traditional Japanese life, such as respect for authority and unwillingness to participate overtly in politics, were left alone in hopes that the more coercive features of the development policy would not be challenged by a restive population. It should be noted, as does Ward, that, while the leaders of Japan's development effort were relatively successful in reaching their first goal—the creation of a national sentiment—they were notably less successful in the second—that of stifling dissent, and perpetuating the traditional Japanese concept of nonparticipation. Thus, even the most vigorous and creative development regime may find that it has only slight influence in the maintenance of traditional ideas in a rapidly developing polity if these ideas are not responsive to the needs of newly mobilized participants. In any event, the significant feature of attitudinal change in Japan was the incremental or piecemeal approach taken by the elite, wherein they sought to change some attitudes, but leave others safely unaltered.[34]

Our task, then, in the closing pages of this chapter, is to explore the factors which impinge on a leader's decisions concerning which sequence of attitudinal change to employ, which orientations he should attempt to alter, when, and to what degree. Our exploration begins with the acknowledgement that, for most cases, the change in political culture is merely a means to a broader end —that of institutional or systemic development, per se. That is, most development leaders, to the extent they seek to guide changes in popular values and beliefs about politics, do so primarily to support the expansion of capabilities of the political order. It follows logically, then, that the sequence of attitudinal changes must be derived from the broader configuration of a state's development strategies (which will be discussed in Part III). Certain changes in orientations or attitudes will be supportive of the expansion of certain capabilities, but for others these attitudinal changes may only be disruptive. For example, if a regime tries to foster an increased popular desire to participate in political inputs before the regime's channels of participation are prepared, the result is almost certainly to be one of frustration and instability as the newly mobilized populace finds the doors closed to their demands.

With this relationship in mind, we may attempt to catalogue some major linkages between some of the attitudinal changes which we have described in this chapter and several of the specific capabilities as they were discussed in Chapter One.

One of the most obvious nexus between attitude and capabilities centers on the spirit of nationalism which all new development regimes attempt to stimulate. For the adequate expansion of the key capabilities of regulation and extraction, an enhanced sense of national consciousness is essential; without such a sense, irredentist minorities and separatist clans or tribes will resist the initial growth of central state power, with the result that the regulative and extractive bases for continued development will not be properly laid. To the extent that the expansion of a state's symbolic capability depends on the content of the symbolic messages (as opposed to the mechanical devices by which they are transmitted), changes in national orientation will also be important. We do not see many direct linkages, either negatively or positively, between orientations toward the nation and the responsive and distributive capabilities.

A positive orientation toward political inputs, in contrast, seems directly supportive of a regime's desire to increase its responsive capabilities. As we described in Chapter One, traditional states which seek to improve their responsiveness quite frequently encounter apathy and lack of interest among the citizenry, as was the case with the Ethiopian leaders who had difficulty stimulating voting interest in their country. Thus, the growth of what Almond and Verba call civic competence could very well be the key to the establishment of a modern responsive capability in a developing state. The other side of the coin contains a note of caution for developing leaders, however, which is that they should be wary of fostering this kind of change in orientation until they are capable of being responsive to it. In the absence of a responsive leadership, increased citizen participation in government on the input side could well inhibit the more coercive aspects of state capabilities—regulation, extraction, and distribution.

Finally, we may cite the relationship between citizen orientation toward political outputs—Almond and Verba's subject or administrative competence —and the more specifically administrative functions of government—extraction and distribution. It seems highly important for a government to be able to sense popular reaction to its decisions regarding resource extraction and distribution if these decisions are to be carried out efficiently and, equally importantly, if the regime is to learn from past errors. The growth of administrative competence, then, serves to facilitate the feedback of information about the results of resource allocation decisions which, in turn, enables a development regime to improve its capabilities in this crucial area.

Lack of space prohibits a detailed analysis of these complex linkages between attitude and political power; Table 2.2 is a first effort at suggesting a complete inventory of these relationships. As with so many of the conclusions we are advancing in these pages, the relationships posited here should most properly be considered as an agenda for future research. The thrust of our basic argument should be clear at this point, however; that is, that a regime's strategy regarding attitudinal modernization must be intimately linked with its strategy of the expansion of systemic capabilities if the overall process of political development is to be solidly supported by concomitant transformations in the political culture.

Table 2.2   Some Suggested Relationships between Five Major Areas of Attitudinal Change and Five Capabilities of the Political System.

	Areas of Attitudinal Change				
Political System Capabilities	Orientation toward the nation	Orientation toward political Inputs	Orientation toward political Outputs	Orientation toward self	Orientation toward others
Regulative	++	-	+	--	-
Extractive	++	-	++	-	-
Distributive	0	-	++	--	?
Symbolic	+	?	?	0	+
Responsive	0	++	0	++	++

Key
++   Attitudinal change strongly supportive of increase in capability
 +   Attitudinal change mildly supportive of increase in capability
 0   Attitudinal change neutral
 -   Attitudinal change mildly negative of increase in capability
 -- Attitudinal change strongly negative of increase in capability
 ?   Relationship not clear

CHAPTER NOTES

1. Daniel Lerner, *The Passing of Traditional Society* (Glencoe, Ill.: Free Press, 1958).
2. David C. McClelland, *The Achieving Society* (New York: The Free Press, 1967).
3. Gabriel Almond and Sidney Verba, *The Civic Culture* (Boston: Little, Brown, 1965).
4. See especially Alex Inkeles, "The Modernization of Man," in Myron Weiner, ed., *Modernization: The Dynamics of Growth* (New York: Basic Books, Inc., 1966),

Chap. Ten. Also, David H. Smith and Alex Inkeles, "The OM Scale: A Comparative Socio-Psychological Measure of Individual Modernity," *Sociometry,* 29, 4 (December, 1966): 353-77.

5. Joseph A. Kahl, *The Measurement of Modernism: A Study of Values in Brazil and Mexico* (Austin: University of Texas Press, Latin American Monographs No. 12, 1968).
6. Taken from Leonard W. Doob, "Scales for Assaying Psychological Modernization in Africa," *Public Opinion Quarterly,* XXXI, 3 (Fall, 1967): 414-21. For additional material on the holding of favorable views toward progress, see James A. Mau, *Social Change and Images of the Future: A Study of the Pursuit of Progress in Jamaica* (Cambridge, Mass.: Schenkman Publishing Company, 1968), esp. Chaps. 5-7.
7. Leonard W. Doob, *Becoming More Civilized: A Psychological Exploration* (New Haven: Yale University Press, 1960), esp. pp. 93-94, 149-50, 153.
8. Robert E. Ward, "Japan: The Continuity of Modernization," in Lucian W. Pye and Sidney Verba, eds., *Political Culture and Political Development* (Princeton: Princeton University Press, 1965), Chap. Two.
9. Ward, p. 56. See also, Lucian Pye, "Identity and the Political Culture" in Leonard Binder, *et. al., Crises and Sequences in Political Development* (Princeton: Princeton University Press, 1971), Chap. 3.
10. Rupert Emerson, "Nationalism and Political Development," *Journal of Politics,* 22, 1 (Feb., 1960): 3-28.
11. Richard H. Pfaff, "The Function of Arab Nationalism," *Comparative Politics,* 2, 2 (January, 1970): 147-68.
12. Emerson, p. 4.
13. Charles C. Moskos, Jr. and Wendell Bell, "Attitudes towards Democracy among Leaders in Four Emergent Nations," *Studies in Comparative International Development,* I, 14 (1965):217-28.
14. For additional evidence in a slightly different context, see Almond and Verba, pp. 64-68.
15. Juan Bosch, *The Unfinished Experiment* (New York: Praeger, 1965), pp. 162-63.
16. Almond and Verba, esp. Chap. Eleven.
17. Myron Weiner, "Political Participation and Political Development," in Weiner, ed., pp. 205-17.
18. Kahl, pp. 18-19.
19. Ward, p. 63.
20. Lucian W. Pye, *Politics, Personality and Nation Building: Burma's Search for Identity* (New Haven: Yale University Press, 1962), p. 26.
21. Donald N. Levine, "Ethiopia: Identity, Authority and Realism," in Pye and Verba, eds., p. 276.
22. Paula Brown, "Patterns of Authority in West Africa," in Irving Leonard Markovitz, ed., *African Politics and Society* (New York: Free Press, 1970), pp. 59-80.
23. Ward, pp. 67-68.
24. Levine, pp. 277-78.
25. Moskos and Bell, p. 227.
26. David Apter, "Some Reflections on the Role of a Political Opposition in New Nations," in Markovitz, pp. 226-41.
27. Immanuel Wallerstein, "The Decline of the Party in Single-Party African States,"

in Joseph LaPalombara and Myron Weiner, eds., *Political Parties and Political Development* (Princeton: Princeton University Press, 1966), Chap. Seven.

28. Almond and Verba, Table VI.5, p. 160.

29. I. Wallerstein, "Ethnicity and National Integration in West Africa," in Marion E. Doro and Newell M. Stultz, eds., *Governing in Black Africa: Perspectives on New States* (Englewood Cliffs, N.J.: Prentice-Hall, 1970), pp. 10-17.

30. Philip M. Hauser, "Some Cultural and Personal Characteristics of the Less Developed Areas," in Jason L. Finkle and Richard W. Gable, eds., *Political Development and Social Change* (New York: Wiley, 1966), pp. 54-64, esp. p. 61.

31. W. Howard Wriggins, "Impediments to Unity in New Nations: The Case of Ceylon," in Finkle and Gable, pp. 563-72. Also, W. Howard Wriggins, *The Ruler's Imperative: Strategies for Political Survival in Asia and Africa* (New York: Columbia University Press, 1969), esp. pp. 29-32.

32. Frank A. Pinner, "Parental Overprotection and Political Distrust," *The Annals,* 361 (September, 1965), pp. 58-70.

33. Richard R. Fagen, "Mass Mobilization in Cuba: The Symbolism of Struggle," *Journal of International Affairs,* XX, 2 (1966): 254-71. Also, Irving Louis Horowitz, ed., *Cuban Communism* (Chicago: Aldine Publishing Co., 1970). Also, James F. Petras, "Socialism in One Island: A Decade of Cuban Revolutionary Government," *Politics and Society,* 12 (February, 1971); 203-24. Also, Richard R. Fagen, *The Transformation of Political Culture in Cuba* (Stanford, Cal.: Stanford University Press, 1969).

34. Ward, pp. 74-82. See also chapter on Japan in Don Adams, *Education and Modernization in Asia* (Reading, Mass.: Addison-Wesley Publishing Company, Inc., 1970), pp. 19-65.

Chapter 3

POLITICAL DEVELOPMENT IN HISTORICAL PERSPECTIVE:

USA/USSR

That the United States and the Soviet Union are competitors in the international arena of the 1970's is, of course, indisputable. In fact, the dominant characteristic of the international system since 1945 has been the degree and scope of competition of these two superpowers. For not only do America and Russia compete in military prowess, economic growth, and cultural expression; each country also puts itself forward as a model from which developing elites in the non-Western world can design a workable development pattern.

The extent of the competition between the two powers in this dimension stems from the remarkable success each has had in developing its own political capabilities. As Huntington and Brzezinski put it,

> The Soviet and American governments thus belong to a small club of successful systems. Simply because they *are* able to govern, they have much in common which distinguishes them from the faltering, incomplete, and ineffective systems found in Asia, Africa, and Latin America. The Soviet and American systems are effective, authoritative, and stable, each in its own way.[1]

Any consideration of political development in its broadest sense, then, must include a discussion of the development patterns of these two super-states; from such a discussion, we may hope to tease out those dynamic features which both systems have in common, those in which they differ, and those which contemporary non-Western elites may seek profitably to emulate in their own drive to modernization.

In any review of the origins of American and Russian political development, one factor stands out clearly enough to warrant mention apart from our more detailed discussion; namely, the differing views in each country toward the concept of limits on the power of government. While the United States began its development effort in a doctrinal environment which prescribed close limits on governmental power, the Soviet Union was endowed with a doctrine which stressed political absolutism, at least in the more coercive aspects of governmental behavior.

The American cultural predilection for placing tight restraints on political power was derived from a deeply rooted resistance to central authority in England. Until the 1830's or 1840's, when rapid population growth began to overtake governmental capabilities, England had been characterized by a mistrust of central government. Walter Bagehot, writing in 1867, stated that "One of the most curious peculiarities of the English people is its dislike of executive government. . . . The natural impulse of the English people is to resist authority."[2] In 1832, England's central government employed a mere 21,000 persons (excluding armed forces), or 0.15 percent of the country's total population of about 14,000,000; in 1831, comparable figures showed that the United States, with an estimated population of 13,321,000, employed in the federal government 11,491 civilians, or 0.086 percent of the total. In both countries, the bulk of the tasks of governance were performed by local ad hoc bodies of citizens, and the central authority did not loom large in the average person's calculations.

The development elite of the United States drew on their British heritage quite heavily when designing the basic law of their political order. In case after case, and in article after article, the fundamental principle enshrined in the American political system was that the government should not be able to act beyond certain well-defined limits. Within the central authority itself, power was fragmented among several different agencies—the Congress, the President, and the courts—each of which was to prevent the other from acting precipitously. John Taylor, a noted liberal writer of the day, expressed the idea along these lines:

> We consider these principles [of division of powers] as opposite and inimical [to the principle of balance of power]. Power is divided by our policy, that the people may maintain their sovereignty; . . . Our principle of division is used to reduce power to that degree of temperature, which may make it a blessing and not a curse . . . We do not balance power against power. *It is our policy to reduce it by division,* in order to preserve the political power of the people, . . .[3]

In addition to this internal fragmentation of power, the drafters of the Constitution also introduced the idea of federal-state division, to split even further the power available to any single governmental agency. In *Federalist #39*, James Madison pointed out that the federal principle restricts even more severely the powers of the central government, since "its [the government's] jurisdiction extends to certain enumerated objects only, and leaves to the several States a residuary and inviolable sovereignty over all other objects."[4] And to cement the concept into the operational bases of American politics, Chief Justice John Marshall enunciated the principle of judicial review of legislative acts in the celebrated case of *Marbury v. Madison* (1803), as follows:

> ... The powers of the legislature [of the United States] are defined and limited; and that those limits may not be mistaken, or forgotten, the constitution is written. To what purpose are powers limited ... if these limits may, at any time, be passed by those intended to be restrained? The distinction between the government with limited and unlimited powers is abolished, if those limits do not confine the persons on whom they are imposed ... It is a proposition too plain to be contested, that the constitution controls any legislative act repugnant to it; ...[5]

The Russian attitude toward governmental power at about the same time could not stand out in clearer contrast. Tsar Nicholas I, who ruled Russia from 1825 to 1855, believed that the monarchy, endowed as it was with a divine mandate, served the country as both the source of all law and the agent of its administration. Through his secret police and ad hoc bureaucracies under his personal control, Nicholas extended his will into virtually every nook and cranny of Russian society which lay within his reach technologically. All major decisions had to be made by him personally; and no substantive area of Russian life could be placed beyond his control were he to so desire. Even in his intelligence service, Nicholas sought "... to penetrate into men's hearts and most secret thoughts."[6]

Nor can we consider Nicholas I as a temporary aberation in Russian politics. When Alexander III came to power in 1881, following the assassination of Alexander II, the full coercive power of the state was unleashed in a fury of laws, regulations, and punishments designed to bring a rebellious society to heel. The press, the Church, the universities, labor groups, political protest movements—all sectors of Russian society which sought to break free from central government control—were suppressed. Alexander III's heir, Nicholas II, sought to carry on the absolutist regime of his father; and even though he was forced by events to permit the creation of a constitutional monarchy in 1905, he personally never reconciled himself to any limits on his power.[7] As he stated in 1895, "Let every one know that ... I shall safeguard the principles of autocracy as firmly and unwaveringly as did my father."[8]

Both Alexander III and Nicholas II, Russia's last two emperors, fell under the powerful influence of one Constantine Pobedonostsev, a prominent jurist and political advisor, whose letters to the two tsars illustrate Russia's absolutist bent. In 1876, for instance, he wrote to Alexander: "The whole secret of Russia's order and progress is above, in the person of the monarch . . . The day may come when flatterers . . . will try to persuade you that it would suffice to grant Russia a so-called constitution on the western model, and all difficulties would disapper . . . This is a lie, and God forbid that a true Russian shall see the day when this lie will become an accomplished fact."[9]

It is indeed difficult, then, to see how the famous Marxist-Leninist dictum that the state should "wither away" could ever have been carried out in absolutist Russia. With the kind of cultural guidance provided by Russia's autocratic heritage, it was easy for Lenin's government to move back toward absolutism following the initial flirtation with rule by the local *soviets* in the heady days after the Bolshevik revolution. Some observers have made the point that Lenin, when he authored his famous tract *The State and Revolution* shortly before the 1917 upheaval, demonstrated great naiveté about the nature of the Russian state. Whereas Lenin predicted the demise of government once class antagonisms ceased to exist, in reality, as Louis Fischer points out, "what commenced to wither away was the idea of withering away."[10] In the context of our discussion here, however, it is probably more accurate to regard Lenin as acting in the cultural tradition of, and within the political guidelines set down by, hundreds of years of unlimited government.

This is not to say, of course, that Lenin and Stalin were just a different type of tsar; quite the contrary, the soviet government has moved dramatically to increase the state's political capabilities in ways that would have been quite alien to Nicholas I. We only wish to point out that the United States and the Soviet Union have sought to expand their political power against the backdrop of two sets of historical experiences which are diametrically opposed: the doctrine of constitutional limitations on power, in America, contrasted with the notion of unlimited state power in Russia.

USA/USSR, I: REGULATION

In contrast to their attitudes regarding the other four political capabilities, Russian leaders have manifested a preoccupation with regulation throughout the entire span of our essay.[11] While the elite of tsarist Russia might have been able to ignore even extractive concerns during practically the entire nineteenth century, they devoted a considerable amount of their resources to the maintenance of order and the regulation of society, down to, as we have already seen, the most minute individual detail.

Prior to 1917, the major threats to the tsarist government occurred in 1825 (the Decembrist plot, an incipient military coup d'etat at the time of the death of Alexander I), and the general period 1895–1905, when severe economic dislocations, peasant and labor restiveness, and failure in the war with Japan conspired to produce a major challenge to Nicholas II's rule. During the 1860's and 1870's, there were also serious peasant and student disturbances which rocked the regime of Alexander II. Otherwise, the nineteenth century produced little in the way of a decline in the Russian government's awesome regulative capability.

The base for the development of this capability was laid by Tsar Alexander I (1801–1825) in his actions designed to strengthen the civil service and other areas of the bureaucracy. Nicholas I (1825–1855) continued this trend with his special emphasis on the secret police, his growing use of extraordinary bureaus to accomplish special tasks under his direct control, and his unremitting application of government censorship of the press. Under Alexander II (1855–1881), the government began to move away from such minute regulation; but the easing of controls on students and peasants had the result of stimulating dissent and rebellion. The last two tsars, Alexander III (1881–1894) and Nicholas II (1894–1917), responded by increasing the pressure on social unrest, and by attempting to recreate the peaceful days of the first half of the century.

Russia's disastrous performance in two wars—the Russo-Japanese War (1904–05), and World War I (1914–18)—led directly to the two great erosions of the state's regulative capabilities. The Romanov Dynasty managed to ride out the rebellion of 1905 only by creating a constitutional monarchy and a representative assembly, the state Duma. While in theory the Duma represented inroads into the regulative capability of the tsar and his bureaucracy, in actual practice Nicholas disregarded much of what the parliament was able to accomplish, which, in itself, was not particularly noteworthy.

From the moment of the overthrow of the tsar in February, 1917, however, Russia's regulative capability fell to virtually nothing. From February to October, 1917, the Provisional Government created by the Duma competed with the Petrograd Soviet of workers and soldiers as the sovereign authority in the country. After the Bolshevik revolution, the control of the formal organs of government lay in the hands of the leadership of the Bolshevik party; but it was not until the end of the civil war, in 1921, that a modicum of regulative power had been restored.[12] Thus, the period 1918–1921 was marked by tremendous effort on the part of Lenin to expand the regulative power of the new soviet state. It is particularly significant that, at about this same time, steps were being taken to centralize the power and control of the Communist Party (CPSU). In 1919, the party leadership created the Political Bureau (Politburo) and the Secretariat in order to facilitate internal control over the organs of the party.[13] Even though Lenin moved to relax controls over important sectors of the economy as part of the New Economic Program (1921–1926), the long-term trend during this period was toward a restoration of central government regulation of most aspects of Russian life.

This trend was accelerated after the death of Lenin (1924) and the consolidation of power by Stalin in 1929. In 1929, several dramatic shifts were registered in Soviet political and economic life which revealed a massive growth of regulative capacity. Forced collectivization of the peasants, industrialization on a crash basis, the emergence of a monolithic CPSU, the bloody purges of the Party Central Committee in 1934, and of the Red Army high command in 1937–38 were all indicators of a growth in regulative capability seldom matched in any other polity.[14]

The picture of Soviet regulative capabilities since Stalin is ambiguous. On the one hand, Khrushchev's struggles for power, which culminated in 1957, seemed to bring a certain relaxation of controls, especially in sectors of the economy concerned with consumer goods, as well as a noticeable broadening of the base of support for the CPSU. In the late 1950's and early 1960's, the Soviet government began to experiment with limited kinds of local government initiatives, with special emphasis on the local control over antisocial behavior. In this, they conjured up images of a similar experiment with local government units, called *zemstvos,* which had been the hope of liberal reformers in the latter half of the nineteenth century.[15]

With the fall of Khrushchev, however, there has appeared to be a resurgence of what some writers refer to as neo-Stalinism, albeit without the arbitrary or capricious exercise of violent coercion.[16] Even assuming the most liberal interpretation of this development, it is still quite clear that the Soviet political system possesses one of the most highly developed regulative capabilities of any polity in the world in the 1970's.

In contrast to the growth of the regulative power of the Russian political system, that of the United States has been slow but steady, with slight incremental accretions building upon a small initial base. The regulative authority of the American polity has suffered its own reversals, as will be revealed below; but these setbacks have been fewer and milder than those experienced by the Russian government.

As we have already indicated, the American political system was brought into being in an atmosphere of limited government, when the doctrine of constitutional democracy was equated with the government's having only minimal power to constrain the citizenry. "That government is best which governs least," Thomas Paine had written; and the first organic law of the new republic, the Articles of Confederation, finally ratified in 1781, was designed to reflect this contention. According to this document, the member states of the Union retained their sovereignty to such an extent that unanimous consent of the states was required to amend the Articles, the power to tax was denied the central government, and the several states were granted the power to levy and collect import duties. Thus, when the delegates of the states met in Philadelphia in 1787 to consider broadening the powers of the central government, and to remedy the defects of the Articles of Confederation, they were actually the first in a long line of political development elites seeking to expand the regulative powers of the political system. And even though the new Constitution gave only a few additional regulative powers to the Congress and the president, such as the power to levy taxes, and the power to regulate trade between the states, the base had been laid for the gradual expansion of the central government's ability to control the behavior of its citizens.

Certainly, in the early days of the Republic this expansion of regulation was not accepted docilely by the state governments or by the people. Repeatedly during the first several decades of America's history, various states or regions denied the right of the central government to intervene in important areas of human behavior. The Alien and Sedition Acts of 1798, passed by Federalists in Congress to give the president the power to deal with conspiracies against the government, was met by the Virginia and Kentucky Resolutions which declared the Acts unconstitutional. In 1832, the right of the central government to enact a tariff which was prejudicial to the rights of some southern states was answered by the famous attempt by South Carolina to nullify the law. There were several attempts at secession from the Union, most notably that of a few leaders of New England in 1804 and again in 1814, when the central government failed to take the measures necessary to protect Massachusetts against British attacks. The most severe threat to the regulative capacity of the federal government took place, of course, from 1861 to 1865, when the states of the Confederacy attempted to break away from a union which they found no longer suited their interests.

Immediately following the Civil War, and for perhaps a decade thereafter, the regulative power of the central authorities increased, due to the stationing of Union troops throughout the South to consolidate the northern victory. As a result of the electoral bargains which brought Rutherford B. Hayes to the presidency in 1876, however, these troops were withdrawn, the white southern leadership returned to a policy of denying blacks their legal rights, and the brief rise in federal regulative capability was reversed.

For about a decade following the Hayes election, federal power remained at a low level, as the presidency and Congress were occupied by mediocre and self-limiting personalities. Central government regulation began to rise slightly in the late 1880's with the passage of the Interstate Commerce Act in 1887 and the Sherman Antitrust Act in 1890. It was not until Theodore Roosevelt came to the presidency in 1901, however, that the central government began to acquire the regulative power which is the mark of a modern activist political system. The first Roosevelt rode at the head of the so-called Progressive movement, which laid the groundwork for most of the expansion of government regulation ever since. Through the passage of such legislation as the Pure Food and Drugs Act and the Hepburn Act (both in 1906), the federal government established the principle that the public interest must be protected, if necessary, through government regulation of private business.

In general, the first steps of the Progressives have been consolidated and built upon by subsequent administrations—Taft, Wilson, Franklin D. Roosevelt, Truman, Kennedy, and Johnson. During the three terms of the Republicans who held office during the 1920's—Harding, Coolidge, and Hoover—

government regulation was allowed to slide backward; and Eisenhower was content merely to exercise the power that he possessed, without seeking to expand it. But, on the whole, the regulative capacity of the American political system has expanded steadily from 1900 to 1970. The most significant increases were achieved during Wilson's first term (1913–1917) and the New Deal (1933–1938). During the first period, the major steps included the creation of the Federal Reserve Board, the passage of the Clayton Antitrust Act, and the establishment of the Federal Trade Commission. Under the presidency of the second Roosevelt, federal regulatory power experienced its greatest expansion, as the government acquired the capacity to control many sectors of American society ranging from the securities market on Wall Street (via the Securities Exchange Commission) to the raging currents of the Tennessee River (via the Tennessee Valley Authority). By 1970, these steps had produced a solid regulative capability, which, although lower than that of the Soviet Union, was still sufficient to control disparate social forces of a large, modern nation while attempting to preserve as much personal liberty as possible.[17]

Chart 3.1 The Growth of Regulative Capability in the United States and the Soviet Union, 1780–1970.

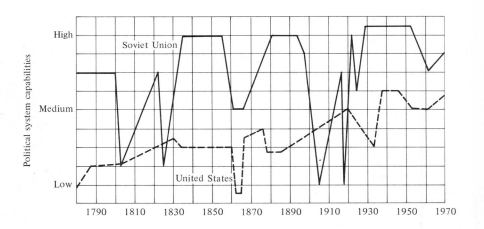

USA/USSR: II, EXTRACTION

When one considers the enormous regulative capability built up by the Russian state in the nineteenth century, it is indeed odd that the same leaders paid so little attention to resource extraction, which, as we have seen, must be developed more or less in tandem with regulative power. In fact, there was little consideration given by the tsars to resource extraction at any time, with the exception of the recruitment of troops necessary to fight the several wars that took place during the period. In fact, one is tempted to conclude that the primitive financial extractive capacities which underlay the Russian political order contributed decisively to the downfall of the imperial government in 1917.

The nineteenth century was not entirely without some effort at extraction of resources. There was a halfhearted attempt by Alexander I's regime in 1812 to levy a mildly progressive income tax as an emergency measure to finance the wars with Napoleon, but the step had no lasting effects. A central banking facility, the State Bank, was established by the reform tsar, Alexander II, in 1860; and a unified budgetary process set up under his regime in 1863. A conscription law was promulgated in 1874 which improved considerably the methods by which the regime recruited soldiers for its massive standing armies.

On the whole, however, the imperial dynasty came to an end in 1917 having built up very little extractive capability. The taxation system still depended too heavily on indirect levies, such as the important tax on alcoholic beverages, which were sharply regressive. For the most part, government spending was based on the creation of inflated currency, rather than upon the development of any real extractive powers. Most importantly, the Russian government did not take advantage of the national crises of the period—the Napoleonic Wars, the Crimean War, and the Russo-Japanese War—to raise revenues. As we noted in Chapter One, the Japanese government was quite skillful in using its emergency wartime powers to increase the tax burden on the wealthier classes, a burden which they did not reduce when the war was over. The tsarist regimes did not follow this policy, choosing instead to finance wars through foreign loans and the printing press; and the result was that the extractive powers of the Russian state remained at a critically low level.[18]

With Lenin's assumption of power, the extractive capability of the Russian state shot up dramatically. The period 1918–1921 was a time of great upheaval and crisis for the new Soviet government, plagued as it was with civil war and foreign intervention on the one hand, and pressures to remake the country's social and economic order in a short span of time, on the other. Lenin, who had come into power predicting the cessation of government in Russia, responded pragmatically by extracting a vast amount of resources from the already heavily burdened Russian country and city populace. During this period, known as "War Communism," Lenin governed the country like a "beseiged fortress." To cite Meyer on this subject,

> Food supplies and raw materials needed for the war effort were taken from whoever had them in his possession, usually the peasants, direct producers of these commodities. Everyone possessing any skill or knowledge or simple muscle power was pressed into service, willing or not. The workers, in whose name the regime claimed to govern, were forced to work under unbelievably hard conditions. Control over many economic enter-

prises, which they had seized in the early months of the revolution, was wrested from their hands, and their unions were subjected to the command of the party.[19]

With the threat of civil war passed, Lenin moved to relax the rigorous controls he had instituted, and the state's extractive powers dropped under the NEP. The respite was only temporary, however, as the Stalinist policies of agricultural collectivization and crash industrialization brought about a rapid renewal of resource extraction powers. This expansion, marked in 1929 by the adoption of Russia's first Five-Year Plan, has continued at a high rate to the present time. In terms of extractive capability, Stalin's government clearly marks the watershed in Russian political development.[20]

Since the mid-1950's, the Soviet government has experimented with different modes of organizing its extractive powers. These experiments have usually been interpreted in the West as signifying the liberalization of the economy, the introduction of the market economy, and so on. A careful appraisal of the changes in economic controls introduced since Stalin's death suggests, however, that the reforms have been intended not to lessen the state's extractive powers, but rather to increase dramatically the resource pool from which the government can extract additional funds.

The most significant changes which the Soviet leaders have introduced revolve around Premier Alexei Kosygin's announcement in 1966 that "by 1968 profits, sales and rate of return on investment will replace fulfillment of quotas as the main standards of success for every Soviet firm."[21] These changes have been heralded as a step away from central direction of the economy. As Goldman points out, however, these reforms merely alter the criteria by which the political system will make the basic extractive and allocative decisions; central planning and a relatively high degree of extractive capability will continue to characterize the Soviet political system for some time to come.[22]

In the United States, extractive capacity tended to grow at a very slow rate prior to the World War I, after which it expanded at a breathtaking pace in response to the financial needs of the American government as it fought a series of bloody and expensive wars. Just as was the case with tsarist Russia, the American political leadership devoted little attention to the extraction of resources through virtually the entire nineteenth century. The development of a full-fledged extractive capability was delayed in the United States until the Progressive era endowed the government with the regulative powers necessary to withdraw from the society those resources vital to the growth of a modern state. Thus, while the regulative needs of the Russian system grew beyond the extractive capability of the tsars to finance them, in the United States the two basic capabilities of political development grew at more or less the same pace.

As we have seen, the Constitution of 1789 gave to the American government the power to tax; but this power was not employed to any great extent until the middle of the Civil War, about 1863. From 1789 until 1816, the tiny federal government budget was funded almost entirely from customs duties (from 99.5 percent in 1789, to 76.2 percent in 1816).[23] After the passage of the Public Land Act of 1820, sales of public land began to contribute a greater share of federal revenue, reaching a high of over 48 percent in 1836. When Ohio was received into the Union in 1803, the federal government established the most important extractive precedent of the period by withholding all ungranted public lands for the welfare of the central treasury; and, until 1863, the sale of these public lands and the customs duties on imports constituted virtually the whole of federal government receipts. In fact, Andrew Jackson derived some amount of pride from the fact that he had run for the presidency in 1828, and had been elected, at least partially on the promise that he would levy no direct taxes on the people.

The Civil War generated such enormous requirements for financing, however, that taxation of manufactured goods, stamps, playing cards, alcohol, and tobacco had to be established. Although the federal budget in 1861 was about what it had been in 1836, or 1816 for that matter, the following war years saw a great increase in federal spending (from $52 million in 1862, to $558 million in 1866, a tenfold increase). This demand was met by additional collections of "internal revenue," or taxation levied on citizens within the country (as opposed to customs duties). While customs duties were raised slightly, the bulk of the new revenues came from domestic taxation, especially on manufacturers.

In the years following the Civil War, manufacturers' taxes dropped off considerably, as did the general need for government revenue. But, the federal treasury had achieved a sort of plateau in both expenditures and taxation, for in neither category did activity drop back to pre-Civil War levels. While customs duties remained about constant, both the federal budget and internal revenue (made up mostly of alcohol and tobacco taxes) went up, so that in 1915 the central government budget stood at about $700 million, of which almost 60 percent was derived from internal taxation.

The approval of the Sixteenth Amendment to the Constitution in 1913, which authorized the federal government to levy a graduated tax on incomes, came just in time, as the First World War created new financial needs for Wilson's administration. From a budget of $697 million in 1915, the United States treasury rose to over $6.6 billion by 1920 (another tenfold increase similar to that experienced during the Civil War). More importantly, from 1915 to 1920, taxes on personal and corporate incomes, and other items, grew from 60 percent of revenues to slightly over 80 percent. It was during this period that the foundation was laid for a rapid expansion of the system's extractive capacity.

Just as we have seen in the case of Japan, periods of war offered to the American government favorable environments in which to augment its extractive powers. Following World War I, there was little increase in the federal budget, and little growth in personal income taxes as a source of revenue, until

World War II and the subsequent conflicts in Korea and Vietnam. Even with the activist programs of the New Deal, Roosevelt's budget level did not exceed that of Wilson's 1920 expenditures until 1941, when the United States stood on the threshhold of war. From 1940 to 1945, however, federal expenditures experienced almost an eightfold increase (from $5.9 billion to $47.8 billion), and this time, personal income taxes bore an increasing share of the burden (43.5 percent of total internal revenue collections in 1945).

Thus, a trend set in wartime—the Civil War, World Wars I and II—has been continued into the post-1945 American political system, thereby allowing the federal government to undertake substantial tasks of social change and welfare which would not have been possible otherwise. Total expenditures have risen; but so has the extent to which these expenditures are financed by taxation (95.8 percent in 1962), and the extent to which these taxes are paid by individual citizens (50.9 percent in the same year). The extractive capability of the United States, while developed slowly, has grown to a formidable source of support for a modern and activist political order.

USA/USSR: III, DISTRIBUTION

There is little doubt that the principle distributive question which faced the Russian state during the nineteenth century was that of the social and economic plight of the serf, which, in turn, was part of the more general problem of the unequal distribution of agricultural land. Certain limited efforts were made by the imperial government between 1801 and 1911 to remedy this situation; the most hopeful was the broad emancipation of the serfs by Alexander II in 1861. As we have noted earlier, however, the expansion of a state's distributive capability is predicated upon a prior growth in extraction; and the

Chart 3.2   The Growth of Extractive Capability in the United States and the Soviet Union, 1780–1970.

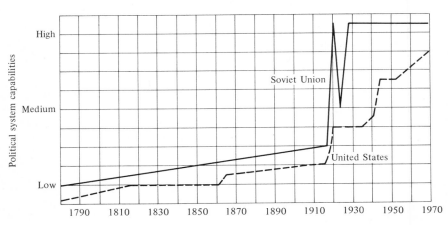

manifest inability of the Russian government to extract meaningful resources prior to the 1917 revolution rendered virtually useless the various actions which the tsars took to redistribute rural properties. The result was usually the raising of peasant expectations to levels which simply could not be fulfilled through traditional means.

It cannot be argued that the tsars did not recognize the magnitude of the problem. Through various decrees in 1801, 1803, 1807, and later, Alexander I eventually granted freedom to about 37,000 serfs. Nicholas I declared in 1842 that "There is no doubt that serfdom, in its present form, is a flagrant evil which everyone realizes, yet to remedy it now would be, of course, an evil even more disastrous."[24] Under Nicholas I, 67,000 serfs gained their freedom, albeit at their own expense. In short, prior to 1861, little headway was made with the problem; and, to a large degree, the prime obstacle was the inability of the tsars to enforce their decrees in this most intractable sector.

The most noteworthy attempt to free the serfs came in 1861 with the emancipation decree of Alexander II.[25] While the decree did set the serfs free to marry, acquire property, and bring action in court, it was notably inadequate in its provisions for transferring ownership of the serf's land to him as a freeman. The process of transfer was lengthy, complicated, and depended upon a great deal of initiative on the part of the former landlord. Worst of all, the peasant was required to pay for the land within a period of 49 years at 6 percent interest! Although the government extended financial assistance to the peasants to help them pay for the property, the impoverishment of the former serfs rendered this portion of the law unattainable. The redemption provisions were canceled finally after the revolutionary disturbances of 1905.

The state's final effort to redistribute land prior to the Revolution took place from 1906 to 1911, when the government of Nicholas II moved to break up the village communes to which much of the formerly serf-owned land had been transferred. Arguing that the communal arrangements were antithetical to a rational exploitation of the resources, the government tried to abolish communal tenure, and establish peasants as individual farmers. Here, as in previous reforms, the objectives could not be reached for lack of expropriation of large landed estates, and the total impact of pre-1917 experiments in land tenure was, if not negligible, certainly inadequate to meet the crisis.[26]

Even under Lenin's policies of "War Communism," full redistribution of resources was not contemplated. Although Lenin did at first advocate expropriation of private estates and redistribution to the peasants, this position was negated by his insistence on sheer extraction of resources during the 1918–1921 period. Due to the extreme pressures placed on the new Soviet government, resources were turned to the defense of the regime and the nation, rather than returned to poorer sectors of society. This phase of Russian economic policy, so critical to the country's development pattern, did not begin in earnest until Stalin came to power.

Beginning in 1929, the most radical kinds of resource redistribution were undertaken by Stalin. In the rural sector, farm plots were collectivized and private ownership was abolished (although eventually small private plots were permitted); government control over these collectives was assured by the establishment of centralized tractor pools, called Machine Tractor Stations (MTS) which quickly became the symbol of Moscow administration throughout the land. Forced-draft industrialization was accomplished by the massive shift of resources from the surpluses created by the rural and managerial classes into heavy industry. In the realm of political power, redistribution also took place in a major way, with power once held by unions, local government agencies, and soviets coming into the jurisdiction of the CPSU. Most definitely, under Stalin, Russian distributive capability—like its extractive capability— took a quantum jump.

Again, since Stalin's death, the story is ambiguous. The debate between the advocates of consumer goods and those of heavy industry has been essentially over another limited reallocation of resources; as in so many other areas of Soviet political life, this debate between "modernism" and "orthodoxy" has yet to be fully resolved.[27] While some slight decline in distributive capability may have occurred under Khrushchev's regime, surely that cannot have been too much in a political order so deeply committed to reshaping the socioeconomic character of its country.

While the institution of serfdom may have presented the Russian leaders with their main distributive problem, at least prior to 1929, in the United States the major reason for the development of the state's distributive capability has been to draw the nation's black citizens into full and equal participation in the social, economic, and political arenas. And, although the Soviet leadership may have reached an uneasy truce with the rural poor of that country by means of the expansion of the distributive powers of the political system, in the United States the problem of maldistribution of resources, opportunities, and status to blacks continues to aggravate the body politic. To be sure, the American political system has developed enough distributive capability to insure adequate participation in the life of the nation to many other socioeconomic minorities (such as Chinese, Jews, or descendents of immigrants from eastern or southern Europe), as well as to its sizeable laboring class. These groups have gained the access to power—both social and political—which signifies the success of a policy of redistribution of resources. As of this writing, however, it must be admitted that the expansion of distributive capacity has not yet gone far enough to grant equality of participation to blacks.

Just as the American government paid little attention to extraction of resources until after the Civil War, so also did they pay scant heed to the grinding problems of racial oppression which were present in the first half of the nineteenth century. Some distribution of resources did, in fact, take place from the federal to the state governments through a scheme engineered through Congress in 1836 by Henry Clay. And, of course, the U.S. government demonstrated substantial power to redistribute resources when it forcibly removed the Indian tribes of the Southeast from their ancestral homes and sent them to the reservations in Oklahoma. As far as the plight of black slaves was concerned, however, most of the distributive reservoir of the central government was exhausted trying to prevent the institution of slavery from expanding into new territory, rather than attempting to eliminate it at its source. This is the esential meaning of the Missouri Compromise of 1820, the Kansas-Nebraska Act of 1854, the Compromise of 1850, and the founding of the Republican party.

The Emancipation Proclamation of 1863 did virtually nothing to redistribute power to anyone; it applied only to those slaves who resided in areas still under Confederate control, and its full implementation had to await the arrival of federal troops. The complete legal effect of emancipation could be gained only after passage of the Thirteenth Amendment to the Constitution. It was hoped by the forces of radical reconstruction that a full guarantee of civil, political, and economic rights could be made to the black citizens through passage of the Fourteenth and Fifteenth Amendments, but even while these emendations were being approved, and even while federal troops were being stationed in the former Confederacy, the southern aristocracy was busy reestablishing its domination over the blacks through the so-called "black codes" of 1865–66.

Once the federal troops were withdrawn from the South, there was virtually no hope of regaining the precious ground gained during the 1860's; and the retrenching federal governments of the 1880's and 1890's turned their backs on the humiliating discrimination of the blacks through the "Jim Crow" era. The famous Supreme Court decision of 1893, *Plessy v. Ferguson,* enshrined the "separate but equal" doctrine for 61 years, despite efforts by Wilson and the second Roosevelt to expand the opportunities for access for black citizens. Even after the 1954 Court decision making it unlawful to maintain dual school systems, and the 1957 Civil Rights Act (the first in this century), blacks still needed to take to the streets to obtain a fair hearing of their case. While considerable improvement was registered through the 1960's in certain areas such as school desegregation and voting rights, an honest appraisal of the problem of racial injustice would have to conclude that the rather substantial distributive power of the American political system had been used to good effect, but not in behalf of the Negro.

Certainly there have been groups which have benefited greatly by this power. Most notable of these has been organized labor, which has emerged from the status of pariah to become one of the foremost sources of economic and political power in the country. The rise of labor as a movement for power would probably be dated from 1842, when the Massachusetts Supreme Court ruled that trade unions were legal, that their members were not collectively responsible for crimes committed by them individually, and that a strike for a closed shop was legal. Through the period from 1870 to 1900, the labor movement struggled—sometimes violently—against the political system in an effort to gain access to the power it needed; their courage and persistence were rewarded finally through the Clayton Antitrust Act of 1914, which Samuel Gompers called "labor's charter of freedom." But the really great strides in labor rights were made under Franklin Roosevelt, who was responsible for more prolabor legislation than any other president. Beginning with the National Industrial Recovery Act (1933) which guaranteed labor's right to collective bargaining, and continuing through the establishment of the National Labor Relations Board (1935) and the passage of Fair Labor Standards Act (1938), the New Deal was clearly organized labor's finest period. Even subsequent attempts to reduce labor's gains, such as the Taft-Hartley Act of 1948, have never sufficed to reduce the enormous distributive power which the American political system had developed and employed for the benefit of its large laboring class.

USA/USSR: IV, SYMBOL CREATION

In contrast to the slight development of extractive and distributive capabilities in tsarist Russia during the nineteenth century, the imperial leadership actually seems to have devoted a significant amount of state power to the expansion of a rudimentary symbolic capability. In both of the categories of symbol creation—the material or infrastructural capacity, and the images themselves —Russian leaders moved ahead, especially between the end of the reign of Alexander I (1825) and the beginning of World War I. The difficulty with the symbolic expansion in Russia lay in the fact that the capability for symbol creation grew neither fast enough nor in the required directions to support the needs of the Russian political order.

Chart 3.3 The Growth of Distributive Capability in the United States and the Soviet Union, 1780–1970.

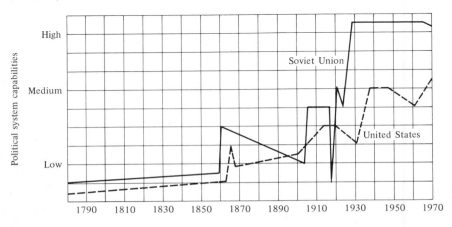

We may date Russia's interest in an improved public school system from

1802, when Alexander I created the first ministry of education in his government.[28] This step was accompanied by sweeping reforms in the administration of state-supported education, most of which failed to have the desired impact for lack of funds. Finally, the reactionary trends in Europe after 1815 produced a wave of repression which negated virtually all the gains which had been registered to that time.

Under Tsar Nicholas I, the infrastructure of symbol creation and communication began to receive more public attention. The first Russian railroad was opened for service in 1837; and the building of hard-surfaced roads through many strategic sectors of the Russian interior also received much support from Nicholas. By 1855, Nicholas had accounted for the construction of over 5,000 miles of roads and about 650 miles of railroads.[29] Most significant, however, was Nicholas' expansion of the school system, and his unabashed use of the schools to propagate the tsar's version of what was termed "official patriotism" or "official nationalism." During the 1830's, the idea emerged that the Russian state should rest on the three pillars of religious orthodoxy, political autocracy, and militant nationalism. To accomplish all this, according to one report written by Nicholas' minister of education in 1843, steps had to be taken "to collect and consolidate in the hands of the government the control of all intellectual resources, theretofore scattered, of all means of general and private education that had . . . partly escaped supervision."[30] To that end, Nicholas assumed the financial support and control over all local schools, expanded the number of years available for the schools at various levels, and established central government control over universities throughout the country. Even with this expansionary program, however, by the mid-nineteenth century, Russian schools could provide education for no more than one-half of 1 percent of its total population.

The trends initiated under Nicholas continued to be barely visible under the imperial regime. Lines of communication, mainly railroads, grew rapidly; but Russia in 1895 still had fewer miles of railway per unit of territory than any other major European country. Schools underwent a series of reforms, which increased slightly the number of children who could receive an education; but the educational system continued to be an instrument used by the aristocracy to perpetuate the country's creaking social structure, and a militant and aggressive nationalism continued to dominate the images formed by the school system.

It seems safe to say that, under Lenin, Russian symbolic capability underwent a sharp decline. This unusual development can be traced primarily to Lenin's distaste for "personality cults" and other forms of personal adulation. Upon his death, however, the use of symbols surrounding his person and his thought grew trememdously.[31] Almost overnight, the ideas of Lenin, as well as images of his person, became key symbols in the Soviet struggle for power. It remained for Stalin, however, to make such impressive use of the symbol creation power of the Soviet state. During the forced industrialization and farm collectivization of the terrible 1930's, Stalin manipulated the threat of external attack, with recollections of Lenin's contributions to Russia, to forestall any incipient growth of opposition within the country. Stalin also engaged in the rewriting of history to adjust the image of Russia and Europe, and to stress the continuity with past glories. This step was especially prominent during the German onslaught of World War II, when Stalin realized that he could not arouse the Russian people to fight Hitler for the glories of socialism, but he could perform this miracle by invoking the images of "Mother Russia." Concurrently, the rapid growth of communications media, radio, the press, the spread of electrification into the rural areas, and the heavy emphasis on school construction helped establish the infrastructure necessary for such a development.[32]

As we have already seen in other instances, the post-Stalin period, and especially the period following the Khrushchev school reforms of 1958, seem to reveal a mild decline in Russia's symbolic capability. While the schools and the media continue to be available for such use, there is some evidence that the Soviet leaders seem to prefer a greater reliance on concrete performance than on symbolic substitutes. Marshall Goldman points out, for example, that the great economic reforms of the late 1960's were discussed with almost none of the characteristic doctrinal debates, and without invoking the great Russian ideological sources, Marx and Lenin.[33] This trend, while ambiguous, may foreshadow as well as accompany the growth of a highly pragmatic "technocracy" in the Soviet Union which eschews symbols for actual production.

In the early days of the development of the American political system, there was similarly little attention given to the enhancement of any symbolic capability. In fact, prior to the Civil War, most American presidents worked to block several significant efforts to increase symbol flow throughout the new nation; and it was not until the great railroad boom of the post-Civil War period that the symbolic capability of the United States began its spectacular and unbroken rise to the high level it occupies today.

The first major step taken by any American government toward an improved symbolic capacity was made in 1803 when, upon the admission of Ohio to the Union, the decision was made to reserve one section of each township to be given to the education fund of the respective state. This provision, seized upon by several states with relish, became the launching device for extensive free public elementary school systems throughout the North, especially in Ohio, Pennsylvania, and Indiana; in New England and the South, however, education continued to be enjoyed principally by the rich.

In other areas of symbol flow, the American government dragged along slowly until the period just before the Civil War, when the expansion of the river and canal system stimulated a rapid increase in internal passenger and cargo movement. The U.S. Postal Service was begun in 1789, and expanded gradually throughout the nineteenth century; but attempts by leaders in Congress to have the federal government intervene in the building or subsidizing of highways or canals were blocked successfully until the 1830's. In 1817, statesmen such as Henry Clay argued for the creation of what he called the "American System," a vast network of roads, canals, and communication channels which would tie the various sections of the country into one unified nation. Opposed by such regionalists as <u>Andrew Jackson</u>, however, the American system was not to be achieved until the Civil War had broken down much of the sectionalism which had held the nation's development in a retarded condition for 50 years.

Two areas—railroads and education—provided the cutting edge of government attempts to extend its symbolic capacity into the interior of the nation after 1870. The first railroad had been inaugurated in 1826, at almost the same time that the first lyceum was founded by Josiah Holbrook for, as he stated, "the public diffusion of knowledge." Yet, on the eve of the Civil War, fewer than 50 percent of the nation's children between the ages of five and seventeen were enrolled in public schools, and fewer than 30,000 miles of railroad were in operation (still four to five times more than in Russia at about the same time).

After the Civil War, however, both rail travel and public education began to experience simultaneous growth of enormous proportions. From 1870 to 1875, almost as many miles of railroad were built as had been constructed in the previous 40 years. Later, as rail construction dropped off, about 1915, the central government began to expand its aid to highway construction; by 1925, the federal government was spending $80–100 million annually on highways, and the level was raised to $200–300 million during the New Deal.

Federal aid to education was not given in the form of direct payments during the nineteenth century; but the rapid expansion of state expenditures, from $63 million in 1870 to almost $215 million in 1900, was made possible by the farsighted decisions to reserve some ungranted land in each town for state education purposes. This growth in spending made it possible to increase the percentage of school-age children enrolled in public elementary and secondary schools from 57 percent in 1870 to 72.4 percent in 1900. Since that time, growth has been slower, but steady in both transportation and education, thus providing a solid base for the symbolic capability of the American political system.

One major innovation of the Roosevelt administration must receive mention here, as it served to open up millions of American homes to symbol flow during the 1930's. We are referring to the Rural Electrification Administration, originally established as an emergency relief agency during the early days of the New Deal, but given status as an independent bureau of the government (along the lines of the TVA) in 1936. In 1933, only one farm family in ten enjoyed electric lights; five years after the REA had been established, the number jumped from 750,000 to 2,250,000; and by 1950, 90 percent of America's farm homes were receiving the benefits of electric power. The implications of this advance, in the age of radio, television, and mass communications, were staggering; and certainly great credit must be given to the REA for having welded the rural 10 percent of the nation firmly into the fabric of American society.

USA/USSR: V, RESPONSIVENESS

Contrary to policies followed by the various Russian governments toward the other four state capabilities, there seems to have never been any concerted effort to improve the system's responsiveness to the demands of any large number of citizens. Whether under the rule of the tsars, or under the regime of the soviets, the average Russian citizen has had very little opportunity to influence his government. There is some evidence that, in the post-Stalin period, certain kinds of interest groupings have emerged within the framework of either the state bureaucracy or the CPSU; but, as we shall argue below, the responsive capability of the Soviet government remains at a rather low level of development.

Chart 3.4 The Growth of Symbolic Capability in the United States and the Soviet Union, 1780–1970.

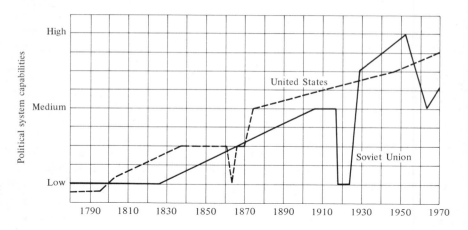

During the nineteenth century, we find almost no interest in trying to respond to any kind of pressures from outside the tsar's immediate circle of advisors until the reign of Alexander II. In 1858, however, Alexander took steps to establish local government units, called *zemstvos,* which were supposed to be endowed with substantial powers of self-regulation. These *zemstvos,* which were to be popularly elected (albeit with a sharply circumscribed electorate) were not only to manage a considerable amount of local concerns, such as roads, hospitals, and law enforcement; they were also to constitute the first layer of a fledgling representative structure which would have offered a channel for citizen participation. Even though opposed by the central bureaucracy and the nobility, the *zemstvos* carried the brunt of the fight for the liberalization of Russian government throughout the latter half of the nineteenth century, and the local and provincial *zemstvos* formed the nucleus of the forces calling for the creation of a constituent assembly during the 1904–1905 revolutionary crisis. In spite of this vigorous effort by local leadership, the *zemstvos* were never able to break through the cadre of imperial advisors to reach the ear of the tsar himself; and after Nicholas II's decision in December, 1904, not to admit *zemstvo* representatives to his major adivsory body, the gulf widened between the Russian state and the local units of government.[34]

The other major effort to develop a responsive capability was the ill-fated State Duma, or parliament, created by Nicholas II in the waning months of 1905 to quiet the forces of revolution. The Duma met in four separate assemblies, April to July, 1906; February to June, 1907; November, 1907 to June, 1912; and November, 1912 to February, 1917. The first two Dumas were dominated by the more radical elements of the Russian political spectrum which were still dedicated to working within some form of constitutional government. The solutions of these two assemblies, especially in the area of the land tenure question, were far too extreme for the ruling dynasty to accept; and the first two Dumas were turned out by imperial decree within a few months of their being constituted. After the dissolution of the second Duma, the government instituted indirect election of delegates for the third assembly, a fact which resulted in a Duma which was more conservative, and therefore more to the liking of the tsar, but also much less capable of responding to the growing demands for radical change. The outcome of this development was that the Duma faded rapidly into oblivion as a potential force for change in Russian society.[35]

Following the Bolshevik revolution in 1917, the responsiveness of the Soviet state grew briefly, as Lenin experimented with representative mechanisms in the Petrograd Soviet, the constituent assembly, and the rapidly growing Communist party. In 1917, it was estimated that the multiple soviets which were springing up throughout the country represented about 23 million Russian citizens, whereas the membership of the CPSU was put in January of that year at 20,000. By the close of 1917, however, party membership had grown to 240,000, and to 750,000 by 1921.[36] The growth of party membership is a deceptive indicator of responsiveness, however; for already by 1921 the CPSU had begun to centralize its internal control mechanisms and to shut off debate. The passage of the antifaction rule at the 10th Party Congress in 1921 marked the turn toward democratic centralism and the weakening of the forces of opposition within the party. Throughout the 1920's, this trend deepened, and the Party Congress began to decline as a source of internal debate. Concurrently, the Central Committee of the party grew in power, in recognition of the lessening sensitivity to "grass roots" demands.[37] Although certain sectors of Russian economic life began to assume some of the functions of interest groups within the Soviet bureaucracy (the military was one prime example), the years from 1925 to 1955 were marked by a low degree of responsive capability.[38]

As part of the general phenomenon of de-Stalinization, the Soviet government moved during the 1960's to become more sensitive to the demands and requirements of its citizens. The CPSU, which in 1963 claimed 10 million members, tried to democratize itself at the 22nd Party Congress by granting greater security to the individual party member, providing for secret ballot on party votes, repudiating mass purges, and ensuring freer debate of the issues.[39] Regional and local party structures have been admonished to seek out indications of public dissatisfaction and report them to the proper authorities for corrective action. Soviet officials have even begun the unusual process of using public opinion surveying to obtain information on the public's desires.[40] Some observers claim that a process is under way in the Soviet Union whereby institutional interest groups are developing and being absorbed into the decision-making apparatus of the state.[41] Certainly, the Soviet leadership is rapidly coming to recognize the need for improving the "feedback" of the decision-making process, so they can better judge the effects of their acts. While this process of developing a responsive capability is certainly underway in Russia, at present we do not see much indication that the Soviet leaders have made a great deal of significant progress.

Were we to select one single sector of political power in which the United States and the Soviet Union stand out clearly as different from one another, it would have to be in the area of responsive capabilities. As we have seen, the Russian leadership has done little to expand this capability, even when they have recognized the value of doing so. In contrast, the United States political system has moved, at times dramatically, but always steadily, to expand its ability to receive and act upon information about the desires and needs of its constituents. While no one would argue that more could not be done to make the American political order more responsive in the latter third of the twentieth century, certainly its capacity to sense the public need compares favorably with that of the Soviet Union in 1970.

It almost seems as if the American political system were created via popular participation. The constitution of the state of Massachusetts was the first to be ratified by a popularly elected body, in 1780; and throughout the new nation, pockets of settlers took it upon themselves to organize local governments which were responsive to the needs of all citizens. The major flaw in this participation lay in its restrictive definition of what a "citizen" was; in order to vote, or to hold public office, one had to be (at least) white, male, over 21 years of age, and the owner of some property. In New York, for example, in 1790, of a total population of about 324,000, only about 12,300 enjoyed the right to vote. Even as late as 1824 (the first year for which we have popular vote statistics for presidential elections), only 3.3 percent of the total population voted for the president, compared with 39.5 percent who voted for either Eisenhower, Stevenson, or six other candidates in 1952. (See Table 3.1.)

Clearly, then, the story of the growth of America's responsive capability can be told as a progressive broadening of the category of citizens entitled to participate in the political process.

The first important step in this process was taken with the creation of the first opposition political party, the Democrat-Republicans of Jefferson and Burr, in 1791. Although attacked by the Federalists, such as Hamilton and John Adams, as being mere "factions" and appealing to the mob, the forerunner of today's Democratic party survived and mobilized enough voters to win the election of 1800, and go on to dominate American politics until the Civil War. During that time, the party saw to it that several important groups were enfranchised, specifically, the small farmer or rural yeoman, the small town merchant, and the slum dweller of the port cities of New York, Philadelphia, and Boston, among others.

The creation of the Republican party in 1854, around the ruins of the Whig party, led to the election of Lincoln in 1860, the extension of the franchise to black slaves, and to a Republican dynasty which lasted until the early part of the twentieth century. Unfortunately, the blacks were unable to keep the access which they gained after the Civil War, and very little was done during the latter third of the nineteenth century to broaden participation in politics. The percentage of the total population which voted for president in 1916 was almost the same as that which had cast a ballot some 40 years earlier, in 1876.

Thanks to the combined efforts of the Progressives and a renewed, nationally based Democratic party, the period following Wilson's first electoral victory witnessed a dramatic expansion of the political system. This expansion was presaged by the growth of organized labor as an electoral force, by the emergence of such big city machines as that of Tammany Hall in New York, and by the populist movement in the late 1890's, which resulted in the creation of the Populist Party in 1892 and the nomination of William Jennings Bryan for the presidency three times, beginning in 1896. The Wilson years, however, produced the Seventeenth Amendment to the Constitution, which permitted direct election of senators, and the Nineteenth Amendment (in 1920) giving women the right to vote. As a result, the percentage of the total population which voted for the president jumped from 18.1 percent in 1916 to 35.6 percent in 1936, where it has remained fairly steady ever since.

Since World War II, the principal innovations in the nation's responsive capability have taken place within the political party structure, as each of the major parties has sought to make its own nominating and issue-selection procedure more responsive to its rank-and-file membership. The national governing boards of the parties have become more open to influence from lower ranks of the party structure; the spread of the presidential preference primary election into more than 25 states has meant that any potential nominee of a major party must demonstrate his popularity throughout the country prior to the national convention; and the process of selection of delegates to the national nominating conventions has itself become more open and democratic.

Chart 3.5 The Growth of Responsive Capability in the United States and the Soviet Union, 1780–1970.

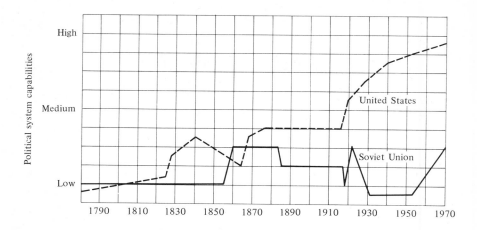

In addition to these changes, new styles of citizen participation have sprung up in the postwar period, demonstrating the American predilection for participatory democracy. Such developments as the creation of Common Cause as a lobby for the public interest, or the efforts of Ralph Nader to crusade on behalf of the consumer, all point to the extraordinary openness of the American system, and the great emphasis placed on sensing and responding to the needs of people scattered throughout the system. The major challenge to American political leaders over the next decade lies in bringing within the system that 20 percent of the population which presently does not share in this great access—those who are traditionally unrepresented, or underrepresented —blacks, women, poor, or youth. If these groups can be brought under the umbrella of the political system, and can begin to share in the broad access enjoyed by other groups, then the responsive capability of the United States will have reached its full, brilliant potential.

CONCLUSIONS

In reviewing our analysis of development patterns in Russia and America, we are led back to a consideration of the differential impacts of the constitutional and cultural environments in which the two systems sought to enhance their capacities. In the United States, while the doctrine of constitutional limitations on power did not prevent the state from expanding its capabilities when conditions warranted, this doctrine did, at least, insure that such development would be gradual, incremental, and undertaken only when significant sectors of the public demanded it. As a result, both regulative and extractive capabilities grew slowly until the turn of the nineteenth century; both grew rapidly and

Table 3.1 Popular Vote for President of the United States, as Percentage of Population, 1824-1968

Year	Total Population (est.)	Total Popular Vote	% of Population Which Voted
1824*	10,924,000	356,038	3.3
1828	12,237,000	1,155,350	9.4
1832	13,742,000	1,217,691	8.9
1836	15,423,000	1,505,278	9.8
1840	17,120,000	2,402,405	14.0
1844	19,569,000	2,700,861	13.8
1848	22,018,000	2,874,572	13.1
1852	24,911,000	3,142,395	12.6
1856	28,212,000	4,044,618	14.3
1860	31,513,000	4,689,568	14.9
1864	34,863,000 **	4,010,725	11.5
1868	38,213,000	5,720,250	15.0
1872	41,972,000	6,469,680	15.4
1876	46,107,000	8,402,329	18.2
1880	50,262,000	9,186,260	18.3
1884	55,379,000	10,055,539	18.2
1888	60,496,000	11,381,427	18.8
1892	65,666,000	12,053,259	18.4
1896	70,885,000	13,910,203	19.6
1900	76,094,000	13,962,065	18.3
1904	82,165,000	13,521,935	16.5
1908	88,709,000	14,888,240	16.8
1912	95,331,000	15,037,535	15.8
1916	101,966,000	18,480,224	18.1
1920	106,466,000	26,728,068	25.1
1924	114,113,000	29,089,084	25.5
1928	120,501,000	36,738,887	30.5
1932	124,840,000	39,721,845	31.8
1936	128,053,000	45,628,516	35.6
1940	131,954,000	49,847,349	37.8
1944	132,885,000	47,821,942	36.0
1948	146,093,000	48,687,607	33.3
1952	155,761,000	61,542,185	39.5
1956	167,259,000	61,807,390	37.0
1960	180,684,000	68,832,818	38.1
1964	192,120,000	70,621,479	36.8
1968	199,846,000	73,186,819	36.6

*1824 is the first year for which popular vote data are available.
**1864 population figure includes the Confederate population.

in tandem thereafter as a modern industrial polity began to emerge. Consequently, the United States government did not have to rely excessively on its symbolic capabilities to survive, although these too were developed as the resources became available. And, most importantly, the regulative, distributive, and symbolic capabilities of the American system did not outgrow the ability of the resource base to support them.

Russian development trends need to be separated into two distinct phases, which correspond to the tsarist and bolshevik regimes. Under both styles of governance, regulative capabilities were maintained at a high level, and responsive capacities were kept low. This, in itself, constitutes a major difference between the Russian and American styles of development. The bolshevik approach to development involved much greater emphasis on extraction and distribution of resources, as befits a modern revolutionary political system. As we have noted, the tsarist regime was finally undone by its inability to extract the resources necessary to pay for its modest and halting distributive efforts. The post-1918 governments did not make that same mistake.

Thus, when boiled down to their essentials, the chief differences between Russia and the United States lie in the emphasis the former places on regulation, and the stress the latter puts on responsiveness. Differences of opinion over extraction, distribution, and symbol creation usually turn out to be differences of degree and of orientation and direction, rather than of absolutes. And, indeed, arguments are frequently put forward to suggest that the Soviet Union and the United States are becoming more like one another, chiefly by virtue of the Russians becoming more responsive, and the Americans becoming more regulative.

Only time will tell us about the validity of this prediction. But, non-Western states interested in finding viable methods for their own development efforts would do well to examine both the Russian and Americans experiences in detail before opting for either; for it seems difficult to imagine the leaders of, say, Ghana, Malaysia, or Uruguay adopting either of these two styles *in toto*.

CHAPTER NOTES

1. Zbigniew Brzezinski and Samuel P. Huntington, *Political Power: USA/USSR* (New York: The Viking Press, Inc. 1964), p. 418. Emphasis in the original.
2. Cited in J. B. Schneewind, "Technology, Ways of Living and Values in 19th-century England," in Kurt Baier and Nicholas Rescher, eds., *Values and the Future* (New York: Free Press, 1969), p. 121.
3. John Taylor, *Inquiry into the Principles and Policy of the Government of the United States* (New Haven: Yale University Press, 1950), pp. 356, 171. Cited in John C. Livingston and Robert G. Thompson, *The Consent of the Governed,* 3rd. ed. (New York: The Macmillan Company, 1971), p. 163. Emphasis added.
4. Cited in L. Earl Shaw and John C. Pierce, eds., *Readings on the American Political System* (Boston: D.C. Heath and Company, 1970), p. 64.
5. Cited in Shaw and Pierce, eds., p. 515.

6. Michael T. Florinsky, *Russia: A History and an Interpretation,* 2 vols. (New York: Macmillan, 1953), p. 772.

7. Florinsky, pp. 1142-43.

8. Cited in Florinsky, p. 1147.

9. Cited in Florinsky, p. 1089.

10. Louis Fischer, *The Life of Lenin* (New York: Harper & Row, Publishers 1964), pp. 115-24, esp. p. 121. Also, Adam B. Ulam, "Lenin: His Legacy," *Foreign Affairs,* 48, 3 (April, 1970): 460-70.

11. We have selected for analysis the period 1801–1970 (Tsar Alexander I–Brezhnev) for Russia, and 1787–1970 (Constitutional Convention–Nixon) for the United States.

12. Alfred G. Meyer, *The Soviet Political System: An Interpretation* (New York: Random House, Inc., 1965), pp. 36-45.

13. Meyer, pp. 167, 168, 172.

14. Alec Nove, "Soviet Political Organization and Development," in Colin Leys, ed., *Political and Change in Developing Countries* (Cambridge: Cambridge University Press, 1969), pp. 65-84. Brzezinski and Huntington, Chap. Seven. Meyer, Chap. Thirteen. Also, Robert Conquest, "Stalin's Successor's," *Foreign Affairs,* 48, 3 (April, 1970): pp. 509-24.

15. Florinsky, pp. 896-902. Meyer, p. 332.

16. Conquest, pp. 509-24. Also, Sidney I. Ploss, "Soviet Politics on the Eve of the 24th Party Congress," *World Politics,* XXIII, 1 (October, 1970): 61-82.

17. At the end of each section of this chapter, the reader will find a chart depicting the course of change in a given capability in both Russia and the United States since about 1780. These charts are meant to be impressionistic, and are included simply to make graphic the arguments developed in the narrative portions of the chapter. The rise and fall of the capability level is pegged to relative concepts of "low," "medium" and "high," rather than to any specific numerical values. They should be taken as illustrative only, meant to portray general trends rather than absolute standards of achievement.

18. Florinsky, pp. 942-45, 1107, 1208-10.

19. Meyer, p. 37.

20. Nove, pp. 74-79. Meyer, pp. 408-9.

21. Marshall I. Goldman, "Economic Revolution in the Soviet Union," *Foreign Affairs,* 45, 2 (January, 1967): 319.

22. See also Marshall I. Goldman, "Economic Controversy in the Soviet Union," *Foreign Affairs,* 41, 3 (April, 1963): 498-512. Also, Leon Smolinski, "What Next in Soviet Planning?", *Foreign Affairs,* 42, 4 (July, 1964): 603-13.

23. Derived from U.S. Department of Commerce, Bureau of the Census, *Historical Statistics of the United States: Colonial Times to 1957* (Washington, D.C.: USGPO, 1960). This document is the source for all U.S. data presented below.

24. Florinsky, p. 755.

25. Florinsky, p. 882-96.

26. Florinsky, pp. 1211-24.

27. Lawrence T. Caldwell, *Soviet Attitudes to SALT* (London: ISS, 1971), Adelphi Papers No. 75, pp. 2-4.

28. Florinsky, pp. 722-27.

29. Florinsky, p. 789.

30. Florinsky, p. 800.
31. Ulam, pp. 460-70.
32. Jeremy R. Azrael, "Soviet Union," in James S. Coleman, ed., *Education and Political Development* (Princeton, N.J.: Princeton University Press, 1965), pp. 233-71.
33. Goldman, p. 498.
34. Florinsky, pp. 896-902, 1155-56, 1170-71.
35. Florinsky, pp. 1177-83, 1184-1200.
36. Florinsky, pp. 1155, 1390. Meyer, pp. 155, 138, 156.
37. Meyer, pp. 159, 162-63.
38. Roman Kolkowicz, "Interest Groups in Soviet Politics: The Case of the Military," *Comparative Politics,* 2, 3 (April, 1970): 445-72.
39. Meyer, pp. 190-91.
40. Meyer, pp. 382-83.
41. Frederic J. Fleron, Jr., "Toward a Reconceptualization of Political Change in the Soviet Union: The Political Leadership System," *Comparative Politics,* 1, 2 (January, 1969): 228-44. Also, Philip D. Stewart, "Soviet Interest Groups and the Policy Process: The Repeal of Production Education," *World Politics,* XXII, 1 (October, 1969): 29-50.

Chapter 4

POLITICAL DEVELOPMENT:

The International Dimension

The development of national political systems does not occur in a geopolitical vacuum; yet, the international impact on political development has frequently been ignored or slighted by analysts who seem to minimize the importance of external influences. In order to remedy this oversight, we shall examine in this chapter the international aspects of national political growth. In our discussion, we shall look at various ways in which a developing political system is linked to its international environment, and how these linkages affect the course of its development process and the improvement of its capabilities.

Since the end of World War II, and the destruction of many colonial empires which came in its wake, the international community has been experiencing its own form of population explosion. Throughout the nineteenth century, although the total population of member states of the international system may have reached 20, the number of effective and influential Powers was probably limited to about five or six.[1] At around the turn of the century, participation had expanded to include many of the Latin American states, and the total system contained perhaps as many as 40 or 50 nations. Today, however, more than 120 political entities claim the right to a voice in the international community.[2]

What is important from the point of view of our discussion here is that the great majority of the new members of the international system are in the process of developing their political capabilities. In contrast to that situation which obtained in the early years of the international system, most of today's members consider themselves relatively less developed both economically and politically, and are engaged in conscious efforts to correct that condition. In the nineteenth century, a state was not admitted to membership in the international system until it had reached a position of relative parity with other members in terms of power, and could defend itself from attack from an already established member of the system, such as in the case of the United States after the War of 1812. The mere acquisition of independent status was not enough to guarantee entry into the international system, as the position of the several Latin American states during the nineteenth century attests. Countries such as Venezuela or Colombia, while sovereign in a legal sense, were not members of the international power community of the period because of their relatively underdeveloped condition.

With the advent of nonpower criteria to determine membership status, the international system has become heavily populated with underdeveloped states. In the post-1945 period, with few exceptions, polities have begun their era of nationhood in a state of underdevelopment. In most cases the first task on their national political agenda is to close the gap between themselves and the already established members of the system. This struggle provides the psychological background against which many of the dramas of development are played out in Africa, Asia, and Latin America.

The decision to initiate a polity's drive to development, to commence the sequence of development decisions, always includes an attempt at self-definition vis-à-vis the international system. As a state's political elite begins its series of development steps, it begins to define its nation's identity or character in terms of external factors. In the case of nations which threw off colonial rule after 1945, this self-definition came naturally and easily in their anticolonial posture. The nonalignment policies and pronouncements of Afro-Asian leaders such as Nehru and Sukarno were intended to serve notice to the world and to their own supporters at home that new, distinct nations had been born with distinctive national characters. The search for national identity in conjunction with the initiation of development has been complicated in Latin America because of that area's relatively long period of postcolonial, independent but underdeveloped status. Nevertheless, in their own ways, Juan Peron in Argentina, Lazaro Cardenas in Mexico, and, of course, Fidel Castro have all attempted to show that they were disengaging from excessive dependence on United States protection (and economic dominance), as a prerequisite to establishing their own sequence of development.

Thus, we cannot ignore the international implications of political development. While preceding chapters have focused on the internal factors which determine the different paths of development, our analysis would not be complete without a parallel examination of external factors which also play an important role in shaping the development sequence.

THE INTERNATIONAL SETTING OF DEVELOPMENT

Among the external conditions which impinge on political development, certainly the *type of international system* must rank as one of the most significant. There is, for instance, a clear relationship between the degree of competition in the international system and the degree of latitude enjoyed by developing states in selecting development alternatives. A balance of power system, with several competing major powers, produces an environment for developing states which is different from that yielded by a rigid, bipolar, "Cold War" system. A third possible arena is offered by the polycentric system which has been operative since the late 1950's or early 1960's, which Stanley Hoffman calls "muted bipolar."[3]

A second major set of constraints which has a bearing on political development arises from the *technological environment,* especially as it concerns military strategy and weaponry. The change from United States superiority in nuclear weapons to something approaching parity with the Soviet Union, a condition referred to as "mutual deterrence," has exerted a strong influence on the activities of the developing nations. At the subnuclear level, the increased capability of the United States to intervene in "brush-fire" wars via its great air and naval mobility has surely influenced development patterns in Southeast Asia, the Caribbean, and the Mediterranean area.

Third, the set of external factors affecting political development should include some reference to the various *models available* to the developing elite. Depending upon the time at which the development program was initiated, a developing elite may be able to choose from a wide variety of examples, based on states which began from similar circumstances, and met varying degrees of success with experimentation in certain areas. For example, those states which began their development sequence prior to 1917—such as Mexico and Japan —had very few models to which they could refer; the incrementalist experience of the United States and Great Britain was hardly useful to them unless greatly modified. After 1940, developing states had not only the Soviet model on which to draw, but also the fascist experiences of Italy and Spain. When this latter concept was largely discredited after World War II, its place was taken by the Maoist rural, peasant revolutionary model; and this example was later modified by Castro in a way which spread in haphazard and unsuccessful fashion to other Latin American countries. Thus, the path which a developing state elects may be determined by the external examples it can follow.

Finally, we may include as an important international variable the *nature of the contiguous environment.* In any given state, the neighbors on its borders constitute an important factor in the perspective of the country's leaders. Whether the contiguous environment dominates the elite's horizon or not will be determined by the ideological and objective concerns of this elite.[4] But, if a developing polity's neighborhood is populated by states which are also undertaking development strategies, the impact on the original state may well be immense. Regardless of the nature of the development sequences undertaken by contiguous countries, the mere fact that they are friendly or hostile, status quo or revisionist, will play a great role in determining the original state's allocation of resources during its development drive. The conflict during the early 1960's between the radical African states of the Casablanca Group and the more moderate members of the Monrovia-Brazzaville Group illustrates the extent to which the character of the contiguous environment may affect the allocation of resources of states within a region.[5]

LINKAGES AND DEVELOPMENT

The several factors which we have examined above, however, may have differential impacts on the internal developmental process of a given polity, depending on a set of linkages, or transmission belts, which bind the nation to its international environment. One of the most important of these is the *degree of penetration* experienced by the developing state. According to James Rosenau, penetration of a political system occurs when "members of one polity serve as participants in the political processes of another." He goes on to specify that this sort of penetration means that nonmembers of the political system enjoy the authority to allocate resources and values within the penetrated polity.[6] It must not be assumed, however, that highly penetrated polities are merely pawns in the international system. As one recent study has pointed out, even in the case of a thoroughly penetrated political system such as Peru, the political leaders were still able to influence other foreign governments, including that of the United States, under certain conditions.[7]

We can distinguish at least four separate degrees of penetration by external actors into our developing political system, each of which brings with it its own peculiar sort of influences on the developmental process.

At the highest level of penetration we find those states which are usually called colonies or, under some conditions, protectorates. States which lie firmly within the sphere of influence of a Great Power would also have to fall in this category.[8] The degree to which the penetrating power uses its authority to participate in the small state's political processes depends to some extent on the Great Power's objectives or aims in maintaining this high degree of penetration. Such penetration is not bought cheaply; especially in the post-1945 era of increasing nationalism, Great Powers have found that the purchase of leverage over internal politics of highly penetrated states is an expensive proposition. For this reason, the motives of the Great Power in sustaining such a high cost will be of great importance in setting the constraints within which a penetrated state can act.

A more moderate level of penetration seems to be present in alliance relationships. Here, the small state is able to muster enough internal power to resist Great Power intrusion into its domestic affairs. Thus, while both Mexico and

Guatemala may be of roughly equal value to the United States, Guatemala has a highly penetrated, sphere of influence political system vis-à-vis the United States, while Mexico's relationships with the U.S. come somewhat nearer being of the moderately penetrated, alliance variety. Similar distinctions could be indicated for other Great Powers as well.

A very few states have tried with success to maintain an independent but involved status with regard to international politics. Certain Great Powers are able to sustain rather high levels of involvement abroad while at the same time enjoying a great deal of independence. Some states, such as Switzerland or Sweden, have been able historically to carry on moderate levels of involvement with other nations without losing independence to any great degree; a few developing states—Brazil and India come first to mind—have also been able to accomplish this feat. However, most states in the developing category, in order to reduce external penetration, have had to pay the price in a form of self-imposed nonalignment. Thus, states such as Burma or Cambodia in Asia, Chile in Latin America, and virtually all the black African nations have been forced to follow this route.

A fourth possibility exists at the theoretical level but, in fact, it may be very difficult to find examples empirically. This is the lowest degree of penetration, which we may call the isolated state. To meet the criteria for this category, a state would have to be strong enough to resist most significant outside influence, a difficult enough task to perform for developing countries; at the same time, however, it must be led by an inward-looking elite which has no desire for external contacts. Geography will obviously play an important role here, since insular states and landlocked, mountainous polities will more easily be able to follow this path. Ceylon and Paraguay, each in its own distinctive way, probably come as close to this model as any state could in a world of modern communications and close interactions.

A second set of linkage factors consists of what Karl Deutsch calls "linkage groups,"[9] collectivities which are part of the domestic political system, but which also maintain certain contacts with other national political systems, and which serve to transmit or channel communications from abroad into the national political arena. Since we may assume that there is no such thing as a completely closed political system in the real world, we must presume that all states possess linkage groups to some degree. However, certain characteristics of these linkage groups will affect the nature of their performance of the transmission belt, or communication function.

First, the internal strength of the linkage groups is an important factor in helping them to play a role in political development. Material and organizational strength will enable these groups to weather storms of protest, and to endure almost certain stress on their position; internal strength of identity and unity will also be important in supporting their role as linkages. Linkage groups are likely to be operating under a great deal of stress, since developing countries are usually interested in establishing an ability to resist penetration from the international system. Groups whose purpose is to break down this resistance, to link the developing polity more closely to the international environment, may be subjected to attack as traitors. This may be the case especially for those local nationals who have worked for foreign corporations, or who were employed in the bureaucracy under a colonial administration, or who have worked for an occupying army in some way. Deutsch also points out the increasing stress on marginal minorities within the national system who may also have ties to foreign states—the overseas Chinese living in Southeast Asia, for example—who are brought under increasing pressure either to assimilate into the national culture or to leave the system.[10]

This discussion leads us, then, to examine the second factor concerning linkage group effectiveness—the strength of the linkages between this group and the national political system. The stronger the ties between a given linkage group and its own national political system, the greater will be the group's ability to act as a channel for communication from the international environment. The prestigous position accorded economists within certain reform-minded governments in Latin America has made easier the transmission of influence from the United Nations Economic Commission for Latin America (UN—ECLA), with the result that ECLA, in the late 1950's and early 1960's was regarded ". . . as the recognized spokesman for Latin America's economic development."[11] The opposite position, however, one in which the linkage group is isolated from, and alienated from the political system, produces an environment which clearly weakens the group's influence. The fragmented societies of the developing world abound with examples of this sort of break in the linkage transmission belt, from the Chinese in Southeast Asia, to the Indians in East Africa, to the American businessman in immediate postrevolutionary Cuba.[12]

A third, and final, factor which has much to do with the transmission effectiveness of the linkage groups is their willingness to accept the status quo in their society. Just as nations outside our political system can hold either status quo or revisionist expectations about the future, so also can groups within the system share these views. Only rarely will the set of linkage groups in a system hold only one dominant view of the future of the system's operations; usually, the groups will have a mixed collection of expectations about what the system holds for them. However, we can predict that all political systems—no matter how well integrated—will contain at least a few revisionist groups and individuals. In addition, a rapidly developing polity is likely to have more than its share of revolutionary linkage groups. The so-called "shadow wars" in such diverse areas as Zambia, Laos, and the Andean regions of Latin America are all eloquent testimony to unsatisfied revisionist demands of unassimilated minorities. The presence of revisionist linkage groups in a developing system becomes of particular importance to the incumbent government when the groups establish links with similarly inclined states abroad. As we shall note below, such a configuration of linkages places a maximum amount of stress on the developing system's regulative capabilities.

REGULATIVE CAPABILITY AND THE
INTERNATIONAL SYSTEM

Having set forth the principal ways in which the international system is linked with, and affects, the developing internal political system, we are prepared to trace some of the effects of these linkages on the improvement of certain systemic capabilities.

We have already noted in another context (see Chapter One) that development elites will emphasize the improvement of a system's regulative capabilities early in the development process. In many cases, the development elite came to power during a period of disruption and unrest, marked by an inability of the old leaders to establish their control over their territorial jurisdiction. All successful development leaders who come to power under these conditions must pay first attention to problems of regulation, if they are to survive long enough to pay attention to other, competing objectives.

The improvement of the regulative capability is really a dual problem for a development elite. On the internal scene, countries which are entering the development process today are confronted with fragments of unassimilated ethnic minority groups over which the central government must extend its authority. On the external side, however, the political systems in today's developing world are almost always characterized by the term "penetrated"; these states must improve their regulative capability to offset this penetration as well.[13] These two aspects of the regulative challenge merge to form one broad problem of establishing governmental authority internally.

For political systems developing during the twentieth century, the presence of revisionist states in the international system has surely increased the problems of internal governance and the improvement of the regulative capability. Already confronted with internal insurgencies growing out of real or imagined deprivations, the governments of developing states have an additional burden thrown on them by aid given to the insurgents by revisionist states—either neighbors or Great Powers. Specific, empirical information on instances of external assistance to local insurgents is understandably ambiguous and subject to varying, emotional interpretations. It does seem clear, nevertheless, that North Vietnamese and (possibly) Chinese activity in Laos in support of the Pathet Lao has made the regulative capability a particularly elusive first step toward development for the Laotian government.[14] In East Africa, the effect of Somali irredentist claims on parts of Kenya and Ethiopia have forced the latter two states to divert valuable resources into the maintenance of control over the disputed area.[15] Latin America has been plagued by this type of interstate behavior practically from the beginning of its period of independence. In the post-World War II period, the center of greatest activity has been the Caribbean and Central America, where a group of democratic, reform-minded states—led by Costa Rica, Guatemala (until 1954), and Venezuela (after 1959)—have carried on a running battle with a group of dictatorial countries—Cuba under Batista, the Dominican Republic under Trujillo, and Nicaragua under the Somoza family. The former group operated through a clandestine agency known as the Caribbean Legion, which was made up of exiles from the dictator-led states, and soldiers of fortune; the latter set of nations allied themselves formally with the Organization of Central American States. The interaction of these conflicting political systems during the 1950's, has yielded much of the insurgency and sub-limited warfare witnessed in the area.[16]

To balance our perspective, however, it must be added that an incumbent government in a developing state does not face alone this challenge to his regulative capability from external sources. Other actors in the international system stand ready to assist that government in establishing his control over recalcitrant insurgent minorities, *especially* if it can be alleged that the insurgents actually are receiving aid from revisionist members of the system. United States assistance to the government of the Republic of Vietnam is only the most dramatic example of this type of status quo penetration; since 1945, United States and other western aid has gone to a wide variety of countries from Colombia and Venezuela, in Latin America, to the Congo (Kinshasa) in Africa, to Thailand and Laos in Asia, for the purpose of assisting the incumbent political system to improve its regulative capability.[17]

One might assume, mistakenly, that the national-international linkage at work here is always between status quo states and incumbents, on the one hand, and reform states and insurgents, on the other hand. To correct that assumption we should point out that the United States enabled and encouraged the Organization of American States to provide regulative aid to Costa Rica during its two periods of conflict with Nicaragua, 1948–1949 and 1955, although the former was a reform state within the Caribbean subsystem, and the latter was a status quo member of that grouping.[18] Similarly, Communist China established close ties with the Sukarno government in Indonesia, even though Sukarno's foreign policy revisionism and close adherence to the Peking position on many foreign issues was not matched by ardent reform at home.[19] The similar demands of foreign policy on Great Powers, and of internal security on developing elites, produce the strange alliances so often seen in the non-Western world since 1945.

Finally, we must make mention of another type of regulation which is practiced upon the representatives of penetrating actors in the developing political system—the expropriation or confiscation of foreign-owned enterprises. In a period of rising nationalist sentiment, many development elites simply find it intolerable that so much of their national destiny should be in the hands of nonmembers of their system. Therefore, they deem it necessary to expropriate properties of foreign nationals, and bring them under the regulative control of the national government. While such a practice could, conceivably, be considered under the heading of an improvement of their extractive capability, the fact is that seldom does such expropriation result immediately in any increase in resources extracted from the economy. The raw materials continue to be sold in traditional markets, unless, as in the case of Cuban sugar, a new, controlled market is found. Frequently, the net output of the expropriated concerns does not rise until well after the initial date of expropriation.

The gains from expropriation, however, are real, even if they are not felt in the extractive areas of the economy. The gains are felt in the symbolic (and real) exercise of the political system's regulative capabilities, and by the acquisition of a sense that the nation is at last in control of its own future. The failure of President Fernando Belaunde Terry of Peru to establish greater controls over the International Petroleum Corporation led to the belief within certain military circles that Belaunde could not properly defend the nation's interests.[20] Likewise, one of the first acts of the new military government in Bolivia, after having overthrown the constitutional president in September, 1969, was to announce a "revision" in the petroleum law, under which Gulf Oil Company had been granted its exploitation concessions in Bolivia. This move was taken, according to the leader of the coup, General Alfredo Ovando Candia, in order to assure". . . autonomous development, free from interference which could damage national sovereignty."[21] Perhaps the most dramatic example of this type of regulative activity, however, was the nationalization of the Suez Canal by Gamal Abdel Nasser in June, 1956. Although certainly of questionable economic significance for the Egyptians, this move not only showed Nasser to be a bold actor on the international scene, but strengthened the feeling of Egyptians that they were no longer pawns to be moved about by the Great Powers.[22]

EXTRACTIVE CAPABILITY AND THE INTERNATIONAL SYSTEM

The impact of the international system on the improvement of a state's extractive capability will certainly be great; but, as with the enhancement of a regulative capability, the developing system may well find the international environment to bring mixed blessings to its development effort.

Most obviously, if a system's developing elite has available to it from external sources certain crucial resources—capital, raw materials, technology, or managerial talent—then the elite will be saved the trouble of making some hard decisions about how to extract these same resources from its domestic reservoir. With certain reservations, one of the major stumbling blocks of economic development programs in many of the non-Western countries appears to be the creation of capital resources. While one might question the setting of a specific rate of capital formation to mark the acquisition of "take-off,"[23] a substantial increase in the formation of capital must in fact take place for economic development to occur. There are, however, only a few sectors of society from which the development elite can extract this capital for subsequent reinvestment.

The leadership of most developing countries seem to assume that capital formation increases will come about as a result of public sector actions. Available evidence indicates that, in those countries with a significantly increased rate of capital formation, the public sector had accounted for at least half of the increase. In addition, public sector ownership of other basic means of production, such as public utilities, transportation, and essential extractive industries, means an even higher contribution of the political system to capital formation and reinvestment.[24]

If, then, the political system is responsible for the mobilization of resources for the economic growth of the nation, from which sectors will these resources be extracted? A number of alternative "mixes" are theoretically available to the developing elite; but the problems of political development immediately appear to render many of these not only unattractive but fatal to a particularly shaky government. In general, the extraction of resources from the domestic environment demands a considerable amount of regulative capability as a necessary (but not sufficient) precondition; and, as we have already seen, governments of developing nations simply do not have the time available to them to improve their regulative capability first before embarking on a program of economic growth and investment.

The international system, then, can provide the funds necessary to establish a self-sustaining program of economic development without forcing the government in question to make the difficult decisions about the sectors which will be forced to sacrifice. The sums in question are not inconsiderable. In 1965, for example, the countries of the developing world (excluding those with centrally planned economies) were the recipients of almost $10 billion in *net* movement of long-term capital. Of this sum, private long-term investment accounted for almost $3 billion. Public funds, from developed market economies, from centrally planned economies, or from multilateral agencies, accounted for the remaining amount of nearly $7 billion. The exact figures for the movement of public capital are shown in Table 4.1.[25]

One concludes, however, that the availability of these funds constitutes an ambiguous advantage for political systems seeking to improve their extractive capabilities. For several reasons, the impact of the international system on the extractive capability of developing states will entail some pitfalls as well.

For one thing, the recipient state will often be asked by the donor to make certain adjustments in policies which the donor deems to be important. To the extent that the availability of aid is dependent on these adjustments, the developing state has been penetrated, often in a manner which is distasteful to the recipient. Nevertheless, the movement of resources in the international

Table 4.1 Net Official Flow of External Resources to Developing Countries (by region) from Developed Market Economies, Centrally Directed Economies, and Multilateral Agencies, 1965. (In millions of U.S. $).

	Developed Market Economies	Centrally Directed Economies	Multilateral Agencies	Total
Latin America*	838	—	160	998
Africa	1,484	204	230	1,918
Asia	2,804	391	424	3,619
Net interregional disbursements	179	—	11	190
Unallocated	125	—	—	125
Total	5,430	595	825	6,850

*Does not include Cuba.
**Does not include Mainland China.
Source: United Nations Statistical Yearbook, 1967.

system remains highly dependent on noneconomic, that is, nonmarket, factors such as political reliability, votes in international organizations, and others. An international system with a varied set of Great Powers will obviously make varying demands on the developing members of the system; clear differences can be seen between the "political strings" placed on aid by the United States, the Soviet Union, and China.

For this reason, some of the developing states have rejected the acquisition of resources from the international system, as a symbol of their newly found ability to resist penetration. Burma, in 1953, and Indonesia under Sukarno both severed aid programs from the United States; Ghana did the same to the Soviet Union following the downfall of Nkrumah.[26] In these and other cases, then, the developing elites must make a fundamental decision—either to diminish their economic development effort or to shift the burden of supporting the effort to domestic groups. In some instances, the elites find that they cannot afford to move in either of these two directions; the inertia created by reliance on the international system for the crucial economic margin of resource extraction is too great a determinant. Their usual recourse, then, is to shift the source of their aid, while still retaining a heavy role for the international economy. This, essentially, is a description of the path taken by Cuba after 1961.

We must not assume, however, that the demands made by the penetrating members of the international system will automatically be detrimental to the efforts of the developing states to improve their internal extractive and regulative capabilities. The "strings" tied to aid may be of two broad types. First, the aid may be used to pressure the developing state to take certain positions in the Great Power conflicts, to accept membership in alliances, to participate in military operations, to accept the presence of Great Power bases on its soil, and so on. In 1954, for example, the United States exerted tremendous economic pressure on various members of the inter-American system to vote in favor of a proposal to condemn international communism in a veiled attempt to unseat the government of Guatemala.[27] Similarly, the Soviets and the Chinese have engaged in what Julius Nyerere has labeled "the second scramble for Africa," employing economic aid and technical and diplomatic missions to move certain African states—Guinea, Algeria, the Congo (Kinshasa)— somewhat closer to their sphere of influence.[28] It is difficult to ascertain what, if any, positive effects these sorts of penetrative demands may have on the improvement of a developing state's extractive capabilities.

These demands, however, should not be lumped together with other kinds of demands made by donors of international resources, which may serve to move the developing state closer to its own goals. Some observers of the foreign aid program of the United States clearly try to draw a distinction between the influence which the donor employs for short-term political purposes, and those which are used for the economic development of the recipient state. In these cases, the donor state uses its aid as a tool to encourage the developing state to make hard development decisions, decisions which are designed to produce exactly the type of capability improvement which the development elite itself desires. The Alliance for Progress concept was aimed at reaching these goals by encouraging the recipient Latin American states to undertake certain difficult reforms regarding land tenure and taxation; in several specific instances —in Colombia, Ecuador, Korea, Pakistan, and Brazil, to name only a few— the United States has withheld aid until the recipient demonstrated the willingness and the ability to undertake additional development measures, in such areas as exchange rates, budgeting, and import duties.[29] Occasionally, this sort of demand provides the necessary incentive for the developing state to make difficult choices, and thus move closer to its development goals; at the least, they provide additional rationales for a development leader to use as an argument for making decisions which he would not otherwise have the power to make, or the leverage to enforce. As Albert O. Hirschman puts it, "It is the role of foreign capital to enable and to embolden a country to set out on the path of unbalanced growth."[30]

Finally, it must be emphasized that penetrative pressures from aid donors to move development elites toward the improvement of state capabilities can serve the cause of political development only if the elites use in a positive manner the time bought for them by such aid. All too often, the evidence indicates, the function of external resources has been to allow the development leaders to postpone the undertaking of vital reforms and, eventually, to forget about them all together. In the field of agriculture, for example, the development of a new strain of wheat, while leading to radically expanded production in developing countries, may have removed the incentives necessary for these countries to embark on badly needed land tenure reform programs. The Food for Peace Program of the United States has permitted national leaders to keep the price of food low in low-income, politically volatile urban areas, but at the cost of undermining market incentives for the expansion of domestic agricultural production.[31] In a different area, the availability of loans from agencies such as the International Monetary Fund for the purpose of alleviating balance of payments problems in developing countries may actually only help the country in question to continue basically unstable exchange rate and fiscal policies at home.

DISTRIBUTIVE CAPABILITY AND THE INTERNATIONAL SYSTEM

The enhancement of a system's distributive capabilities blends almost imperceptibly with the growth of extractive powers. Without a significant extractive capability, a political elite cannot hope to undertake the concrete distribution of resources from one sector to another. In addition, the enhancement of a system's extractive powers is usually justified by proclaiming a need to increase either the polity's regulative or its distributive capabilities. Indeed, the distinction between extraction and distribution rests mainly on the intentions of the political leadership; and, for this reason, such distinction erodes easily when confronted with empirical data.

In no area is this blurring of capabilities more evident than in evaluating the impact of the international system on political development. Whatever the international environment does to lessen the burden of extraction will also ease the difficulties encountered in the redistribution of resources. In fact, as we emphasized, foreign aid makes resource extraction easier for a developing polity precisely by making it appear as if there is no shift in the distributive policies of the regime domestically. Therefore, the example which we propose to discuss below—land tenure reform—could also have been included in the analysis of extraction capabilities.

For reasons which we have discussed elsewhere, land tenure reform is often cited as a key to political and economic development. The economic implications of agrarian reform may indeed be enhanced merely through nonconfiscatory measure, such as cadastral and taxation improvement, increased long-term credit, feeder roads, and others. In terms of political power, however, in some countries, the road to development is blocked without the seizure of large estates and the transfer of this property to large groups of previously landless tenants. Thus, a thorough-going agrarian reform program virtually demands the expansion of a political system's distributive capabilities. The external environment can contribute a great deal of help to a developing elite in its efforts to transfer the ownership of the nation's agricultural lands.

In both Europe and Asia, in the wake of World War II, the victorious Great Powers pressed vigorously for the institution of agrarian reform programs in the occupied states. In Eastern Europe, particularly in Poland and Hungary, the advancing Red Army of the Soviet Union guaranteed the success of the local communist programs of expropriation of large rural estates; in all, some 48 million acres were expropriated by the communist governments installed by the Soviet Union, with about 30 million of these acres subsequently redistributed to about 3 million peasant families.[32] In Japan, immediately following the occupation of that country by the United States armed forces at the end of the War, the enactment of a far-reaching agrarian reform law was facilitated greatly by the directive issued by General MacArthur in December, 1945, which stated that, "The Japanese Imperial Government is directed to take measures to insure that those who till the soil of Japan shall have more equal opportunity to enjoy the fruits of their labor."[33] Although both the Eastern European leaders and the Japanese government probably would have enacted some kind of limited land tenure reform eventually, even without pressure from occupation forces of foreign governments, there can be no doubt that the influence of the Russian and American occupation both speeded the reforms and, in the case of Eastern Europe, increased their scope tremendously.

At the opposite end of the spectrum of external influence, we can locate the activities of various international organizations and agencies which have an organizational interest in the land tenure reform programs of developing countries. The Food and Agriculture Organization of the United Nations, for example, has operated since 1945 in the role of the international "extension agent," to the world's depressed agricultural areas. The work of the FAO is restricted to activities which seem to impinge on national sovereignty only in a limited way, such as the provision of technical aid and the collection and dissemination of information. In such areas as the management of agrarian reform pilot projects, however, the FAO has contributed greatly to our understanding of the needs and results of land tenure reform under a variety of conditions.[34] The International Bank for Reconstruction and Development has also been active in the area of supplying technical advice, which has occasionally been used by the recipient government as the rationale for embarking on certain reform ventures when internal political considerations might have been balanced against them.[35]

Somewhere in between these two types of external pressures for agrarian reform, we find the moderate nudges administered by Great Powers who feel that some improvement in the land tenure situation in developing countries would contribute to the achievement of their ideal of a stable international system. In Taiwan, scene of the second successful noncommunist land tenure reform program (after that of Japan), the presence of the Joint (Chinese-American) Commission on Rural Reconstruction afforded the Nationalist Chinese not only social and technological advice, but economic assistance as well.[36] In Latin America, the United States (prompted by the Cuban experiment) was able to persuade several members of the inter-American community, through the Alliance for Progress, to commit themselves ". . . to encourage . . . programs of comprehensive agrarian reform leading to the effective transformation . . . of unjust structures and systems of land tenure and use . . ."[37] Admittedly, many of the governments of Latin America responded with formal laws embodying widespread reforms, or created special agrarian reform agencies to satisfy their commitments; but, subsequent moves to implement these programs were quite often lacking.[38] Nevertheless, in those cases where there was already some internal potential for the expansion of the distributive capability, as in Colombia, the additional incentives of United States economic aid were enough to move some political systems across the threshhold of reform, and to begin to undertake some redistribution of agricultural holdings.[39]

SYMBOLIC CAPABILITY AND THE
INTERNATIONAL SYSTEM

The external environment provides the elite of a developing state with great assistance in the expansion of its symbolic capabilities. Both in providing substantial channels for the expression and transmission of created symbols, as well as in offering a useful target for the creation of national symbols, the international environment has a net positive impact on the symbol creation capability of the developing state.

One of the most important channels for the expression of national symbols, of course, is the multitude of international organizations which have arisen since World War II. From the United Nations and its various specialized and regional agencies, such as the Economic Commissions for Latin America, Africa, and Asia and the Far East, through such purely regional groupings as the Organization of American States, or the Organization for African Unity, the developing states have before them numerous opportunities for the creation of symbolic positions on issues which do not touch them directly.

The ready availability of the international environment as a sounding board for the creation of systemic symbols has meant an easier task, relatively speaking, for developing states in the post-1945 period, at least as far as symbolic capability is concerned. States which initiated their development process prior to 1945 were confronted with a much more restricted environment in which to expand the symbolic capability. Developing states like the Soviet Union, because of its Great Power status, possessed a large amount of international symbolic capability already; and, in addition, their revolutionary philosophy facilitated the creation of additional symbolic capabilities with little expenditure of internal resources. Smaller developing states of the period, however, such as Mexico, were forced to develop their symbolic capability almost completely internally, with the result that many difficult choices had to be made about the allocation of resources in accord with the symbols they created. Since 1945, developing states have been given an environment in which symbol creation is an inviting path of development.

Generally speaking, the symbols which the developing smaller states have attempted to create have had two pragmatic objectives: (1) to solidify internal support for, and to legitimatize the regime; and (2) to protect them from overt interference from Great Powers or, simply, from stronger neighbors.

The management of foreign policy for a developing state is critical from an internal viewpoint, since it is in the state's relations with other systems that the developing elite gets its first chance to define the "we" and the "they" of their society. Most of the political communities of developing systems are highly fragmented, "mosaic" societies, divided among themselves along ethnic, religious, linguistic, and other lines.[40] The need to create a foreign policy, to establish an identity vis-à-vis the outside world, offers the developing elite an opportunity to expand its symbolic capabilities at virtually no internal cost. Now, for the first time, the citizens of Kenya or of Malaysia or of Peru can so identify themselves, very simply, by distinguishing between themselves and the foreigner, the stranger. As Good has written, "Domestic issues divide the nation and disclose how little developed is its consciousness of itself; foreign issues unite the nation and mark it as a going concern."[41]

We must introduce an important caveat to the understanding of the international symbolic capability, however. The utility value of drawing a distinct line between the "we" and the "they" depends to a great extent on the configuration of the linkage groups which the developing political system contains. If the set of linkage groups contains large segments of society which have obvious revolutionary expectations, then the adoption of firm and highly controversial stances in foreign affairs can prove to be the downfall of the regime. In Latin America, leaders of shaky reform regimes have hesitated to condemn Fidel Castro and United States intervention in the Dominican Republic for fear of severe internal repercussions. In Africa, the leaders of insecure governments have condemned separatism or secessionist desires throughout the continent, regardless of the inherent justice of the position, out of fear that they may be stirring latent aspirations in a similar direction in their own country.[42] Thus, the opportunity offered by the international environment for the creation of symbols is not always an advantageous one, and the astute political leader must take his internal power structure into account before he steps out onto the stage of international politics.

The second function which developing states have sought to derive from an expanded symbolic capability in the international system has been to protect themselves from overt penetration from large, ambitious neighbors. The leaders of the developing states have recognized that, with few exceptions, they are deficient in the resources necessary to extend their regulative capability into the external environment. In other words, they cannot protect themselves from any determined Great Power or major regional state. Rather than devote precious resources to try to develop a militarily credible defense force, they have chosen to substitute the endorsement of suitable symbols which, they hope, will constrain states which otherwise might covet their territory. They seek, in short, to substitute symbolic capability for regulative capability.

In Latin America, the smaller states in the region have consistently fought for the concept of nonintervention in hopes that somehow the enormous power gap between themselves and the United States could be bridged in this manner. During the period of increased United States armed interventions in the Caribbean, prior to 1920, the Latin American countries began to pressure their powerful neighbor into acceptance of the nonintervention doctrine; but it was not until the adminstration of Franklin D. Roosevelt that such a position became United States Policy.[43] By 1948, the Latin American states had persuaded the United States to sign the Charter of the Organization of American States with the following provision: (Article 15)

> No State or group of States has the right to intervene, directly or indirectly, for any reason whatever, in the internal or external affairs of any other State. The foregoing principle prohibits not only armed force but also any other form of interference or attempted threat against the personality of the State or against its political, economic and cultural elements.

The Afro-Asian equivalent of the nonintervention doctrine has been the concept of nonalignment. Western observers, in characterizing the doctrine of nonalignment as a cynical attempt to play one side of the Cold War against the other, have usually overlooked the fact that the African and Asian leaders are using the concept as a moral shield, behind which they can consolidate their regimes. In Asia, states such as Cambodia and Burma had reason to fear not only the prospect of being involved in a general Great Power confrontation, but also being penetrated by their more powerful and aggressive small neighbors.[44] In Africa, leaders from Ghana, Tunisia, Egypt, and Kenya, among many others, attributed their desire to be nonaligned to their fear of neocolonialism and Balkanization.[45] In all these cases, as in those from Latin America, the developing states sought to expand their symbol creation capability externally in order to save what little regulative capability they were able to muster for internal purposes.

RESPONSIVE CAPABILITY AND THE INTERNATIONAL SYSTEM

The impact of the international system on the growth of responsive capabilities of a developing state is certainly ambiguous, at best. One of the recurrent general statements which one encounters in the writing on the subject has been that development elites can employ foreign crises to divert the attention of the masses away from their true sources of discontent, and thereby delay the moment of truth when the government must come to grips with their demands.[46]

Sukarno of Indonesia has been frequently selected as one of the most prominent users of foreign policy as a device to divert the attention of his people away from real internal problems. As Robert Shaplen describes it,[47] from 1961 until his downfall in 1965, Sukarno moved from one foreign policy crisis to another, each one designed to whip his followers into a frenzy of support for this charismatic leader. Beginning with the confrontation with the Dutch over West Irian, and continuing with the shadow war with Malaysia and Indonesia's withdrawal from the United Nations, Sukarno consistently neglected serious problems festering within the Indonesian body politic to turn his attention abroad. Finally, the collection of problems—falling production, rising prices, and generally worsening economic conditions and lack of confidence in the government—became so severe that leaders of Indonesia's armed forces appeared to be moving in the direction of ousting Sukarno. Whether or not the army actually was planning a coup, the Indonesian communists *thought* so, which prompted the latter group to launch their abortive coup in late September, 1965.

Franklin B. Weinstein, in a recent article on Indonesian foreign policy, uses a somewhat different approach to reach a similar set of conclusions.[48] Weinstein argues that the Indonesian political culture leads the elite members to be cautious about dealing with a hostile world, a world full of threat and danger. During the period of confrontation, roughly 1962 to 1966, when the internal political structure was the arena of competition among Sukarno, the army and the Communist Party (PKI), this perception of the outside world brought about a policy of nationalistic xenophobia. It was literally impossible for any of the competing members of the elite to appear to be softer towards the external environment than either of their two opponents. Once the internal struggle for power was resolved in favor of the army, it was no longer necessary to use foreign policy for domestic political leverage. As a consequence, Indonesia's foreign policy became much more conciliatory toward the United States and other sources of badly needed capital. Weinstein adds, however, that elite members have changed policy without undergoing significant change in their views about the essentially hostile nature of the international environment.

Some recent research of a systemic nature, however, leads the observer to be skeptical of too-close an identification between internal unrest and foreign policy adventurism. Burrowes and O'Leary, for example, attempted to test empirically the hypothesis that "international instability fluctuates with the domestic insecurity of national elites," by examining in detail international and domestic political conflict in the Middle East.[49] Their findings reveal that, in the case of Syria, the relationships between internal and external conflict patterns were few, fairly weak, and insignificant when compared with the strong intercorrelations within each subset of internal and external conflict indicators. As the authors rather cautiously point out, "If Syrian leaders did with any regularity use external politics to manage domestic conflict during this period of Syria's history, that fact was not captured by the data and the techniques used in this study."[50] When one considers, however, the high levels of both internal and external conflict in this region during the period studied, it seems that the hypothesis linking internal and external conflict behavior would have been strengthened if it had merit. Clearly, much more empirical evidence needs to be collected; but, we have seen enough for the moment to begin to call into question the conventional wisdom about the impact of the international system on the displacement of internal demands for political action.

In summary, then, for developing states, membership in the international community after 1945 has been a mixed blessing. On the positive side, the international environment has been the source of increased financial resources, thus facilitating the expansion of extractive and distributive capabilities without sacrificing critical levels of internal support for shaky regimes. The Cold War environment since the mid-1950's has likewise encouraged the developing states to expand their symbolic capabilities, similarly with very little cost internally. Finally, although the evidence is not clearcut, the formulation of foreign policy gives insecure developing elites the opportunity to divert attention away from real grievances at home.

On the negative side, however, the presence in the international system of significant revisionist states, and their linkages with similarly inclined alienated minorities within the developing states has magnified the problem of establishing firmly the regulative capability so badly needed at the beginning of a development effort. In addition, the recipients of external resources have frequently been called upon to undertake certain reforms at home in order to qualify for the continuation of aid; and this also has increased the level of informal penetration which seems so characteristic of developing political systems.

We may conclude that the international system is a net positive influence on the typical developing state, at least in the short run. Eventually, however, the successful developing state will be forced to turn inward and rely on its own resources for continued political development. The aid provided by the international community can, at best, be only a temporary expedient, which must be followed by concrete gains in systemic capabilities at home if the development effort is to succeed.

CHAPTER NOTES

1. Amry Vandenbosch, "The Small States in International Politics and Organization," *Journal of Politics,* 26, 2 (May, 1964); 293-312.
2. Chadwick F. Alger and Steven J. Brams, "Patterns of Representation in National Capitals and Inter-governmental Organization," *World Politics,* XIX, 4 (July, 1967): 646-63.
3. Stanley Hoffman, *Gulliver's Troubles, or the Setting of American Foreign Policy* (New York: McGraw-Hill, Inc. 1968), Chap. Two.
4. William G. Fleming, "Sub-Saharan Africa: Case Studies of International Attitudes

and Transactions of Ghana and Uganda," in James N. Rosenau, ed., *Linkage Politics* (New York: Free Press, 1969), Chap. Five.

5. I. William Zartman, *International Relations in the New Africa* (Englewood Cliffs, N.J.: Prentice-Hall, 1966), Chap. One.

6. James N. Rosenau, "Toward the Study of National-International Linkages," in Rosenau, ed., *Linkage Politics,* P. 46.

7. See Rod Bunker, "Linkages and the Foreign Policy of Peru, 1958–1966," *Western Political Quarterly,* XXII, 2 (June, 1969): 280-97.

8. John P. Vloyantes, "Spheres of Influence and International Relations: A Proposed Framework for Analysis" (Paper prepared for delivery at the Mid-West Political Science Association Conference, Ann Arbor, Michigan, April, 1969), pp. 1-8. Mimeo.

9. Karl Deutsch, "External Influences on the Internal Behavior of States," in R. Barry Farrell, ed., *Approaches to Comparative and International Politics* (Evanston, Ill.: Northwestern University Press, 1966), pp. 5-26, esp. pp. 8-19.

10. Deutsch, p. 17. See also Robert Shaplen, *Time Out of Hand: Reaction and Revolution in South East Asia* (New York: Harper & Row, 1969), pp. 164-67, for a description of the persecution of the Chinese minority in Indonesia.

11. Albert O. Hirschman, "Ideologies of Economic Development in Latin America," in Hirschman, ed., *Latin American Issues: Essays and Comments* (New York: Twentieth Century Fund, 1961), p. 13.

12. See W. Howard Wriggins, *The Ruler's Imperatives: Strategies for Political Survival in Asia and Africa* (New York: Columbia University Press, 1969), Chap. Two. Also Leland Johnson, "U. S. Business Interests in Cuba and the Rise of Castro," *World Politics,* XVII, 3 (April, 1965): 440-59.

13. The penetrative pressure from already developed neighbors may be in many cases the stimulus needed to encourage the initiation of a development sequence in the penetrated state. See S. N. Eisenstadt, *Modernization: Protest and Change* (Englewood Cliffs, N. J.: Prentice-Hall, 1966), pp. 18-19.

14. Shaplen, Chap. Seven.

15. Vernon McKay, "International Conflict Patterns," in McKay, ed., *African Diplomacy* (New York: Praeger, 1966), pp. 7-8.

16. See George I. Blanksten, "Foreign Policies in Latin America," in Roy C. Macridis, ed., *Foreign Policy in World Politics* (Englewood Cliffs, N. J.: Prentice-Hall, 1967), 3rd ed., pp. 363-67.

17. Joan M. Nelson, *Aid, Influence and Foreign Policy* (New York: Macmillan, 1968), pp. 19-23.

18. David W. Wainhouse, *et al., International Peace Observation* (Baltimore: The Johns Hopkins Press, 1966), pp. 106-14.

19. Shaplen, pp. 78-87. Wriggins, p. 231.

20. See Richard Goodwin, "Letter from Peru," *The New Yorker,* May 17, 1969, pp. 41-109.

21. *Comercio Exterior* (Mexico City), XIX, 10 (October, 1969): 792.

22. Wriggins, p. 224.

23. As does Walt Rostow, *The Stages of Economic Growth* (Cambridge, Mass.: Massachusetts Institute of Technology Press, 1961), p. 39.

24. John Adler, "Public Expenditures and Economic Development," (Santiago, Chile: Organization of American States, Published for the Joint Tax Program of the OAS,

the Inter-American Development Bank and the Economic Commision for Latin America, December, 1962), pp. 10-13. Mimeo.

25. Data gathered from *United Nations Statistical Yearbook, 1967* (New York: United Nations, 1968), pp. 688-95.

26. Werner Levi, *The Challenge of World Politics in South and Southeast Asia* (Englewood Cliffs, N. J.: Prentice-Hall, 1968), p. 107. *The New York Times,* March 2-3, 1966.

27. J. Lloyd Mecham, *A Survey of United States-Latin American Relations* (Boston: Houghton Mifflin company, 1965), p. 217.

28. Emmanuel John Hevi, *The Dragon's Embrace: The Chinese Communists in Africa* (New York: Praeger, 1966), Chap. Four. See also Julius Nyerere, "The Second Scramble" in Rupert Emerson and Martin Kilson, eds., *The Political Awakening of Africa* (Englewood Cliffs, N. J.: Prentice-Hall, 1965), pp. 162-65.

29. Nelson, Chap. Four.

30. Albert O. Hirschman, *The Strategy of Economic Development* (New Haven: Yale University Press, 1961), p. 205. For Hirschman, unbalanced growth is the proper kind for development purposes.

31. The *Economist* (London), V. 228, September 28, 1968, pp. 60-61. See also Cristoph Beringer, *The Use of Agricultural Surplus Commodities for Economic Development in Pakistan.* (Karachi, Pakistan: The Institute of Development Economics, January, 1964), esp. pp. 45-60.

32. D. F. Fleming, *The Cold War and Its Origins* (Garden City, N. Y.: Doubleday & Co., Inc., 1961), Vol. I, pp. 256-58. Also, Michael B. Petrovich, "Some of the Problems of Land Tenure in Eastern Europe," in Kenneth H. Parsons, and others, *Land Tenure:* Proceedings of the International Conference on Land Tenure and Related Problems in World Agriculture (Madison: University of Wisconsin Press, 1956), pp. 401-6.

33. Keiki Owada, "Land Reform in Japan," in Parsons, p. 221. Also, R. P. Dore, *Land Reform in Japan* (London: Oxford University Press, 1959), esp. Part II.

34. Thomas F. Carroll, "The World Land Tenure Problems and the Food Agriculture Organization," in Parsons, pp. 69-83.

35. Albert O. Hirschman, in *Journeys Toward Progress* (New York: Twentieth Century Fund, 1963), pp. 116-41, discusses the World Bank missions to Colombia in 1949 and 1956, and the impact they had on the land taxation programs in that country.

36. Wolf Ladejinsky, "Agrarian Reform in Asia, " *Foreign Affairs* 42, 3 (April, 1964): p. 457.

37. *Alliance for Progress.* Official Documents Emanating from the Special Meeting of the Inter-American Economic and Social Council at the Ministerial Level. Punta del Este, Uruguay, August 5-17, 1961. (Washington, D. C.: Pan American Union, 1961), p. 11.

38. Charles W. Anderson, in *Politics and Economic Change in Latin America* (Princeton, N. J.: D. Van Nostrand, 1967), p. 144, mentions Honduras as a specific case of this type of "paper" administration of the agrarian reform program.

39. Hirschman, p. 156.

40. Wriggins, p. 22. Charles W. Anderson, Fred R. von der Mehden, and Crawford Young, *Issues of Political Development* (Englewood Cliffs, N. J.: Prentice-Hall, 1967), Chap. One.

41. Robert C. Good, "State-Building as a Determinant of Foreign Policy in the New States," in Laurence W. Martin, ed., *Neutralism and Nonalignment: The New States in World Affairs* (New York: Praeger, 1962), p. 8. See also Levi, Chap. Two.

42. Zartman, Chapter Three. For a discussion of the interaction between internal Mexican politics and Mexico's policy toward Castro's Cuba, See Howard F. Cline, *Mexico: Revolution to Evolution, 1940–1960* (London: Oxford University Press, 1963), Chap. XXXIV.

43. Bryce Wood, *The Making of the Good Neighbor Policy* (New York: Columbia University Press, 1961).

44. Levi, pp. 87-89.

45. Vernon McKay, "International Conflict Patterns," in McKay, pp. 16-19.

46. Wriggins, pp. 230-31.

47. Shaplen, pp. 75-82.

48. Franklin B. Weinstein, "The Uses of Foreign Policy in Indonesia: An Approach to the Analysis of Foreign Policy in the Less Developed Countries," *World Politics,* XXIV, 3 (April, 1972): 356-81.

49. Robert Burrowes and Michael O'Leary, "Conflict and Cooperation Within and Between Nations: Israel, the United Arab Republic and the Major Arab States of South West Asia, 1949–1969." Prepared for delivery at the International Studies Association convention, San Francisco, March 27-29, 1969, p. 2, Mimeo.

50. Burrowes and O'Leary, p. 5.

Part 2

POLITICAL INSTABILITY

Chapter 5

DEVELOPMENT AND POLITICAL INSTABILITY

Are social observers accurate when they assert that the process of political development *always* brings with it a certain amount of personal or systemic disorder? Is there something *inherent* in the process of political development which tends to produce increased levels of civil strife and dislocation? Merely to advance these questions as if they were still not resolved is to challenge one of the conventional wisdoms of contemporary political development theory. And yet, as we hope to show in the following pages, the issue is actually quite in doubt, and quite definitely within the scope of human intervention and control.

DEVELOPMENT AND INSTABILITY

There seems to be little question that most observers consider the modernizing process to be highly destabilizing to political institutions, and to the broader social system of which they form a part. Virtually every social scientist interested in the phenomenon of modernizing traditional political systems assumes that the very process of rapid change will affect adversely the psychological balance of the participants in the process, with temporarily destructive results for the system itself.

S. N. Eisenstadt, for example,[1] states that "Disorganization and dislocation . . . constitute a basic part of modernization," and that this process brings with it "of necessity" the growth of "social problems, cleavages and conflicts between various groups, and movements of protest . . ." The causal factors are the well-known components of modernization: urbanization (which destroys rural family and clan ties), industrialization (which has undermined traditional occupational security and work discipline mores), political centralization and democratization (which have dislodged traditional elites from their favored positions), secularization (which has weakened the position of long-established values and standards of performance), and social mobilization (which has heightened mass awareness of deprivations and of sociocultural cleavages in the society).

All these dislocations and disorganizations, according to Eisenstadt, produce the continual growth of "social problems," which he defines as "breakdowns or deviations of social behavior, involving a considerable number of people, which are of serious concern to many members of the society in which the aberrations occur."[2] These problems are especially likely to occur in those areas of human behavior where institutionalization is weak: performance of sexual roles, maintenance of family relationships, and the occupational structure. The result will be increased incidences of abnormal behavior: crime, suicide, alcoholism, sexual deviance, and others. In all cases, however, the disorganization and resultant social problems have arisen because the process of rapid change has destabilized or disoriented the personality structure of the individual actor in the system.

C. E. Black, in his analysis,[3] speaks of "the agony of modernization," a process which may in the long run hold out the hope for great human progress, but only at "a high price in human dislocation and suffering." Black is concerned, as was Eisenstadt, about the personal disorientation incurred as a result of changes in values and standards of judging performance, which come with modernization. He decries the seemingly inevitable growth of personal maladjustment as a component of the development process, and he suggests that, although the more complex types of personality disorder such as neuroses and paranoia may be present in traditional societies, they burst forth more frequently in visible manifestations of deviant behavior when confronted with the disrupting challenges of the modernization process.

Black argues that merely because a modernizing personality begins to have more faith in his ability to control his environment he does not therefore become more at peace with himself psychologically. Development makes him less certain of his goals in life; the modern society produces an "atomized" individual with little sense of community; and "personal insecurity and anxiety" become the "hallmarks of the modern age." Lamenting the absence of confirming empirical evidence, Black still asserts that ". . . all categories of social disorganization—crime, delinquency, divorce, suicide, mental illness— have seen an increase in frequency as societies have become more modern." And, finally, he concludes that "No large numbers of individuals have been able thus far to adjust satisfactorily to the modern environment . . ."

A third analyst, Samuel Huntington, in his excellent extended essay on "political decay,"[4] finds there to be a strong correlation between rapid political mobilization and political instability. According to Huntington, the one inescapable component of political modernization is the expansion of political participation, the rapid mobilization of ever-increasing numbers of individuals who beat at the doors of the slowly evolving political structure with incessant demands for change. The integral parts of social mobilization—heightened awareness of relative levels of poverty and unequal distribution of wealth, increased exposure to political activism and its practical results, and an enhanced sense of the latent power which lies in the hands of the mob—are supposed to produce the systemic disruption which accompanies the modernization process.

Huntington's use of suprasystemic level empirical data seems to confirm repeatedly the positive correlation between economic development, social change, and political mobilization on the one hand, and violence and system instability on the other. He does hold out the hope, however, that systems experiencing high levels of instability may eventually reach a stable plateau of political and economic growth; "modernity," he says, "means stability and modernization instability."[5] By achieving the status of modernity, then, a system may actually return to its premodernization level of stability. The remainder of his study is devoted to explaining how the path to modernity leads to the growth of politically relevant institutions, especially the political party.

DEVELOPMENT AND STABILITY

In recent years, however, fragments of empirical evidence have begun to appear which, at the least, begin to cause us to doubt the conventional wisdom concerning the *inevitable* instability of the development process. Because of the much more limited scope and exposure of these analyses, they will be presented here in substantial detail.

One of the most interesting cases of directed cultural change that we have on record is that of the small village of Vicos, in highland Peru. The Vicos project, initiated by a group of social scientists from Cornell led by Allan R. Holmberg, has aimed at redirecting the technical and social base of life for the purpose ". . . of transforming one of Peru's most unproductive, highly dependent manor systems into a productive, independent, self-governing community adapted to the reality of the modern Peruvian state."[6] To accomplish this task, Holmberg and his associates, including several Peruvian social scientists, set out to alter many of the traditional concepts and mores of the some 1,700 Quechua-speaking Indians who lived in the village. Most, if not all, of the traditional ways of doing things were attacked at Vicos, including the remuneration for labor, the method of governing the town, the attitude toward group activities for the good of the community, the ownership of property, as well as subtle psychological areas such as confidence in associates and ability to predict the future with assurance. In short, since 1952, a thoroughly traditional community has been catapulted into the modernizing trends of the world around it. If the commonly held notions about the destabilizing effect of modernization are correct, we should expect to find the inhabitants of Vicos to be hyper-unstable after such a dizzying ascension to the heights of modernity.

Actually, however, the psychological impact on the natives of the village has been ambiguous, and in certain cases even tends to support the conclusion that the modernization of the system has enhanced psychological stability. To be sure, a survey taken in 1963 detected an increase in anxiety in the community.[7] When questioned, the male heads of household indicated a "substantial increase" in such psychosomatic indicators as trembling hands, palpitations of the heart, nightmares, headaches, loss of appetite, and difficulty in falling asleep. The analysis reveals that this increase is in accord with changes recorded in similar transitional villages in Peru.

Of great significance to our study, however, is the fact that certain types of what may be termed "social pathology" had definitely *decreased* during the period 1953–1963. The divorce and separation rate, for example, had been reduced by 50 percent. Petty theft, especially of livestock and other items of private property, had declined considerably. Assaults connected with robbery had declined, although assaults associated with disputes over land ownership had risen. Suicides, homicides, and infanticides continued to occur at a rate consistently so low that collection of statistics was not warranted. Most impressive is the drop in the use of *coca,* the drug-like leaf which Andean Indians chew to deaden the pangs of hunger and to aid them in withdrawing from the pain of their environment. Since the inception of the Vicos project, the use of *coca* has decreased sharply, and its use has even been prohibited in certain of the community agricultural projects. If one could hazard some tentative conclusions on the basis of this partial information, he might say that modernization had made the *vicosinos* more aware of the ills of their environment, as well as somewhat apprehensive about the way to remedy these ills; but, at the same time, they had become more confident in their ability ultimately to win out over the challenges of their surroundings.

From the small Ghanaian village of Larteh comes additional evidence, as supplied by David Brokensha.[8] This village of some 6,000 or so inhabitants (as of 1960) has been exposed to various types of strong modernizing influences since the mid-nineteenth century. Nevertheless, according to Brokensha, the village has been characterized by its ability to absorb social change in many important areas of village life, to accommodate these changes into their traditional modes of living, and to accomplish all this with virtually no evidence of social or psychological strain.

The sources of social modernization in Larteh are varied. They begin with the introduction of Christianity, through the founding of the Basel Mission and its related school in 1858. Although the mission experienced rather slow progress in the beginning, growth in converts had become substantial by the turn of the century. When, during World War I, the predominantly German mission was forced out of Larteh, it left behind a legacy of some 2,000 Christians, and a wealth of influence in other important areas, such as education, building construction, and community development.

The second major source of modernization came from the introduction of cocoa farming into the Larteh region about the turn of the century. The modifications brought about by this stimulus are equated by Brokensha to the influence of the horse on the life of the American Plains Indian, which is to say that they were (and continue to be) substantial. Larterians had had some exposure to the cash economy prior to the cultivation of cocoa, through experience with palm oil, rubber, and coffee; so the linkages of the cash nexus did not prove to be unsettling in themselves. The cocoa-oriented economy did foster significant changes in migration and demographic patterns, as more Larterians moved to the west where lands were more plentiful and easier to acquire. In the village, itself, however, the cocoa crop provided ready cash to build roads, schools, and churches. Indeed, the cocoa money, reinvested in education, served to further the trend of modification and social change initiated by the economic dislocations themselves.

Brokensha musters impressive evidence to show how the Larterians have managed to adjust evenly to these new challenges. Violent assaults, suicide, and homicide have been practically unknown, as Larterians place great value on nonviolence, and anger and violent actions are considered especially reprehensible. It is noteworthy that there appeared to be a higher incidence of suicides in the latter part of the nineteenth century, when witchcraft and sorcery were more important than they are today. Brokensha reports that, from June, 1959, to May, 1963, there were only 40 cases of crime in Larteh, or an average of about one per month, including 16 cases of theft, ten of assault, but only one attempted suicide and one homicide. Rape or attempted rape appear to be completely unknown.

Another sign of the social vigor and good health of Larteh lies in their devotion to community support for public works projects. Larterians have shown themselves to be active in their support for communal projects, such as roads, bridges, schools, and churches; and they have compiled an impressive record of donations (fueled by the cocoa trade) and work contribution for the welfare of the community. Many of their projects have anticipated national government intentions; they have been initiated by local Larterian volunteer organizations, only to be turned over to Ghanaian national agencies for subsequent direction.

Several brief examples will serve to illustrate how Larterians have been able to achieve a blend of traditional and modern in their social and political life. Brokensha describes a political rally for the Larteh branch of the Convention People's Party of Kwame Nkrumah in 1961. Although the rally was sponsored and directed by a modern (and modernizing) national political party, tradi-tional chieftains were accorded places of respect and honor, and the traditional Larteh band was on hand to supply music and entertainment as it had at virtually every public function in the village since 1913. Nkrumah's CPP was clearly being presented in traditional surroundings, even though the messages of the rally were modern. In the realm of medicine, there has been established at Larteh the Ghana Psychic and Traditional Healing Association, sponsored by the CPP's Minister of Health and encouraged at the time by Nkrumah's party. The purpose of the Association appeared to be the blending of witch-craft and mystic healing into modern medicine, especially as regards psychiat-ric disorders, which are felt to be especially susceptible to faith or spiritual treatment.

Brokensha's study appears to highlight Larteh's excellent educational sys-tem as the principal factor in easing the process of social transformation. Extensive educational facilities have been available to Larterian children since the founding of the first mission school in 1858; and Larteh's illiteracy rate of 29 percent (for males) compares favorably with Ghana's overall national rate of 71 percent. Whatever the cause, Larteh's experience is impressive evidence that social change need not produce psychological conflict. To cite Brokensha,

> . . . The outstanding feature of social change at Larteh . . . is not conflict but adaptation and accommodation . . . Larterians have accepted, with few violent reactions, many intrusive elements in their culture, and far from being in constant conflict, socially or psychologically, they have displayed a resilience and tolerance, in keeping with their values of calmness, deco-rum, and propriety . . . In this respect Larteh is typical of many other West African communities.[9]

Evidence of a more impressionistic nature about the capacity of the human psyche to withstand or absorb rapid change can be found in a series of case studies compiled by Arthur E. Niehoff.[10] These reports from the field by experienced social change agents clearly indicate that the responses of tradi-tion-bound peoples to the challenges of change constitute a complex set of emotional and pragmatic behavioral alternatives. In a small village in India, for example, the authors[11] found an entire people up in arms because an outsider was attempting to innoculate them against smallpox. The village priest had condemned the visitor, with the results that no one would submit to having his arm scratched. When the priest's nephew fell ill, however, he quickly changed his attitude toward the new medicine, and demanded that the visitor innoculate the boy, giving as his reason the belief that the medicine *might* work and he did not want to let the child die without having tried all other feasible remedies (a remarkably pragmatic calculation). With the priest's support, the visitor was able to vaccinate the entire village; and, in the long run, both the priest and the townspeople became ardent supporters of the "Western" public health methods.

In a second case, the author reports on the successful attempt at village resettlement, ordinarily one of the most difficult types of social change to engineer. In this case,[12] involving the relocation of an entire village in Nigeria, the project got off to a bad start because of the poor design of the houses in the new area, and because of the ancestor links which the villagers still claimed with the traditional village site. On top of these problems, the resettlement authority seemed reluctant to permit participation by the relocated villagers in the design of their new homes. However, once this barrier was eliminated, and permission was granted to revise the design of the houses, the villagers became extremely enthusiastic about their new village site, and abandoned willingly the graves of their ancestors for the new location. As of final writing, the author reports that the new village has become a source of great pride to the resettled Nigerians; and he attributes the success of the transition to the opening of channels of participation and communication between the resettlement authority and the villagers who were being resettled.

Finally, Niehoff himself writes of the success he enjoyed in enlisting the aid of Buddhist monks in supporting a wide variety of social, political, and technological changes in Laos.[13] According to Niehoff, many Western agents of change fail to appreciate the great potential which Buddhism offers for gaining support for change. Most outsiders apparently believe that Buddhism as a faith advocates passivity, fatalism, and resignation, rather than innovation and change. Further, it is believed that Buddhist monks, in particular, wish to withdraw from affairs of this world and pass their days in quiet contemplation. Nothing could be further from the true state of affairs, declares Niehoff. He goes on to cite several examples where Buddhist clergy have taken the lead in advocating projects involving social or technological change in Laotian villages. Some of the projects involved the digging of wells; others, simply the organization of community development associations. In other cases, the Buddhist organizations participated actively in the political upheavals which afflicted Laos in the late 1950's and early 1960's. In brief, Buddhism offers the outside agent of social change a ready elite or cadre of local supporters who, contrary to conventional wisdom, are quite prone to accept innovation and change.

The evidence so far presented, although of a somewhat subjective nature, seems to indicate that rapid social and political change may, under a variety of circumstances, actually enhance psychological security, rather than promote psychic instability. Our proposition has been strongly confirmed by several quantitative tests designed to elicit a more nearly objective measurement of the psychological phenomenon of response to rapidly changing surroundings. Each test deals with a different aspect of the modernization process: expansion of communications, the cash nexus, rapid urbanization, and industrialization.

Daniel Lerner, in his seminal work on political development and social modernization in the Middle East,[14] advances data based on personal interviews of a number of citizens of Turkey, a sample drawn from a wide variety of social and economic groupings. Among other things, Lerner was interested in probing the extent to which an individual becomes more self-confident, less fatalistic, and more certain of a favorable outcome in life as he becomes more modern; that is, as he becomes more capable of projecting his personality across psychological barriers which constrict the traditional psyche. To test this transition, Lerner constructed a "Dysphoria Index" which consisted of several simple questions designed to test (1) whether the person felt generally happy or unhappy most of the time; (2) how he felt about news items to which he was exposed; and (3) how confident he felt about being able to change things he did not like. There appeared to be a clearcut and consistent pattern from traditional to modern mentality, with self-confidence and contentment increasing as the individual moves from traditional to modern and, hence, to become more exposed to communications media. The exact results are provided in Table 5.1.

Table 5.1   Daniel Lerner's Dysphoria Index of a Selected Sample of Turkish Citizens.

	Moderns	Transitionals	Traditionals
Feels unhappy generally	15%	20%	33%
Felt unhappy about last news	39%	46%	62%
Felt unable to solve Turkey's problems	45%	53%	86%

Significantly, Lerner adds that his data are not intended to show that a modern life style is Utopian, or that modern countries are perennially happy and well adjusted. On the contrary, even the moderns demonstrated that problems of psychic adjustment tend to persist, and to change character. Nevertheless, as Lerner points out, tradition-bound peoples are generally so plagued with doubts and lack of self-confidence, and find their plight to be so personally unrewarding, that they are willing to undergo the temporary dislocations of transition for the promised benefits of modernity. Finally, the actual transition itself from tradition to modernity appears in Lerner's formulation as somewhat more distressing than modernity itself, but less distressing than the state of tradition and social and psychological immobility.

A somewhat different study focuses on the rural traditional society in Venezuela, and how subsistence farmers enter the cash economy.[15] Among other data, the study presents some striking contrasts between the rural subsistence farmer in Venezuela and his (supposedly) more modern counterpart, the wage-earning agricultural laborer. In virtually every case in which these two groups were asked about their values, norms, beliefs, and hopes for the future, the more modern group answered with more confidence, with less anxiety, and with less general malaise about their life and immediate surroundings. For example, almost 62 percent of the subsistence farmers replied that their personal life was unhappy, as contrasted with only 50 percent of the agricultural laborers. More than 22 percent of the subsistence class indicated that "problems are frequently worse than one can bear," but only about 9 percent of the wage-earning laborers felt this way.[16] Similarly, agricultural laborers showed themselves to have more confidence in the nonfamily personal contacts which they enjoyed, and were decidedly more modern in their outlooks on religious subjects such as birth control and divorce.

The Mathiason study goes on to show, however, that the rural subsistence farmer is not likely to remain in his downtrodden, semimodern setting for long, because of the highly politicized role which he is expected to play in Venezuela. With the volatile urban areas usually voting for the more mercurial candidates, the stable long-established political parties have had to base a great deal of their support on the rural agrarian society. As far back as 1936, shrewd political leaders began to mobilize the rural voters through active agrarian syndicates or unions, which today have a great hold over the political participation of the farmers in Venezuela. For this reason, even though the highly traditional subsistence farmers hold fairly unstable views of the life situation, they also possess a paradoxically high opinion of their own political efficacy. This feature helps to explain the general rejection of the use of violent protest against the government as justifiable. Thus, we can look forward to a rapidly modernizing rural sector in Venezuela, but one which will in all likelihood be increasingly stable in outlook, because of the instrumental nature of their mobilization experience.

As far as the impact of urbanization is concerned, there is a growing body of literature attesting to the *stabilizing* features of the rapid migration of traditional, rural peasants to the glittering city.[17] Running counter to the notion of the urban slum as a festering sore, ready to infest the body politic of the typical Asian, African, or Latin American state, we find newly emerging research demonstrating that migrants to large cities in these areas do not find the city to be such a hostile and destabilizing place as was once believed.

This author recently concluded a detailed analysis of forms of political instability in 11 states of the Caribbean and Central America, covering the period 1948–1964.[18] Our data, based on some 2,313 separate political events yielded three indices of instability for each country, as well as for each region: capital city, urban area other than the capital, and rural. One index, based on the duration of each event, the number of persons involved, and the number of persons killed, portrays the scope of the event, as well as its impact on the overall political structure of the system. Two additional indices measure the level of psychological stress which, we infer, accompanied each act of instability: the first was based on the coder's subjective evaluation of the intensity of aggressive behavior which characterized each event; and the second focused on the 12 principal types of unstable political acts.

The results of our inquiry support the contention that urbanization need not necessarily lead to psychological disorientation. The data reveal that the capital city is, to be sure, the area which has the highest incidence of instability.

For the Caribbean region as an average, the capital city is about 8.5 times as unstable as the other urban areas, and over nine times as disruptive as the rural areas. This appears to be the result, however, of some factor other than the "urban-ness" of the capital, since the "urban-other" and the rural areas registered almost identical scores. In five of the eleven states, in fact, the rural areas actually score higher than do the urban-other locations. If there is some factor which makes the capital city the cockpit of political upheaval in the Caribbean, then it must be more closely related to the role of the capital as the seat of government, and not to the induced stress of urbanization.

When we turn to the two indices of psychological stress, a clear picture emerges of rural disruption and disorder, when compared to the (relatively) tranquil capital and urban-other sectors. On one scale, for example, we found that in seven out of eleven states the rural areas were the scene of greatest psychological discontent. The second index confirmed the conclusion even more strongly, in that it picked up rural predominance of psychological stress in nine of the eleven cases.

We conclude, therefore, that the urbanization component of the modernization process follows the pattern of the communication and cash economy factors, in that it has a complex and ambiguous impact on the personality structure of those caught up in the winds of change. Most importantly, however, we have found that, by itself, rapid urbanization cannot be isolated as a causal factor in psychological instability in developing polities.[19]

By far the most definitive challenge to the theories of the inevitability of an unstable modernization process comes from the recent work of Alex Inkeles and David H. Smith.[20] Inkeles and Smith have collected a substantial amount of empirical data based on extensive interviews with some 6,000 men in six different countries—Argentina, Chile, East Pakistan, India, Nigeria, and Israel. The interviews, as reported in the cited articles, were intended to test the impact of modernization, and especially of industrialization on the mental health of the interviewees, by asking them about the incidence of symptoms of psychosomatic disorders. Respondents were asked to indicate the frequency of their experiencing such symptoms as trembling limbs, insomnia, nervousness, biting fingernails, loss of breath when not exercising, frightening dreams, inability to face recurrent chores, and others. The results were then correlated with work experience, length of time exposed to modernizing influences, and other possible sources of maladjustment. Their impressive study finds that "On balance, the data simply do not support the assertion that these modernizing influences [urbanization, industrialization, and mass communication] work consistently and importantly to generate poor personal adjustment as measured by psychosomatic symptoms . . . the theory which sees the transition from village to city and from farm to factory as *inherently* deleterious to mental health must be, if not wholly discarded, at least drastically reformulated."[21]

We do not intend to suggest at this point that all the broader, more impressionistic formulations about the instability of the development process should now be discarded. Nor do we mean to imply that development and modernization are always going to have a stabilizing effect on the participants. We simply would like to emphasize, along with Inkeles and Smith, that certain types of development processes may be destabilizing, while certain other types may have exactly the opposite effect on individual personalities. Similarly, certain personality structures may facilitate the individual adjustments required by rapid change, whereas other such structures may impede personal adjustment. As those authors make clear, they are merely trying to caution the casual observer against assuming that individual stress is an *inherent* or *universal* ingredient of modernization; instead, they urge that analysts at least ". . . allow for the possibility that there can be industrialization and urbanization without ever-heightened levels of psychic distress in the population."[22]

SOURCES OF MISUNDERSTANDING OF INSTABILITY

There are several reasons why observers may have exaggerated the inherent nature of instability in the development process. First, from a purely mechanical point of view, our recording of statistics in traditional, underdeveloped societies is apt to be rather primitive, thus making difficult the drawing of comparisons with contemporary social systems. Given access to reliable statistics from political systems prior to 1900, we might very well find that the propensity for instability in many of them was limited only by the technological means for registering that instability in a satisfying manner.

The burgeoning literature dealing with the complex concept of anomy, or a condition of social normlessness and lack of regulation, illustrates well the problem of limited statistical horizons. As has been convincingly pointed out,[23] the writings of Durkheim, Merton, and Srole, which have allegedly proved that the various components of social modernization—urbanization, industrialization, and increased communications—lead to psychological maladjustment, are actually based on data which do not permit the comparison of a contemporary, modern political order with one representative of traditional societies. Thus, an assertion that men in industrialized, urban environments tend to score "high" on anomy scales is meaningless without first comparing these men with those of other societies and other time frames.

A second source of our misunderstanding of the development process lies in our exaggeration of the difference between modernity and tradition as states of mind. Underlying much of the writing on political modernization is the notion that the traditional state and the modern state are two ideal types, that in order to change from the former to the latter massive psychological and procedural transformations must be undergone, and that, at the end of the painful transition, the formerly traditional state will retain not a single vestige of its former "traditional" self, having now become entirely modern.[24] Because

of the universalistic and undifferentiated nature of change, political development is perceived as engendering great stress.

Certain cases seem to show, however, that the transition from traditional to
modern may involve only the *selective* alteration of norms and institutions.
Traditional institutions, such as India's caste system may actually carry with
them the seeds of democratic development by facilitating the expansion and
mobilization of new political participants within a familiar and meaningful
system of human relationships.[25] In some instances, rural village institutions,
such as those of Japan, may possess such inner strength and flexibility that
modernizing forces are shaped and turned to local needs, thus enhancing
rather than aggravating psychic stability.[26]

Third, there seems to be little doubt that many social scientists have tended
to idealize the psychological peace and harmony of traditional societies. Inkeles and Smith cite this belief as one of the principal reasons for assuming that
the transition from rural and traditional to urban and modern must be a
disruptive experience. On the contrary, they indicate, life in rural and traditional environments can be extremely unsettling for the average peasant, ". . .
who suffers deep insecurity both in his relation to nature, . . . and in relation
to the powerful figures in his village . . ."[27] Caught in the grip of his environment, the typical peasant is apt to be distrustful, a believer in witchcraft and
sorcery, fearful of his surroundings, and a frequent user of local drugs (such
as the *coca* of the Andean residents) to escape from reality.

I. R. Sinai has painted for us a picture of the assault on the personality of
the typical traditional peasant of Asia in his book *The Challenge of Modernization.*

> Enveloping all these communities (of peasants) there is a sense of life
> robbed of all significance. Man is both degraded and mocked. The peas-
> antries are all haunted by the fear that the earth will lose its fertility . . .
> They are obsessed by an almost panic concern to maintain the size of their
> populations. Surrounded by malignant demons and spirits, threatened by
> the unruly forces of nature and society, they were led to seek the interven-
> tion of occult powers whom they must try to propitiate or coerce by means
> of offerings, spells, worship, to protect their precarious though unchanging
> position in the natural and social order . . . war, famine and disease deso-
> lated them, conquerors swept over them, tax collectors . . . robbed them,
> but these villages remained unchanged and unaffected, always ready to
> resume the old burdens and to submit tamely to the same degrading
> routine.[28]

It is indeed difficult to see how the transition to modernity could be anything
other than stabilizing and reassuring for individuals from such a threatening
environment.

A recent examination of the modal personality in Iran portrays vividly the
psychological effects of life in tradition-bound society.[29] The Iranian individ-

ual, according to this study, lives in a constant state of crisis, crisis which is as unremitting as it is overwhelming. The immediate result has been the growth of interpersonal relations along lines of gross unpredictability. As the author puts it, ". . . the individual is not provided with any reasonable assurance that if he behaves in a particular way toward a particular individual . . . that he can expect a particular reaction in return, save that the reaction will be unanticipated and unpredictable, and probably to his disadvantage."[30] As a consequence, the typical Iranian adopts a variety of self-defeating defense mechanisms to protect his personality from the assault of an unpredictable and hostile psychological environment. These mechanisms range from isolation and an exaggerated sense of individualism, on the one hand, to explosions of violent aggression on the other. However these mechanisms may be manifested in practice, they reflect the torment of the traditional personality as he confronts an unyielding social universe. More importantly, they reduce the Iranian's chances for full exploitation of the diverse attributes of modernity when, and if, they arrive.

There seem to be several factors working against a full appreciation of the stressful nature of traditional society. For one thing, traditional political groupings appear to have found remarkably good mechanisms for coping with severe mental disorders and potentially disruptive social behavior, without having recourse to modern medical treatment facilities. Severe psychological disturbances are often treated in traditional, village communities as constituting a threat to the spiritual well-being of the entire group; and the presence of a disordered personality triggers a collective mechanism which causes the entire community to feel a responsibility for the care of the sick person.[31] Instead of isolating the disturbed person from society, the traditional community launches a village-wide effort to reintegrate the individual into the collectivity, thereby meeting the assault of the demonic spirit which has temporarily invaded his body and mind. Actions which would be termed "treatment and rehabilitation" in a Western context are seen as part of the exercise of a communal responsibility to help the afflicted individual ward off the evil spirits.[32]

Certain attributes of traditional culture also serve to drain off the more aggressive aspects of personality disruption with minimum disorder for the community as a whole. Some traditional cultures seem to have facilitated the act of suicide by endowing certain extremely high risk feats with glory and symbols of bravery and adventure, thereby removing the stigma attached to what is considered an antisocial act in the modern community.[33] In the Kayah culture of Burma, great social pressure is brought to bear on the parties to any dispute to compose their differences either through direct discussion or, if that fails, through third-party mediation. The people of this tribe seem greatly concerned about the possibility that internal disruptions will so weaken them that they will fall prey to aggressive neighbor; hence, the need to present a common front to the outside world. The result is the bottling up of agressive emotions for the sake of communal tranquility.[34] Whatever may be the mechanisms in traditional society for coping with personality disorders, the end result is to hide from view the true nature and extent of psychological stress in these political systems. As a consequence, we have been led to overestimate the psychic peace of the traditional village.

Finally, we have been inhibited from probing the exact nature of psychological instability of traditional polities by the protestations of anticolonial spokesmen of newly formed states, who have argued that many, if not all, of their ills could be laid at the doorstep of Western-style industrialization, urbanization, and political mobilization. For these leaders, such as Gandhi and Nehru of India, Leopold Senghor of Senegal, Julius Nyerere of Tanzania, or Victor Raul Haya de la Torre of Peru, the "Golden Age" in the cultural life of their communities could always be traced back to a time before the coming of the exploitative modernizers from Western Europe and North America. Their argument focuses on a dream of undoing the evil done by Westernization and modernization and returning to a more peaceful, more traditional, more "native" form of political organization and culture.[35] One can easily adopt a cynical view of these arguments, attributing them to political opportunism, designed to whip up popular enthusiasm for the anticolonial struggle. To do so would be to underestimate the powerful longing of non-Western leaders to guide a development process which is distinctive, stimulating to national pride, and harmonious with local tradition. Whatever the source of these expressions of faith in tradition, they have served to reinforce an already present sense of cultural relativism among Western social observers, which, in turn, has led us to have grave doubts about the wisdom of any policy which would seek to undermine the peace and psychic tranquility of political tradition.[36]

Thus, the destabilizing effects of political change have been exaggerated as a result of an idealistic view of traditional life. In addition, however, modern political analysis, drawing on its heritage of systems theory and its consequent emphasis on stability, has tended to focus conceptually on the *system* (or social aggregate) and the way it changes, rather than on the *individual* and the way in which he perceives, and reacts to, change. Because of its origin in the concept of the organismic system, and its heritage in the biological sciences,[37] systems theory, when applied to political analysis, has usually led observers to conclude that political disorder was a disease of the body politic, a pathological state, a condition found only in a sick society, or among social deviants. Gabriel Almond, for example, in his celebrated introduction to *Politics of the Developing Areas,* regarded virtually any violent act as (1) an example of anomic behavior and (2) an inherently dysfunctional act since it tended to break down the all-important boundary between the polity and the society.[38] It is noteworthy that Almond, in a later formulation, admits the possibility that violence may not be pathological under certain conditions. Referring specifically to the case of Peru, as investigated by James L. Payne,[39] Almond accepts the possibility that political instability is culturally and psychologically determined, rather than a function of some objective standards of system performance. As he makes clear, in the circumstances of Peruvian politics, " . . . rather than constituting a threat to the system's usual performance, mass violence has become a part of the regularized pattern of performance, a structured channel of access into the political system."[40]

Generally, however, a system-level focus has tended to mislead us in an examination of political instability. By directing our attention to the social aggregate, political systems research has both exaggerated and underestimated components of the problem of instability. Systems theory has exaggerated the presence of unstable behavior by comparing all political communities against an ideal type of system which was free of conflict and aggressive behavior; it has underestimated the extent to which human collectivities can adapt to stressful conditions.[41] It is our conviction that the study of political instability must adjust its focus to the level of individual perceptions; stability and instability reside in the mind of the actor, not in some abstract notion of "system," and it is in the perceptions of the actor that we as analysts shall find the answers to the questions with which we began this chapter.

Specifically, we propose the following definition of political instability, by way of introduction to Chapters Six and Seven. We conceive of political instability as being a function of two variables: (1) the level, source, and type of psychological stress produced by the process of political development; and (2) the techniques used by political actors to resolve their stress. The remainder of Part Two will be devoted to an examination of these variables.

CHAPTER NOTES

1. S. N. Eisenstadt, *Modernization: Protest and Change* (Englewood Cliffs, N.J.: Prentice-Hall, 1966), esp. Chap. Two.
2. Eisenstadt, pp. 22-23.
3. C. E. Black, *The Dynamics of Modernization: A Study in Comparative History* (New York: Harper & Row, 1966), esp. pp. 26-34.
4. Samuel P. Huntington, *Political Order in Changing Societies* (New Haven: Yale University Press, 1968), esp. Chap. One.
5. Huntington, p. 43.
6. Allan R. Holmberg, "The Changing Values and Institutions of Vicos in the Context of National Development," *The American Behavioral Scientist,* VIII, 7 (March, 1965): 3.
7. J. Oscar Alers, "The Quest for Well-Being," *The American Behavioral Scientist,* VIII, 7 (March, 1965): 20-21.
8. David Brokensha, *Social Change at Larteh, Ghana* (Oxford: Clarendon Press, 1966), esp. Chaps. 2, 3, 4, 6, 7, 8, 11, and 12.
9. Brokensha, p. 269.
10. Arthur E. Niehoff, *A Casebook of Social Change* (Chicago: Aldine, 1966), p. 305.
11. Eugene P. Link and Sushila Mehta, "A New Goddess for an Old," in Niehoff, pp. 219-24.

12. B. K. Cooper, "New Eruwa," in Niehoff, pp. 120-23.
13. Arthur Niehoff, "Theravada Buddhism: A Vehicle for Technical Change," in Niehoff, pp. 234-45.
14. Daniel Lerner, *The Passing of Traditional Society: Modernizing the Middle East* (New York: Free Press, 1958), esp. pp. 131-46.
15. John R. Mathiason, "The Venezuelan Campesino: Perspectives on Change," in Frank Bonilla and Jose A. Silva Michelena, eds., *The Politics of Change in Venezuela: Volume I, A Strategy for Research on Social Policy* (Cambridge, Mass.: MIT Press, 1967), pp. 120-55.
16. Mathiason, Table 5.1, p. 129.
17. See Wayne A. Cornelius, Jr., "Urbanization as an Agent in Latin American Political Instability: The Case of Mexico," *American Political Science Review,* LXIII, 3 (September, 1969): 833-57, for a brief but complete discussion of the debate over the role of urban areas in political instability.
18. Robert P. Clark, Jr., "Dimensions of Political Instability in the Caribbean," paper presented to the Southern Political Science Association meeting, November, 1971.
19. Somewhat the same conclusions were arrived at by Joan Nelson in her article "The Urban Poor: Disruption of Political Integration in Third World Cities?", *World Politics,* XXII, 3 (April, 1970): 393-414.
20. For the most complete summary of this work, see Alex Inkeles and David H. Smith, "The Fate of Personal Adjustment in the Process of Modernization," a manuscript prepared for delivery at the 1968 Tokyo-Kyoto Meetings of the International Anthropological Association. For a briefer summary, see Alex Inkeles, "Making Men Modern: On the Causes and Consequences of Individual Change in Six Developing Countries," *American Journal of Sociology,* 75, 2 (September, 1969): 208-25, esp. pp. 223-25.
21. Inkeles and Smith, "The Fate of Personal Adjustment in the Process of Modernization," *op. cit.,* pp. 50-51. Emphasis added.
22. Inkeles and Smith, p. 54.
23. By Herbert McClosky in his article "Psychological Dimensions of Anomy," in McClosky, *Political Inquiry: The Nature and Uses of Survey Research* (London: The Macmillan Co., 1969), pp. 126-33.
24. See Lloyd I. Rudolph and Susanne Hoeber Rudolph, *The Modernity of Tradition: Political Development in India* (Chicago: University of Chicago Press, 1967), esp. pp. 3-14.
25. Rudolph and Rudolph, Part One.
26. Toshinao Yoneyama, "Comparisons of Modernization in Two Japanese Villages," in Julian H. Steward, ed., *Contemporary Change in Traditional Societies: Volume II, Asian Rural Societies* (Urbana: University of Illinois Press, 1967), pp. 329-43.
27. Inkeles and Smith, "The Fate of Personal Adjustment in the Process of Modernization," p. 55.
28. I. R. Sinai, *The Challenge of Modernization* (New York: W. W. Norton & Company, Inc., 1964), pp. 34-35.
29. Norman Jacobs, *The Sociology of Development: Iran as an Asian Case Study* (New York: Praeger, 1966), esp. Chap. Nine.
30. Jacobs, p. 250.

31. Benjamin D. Paul, "Mental Disorder and Self-Regulating Processes in Culture: A Guatemalan Illustration," in S. N. Eisenstadt, ed., *Comparative Social Problems* (New York: Free Press, 1964), pp. 87-94.

32. Horacio Fabrega, Jr. and Duane Metzger, "Psychiatric Illness in a Small Ladino Community," *Psychiatry,* 31, 4 (November, 1968): 339-51.

33. Raymond Firth, "Suicide and Risk-Taking in Tikopia Society, *Psychiatry,* 24, 1 (February, 1961): 1-17.

34. F. K. Lehman, "Burma: Kayah Society as a Function of the Shan-Burma-Karen Context," in Steward, pp. 32-33.

35. For speeches and documents of all these men, see the useful compendium by Paul E. Sigmund, ed., *The Ideologies of the Developing Nations,* rev. ed., (New York: Praeger, 1967).

36. See Lucian Pye, "The Foreign Aid Instrument: Search for Reality," in Roger Hilsman and Robert C. Good, eds., *Foreign Policy in the Sixties: The Issues and the Instruments* (Baltimore: Johns Hopkins Press, 1965), Chap. Six.

37. Karl W. Deutsch, *The Nerves of Government* (New York: Free Press, 1966), 2nd ed., pp. 30-34.

38. Gabriel Almond, "A Functional Approach to Comparative Politics," in Gabriel Almond and James Coleman, eds., *Politics of the Developing Areas* (Princeton, N.J.: Princeton University Press, 1960), pp. 3-64, esp. pp. 34-35.

39. James L. Payne, "Peru: The Politics of Structured Violence," *Journal of Politics,* 27, 2 (May, 1965): 362-74.

40. Gabriel Almond and G. B. Powell, *Comparative Politics: A Developmental Approach* (Boston: Little, Brown, 1966), esp. pp. 81-82.

41. David Easton, *A Framework for Political Analysis* (Englewood Cliffs, N.J.: Prentice-Hall, 1965) esp. Chap. Six.

Chapter 6

SOURCES OF INSTABILITY:

The Stress of Development

The roots of political instability in rapidly developing polities can be traced to psychological distress of individual political actors. Whether or not the process of political development unleashes acts of disorder and disruption depends, in the first analysis, on whether or not the process proves distressing psychologically to the members of the political community.

THE CONCEPT OF STRESS

There appears to be little consensus within the psychological community on the exact definition of the concept of stress.[1] Some writers emphasize the condition of the individual; others, the agent which produced the condition initially. Some, following Hans Selye, are concerned with the response of the stressed organism to the stress-producing agent, and the organism's efforts to adapt itself to the threats of the agent.[2] If psychologists have yet to agree on such a fundamental concept, political scientists still treat the notion as being useful for analysis only at the level of the social aggregate; that is, the political system. Analysis of political stress on individuals is virtually unknown. Therefore, we may be permitted a certain degree of latitude in formulating our operational definitions in this field to correspond to exigencies in political research. For our purposes, stress will be defined as the process by which an

118

individual senses a threat to his well-being and/or stability, and reacts to defend himself from the threat.[3]

The exact nature of the threat to a person's well-being or stability centers on two components of the threatening condition. The first, the stress agent, or that condition which induces in the individual the idea that his well-being is under attack, will be the subject of an extended discussion below. The second, the stressed state of the individual, refers to the "condition of feeling stressed" experienced by those persons under assault.

We must advance with great caution in our analysis of this stressed condition. At the present "state of the art" in political stress analysis, any statements we could make about the presence or absence of stress must be based on inferences we draw from observances of overt behavior. For example, if we see a person in the window of a burning apartment building, and the person is screaming for help, what we observe are only two variables: a stress agent (fire), which is intuitively defined; and a stress response (screaming) also intuitively defined. We can only infer the presence of stress in the screaming person. While this example seems ridiculously simple, many empirical cases drawn from the political realm present us with very difficult cases of inference from observable stimuli and responses.

To be specific, we should be very cautious about inferring psychic stress in political actors from non-Western political cultures when we see them confronted with conditions which Western behavioral science defines as stressful. In the absence of acute sensitivity to the parameters of the subject culture, we are apt to run the risk of interpreting as stressful a particular act which in the host society may appear to be completely normal.[4] The arbitrary practice of violence by political actors, for example, seems to Western observers to be the occasion for severe psychological disruption, as the initiators of unrest attempt to inspire fear and submissiveness in their targets. E. V. Walter, in his exploration of primitive terror and despotism,[5] cites the case of the Zulu leaders of the mid-nineteenth century, who apparently exercised complete freedom to execute any of their followers without cause. Far from inspiring psychic stress, however, this constant threat of being done in by the chieftains seems not to have bothered the Zulus at all. As one British writer of the period put it, although typical Zulu citizens live with death constantly hovering above them, ". . . they think no more of their end by order of their chiefs or by violence, than most of ourselves do of 'shuffling off this mortal coil' in the quietude of our beds and through natural causes."[6] In a rather different political context, that of Peru in mid-twentieth century, James Payne points out that political violence, far from being symptomatic of anarchy or chaos, is actually an integral and necessary segment of the political process. Indeed, only by making violence the focal point of analysis can one extract conclusions about Peruvian political behavior which makes such behavior understandable and predictable.[7]

For this reason, we cannot be very precise in advancing an operational definition of psychological stress. We do know that a stressed condition can be inferred when we observe a disturbance or threatened disturbance of crucial psychological variables from within their normal limits. Although we do not, at present, know what all these crucial variables are, we do know that they are of two broad classes. First, psychological stress can be induced when abnormal functioning is observed in those variables which have a bearing on the physical well-being of the individual; biological drives seem to be the principal mechanisms at work here. Second, a stressful state can be inferred from the displacement of variables from the norm which threatens some aspect of the personality structure or the ego of the individual, thereby arousing anxiety, failure, or frustration.

The final component of our operational definition above had to do with the efforts of the individual to defend himself from threats to his well-being or stability. This defense process consists of a set of stress responses (following Selye's definition), which the individual engages in to protect himself from the threatening environment. Insofar as one's personality structure provides him with his repertoire of acceptable and accessible stress responses,[8] the personality of relevant political actors is integrally linked to the system's ability to respond to stressful conditions. The broader the repertoire of stress responses in any given society, the better able that society will be to react to the stress of rapid political change without succumbing to the destabilizing effects of disorder and upheaval.

We should make very clear from the beginning our belief that *all* politics, whether of the developmental variety or not, involve a certain amount of induced psychological stress. As James C. Davies points out,[9] action in the political sphere of society is resorted to by insecure individuals only after extra-political solutions to restore their security have been tried and found wanting. Most persons prefer to resolve their conflicts through interpersonal and intergroup action, bargaining and compromise; it is only after these efforts have failed that a person decides to move into the political arena for satisfaction. The result, then, is that politics become the mechanism by which society resolves its problems which cannot be resolved through interpersonal negotiation, or, put another way, "on the merits of the issue." Men seem to have recognized that they need some institutionalized method of resolving conflicts which resist personal accommodation; the political system provides them with that mechanism. The net outcome, however, is that political issues are always going to involve highly conflictual, hence highly stressful, personal relationships.

Developmental politics, to return to our principal theme, appear to engender especially high levels of psychological stress. Some reasons for this feature of the process of political change will be advanced shortly. But we wish to point out that we do not consider politics of developing countries to be generically different from that process in more highly developed polities. As we sought to argue in Chapter Five, the psychological stress of development need not lead inevitably to high levels of systemic instability and disorder. Just as the developed polity has managed to cope with the stress of changing attitudes and expanding political boundaries, so also must the developing state learn to manage these forces. Indeed, stagnation awaits any development elite which fails to provide channels for the control of change-induced stress.

At the most basic level of political awareness, stress can be expected to appear whenever a political actor senses a discontinuity in his environment.[10] This sense of discontinuity arises from his perception that a crucial variable in the political system has changed the way in which it operates. In other words, the individual must perceive that the manner in which variable A functioned in time T_i is not the same as the manner in which it will function in time T_{ii}, and that the discontinuity thus produced will significantly affect his well-being and/or stability. Most importantly, the actor must experience an awareness that, because of this discontinuity, he is much less able to predict the functioning of the variable in the future in a manner favorable to his interests.

TYPES OF STRESS: COGNITIVE DISSONANCE

Whatever the specifics of political discontinuity, all potential stress-producing change may be reduced to two general types. The first is what we shall call(after Leon Festinger) *cognitive dissonance,* or stress engendered by an incongruence between image and expectation on the one hand, and perceptions of reality on the other.[11] Kenneth Boulding has noted that wherever there is not chaos, there are some expectations about the future.[12] These expectations, shared by political actors, are based on the images they hold about system functioning in the future, and are, to a large extent, the essential glue which holds a social system together.

Boulding goes on to point out that the actors in the system can tolerate variance in the functioning of the system's variables (our levels of change, described below) within a certain range without being subjected to personal stress. When variables change beyond this range of expectation, the actors experience what Boulding calls "astonishment," or failure of expectations. If the variable in question continues to operate in a manner which invalidates the actors' expectations, then one of the following events must occur: (1) either the actors will alter their images (a relatively rare act of self-discipline in the short-run); (2) the variable's functioning will be altered to conform to the actor's images; or (3) the actors will succumb to the stress and begin to behave in a psychologically unstable manner.

As we noted in Chapter Two, however, the process of political development seems to dictate the transformation of a great number of key political and social values across the population. Attitudinal modernization appears to bring in its wake the inevitable crisis between the nation's elders, who hold to the traditional mores of the society, and the youth of the country, who are responding to the challenges of a changing environment. This generational division is further complicated by the stress-producing schisms within the older group itself, and, even within many individuals, as they struggle to regain a foothold in a rapidly changing political process.

I. R. Sinai provides us with a vivid picture of an Indian intellectual as he agonizes through the maze of contradictions found in the modernization process of his country.

> ... people like me are heirs to two sets of customs, are shaped in our daily lives by dual codes of behavior. For example: my generation on the one hand declared its agnosticism and on the other tamely succumbed to the old rituals; we yearned for romantic love but were reconciled to marriage by the well-established method of matching horoscopes to a girl selected for us by our parents; outside our homes we smoked, consumed alcohol, and ate meat, when available, but at home we were rigidly puritan and vegetarian; we glibly talked about individual salvation although we belonged to a very closely knit joint-family system.[13]

For this Indian, expectations about social structures, mores, acceptable life goals, and interpersonal relationships had become incongruent with his perceptions of reality, and the result was psychological stress.

That this lack of congruence between expectations and reality can be severely disruptive can be illustrated with several examples drawn from states in the process of rapid, disjunctive modernization.

While not a non-Western country in the usual sense, Spain in the days immediately preceding its bloody civil war was surely a country caught in the grip of severe instability, brought on by the tremendous gap between what the laboring class had been led to expect from the Catholic Church, and what in fact the Church had done to advance the material interests of the upper class of the country. When the civil war began in July, 1936, those Church buildings and personnel which had the misfortune to find themselves in Republican territory were subjected to massive attacks, destruction, torture, and murder, in reprisal for their alleged betrayal of the principles of Christianity. As Hugh Thomas relates:

> Throughout Republican Spain, churches and convents were indiscriminately burned and despoiled. Practically nowhere had the Church taken part in the rising [of the Nationalist, anti-Republican forces. R.C.] Nearly all the stories of firing by rebels from church towers were also untrue. But the churches were nevertheless attacked as the outposts of upper or middle-class morality and manners. Destruction rather than loot was the aim.[14]

In addition to attacking Church property, the militia gangs from Republican unions also attacked Church officials with a brutality and sadistic cruelty which reflects the intense hatred engendered by the Church's role in the class struggle in Spain. Thomas reports that, of the nearly 86,000 persons murdered or executed in Republican Spain during the war, almost 8,000 were religious officials, including over 5,000 priests, nearly 300 nuns (many of whom were raped before their execution), and 12 bishops.

While the violence directed against the Church in Spain may be said to have a class basis, pitting as it did the workers against a bastion of upper class spiritual values, the widespread violence in Colombia from 1946 to 1953 seems unrelated to class antagonisms. This eruption of rural warfare, known by the generic term of "La Violencia" in Colombia, took about 135,000 lives between 1949 and 1958. Because the conflict cut across class lines, and saw peasant struggling against peasant, it is an example of stress arising from highly exacerbated attitudinal differences and discontinuities.

As Richard Weinert describes it,[15] the violence in Colombia must be traced to the conflict between the modernizing forces of the country, generally regarded as part of the Liberal party, and the traditionalists, who felt that modernization was an assault on their sacred, traditional order. The drive to value modernization, which began in Colombia in the 1930's, brought forth countless individuals who felt their reliable way of life slowly crumbling away from them. The bitter antagonists of the Liberals, the Conservative party, were able to mobilize a sizeable segment of the peasant class against the Liberal-led modernization drive. Seizing on a Colombian legacy of accompanying the transfer of power with violence and upheaval, the Conservatives sought to halt the modernization effort by launching aggressive attacks against Liberal strongholds in rural areas. That the violence involved struggle between rural peasants on both sides seems not to have made much difference; the attacks, also notable for their brutality, cruelty, and overtones of sexual abuse,[16] appear to have been aimed at wiping out the advocates of a particular value structure, one which was undermining the traditional style of life in the country.

More recently, Indonesia has been wracked by mass killings which have had heavy overtones of the bloody confrontation of competing and antithetical value systems. The killings began after the failure of the attempted coup d'etat launched by the Indonesian Communist Party (PKI) against the Indonesian army in September, 1965. In retribution, and in light of Indonesian leader Sukarno's inability or unwillingness to punish the Communists, the army initiated a series of raids against PKI headquarters and strongholds. The result was the unleashing of intense popular hatred of the communists by the more traditional, mystical Hindus, who vented their anger by killing an estimated 250,000 to 350,000 Communist leaders and militants, as well as many sympathizers.

On the island of Bali, as Robert Shaplen reports, the massacres were especially vicious.[17] Here, where traditional Hindu mysticism had persisted in more or less unmolested form for centuries, the PKI had attempted to convert the Balinese to Communism by a combination of vague promises for land reform and by making a mockery of the local customs and traditions. The Communist leaders had sharply criticized the festivals of the religious Balinese, and had taunted them for the peculiar nature of their mystical ways of life. The PKI leaders had also employed various forms of terror in order to spread their messages among the Balinese people; and, when the mass killing of Communists began, in December, 1965, the Balinese wrought vengeance on the Communists with incredible fury and emotion. Some 40,000 people were killed in about two months, many at random by special squads of black-shirted thugs; and the bloodletting did not cease until the Indonesian army sent in paratroopers to restore order.

TYPES OF STRESS: DEPRIVATION

The second broad type of stressful political change may be encompassed in the word *deprivation.* In this case, the actor perceives himself as being physically or affectively interfered with, severely restricted in activity, in stimuli, or in social relations, or, in extreme cases, actually deprived of the physical factors required for survival. The individual senses that his environment has become threatening, and that a critical region has been approached in which his well-being and stability can no longer be taken for granted.

Ted Gurr has examined in great detail the nexus between the psychological phenomena of frustration-aggression and relative deprivation, on the one hand, and the recourse to civil violence on the other.[18] Gurr argues that the frustration-aggression mechanism appears to be the chief causal variable in determining the level of violence-producing tension in human beings; and, he says that this mechanism is triggered by the presence of relative deprivation. Relative deprivation, which Gurr defines as "the perceived discrepancy between value expectations and value capabilities," thus appears to be a principal factor in impelling men to such levels of instability that they are led to inflict damage on each other.

Gurr has identified at least three broad patterns of relative deprivation; each involves a rapid widening of the gap between one's expectations and his capabilities, and examples of each can be found in political systems undergoing an unstable form of political development. The first type of deprivation, which Gurr calls aspirational, comes about when value expectations are increasing rapidly and value capabilities remain relatively stationary. In July, 1962, the armed forces of Peru deposed the outgoing civilian government of Manuel Prado in order to assure the subsequent election of Fernando Belaunde Terry, who had barely missed securing a plurality of the votes in the national presidential election in June. The armed forces leadership of the country, fearing a victory by long-time enemy Victor Raul Haya de la Torre, leader of the mass-based Aprista Party, moved to cancel the 1962 elections, apparently won by Haya, and to install Belaunde in elections held the next year. At that time, the army held very high aspirations for the Belaunde government (as did the government of the United States). In the first place, Belaunde's brand of reform promised to bring the modernization of the country's economic and social system, which, the army leaders believed, would forestall the popular uprising which had been threatening Peru for decades. Further, Belaunde pledged to secure national control and ownership over the petroleum reserves of the country by nationalizing the holdings of the International Petroleum Corporation (IPC). On both counts, while the army's expectations soared, their nation's capabilities remained stationary. By 1967, the country's economic problems had worsened to such an extent that urban unrest, inflation, and strikes alternated with alarms of guerrillas filtering in from the rural areas. In the area of national control over natural resources, the Belaunde government proved as unable to deal with IPC as previous Peruvian governments had been. The armed forces leaders drew the obvious conclusion: that civilian politics as usual were failing to meet their high expectations which had prompted them to put Belaunde into power in the first place. Accordingly, on October 3, 1968, the armed forces of Peru overthrew the Belaunde government and moved to establish an army regime of long-standing, endowed with the necessary power and ideological conviction to deal decisively with Peru's aggravated economic and social problems.[19]

Progressive deprivation, Gurr's second model, is seen to develop from the much more complex situation in which value expectations and value capabilities rise sharply together for a period, followed by a sharp drop in capabilities, thereby opening a widening gap between the two variables. Thus, progressive deprivation is reminiscent of James Davies' famous "J-curve" hypothesis.[20] Australian New Guinea, after World War II, has been the scene of rather widespread disorders, riots, and protest movements; and, to a large extent, the cause can be traced to the treatment the New Guinea natives received from American soldiers during their wartime occupation of the area. Especially on the island of Manus, the natives came under the influence of the American troops who treated them as equals, even to the point of sharing scarce rations with them. The presence of the Americans inspired the Manus-islanders to aspire to higher economic gain and to correct formally political and social treatment. When the Americans left, in 1946, the old aspirations remained, and continued to climb. The Australians, upon returning, continued their prewar methods of governance, which prompted economic growth, but which reversed the trend toward equality of treatment. An invisible racial policy descended upon the island again. As an example, Australians and Europeans were allowed to purchase and consume alcoholic beverages; the native population was forbidden to do so. The result has been the onset of political and economic protest organizations built around the grievances of natives, and designed to rectify the inequities of the colonial system. As aspirations or expectations continued to rise, capabilities turned downward, with the consequent increase in psychological stress and unstable behavior.[21]

When observed at the aggregate level, (measured in terms of gross national product per capita), the case of Cuba in the years prior to the invasion of Fidel Castro also seems to support the hypothetical model of progressive deprivation. As Tanter and Midlarsky have indicated,[22] Cuban GNP/Cap increased steadily every year from 1948 through 1951, and then turned downward sharply from 1951 through 1953 (the year of Castro's first assault on the Cuban government in his attack on the Moncada barracks). Tanter and Midlarsky reason that this dramatic illustration of progressive deprivation in the economic sphere prepared Cuba for the onset of the guerrilla revolutionary war which followed soon after, and made them more receptive to Castro's movement. The authors also go on to conclude that the radical drop in Cuba's economic fortunes supplies some evidence to explain the ferocity of the Cuban revolutionary war, as measured in terms of deaths per 1,000 population. Once again, the concept of progressive deprivation provides a useful analytical tool for understanding social unrest and psychological stress.

The third form of relative deprivation, which Gurr has labeled decremental deprivation, involves the maintenance of stable value expectations by a group confronted with declining value capabilities. This role is most often portrayed as being played by economic elites such as the landed aristocracy of a developing country. Actually, such diverse groupings as tradition-oriented intellectuals or religious cliques can be caught in the same dilemma. Small farm villages in East Africa—Kenya and Tanzania, especially—seem to be suffering from increased pressure on scarce land resources. In some cases, economic aspirations may be rising slightly; but, in many instances, the villagers of such tribes as the Nyakyusa of what is now Tanzania would be content merely to maintain their present standard of living. A rapidly increasing population, however, creates a severe land shortage, with every available parcel of land under intense cultivation. Conflict arises from the fact that their traditional method of allocating land resources, which did not hinge on a son's inheritance rights, apparently do not suffice to insure a rational exploitation of the land. Similarly, the calls by Tanzania's President Julius Nyerere to recreate a kind of communal, rural socialism in his country have also failed to guarantee a full and equitable distribution of rapidly dwindling agricultural resources. Thus, in the face of declining capabilities (land) and stable expectations (standard of living and a nonadaptive value structure), the typical East African farmer is confronted by stress induced by deprivation of the decremental variety. The result has been internal conflict within family and kin group, with the consequence that these essential elements of Tanzania's rural social structure are beginning to erode under the strain of land shortage.[23]

It should be apparent from the above examples that political development will always bring a certain amount of deprivational stress in its wake. As we saw earlier, political development involves the expansion of systemic capabilities into areas of resource and value allocation previously left untouched by the traditional, less developed political system. In some cases, this expansion may actually result in the shift in the ways in which these resources and values are assigned to various sectors of society. In other instances, the only immediate changes may occur in the expectations about impending changes. In either case, political modernization seems destined to provoke symptoms of stress as an outgrowth of deprivation of either the aspirational, progressive, or decremental types.

As some observers have made clear, cognitive dissonance and deprivation are not mutually exclusive concepts or sources of stress. There is likely to be considerable overlap between the two when actually applied to empirical, "real-world" cases. Gurr, in a brief discussion of cognitive dissonance, points out that deprivation has a somewhat more tangible quality to it, in that it refers to "welfare, power, and interpersonal value expectations," while cognitive dissonance can be observed at work in reference to any cognitive elements, not just values or conditions of life.[24]

Stephen B. Withey, a psychologist, has provided us with a useful discussion of the difference between these two types of stress-producing changes.[25] In both types of cases, the change involves a restructuring of the observer's environment, a restructuring which he perceives as threatening. In the first instance, stress is produced by a failure of the adjustive feedback mechanism to produce the requisite information for the observer's adjustment process. In the second, the notion of critical regions applies, and threat is perceived as an invasion of these zones. As an illustration, Withey cites the driver of an automobile who is confronted with two different sorts of changes in the perceived environment. First, he loses his way, his map proves to be faulty, his compass ceases to function, he becomes disoriented, and he stops to collect his thoughts. He has just undergone cognitive dissonance stress. Subsequently, back on the road, the car's radiator begins to overheat, causing him to doubt the vehicle's ability to continue to function, and again he stops to allow it to cool. He has now been subjected to stress of the deprivation variety. Both varieties of change have required adjustment; both have produced stress.

THE LEVEL OF STRESS

From the question of the source of psychological stress in a developing polity, we turn now to another important factor affecting political instability: the level of stress. With all other factors held equal, we hypothesize that the greater the degree of psychological stress engendered by political change, the greater will be the tendency for this stress to result in overt behavior which is disruptive for the system as a whole.

The concept of level of psychological stress presents a political scientist with some very thorny methodological problems. Psychologists and physiologists can define stress as an alteration of the functioning of the central nervous system, and can measure stress by use of the electroencephalogram (brain waves) and by galvanic skin reflex.[26] A similar operational definition in political science would not be particularly useful since it seems unlikely that we could secure the cooperation of relevant political actors at moments of acute stress in subjecting themselves to various telemetering tests of their central nervous system. Thus, for the time being, until better measurement devices are developed, we must fall back on the hypothetical construct of inferred stress, derived from an observance of what we define intuitively as a stressful condition (the reader is reminded of the caveats lodged against this approach earlier in this chapter).

For our purposes here, then, we propose to define the level of psychological stress as a function of the depth and importance of the political change which the political actor is observing. The more profound the change in his environment, the more stressed the actor will feel. In this context, we advance the following list of political variables, together with some empirical examples of the ways in which they might change. While we do not maintain that this list is exhaustive, and that other variables could not be added, we do think that the set of variables covers fully the *range* over which a political system is likely to experience change. Finally, as presented here, this list of key or essential variables is little more than an agenda for additional research into the linkages between political development and psychological stress.

1. **Changes in Ruling Personnel**   This category is intended to contain those instances in which the only change concerns the occupant(s) of the chief decision-making role(s) in the system. It is usually assumed that this sort of change occurs rather regularly in systems which are democratic; but, experience suggests that elections in democracies are often accompanied by changes which extend beyond the level of ruling personnel into other, more fundamental variables. On the other hand, despotic systems which undergo palace coups, purges, or high level power struggles which do not result in any policy changes may fit this category very well. Such a case was the murder of Colonel Carlos Delgado Chalbaud, head of the provisional military government in Venezuela, in November, 1950. Following Delgado's death, Colonel Marcos Perez Jimenez, another member of the military *junta,* assumed complete power which he retained until 1958.[27] In spite of the change from Delgado Chalbaud to Perez Jimenez, there were virtually no additional changes in the Venezuelan political system.

2. **Changes in Constitutional Procedure, or in the Accepted "Rules of the Game"**   The political actor is likely to view this type of change as somewhat more disruptive, since it alters the informal or formal rules and prescriptions by which policies are determined and decisions are made in the system. Certain changes in the methods of personnel recruitment can also be

introduced under this category, if the effect is not to alter the functioning of more fundamental variables. The adoption of a new constitution for the state would fit into this category, as well. Illustrative of this sort of transition is the set of changes in operating rules and regulations undergone by native bureaucracies and public administration cadres in states soon after gaining their independence. Changes in personnel are obviously in store for the local bureaus; the transition from colonial administrators to local officials, especially at the village and district level, is crucial for the prompt establishment of a sense of self-control over the destiny of the new state. Beyond these changes, however, the exposure of the bureaucracy to national political pressures, from which they were immune during colonial times, will surely alter their preindependence mode of operations. Judicial and police functions, for example, will be transferred to more specialized agencies; recruitment standards will be adjusted; and lines of authority and spheres of competence will have to be established anew. The bureaucracy, in spite of its inherent conservatism, will face multiple adjustments in new states following the granting of independence.[28]

3. Changes in Functional Equivalents   At this third level of change, certain functions of the political system are transferred from one set of structures or institutions or individuals, to another. Even under normal circumstances, this type of change may be quite unsettling to the average political actor, as it represents the most extensive kind of alteration which can be accommodated entirely within the political system. Nevertheless, even when this sort of change is undergone in a brief span of time, the results do not necessarily have to be destabilizing if the relevant political actors are accustomed to other transitions at the same level.

A very important example of a change in functional equivalent in non-Western developing political systems is the military coup d' etat.[29] In this example, seen from Peru, Bolivia, and Argentina; to Ghana, Nigeria, and Dahomey; to Burma, Indonesia, and South Vietnam, the military as an institution becomes highly dubious about the continued ability of civilian authorities to perform the functions assigned to them by formal or informal rules. In a swift and short armed action, then, the armed forces depose the civilian leadership and arrogate to themselves the functions formerly allocated to the ousted groups. Thus, changes in functional performance have taken place, with such functions as interest aggregation and rule output being performed within the institutional boundaries of the armed forces.

4. Changes in Boundaries of the Political System, and in Boundary-Maintenance Devices   The changes envisioned in this category appear to have greater potential for the unsettling of the actors in the system because, for the first time in our typology, we encounter alterations which affect directly the relations between the political system and the larger social system which surrounds it. Two specific types of changes can take place under this rubric. First, the entire political system may be expanded by the inclusion of new activities, roles, institutions, or individuals. The boundary of the political system may be expanded to enclose relatively more of the social system than was the case prior to the change. As we have indicated earlier, the expansion of the scope of the political system seems to be one of the indispensable features of a program of political development; especially in the crucial areas of regulation, extraction, and distribution capabilities, development simply cannot be undertaken on the old base of the formerly constricted political system. Thus, in any truly developing political system, we should expect changes of this sort —involving the expansion of system boundaries—to be highly visible.

One very important type of boundary expansion often seen in the course of political development involves the expropriation of economic activities formerly owned by private sector corporations, either national or foreign. In Mexico, for example, the achievement of "take-off" in the area of extractive capabilities was probably enhanced by the expansion of the political system into petroleum exploitation, as represented by the expropriation of United States firms in 1938.[30] Similarly, President Nasser's seizure of the Suez Canal in 1956 was a critical step in the expansion of the Egyptian political system's boundaries into areas formerly controlled by non-Egyptians.[31]

A second important type of change concerns the devices established to maintain the boundary by controlling the channels of communication from one system to another.[32] This also is an important step for developing polities, for, as Samuel Huntington points out,[33] political systems faced with mounting numbers of newly mobilized participants with increasingly pressing demands for action simply must provide for the channeling of these demands into the political system in such a way that they can be converted into corrective action. A newly mobilized individual cannot be demobilized; his education and exposure to mass media cannot be taken away from him; so the political system must create new channels whereby this individual can become a meaningful (for him) participant in the communication which crosses the boundary of the political system.

The political party is the institution most often mentioned in connection with the creation of new boundary-crossing communication channels. Huntington stresses this point repeatedly in his analysis of political development,[34] as he states unequivocally that "The principal institutional means for organizing the expansion of political participation are political parties and the party system."[35] Indeed, a good number of the more successful development elites owe their good fortune to the timely creation of strong political party organizations. Whether in Mexico, with the single-party dominant system of the PRI (Institutional Revolutionary Party),[36] in the Democratic Republic of Vietnam, with Ho Chi Minh's creation, the Dong Lao-Dong (Vietnamese Workers' Party, or Communist Party),[37] or in Tunisia, with the Neo-Destour Party of Habib Bourguiba,[38] the active mobilization of the masses through a vigorous political party seems to be the hallmark of the development leader who is expanding his political system and its capabilities without engendering undue psychological stress on the system's participants.

We must note, however, that other devices exist to bridge the gap between the political system and its newly mobilized participants. In some countries, particularly in Latin America, peasant leagues are active in the political education and mobilization of the rural dweller and worker. In few cases are these leagues fully autonomous, usually owing their organizational life to some higher, more inclusive structure, such as a political party or government ministry. Regardless of their broader institutional ties, however, they still provide the emerging peasant with his first taste of political modernization in many cases.[39] The public sector's bureaucracy may also serve this vital boundary-maintenance function, as development elites have discovered in various countries of Africa and Asia.[40]

5. Changes in the Allocation of Power and/or Resources Among Social Classes
At this level of political change, we encounter some of the supposed attributes of a "true" revolution, as opposed to a simple palace coup or internal power struggle affecting only the traditional elite.[41] Fundamental changes are experienced in the way in which political power and command over resources are distributed among various social classes in the system.

The speed with which this type of change is initiated and consummated will have much to do with the way in which it affects the psychological stability of the participants. If the changes are carried out in a very brief span of time, and the total quantity of resources available for distribution is not increased, then the sums allocated to one class must be extracted from another class, with all that that implies for the stability of the latter. However, if changes are spaced over a long period, and the overall sum of resources available grows commensurately, then the psychological disturbances generated by the change are likely to be internalized rather easily by the newly deprived groups. Finally, if the changes in allocation involve primarily symbolic rather than material resources, the stress felt by participants will be more likely to have its origins in cognitive dissonance, as opposed to deprivation, with additional implications for overall systemic stability.

The experience of the Democratic Republic of Vietnam, after 1954, offers us one of the most dramatic examples of resource and value reallocation seen in the contemporary non-Western world. The DRVN aggressive agrarian reform program had its origin in a "Population Classification Decree" promulgated in the midst of the French-Indo-Chinese War, on March 2, 1953. This decree was aimed at classifying the entire rural population of the nation, and, in so doing, to indicate which groups would be forced to yield their agricultural holdings to the reform agency, the Central Land Reform Committee. In its initial phase of implementation, from 1953 to about 1956, the program had as its goal no less than the total elimination of the landowning class, through three steps: (1) mobilization, or psychological preparation, of the peasants for mass trials; (2) liquidation of landlords and rich peasants, and the expropriation of large estates as well as lands which belonged to churches, and to foreigners; and (3) redistribution of the land to landless peasants.

The local cadres of the land reform agency undertook their task with great vigor, especially after the departure of the French in 1954. Death sentences were handed out liberally by special "People's Agricultural Reform Tribunals"; some observers estimate that as many as 50,000 North Vietnamese were executed, and possibly as many as twice that number imprisoned in forced labor camps, in the course of the implementation of the decree. At last, the threat of severe and arbitrary action against life and property became so widespread that Ho Chi Minh himself acted to slow down the process of land expropriation and distribution, too late, however, to prevent a popular explosion of peasants and small landowners in the former Viet-Minh stronghold of Nghe-An province. There the farmers rioted in protest against the reform, whereupon the DRVN government dispatched the entire 325th Division of the Vietnamese People's Army to crush the rebellion.

Once the open opposition had been defeated, however, the communist leadership moved to soften the impact of the land reform program. New cadres, trained to be sensitive to the needs of the peasants, were sent out to points of greatest friction to redress grievances; some prisoners were released from detention camps; and bureaucratic remedial actions were taken against the leaders of the Central Land Reform Committee. Since the rebellious province included a substantial Catholic population, and there was some indication that religious grievances played a part in the uprising, new aid was given for the reconstruction of Catholic churches. By this judicious combination of coercion and payoff, the North Vietnamese government managed to survive what was probably the most serious challenge to their control over the countryside since 1954.

The expropriation and redistribution of land in small plots to individual farmers was to be only the first phase of the agrarian reform program, however. By the late 1950's, it was clear that this successive redivision of private land had reached the point where each individual farm family lacked the land necessary even to reach the subsistence level of production. Therefore, the reconsolidation of land into cooperatives began in earnest in 1958; by March, 1963, cooperatives included 87.7 percent of all rural families. The radical change in policy apparently had a highly distressing effect on the peasants, as well as on the government cadres who were charged with the implementation and explanation of these new policies. Nevertheless, with the memories of the unsuccessful 1956 rebellion still fresh in the minds of the peasants, this change was undertaken with much less friction or resistance.[42]

6. Fragmentation in the Territorial Jurisdiction of the Political System   We have in mind here the ultimate internal political change—secession

or separatism. This category comes as close as any imaginable to the organic concept of systemic "death," because the malcontents are so disaffected that they do not even want to fight over control of the system in question. The viewpoint of a secessionist differs markedly from that of a revolutionary in ways which seem appropriate for discussion at this time. First, we should note that in general a secessionist and a revolutionary probably do not differ too much in their degree of alienation from the system. Both the revolutionary and the secessionist have reached the point where they are no longer able to predict the enjoyment of any positive benefits from continued participation in the present system as they know it. The dividing line between secession and revolution arises, instead, from other differences in perceptions.

The secessionist in his insurgency faces a different cost-benefit ratio from that faced by the revolutionary. The secessionist perceives that he cannot capture the central machinery of the political system at any cost which is acceptable to him, so he instead decides to sever all relations with the current system and to replace it with one in which his group is overwhelmingly dominant. The revolutionary, facing a different cost-benefit ratio, opts to try to take control of the present system. In both cases, strategic and tactical considerations of a military nature may weigh more heavily than ideological questions of cultural affinity (or lack thereof). Second, the secessionist's viewpoint of the cost-benefit ratio will surely be affected by the fact that one of his objectives is to establish a system in which he will not have to share either power or territory with those not of his group. The revolutionary is obviously willing to share, if only because he intends to occupy some of the dominating role(s). Finally, the stakes of a secession are radically different from those of a revolution, in that the former constitute two entirely new(or wholly transformed) systems, while the latter are focused on the existing system (albeit in radically changed form).

The attempt of the Ibos to secede from Nigeria and form the independent state of Biafra in 1967 is illustrative of the process by which a military coup transforms itself into a secessionist movement. As we shall discuss in greater detail in Chapter Eight, Nigeria, once considered to be black Africa's most stable and promising new nation, carried from its inception the tribal and linguistic divisions which offered the potential for fragmentation. At first, the British-imposed federal system had established a stable if uneasy balance among the rival regional forces. So long as economic progress continued unbroken, tribal animosities could be curbed for the good of the national entity. As economic cramp began to set in, however, a struggle ensued between the upwardly mobile and energetic Ibos and other tribes over the role which the former would play in a future Nigerian union.

In January, 1966, many Ibo leaders apparently still hoped to be able to carve out for their people a major role in the governance of a united Nigeria. The military coup of that month, although national in its inception, brought many Ibo army officers into prominence in the central government. After a brief period of intense disruption, a provisional military government was installed under an Ibo, Major General J. T. U. Aguiyi-Ironsi. Through a series of decisions, culminating in the unification decree of May, which abolished the federal regions and unified the civil service, Ironsi appeared to be moving Ibos toward greater control over all of Nigeria.

In July, 1966, the military launched a second coup which drove the Ibos from power. Many leaders of the Ibo community began to return to their eastern homes, spurred by widespread massacres of Ibos in the hostile northern provinces. The combination of the coup and the massacres were enough to convince Ibos that they could no longer look forward to a secure share of the power and economic benefits of the Nigerian system.[43] Finally, in May, 1967, after several attempts at negotiation with the authorities in Lagos, the Ibo leader, General Odumegwu Ojukwu, declared that his region had seceded from the Federation, and that the new nation of Biafra had come into being. The result was a bloody, 30-month long civil war.

We have attempted to set forth the political variables which are likely to undergo change in the process of modernization. The above list is intended to reflect gradually increasing levels of disorder in the political system, as viewed by the individual actor. Yet, these variables do not change in isolation, but in varying combinations and sequences. It is difficult to generalize on this point, but we find it reasonable to assume that individual actors will become more destabilized, anxious, or uncertain about the future as change penetrates through successive layers of the political and social system. Therefore, we have arranged the variables in order of relative importance to the stability of the

Table 6.1   Levels of Political Change. ('X' denotes change in variable)

Types of Transitional Systems						*Variables Subjected to Change*
Stable	*Evolutionary*	*Disrupted*	*Malfunctioning or Expanding*	*Revolutionary*	*Fragmenting*	
X	X	X	X	X	X	Ruling personnel
	X	X	X	X	X	Constitutional procedure
		X	X	X	X	Functional equivalents
			X	X	X	System boundaries
				X	X	Allocation of values
					X	Territorial jurisdiction

system, and have indicated in Table 6.1 the possible combinations of political change.

THE RESOLUTION OF STRESS

So far, we have considered the source and level of political stress. A third important factor determining the impact of stress on political development concerns the techniques which a social group can call upon to resolve a distressing conflict or situation. As we hypothesized above, societies with repertoires of stable stress responses have a better chance of withstanding the pressures of political development than do polities where stress responses are primitive, violent, or disruptive.

To illustrate our point, let us examine the different ways in which eight nations in the Caribbean cope with stress.[44] As we have said, each political culture develops its own repertoire of stressful behavior patterns which are accessible and acceptable to most members of the society. Each of these behavior patterns permits relatively greater or less adaptation of the system to stressful conditions such as rapid modernization, external threat, natural disaster, and so forth.[45] The exact nature of these stress responses determines how much of the stress is accommodated through politically relevant action, and, hence, how much of a tension-reduction burden is placed on individual, group, and polity actors.

To summarize briefly the broader study, our examination of stress responses in the Caribbean uncovered at least four general categories of behavior used to cope with conflictual conditions. Some individuals chose to *avoid the stressful situation* altogether by physically moving away from the source of conflict. These actors resolved stress either by emigrating to another country, or by migrating to another place within the same country.[46] Others dealt with stressful conditions by *directing the tension inwardly* against themselves, or by *displacing it against persons who were close* to them socially. We find these individuals counted in statistics covering suicides, homicides, alcoholism, divorce, and so forth.[47] Still another group of political actors chose to resolve stress by *participating in overt political activities which carried only a moderate level of personal risk.*[48] Examples of such action would be voting in elections, and taking part in strikes and demonstrations unmarred by violence. A last group elected *participation of a violent nature* in the political process as their response to conflict. These high risk actors were the agents of terrorism, sabotage, coup d'etats, army revolts, guerrilla warfare, violent strikes and demonstrations, and civil wars, among others.

Our findings, covering the period from 1948 to 1964, reveal at least three clear "styles" of responding to conflict in the Caribbean. In Mexico, Costa Rica, and Venezuela, the three most highly developed and most stable democracies of our group,[49] activist citizens channeled between 65–70 percent of their stressful behavior into voting and other moderate risk activity. Most importantly, the more destabilizing forms of stress response—suicides, homicides, and political violence—were resorted to by a mere 2–4 percent of the population in these countries.

In clear contrast to the first group, in the Dominican Republic, Guatemala, El Salvador, and Honduras, a majority of the distressed citizens chose to avoid conflict completely by migration. In the first three countries of this group, migration or emigration accounted for about 55 percent of the total stress responses, while in Honduras the level reached 65 percent. Apparently, the heavy reliance of these systems on migration helps account for the relative stability of their development processes up to a point, especially in the case of El Salvador. One wonders, however, just how much active participation we can expect in the future in political cultures which endorse avoidance as the appropriate style for coping with conflict.

Cuba under Fidel Castro stands out as a unique (for Latin America) approach to stress response. Since there have been very few channels open for moderate risk participation in Cuba from 1959 to 1964, distressed Cuban citizens have sought psychological release in other ways. The overwhelming majority (over 75 percent) of those who have taken some action to resolve stress have done so by leaving the country or by migrating within the island; but extraordinarily high percentages of Cubans have either directed their tension inwardly or have engaged in risky adventures in violent politics. The combined score for suicides, homicides, divorce, and deaths from hypertension for Cuba, for example, was five times higher than the eight-nation Caribbean average.

We find, then, a close correlation between the style of stress response of a political culture, and the stability of the development process which that culture will support. If the style of conflict resolution tends toward participation in only moderately risky endeavors, such as voting, then the polity may expect a relatively stable history of change. If, on the other hand, the political culture sanctions stress responses which provoke greater instability in the system—such as homicide or rebellion—the developing country can look forward to a rather dismal future as it struggles to attain self-sustaining change. It is appropriate that we suspend our discussion at this point; in Chapter Seven, we will take up again the question of risk-taking, and its relationship to political culture and political development.

THE MANAGEMENT OF STRESS IN DEVELOPING COUNTRIES

By way of conclusion to Chapter Six, we shall examine some techniques and guidelines by which a development elite may carry out a political reform program while managing the potential disruptive effects of psychological stress. We use the term "management" to reflect our conviction that stress is an ever-present feature of political conflict; stress can be minimized and channeled, but it can not be eliminated from any functioning political system. The following comments, then, are intended to suggest ways of directing stressful decisions in order to minimize the chance that they will result in overtly disorderly behavior.

1. The Avoidance of Dissonance Stress   One of the foremost sources of dissonance stress in non-Western political systems is the inherent contradiction between the demands of the leadership for modern behavior in the political realm—centralized political authority, loyalty to the nation-state, replication of parliamentary and constitutional democracy—and their exaltation of the society's traditional modes of communal decision-making and allocation of resources and values. I. R. Sinai has written of the stress engendered in India by the gulf between the Gandhian call for a return to traditional Indian spiritual virtues, on the one hand, and the relentless exigencies of a modern nation-state, on the other. Indonesia, in its own special way, suffers from the same problem of requiring that the intellectuals pay homage to the Western style of politics while inspiring the mass of the Indonesian population to return to the sanctified traditional ways of Indonesian communal politics, with its emphasis on consensus, endless talking around the issue, and the absence of any definitive solutions to pressing political, economic, and social problems.[50] For the development elite of any country faced with similar problems the lesson is clear: dissonance stress can be avoided only if the leadership resists the temptation to exalt the traditional modes of political behavior, and instead makes clear to all political actors that modernization will inevitably require certain concessions of thought and habit; further, the sooner these concessions are made, the easier the transition will occur.

2. The Avoidance of Deprivation Stress   Deprivation stress, brought on by the opening of a gap between expectations and capabilities, will be treated most successfully through government policies which aim at enhancing a sense of one's capabilities, rather than those which reduce his sense of expected returns from the system. Apart from the inherent difficulty in altering downward a person's aspirations, such a policy would be self-defeating for a development elite to assume. The enhancement of an individual's capabilities, on the other hand, can be accomplished by insuring that his initial contacts with a rapidly developing political world provide him with psychologically gratifying instrumental experiences. In other words, he must be made to feel that he is capable of controlling, in some small degree, the policies which impose upon him new and unusual burdens. Mathiason's study on the Venezuelan peasant confirms this thesis; the extensive opportunity for political participation offered to the peasant through political parties and peasant leagues has plunged the Venezuelan rural sector suddenly into the modern world with little of the psychological stress normally associated with such a heady enter-

prise. Thus, we conclude that a rapidly developing elite which finds that it must make sharp changes in resource and value allocation should endeavor to do so in such a way that those affected are given an opportunity to participate instrumentally in the decision-making process from which the changes emanate.

3. The Avoidance of a Sense of Discontinuity

If discontinuity lies at the root of all stress sensations, public policy should be directed at reducing the sense of discontinuity, or failing that, at enhancing the individual's competence to cope with a discontinuous environment. The first objective, reducing the degree of perceived discontinuity, may be reached by minimizing the fluctuations, oscillations, false starts, and underachieved goals of development programs. The betrayal of goals, no matter how lofty and well-intentioned, does much to convince the tradition-bound citizen that the new government is just following the nation's politics "as usual"; and he will likely try to take refuge in some low-risk mode, such as withdrawal. Far better for the development elite to set goals realistically, and to meet them consistently; the sense of uncontrollable discontinuity will decrease accordingly. In addition, the development leadership can smooth over this feeling that he is capable of adjusting to a new and constantly changing environment. The lesson from the village of Larteh, Ghana, appears to be exactly that—that rapid change can be borne by the populace if their educational level is relatively high.

4. The Direction of Stress Toward Stable Adjustment.

Presuming, in spite of the above admonitions, that political development will probably be accompanied by certain levels of stress, no matter what, the development elite would do well to turn their policies in such a way that such stress leads to a minimum amount of overt upheaval. It is difficult to predict exactly how much the modal personality will attempt to resist stress agents. Our experiment with

Chart 6.1 An Hypothesized Relationship Between Socio-
Economic Status and Risk-Taking Propensity.

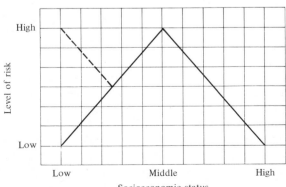

the several states of the Caribbean above, however, leads us to believe that, just as each nation has its own distinctive repertoire of stress response, so also will each socioeconomic class *within* the nation exhibit a unique "style" of reacting to stress. Whereas one class may respond to stress through some form of moderate-risk participation, another class, at the opposite end of the spectrum, may respond through withdrawal, while a third may react violently, through high-risk attacks on the system. The job of the development leadership lies in attempting to place the burden of stressful decisions on those sectors which are most likely to react in a manner which does not destabilize the system.

The difficulty of predicting the stress response of each socioeconomic class of each polity in the non-Western world is obvious; empirical confirmation of these hypotheses must await the development of research tools not presently at our disposal. While we are waiting, however, the following may serve as suggestive of a place to begin our inquiry. Confining our analysis to simply the high and low risk alternatives for the moment, we see from Chart 6.1 that there is a curvilinear relationship between the socioeconomic status of a certain group (SES) and the propensity of that group to opt for high or low risk alternatives. Specifically, groups with a low SES, those who live under conditions of fatalism and who lack faith in the ability of man to control his surroundings, will be more apt to select internalized forms of stressful behavior (see Table 6.2). Occasionally, however, these same persons, when provoked by some extreme type of deprivation, such as food shortages, may explode into severely disruptive behavior. The lower end of the SES axis, then, has a "two-tailed" appearance. At the upper end of the scale we find individuals with relatively greater education, resources, and experience with reaction to political stress. We may surmise that these individuals would have a greater ten-

Table 6.2 Repertoires of Stressful Behavior Modes According to Socioeconomic Status: A Suggested Typology.

Socioeconomic Status	*Type of Stress*	
	Dissonance	*Deprivation*
High (landed gentry)	Withdrawal (low)	Exile (low)
Upper middle (army, bureaucracy)	Alcoholism, psychosomatic discharge (low)	*Coup*, revolt (high)
Middle (students)	Riot (high)	Riot (high)
Lower middle (urban labor)	Alcoholism, divorce (low)	Strikes, riot (high)
Lower (peasants)	Psychosomatic discharge, primitive drugs (low)	Withdrawal, family disintegration (low)
	Occasional spasm of violence (high)	Riots, land invasion (high)

dency to react to stress through internalized behavior, such as a change in their goal structure, or through avoidance behavior such as going into exile. Groups in the middle, such as university students, are alert to their ability and opportunity to effect change, but are frustrated by their lack of access to the concrete levers of power. For them, high-risk activism may be a more feasible route to select. Table 6.2 summarizes these varying responses to stress according to socioeconomic status. As we stated earlier, this typology can be regarded as no more than suggestive at this stage of our investigation; but, to some degree, successful development elites must make rough calculations of this nature if they are to direct political stress into channels which do not unduly hinder the progress of the development effort by leading to political instability.

CHAPTER NOTES

1. Fred E. Horvath, "Psychological Stress: A Review of Definitions and Experimental Research," *General Systems Yearbook,* Vol. 4, 1959, pp. 203-29.
2. Hans Selye, *The Story of the Adaptation Syndrome* (Montreal, Canada: Acta, Inc., 1952), esp. Chap. One.
3. This definition draws heavily from William Caudill, *Effects of Social and Cultural Systems in Reactions to Stress* (New York: Social Science Research Council, 1958), SSRC Pamphlet #14, pp. 4-10.
4. A. Irving Hallowell, "Psychic S'resses and Culture Patterns," in S. N. Eisenstadt, ed., *Comparative Social Problems* (New York: Free Press, 1964), pp. 73-77.
5. Eugene Victor Walter, *Terror and Resistance: A Study of Political Violence,* (New York: Oxford University Press, 1969), esp. Chap. Nine.
6. David Leslie, *Among the Zulus and the Amatongas,* (Glasgow: 1875), p. 62, cited in Walter, p. 224.
7. James Payne, "Peru: The Politics of Structured Violence," *Journal of Politics,* 27, 2 (May, 1965): 362-74.
8. Raymond B. Cattell, *The Scientific Analysis of Personality* (Chicago: Aldine, 1965), pp. 28-32.
9. James C. Davies, *Human Nature in Politics* (New York: Wiley, 1963), pp. 6-11.
10. The subject of discontinuity in political perception is treated extensively in Richard E. Dawson and Kenneth Prewitt, *Political Socialization* (Boston: Little, Brown, 1969), esp. Chap. Six.
11. Leon Festinger, *A Theory of Cognitive Dissonance* (Evanston, Ill.: Row, Peterson & Company, 1957), pp. 279.
12. "Political Implications of General Systems Research," *General Systems Yearbook,* Vol. 6, 1961, pp. 1-8.
13. I. R. Sinai, *The Challenge of Modernization* (New York: Norton, 1964), p. 64.
14. Hugh Thomas, *The Spanish Civil War,* (New York: Harper & Row, 1961), esp. Chap. 20.
15. Richard Weinert, "Violence in Pre-Modern Societies: Rural Colombia," *American Political Science Review,* LX, 2 (June, 1966): 340-47.
16. Norman A. Bailey, "*La Violencia* in Colombia," *Journal of Inter-American Studies,* IX, 4 (October, 1967): 561-75.

17. Robert Shaplen, *Time Out of Hand: Revolution and Reaction in Southeast Asia* (New York: Harper & Row, 1969), pp. 110-27.
18. Ted Robert Gurr, *Why Men Rebel* (Princeton, N.J.: Princeton University Press, 1970), esp. Chap. Two. Also, Ted Robert Gurr, "A Causal Model of Civil Strife: A Comparative Analysis Using New Indices," *American Political Science Review,* LXII, 4 (December, 1968): 1104-24. Also, Ted Robert Gurr, "Psychological Factors in Civil Violence," *World Politics,* XX, 2 (January, 1968): 245-78. Gurr's work has been confirmed in its broadest aspects by the following studies. Ivo and Rosalind Feierabend, "Aggressive Behavior within Polities, 1948–1962: A Cross-National Study," *Journal of Conflict Resolution,* X (September, 1966), pp. 249-71. And Ivo K. Feierabend, Rosalind L. Feierabend, and Betty A. Nesvold, "Social Change and Political Violence: Cross-National Patterns," in Hugh D. Graham and Ted Gurr, eds., *Violence in America: Historical and Comparative Perspectives* (Washington, D.C.: USGPO, 1969), Vol. II, Chap. 18.
19. For background information on the Peruvian election crisis of 1962, see Arnold Payne, *The Peruvian Coup D'Etat of 1962: The Overthrow of Manuel Prado* (Washington, D.C.: Institute for the Comparative Study of Political Systems, 1968). For a thorough account of the 1968 crisis, with an emphasis on the petroleum controversy, see Richard N. Goodwin, "Letter from Peru," *The New Yorker,* May 17, 1969, pp. 41-109.
20. James C. Davies, "Toward a Theory of Revolution," *American Sociological Review,* XXVII, 1 (February, 1962): 5-19.
21. Erik Allardt, "Reactions to Social and Political Change in a Developing Society," in K. Ishwaran, ed., *Politics and Social Change,* Vol. IX of *International Studies in Sociology and Social Anthropology* (Leiden: Brill, 1966), pp. 1-10.
22. Raymond Tanter and Manus Midlarsky, "A Theory of Revolution," *Journal of Conflict Resolution,* XI, 3 (September, 1967): 264-80.
23. For a description of the land shortage problem in East Africa, see P. H. Gulliver, "Land Shortage, Social Change and Social Conflict in East Africa," *Journal of Conflict Resolution,* V, 1 (1961): 16-26. See also David Feldman, "The Economics of Ideology: Some Problems of Achieving Rural Socialism in Tanzania," in Colin Leys, ed., *Politics and Change in Developing Countries* (Cambridge, England: Cambridge University Press, 1969), pp. 85-111.
24. Gurr, *Why Men Rebel,* p. 41.
25. Stephen B. Withey, "Reaction to Uncertain Threat," in George W. Baker and Dwight W. Chapman, eds., *Man and Society in Disaster* (New York: Basic Books, 1962), Chap. Four.
26. S. I. Cohen, A. J. Silverman, and B. M. Shmavonian, "The Measurement of Human Adaptation to Stressful Environments," *General Systems Yearbook,* IV (1959), pp. 231-41. Also Richard S. Lazarus, "A Laboratory Approach to the Dynamics of Psychological Stress," in George H. Grosser, Henry Wechsler, and Milton Greenblatt, eds., *The Threat of Impending Disaster: Contributions to the Psychology of Stress* (Cambridge, Mass.: M.I.T. Press, 1964, pp. 34-57. See also Peter G. Bourne, *Men, Stress and Vietnam* (Boston: Little, Brown, 1970) for examples of other methods of measuring stress.
27. Philip B. Taylor, Jr., *The Venezuelan Golpe de Estado of 1958: The Fall of Marcos Perez Jimenez* (Washington, D.C.: The Institute for the Comparative Study of Political Systems, 1968), pp. 35-36.
28. J. Donald Kinsley, "Bureaucracy and Political Development, with Particular Ref-

erence to Nigeria," in Joseph LaPalombara, ed., *Bureaucracy and Political Development* (Princeton, N.J.: Princeton University Press, 1963), Chap. Ten.

29. The literature on the role of the military in developing systems is extensive. See especially the following: Edwin Lieuwin, *Generals vs. Presidents: Neo-militarism in Latin America* (New York: Praeger, 1964). Samuel P. Huntington, ed., *Changing Patterns of Military Politics* (New York: Free Press, 1962). John J. Johnson, *The Military and Society in Latin America* (Stanford, Cal.: Stanford University Press, 1964). Edward Feit, "Military Coups and Political Development: Some Lessons from Ghana and Nigeria," *World Politics,* XX, 2 (January, 1968): 179-93. Morris Janowitz, *The Military in the Political Development of New Nations* (Chicago: University of Chicago Press, 1964). Henry Bienen, *The Military Intervenes; Case Studies in Political Change* (New York: Russell Sage Foundation, 1968).

30. Howard F. Cline, *Mexico: Revolution to Evolution, 1940–1960* (London: Oxford University Press, 1962), Chap. XXIX.

31. Tom Little, *Egypt* (London: Ernest Benn, Ltd., 1958), Chap. 23.

32. For an important discussion of boundaries and boundary-maintenance devices, see David Easton, *A Framework for Political Analysis* (Englewood Cliffs, N.J.: Prentice-Hall, 1965), Chap. Five.

33. Samuel P. Huntington, *Political Order in Changing Societies* (New Haven: Yale University Press, 1968), esp. Chap. One.

34. Huntington, esp. Chap. Seven.

35. Huntington, p. 398.

36. Cline, Chap. XV.

37. Bernard B. Fall, *The Two Viet-Nams: A Political and Military Analysis,* 2nd rev. ed. (New York: Praeger, 1967), pp. 179-83.

38. W. Howard Wriggins, *The Ruler's Imperative: Strategies for Political Survival in Asia and Africa* (New York: Columbia Univeristy Press, 1969), pp. 109-12. Also Clement Henry Moore, "The Neo-Destour Party of Tunisia: A Structure for Democracy?", *World Politics,* XIV, 1 (October, 1961): 461-82. Reprinted in Jason L. Finkle and Richard W. Gable, eds., *Political Development and Social Change* (New York: Wiley, 1968), pp. 535-50.

39. John R. Mathiason, "The Venezuelan Campesino: Perspectives on Change," in Frank Bonilla and Jose A. Silva Michelena, eds. *The Politics of Change in Venezuela: Volume I, A Strategy for Research and Social Policy* (Cambridge, Mass.: MIT Press, 1967), pp. 120-55. See also Neale J. Pearson, "Latin American Peasant Pressure Groups and the Modernization Process," *Journal of International Affairs,* XX, 2 (1966): 309-17.

40. LaPalombara. Also Jose Veloso Abueva, "Bureaucratic Politics in the Philippines," in Lucian W. Pye, ed., *Cases in Comparative Politics: Asia* (Boston: Little, Brown, 1970), pp. 223-38.

41. See, for example, the typology of revolutionary forms proposed by Tanter and Midlarsky, "A Theory of Revolution."

42. For a discussion of the DRVN land reform program, see Bernard Fall, p. 168. See also Bernard Fall, *Viet-Nam Witness: 1953–1966* (New York: Praeger, 1966), Chap. 8, 10. Also, Joseph Buttinger, *Vietnam: A Political History* (New York: Praeger, 1968), pp. 424-29.

43. James O'Connell, "The Ibo Massacres and Secession," *Venture,* 21, 7 (July/August, 1969): 22-25.

44. These conclusions are based on a more detailed study made by the author on "Dimensions of Political Instability in the Caribbean." Paper presented to the Southern Political Science Association Meeting, November, 1971.

45. Leonard W. Doob, *Becoming More Civilized: A Psychological Exploration* (New Haven: Yale University Press, 1960), p. 211. For additional evidence on this point, see the comparison of U.S. and Vietnamese psychiatric casualties in Bourne, Chap. Five.

46. See Juan C. Elizaga, "Internal Migrations in Latin America," and John D. Durand and Cesar A. Pelaez, "Patterns of Urbanization in Latin America," both in Clyde V. Kiser, ed., *Components of Population Change in Latin America. The Millbank Memorial Fund Quarterly,* XLIII, 4 (October, 1965): 144-59, and 166-91. Also, Deena R. Khatkhate, "The Brain Drain as a Social Safety Valve," *Finance and Development,* 7, 1 (March, 1970): 34-39.

47. For a detailed discussion of various levels of tension-reducing devices, which operate at the internal level, see Karl A. Menninger, "Psychological Aspects of the Organism under Stress," *General Systems Yearbook,* II, 1957, pp. 142-72. See also F. M. Martin, "Stress Disorder in Society," in *The Nature of Stress Disorder* (Springfield, Ill.: Charles C. Thomas, Publisher, 1959), p. 132.

48. For a discussion of various levels of risk-taking, see John W. Atkinson, "Motivational Determinants of Risk-Taking Behavior," in Atkinson, ed., *Motives in Fantasy, Action, and Society: A Method of Assessment and Study* (Princeton, N.J.: D. Van Nostrand, 1958), pp. 322-39.

49. Russell H. Fitzgibbon and Kenneth F. Johnson, in their article "Measurement of Latin American Political Change," in John D. Martz, ed., *The Dynamics of Change in Latin American Politics* (Englewood Cliffs, N.J.: Prentice-Hall, 1965), pp. 113-29, ranked Costa Rica in second place, Mexico in fifth, and Venezuela, eighth among *all* Latin American countries on a scale of political change relevant to democracy. No other country in our sample scored higher than eleventh.

50. Sinai, pp. 71-92.

Chapter 7

SOURCES OF INSTABILITY:

Development and Risk

Psychological stress, brought on by rapid political change, is a necessary but not sufficient condition for the growth of political instability. As we noted in passing in the closing portion of Chapter Six, this psychological stress must be resolved in a high-risk manner in order for the results to be destabilizing for the system as a whole. The propensity of a political order to resolve stressful situations via high-risk alternatives will determine whether or not the stress of development turns into instability.

HIGH-RISK SOCIETIES

We must concern ourselves, then, with the presence or absence of an abnormally large number of high-risk actors in any given political system. All societies contain at least a few individuals whose personality structures include high-risk behavioral alternatives. As we intend to show, however, there are social systems which produce higher than average percentages of high-risk individuals. These high-risk societies contain such a high percentage of high-risk individuals that their *modal personality* would be characterized by a propensity to take high risks.[1]

We should note here that the concept of high risk does not necessarily mean that a political actor risks his life, or engages in violent behavior to achieve political gain, although frequently these two aspects of risk do accompany high risk political activity. We have in mind here the notion of high risk, as employed in the studies of Atkinson, McClelland, and others.[2] According to this formula, the motivation of an individual to select a certain alternative route to solving a problem over other, competing alternatives is a function of three variables: the strength of the need which must be gratified, the expectancy held by the actor that the alternative under consideration will lead to the desired goal (also referred to as the subjective probability of success), and the value of that goal to the actor. Leaving aside the first variable, strength of drive, which has been dealt with in the previous chapter, we find that the choices a political actor makes about avenues of action depend on the degree to which the actor thinks that he will succeed, and the value which he places on such success.

Typically, then, an act which carries with it a very low probability of success (a high-risk act) will also provide the actor with a very high degree of satisfaction if he completes it successfully, simply because very few other people could have performed the act without failing. A low-risk act, on the other hand, while having a high level of probability of success, carries almost no incentive because success is guaranteed. Moderate-risk acts, in the middle of the spectrum, constitute alternatives for which the subjective probability of success and the incentive to succeed are roughly similar.

David McClelland, examining the issue from the point of view of entrepreneurs, and their roles in economic development, formulates the problem along similar lines.[3] The businessman, in administering a complex economic enterprise, confronts daily decisional situations ranging from those involving little or no risk, in which actions are routinized or prescribed by tradition or specialized knowledge, to those which are completely without precedent, and which are seemingly dependent on "luck" or "fate" for a satisfactory outcome. These latter, of course, are his high-risk alternatives. The businessman, having a personality structure which drives him to want to achieve (McClelland's principal hypothesis), opts however for the choices in the middle of the spectrum, those which involve moderate risk, in which both skill and luck play a part in the successful outcome. McClelland argues that the businessman, being a high achiever, needs to feel that his skill is being utilized to the maximum, a feeling which he cannot obtain from selecting either routine or totally innovative alternate solutions.

As noted earlier, a propensity to enter situations which endanger one's life is not necessarily indicative of a high-risk personality. The type of psychological high-risk to which we are referring has to do with the setting of impossibly high goals. Thus, although the United States space program certainly carried with it a high degree of risk of life for the astronauts, there is also a very high degree of success guaranteed. As we would expect, then, the original Mercury astronauts possess personality structures which could only be described as moderate-risk.[4]

It also appears that a propensity to engage in violence for political gain is not necessarily indicative of a high-risk individual. The crucial factor to be considered is whether or not the actor enters into the disruptive activity with little or no chance of success. The expectations of the actor about the success or failure of his violent behavior determine whether he is a high-risk personality type or not.

Lucian Pye, in his detailed examination of communist guerrillas in Malaya, found that his survey sample, based on some 60 former guerrillas who had surrendered to the British, were predominantly what we would call moderate-risk personalities.[5] Although they had been highly stressed, and thus enticed to explore violent action for political gain, they were also interested in immediate achievement of what they thought were realistic goals; and they defected when they realized that these goals could not be achieved through guerrilla action. Similar conclusions could be drawn of V. I. Lenin, in the days immediately prior to the Bolshevik revolution. Although Lenin resorted to violent action to overthrow the Provisional Government of Kerensky, an analysis of his thoughts and words in the early days of November, 1917, reveals that he was rational and precise in his power calculations, and confident of being able to achieve at least his initial objective—the destruction of the Kerensky government.[6]

Adopting the high-risk alternatives in political action means, in our formula, setting political goals radically high, so high in fact that the actors who set them understand that they are unattainable. We shall explore below some of the psychological and cultural mechanisms at work to move political actors toward decisions of this sort. An empirical example presented at this point may serve to clarify our meaning. One wonders how the movement to protest United States participation in the war in Vietnam managed to maintain its momentum in the face of little change in overt United States government policy prior to 1969. The clue is supplied by psychologist Kenneth Keniston in his study of the participants in the Vietnam Summer Project in 1967.[7] Keniston reports that the success of the Vietnam Summer Project is impossible to evaluate; on some scales, it would score rather high, principally because of its organizational success. However, it failed to stop the war; and, if that were its purpose, it would have to be considered a failure. Nevertheless, Keniston, in a revealing statement, indicates that, although the Project failed to stop the war, " . . . none of those who planned or led the project expected that it could accomplish that objective." That, in essence, is the core of a high-risk personality, one who adopts impossibly difficult tasks or goals so that he will not betray his fragile psychological commitment to success when failure comes. As the Yippie Movement sometimes puts it, "Be Realistic! Demand the Impossible!"[8]

Keniston, at a later point in his study, indicates that before revolutionary activity is possible, a potential political radical must make certain psychological commitments to himself and to his cause, commitments which involve his expectancy of success. For the small minority of revolutionary activists, the path to radicalism lies through a realistic perception that victory is possible, and desirable. For a much larger majority, however, the decision to become a radical is based on the more complex rationale that victory is neither possible, nor essential for the individual to be gratified psychologically. For this group, which typifies our failure-threatened personality, failure is considered a natural and inevitable component of their struggle; victory is not necessary, for they are buoyed up by their conviction that they are involved in a morally correct campaign. Thus, when failure comes, as it must inevitably, their personality structures are buffered against the strain. If it were otherwise, they would not be able to stand the frustration and constant sense of failure which accompanies the radical movement in the United States in the 1970's. Keniston cites one of his subjects when asked how he dealt with failures:

> . . . I just wouldn't drop out. . . . If you keep reading or seeing the kind of things that go on in the world or in this country—I would feel much too guilty to really drop out. I don't expect success to come very soon, so I'm sort of protected against that . . . In the meanwhile, I have a good life, lots of friends. If you just don't decide to expect overwhelming success, you're okay.[9]

From the opposite end of the American political spectrum comes evidence to support the notion that members of radical groups tend to be of the high-risk variety. Fred Grupp, in a recent article, has identified several reasons why members of the John Birch Society continue to contribute their time, energy, and money to the JBS in the face of almost total failure to achieve any of the Society's principal goals.[10] Grupp found that, whereas about three out of every five JBS members joined for ideological reasons (61 percent), only one out of five professed satisfaction with the Society over achievement of their ideological goals (19 percent). Nevertheless, these members remain dedicated to the Society because they profess to find the mere activity of the Society—passing out pamphlets, calling people on the telephone, writing letters, and so on—to be satisfying and rewarding, regardless of whether they change anything or not.

SOURCES OF HIGH-RISK BEHAVIOR

There are several important sources of high-risk behavior in all political systems; because our focus in this section is on the personality structure of the destabilizing political actor, however, we will devote most of our discussion to the psychological origins of such activity. As in the case of psychological stress, most of the relevant empirical examples will be drawn from nations and societies in the non-Western world, particularly those which have suffered from high levels of civil disruption during the course of the development process.

The psychological mechanism which impells men toward a high-risk solution to a problem has been extensively investigated by psychologists under laboratory conditions;[11] there remains, however, the major task of applying their findings to the world of political risk-taking. Accordingly, the analysis which follows is intended to be suggestive of an agenda for future empirical research in the area of the personality structure of political risk-takers.

The choice by a political actor of a high-risk solution to a problem can be traced to his feelings regarding success and failure. Failure or success can best be defined psychologically according to whether or not actual performance falls within the range of expected performance. A person performs a task with a certain level of expected achievement in mind. If he falls within this expected range of accomplishment, he feels neither success nor failure. A sense of failure occurs only if he falls below his expected level of achievement. The meaning of failure in this sense, then, " . . . is the lowering of the self-estimate because a performance did not follow a prediction made on the basis of the self-evaluation."[12]

Individual orientation toward success or failure can be summed up in the two personality types described by Atkinson and Feather,[13] and by McClelland.[14] On the one hand, the person with a high need for positive achievement will select tasks of moderate risk, since these offer him the greatest opportunity to affect the outcome of the problem through his own skill and talent. The other type of personality, the failure-threatened personality, is of greater concern to us here.

The failure-threatened personality is a person more strongly motivated by a desire to avoid failure than by a need to attain positive success. His behavior is governed by a need to avoid undertaking any task on which he could fail. As a result, if he is not confronted with any stressful incentives, if he does not perceive the need to do anything, he will never voluntarily undertake any task in which there is uncertainty of outcome. His normal routine of behavior will focus on low-risk acts, those which involve no chance of failure because of their simplicity. Once galvanized into overt action, however, the failure-threatened personality undertakes tasks which are so extremely difficult that the mere appearance of trying to accomplish something difficult will be respected by society, and the individual suffers no deflation when the expected failure occurs. In psychological terms, since he already knew that he was not going to succeed in reaching his stated goal, he does not risk personal failure because he does not fall below his expected performance level.

Three indicators of a high-risk personality help us to locate such behavior in the political realm. First, when one failure comes after another, the failure-threatened personality reacts not by *lowering* his goals and making them more realistic, as we would expect; on the contrary, he successively *raises* his sights after each failing effort. Each failure sensitizes him to the vulnerability in his ego, which triggers the defense mechanism of constantly setting his goals at an impossible height. Thus, he insures that he will never run the risk of psychological failure by lowering his expectations of performance. Second, the failure-threatened personality seems to be much more conscious of peer group pressures and standards of performance than does the achievement-oriented individual. Although high achievers (and, therefore, moderate-risk actors) compete with an internal standard of accomplishment, failure-threatened individuals operate in terms of external standards, usually set by some group of which they are a member. Finally, after each example of failure, the high-risk personality will disown any responsibility for the failure. Instead, he places blame on uncontrollable forces which have mysteriously affected the outcome. Such forces as destiny, luck, will of the gods, the Establishment, the power structure, communism, capitalism, and many others share the burden of guilt; the failure-threatened personality continues serenely along his high-risk path, sheltered by the defense mechanism of rationalization and displacing the blame onto impersonal, slightly mystical evil-doers.

TWO CASE STUDIES

The childhood of Jerry Rubin, one of the founders of the Yippie Movement, provides some interesting glimpses at the interplay between a series of frustrating failures in life, on the one hand, and a continual raising of political goals, on the other.[15] Born into a lower class Jewish family in Cincinnati, Rubin grew up with a heightened anxiety about achieving great things and thereby leaving behind the ethnic and economic stigmas of his heritage. But, beginning in grade school, at about the age of nine, one failure after another greeted his efforts. His father was a great sports fan, and Jerry yearned to be a major league baseball player. Too small and ill-coordinated, he was rejected by local teams of youngsters, and fell into the habit of being the team manager. His desire to gain entrance into the best high school in Cincinnati was blocked when he failed the school's entrance examination. As editor of his high school's newspaper, he drove hard for a high rating from the National Scholastic Press Association, only to fail by a small margin. Poor grades made him ineligible for election to an honor society for journalism students. Significantly, his first venture into politics was to support the candidacy of Adlai Stevenson in 1952, a failure which began to instill in Rubin a lack of faith in moderate politics. Finally, when the politics of mass demonstration began to play a major role in American society, Rubin was psychologically ready to let himself be mobilized. Interspersed with activities with the Vietnam Day Committee and other protest movements at the University of California at Berkeley, however, lay one last attempt at moderation: Rubin managed the campaign of Robert Scheer for the Democratic nomination for congress from California's Seventh District. This, too, ended in failure; and Rubin turned more and more to the Students for a Democratic Society, the National Mobilization to End the War in Vietnam, and, finally, his own creation, the Youth International Party.

Culturally, as well as geographically, rural Venezuela seems quite remote from the middle class Jewish suburbs of Cincinnati, Ohio. Yet, across this chasm we find repeated the same sequence of failure and increased goals in the case of a young Venezuelan revolutionary.[16] This 22-year-old radical student activist and labor organizer had served as a member of the Venezuelan Communist Youth, and had been arrested by the police for agitating factory workers into violence against the government. Because the interviews were carried out by an experienced psychoanalyst, we have a more complete picture of the failure-threatened personality. His earliest recollections of his mother were all concerned with placating her anger, and of being punished severely for insignificant acts of mischief. He greatly desired the love and affection of his parents, but was denied these rewards contingent upon performance of excessively demanding tasks, or upon conforming to unrealistic standards. As a result of his parents' separation, the youth was forced to discontinue his education, a fact for which he blames his father. The subject also manifested a rare willingness to discuss his failure to live up to the very demanding standards of sexual performance implicit in the Latin American concept of *machismo* (masculinity). The first sexual experience of the student occurred at the age of eight, and was an obvious failure, due to its premature timing. Subsequent attempts to foster a durable relationship with women were also failures. A childhood romance was broken up by the girl's hot-tempered father; and there is an indication of impotence in attempted relations with prostitutes. The interviewer notes that the subject devotes quite a large amount of psychic energy to psychosexual repression.

The informant's political activity began on a radical note, influenced by the underground revolutionary efforts by his father in an earlier period. These influences were augmented by his participation in a Communist cell in the underground movement against the dictatorship of General Marcos Perez Jimenez (overthrown in 1958). Yet, in the hyper-politicized atmosphere of the Venezuelan dictatorship of the mid-1950's, such a beginning would not necessarily have been considered a high-risk choice. The interesting fact about our informant is that he continued his underground work, even after a democratic government had come to power. His major clandestine activities consisted of organizing workers, in studying and writing on revolutionary subjects, and in extending the influence of the Communist party into various unions. He was not, however, a member of the armed insurgent group which from time to time threatened the Venezuelan government in the 1960's. His personality structure furnished the framework within which he sought ever higher and less relevant goals in a rapidly developing political order, thereby becoming a destabilizing element in that order.

SOURCES OF THE FAILURE-THREATENED PERSONALITY

We have already alluded to several aspects of child-rearing and acculturation practices (such as setting difficult goals) which seem prone to bring forth a failure-threatened personality. Previous efforts to define systematically the causal child-rearing patterns in a failure-threatened individual have focused on several typical combinations of reward, punishment, and indifference which allegedly produce children with great fear of failure.[17] The application of punishment for failure, coupled with either indifference toward trying or with punishment for not trying, and the absence of any reward for success or for trying, seems to be the ideal "mix" for training the failure-threatened personality. We think, however, that we can uncover some linkages between high-risk actors and the breakdown of a political development effort by outlining some child-rearing practices of non-Western countries which seem to us especially prone to produce individuals with high fear of failing.

CHILD-REARING PRACTICES: INDONESIA

We may begin our survey with an example of child-rearing which is based on an unpredictable mixture of permissiveness and severity of punishment. In Indonesia, the child is given special latitude from birth to the age of about seven to nine years.[18] Formal discipline is very weak; the parents intervene very little in the child's desires or whims. Parental guidance is slight. Thus, preparation for later life is inadequate for the shock of the abrupt transition into the adult world. This transition occurs suddenly with no warning at the age of about nine years; and the child is vaulted into the world of adults, both socially and sexually. No effort is made to help the child to adapt; he is expected to make the change easily and without complaint. In overseeing this transition, the Indonesian parent rarely, if ever, makes use of love or affection; most controls are based on punishment, both physical and psychological. Sexually, Indonesian children are stimulated quite early by their parents, and they are taught to adhere to adult sexual standards long before they are ready physiologically. A final touch is added by the typical Balinese mother, who derives great joy out of deliberately exciting the small child and then suddenly withdrawing the exciting object from the child's reach. As the child matures, the teasing continues, and begins to become more sullen and less happy. All these factors combine to produce a typical Indonesian child who cannot help failing repeatedly at an early age. By combining undue permissiveness and arbitrary punishment with the taunting of the mother, the Indonesian family succeeds in training their children to be dominated by fear of failing, to distrust their environment,[19] and to be excessively cautious of undertaking any personal commitment to a less-than-certain enterprise.

CHILD-REARING PRACTICES: BURMA

A similar pattern of family training seems to be present in Burma, as reported by Lucian Pye.[20] Burmese children are treated with a great deal of indulgence and affection early in their lives; especially in the feeding and coddling activities, the young are the objects of family attention and concern. Soon after this stage, however, the family environment begins to take on a very threatening, hostile, and unpredictable form. The mother becomes quite whimsical about rewarding the child; teasing and ridicule are interspersed with attention and indifference, in a manner unrelated to the child's actual performance. Early on, then, the Burmese child learns that there are no discernible relationships between performance and reward.[21] The family structure becomes increasingly demanding and unyielding for the child as he grows older; but the increasing demands of his parents for obedience and conformity are not matched by increased clarity of the standards to which he is to conform. He is only instructed that, as he matures, he is to avoid annoying the parents; for guidance as to *how* to accomplish this, he must rely on intuition. As a consequence, the unpredictable and arbitrary family environment forces the child into a mold of low-risk activity which requires little or no innovation. In addition, Burmese parents rely heavily on fear—either of themselves or of the unknown—to force strict compliance to their wishes. Weird spiritual forces are always lurking about to carry off the child if he does not conform to the instructions of the parents. Parental punishment of a physical nature is added to supplement the threats of bogey men and witches. Thus, as in Indonesia, a highly permissive infancy gives way to a demanding and rigid youth, with punishment and reward bearing little understandable relationship to performance, and with the most fundamental of all human relationships—that of mother to child—undermined by the capricious behavior of the former.[22]

SOCIAL PRESSURES: THE ARAB WORLD

Inasmuch as child-rearing in Egypt, and the Arab world in general, shows some strong similarities with the Asian examples given above,[23] we may more profitably examine the broader context of acculturation in Arab lands for a further look at processes which engender fear of failure.[24] In Arab societies, the extensive network of rigorously binding social connections and commitments appears to reinforce the fear of failure first instilled by the child-rearing practices of the family. Duties and privileges of an Arab to other members of his social network are sacred and compelling; social groupings are characterized by strong mutual expectations about behavior. The various groups of which the Arab individual is a member intervene in his personal decision-making process, guiding him and denying him, in accordance with his commitments to the group. The Arab is not a free agent in his society; before acting, he must consult numerous relatives and senior members of his social aggregate. In addition, the group's members constantly pronounce on the individual's performance; so much so, in fact, that he finds compliance with their numerous demands to be virtually impossible. Punishment by the group for failure, however, is severe and harsh. " . . . Punishment may take the form of one of the following or a combination of them: . . . reproaching, . . . shaming, scolding, face-to-face insults, belittlement which is often accompanied by swearing, ... ridicule, criticism, and the like."[25] Society at large, then, takes on the attributes of a harsh and unyielding parent, even after the Arab child has left the family environment. Society is also regarded as the enemy of the Arab, always ready to punish him for transgressions, yet seldom prepared to reward him for success. The Arab confronted with this dilemma, typically seeks a low-risk solution. Instead of straining to achieve a positive end, the Arab seeks to avoid doing the disapproved, in order to escape the blame and punishment which surely await him. One of the principal social mechanisms at work in Arab society is that of shame or reproach for failure; and the member of Arab society, in trying to adjust to this mechanism, adopts behavior patterns which are typical of the failure-threatened personality: secrecy in action; displacement, scapegoating and dislike of foreigners; blaming unknown or unseen forces, such as the will of Allah, for failure; high degree of overt self-confidence; and a sense of fatalism, predestination, and resignation before the forces of destiny.

MACHISMO: MEXICO

If the failure-threatened personality grows out of child-rearing practices in Asia, and out of rigid social bonds in the Middle East, the excessive demands of the male's sexual role appear to be an important agent working toward the development of such a personality structure in Latin America. While the discussion below will center on Mexico,[26] the conclusions reflect conditions in Latin America in general.

As we have already seen in the case of the Venezuelan revolutionary youth, the cult of manliness is a dominant cultural factor in most Latin American political systems. As Carl Batt puts it, the drive to dominate others, and, thereby, to prove yourself a man, is " . . . almost the conscious cultural imperative of Mexican life."[27] This drive to prove ones' masculinity is derived, in turn, from the heavy emphasis placed during childhood on sexual performance and the open bragging of boys about their sexual prowess. From a very early age, the young Mexican boy is guided firmly in the direction of the behavior that is expected of every *macho* (male). At about this time, the boy is subjected to what appears to him to be a paradox: he is expected to be manly, yet to submit to the desires of his father. Great emphasis is placed in later years on actual activity, the size of the young boy's sexual organs, and on the telling of his accomplishments among his peers. As a consequence of all this stress on a child's sexual performance, he is confronted with role expectations which he cannot possibly live up to. The psychological setting laid for the development of a failure-threatened personality. As sexual role performance consistantly falls below expectations (as it must if only because of physiological immaturity), the boy's goals grow and grow, in order to avoid the stigma of self-evaluated failure. Again to cite Batt:[28]

When masculinity is highly rated in a culture, a child may see the masculine role as an impossible attainment . . . In an attempt to hide his feeling of inferiority and womanliness, he may overcompensate through hyper-masculine wishes and actions. . . . Often, unattainable, childishly evaluated masculine goals develop and a craving for their satisfaction and for personal triumph. The consequent inevitable defeat only increases the original sense of inferiority and unmanliness, and the resultant envy, defiance, vengeance, resentment, and general hypersensitivity of character. By the time of attainment of maturity, the typical Mexican male is caught firmly in the pattern of sexual failure and frustration followed by increased drive toward greater sexual prowess. Unable to find a satisfactory accomodation with his wife, he turns to impersonal sexual engagements with mistresses or prostitutes, and, thereby, shields himself from the agony of defeat in this all-important sector of his life. In this way, the cult of manliness offers a fertile cultural field for the development of a high-risk social and political order.

THE KIBBUTZ

Up to this point, we have been examining child-rearing practices which, we infer, tend to produce accidentally a higher than usual percentage of failure-threatened personalities. Let us consider, then, one of the few available examples of a child-rearing system designed specifically to yield personality structures which shy away from moderate-risk tasks. The Kibbutz of Israel, now in existence for some 60 years, is a voluntary collective form of communal living, in which adherence to group norms and a willingness to subordinate oneself to group demands are essential personality characteristics.[29] These communal farms, which now contain about 100,000 persons, are based on the imperative of the social aggregate, to which most individual whims and desires must be subjected. Clearly, then, their educational system must avoid any practices which would produce high achievement or moderate-risk personalities. From birth, the child is separated from the mother, and returns to the family only on brief daily visits. Discipline, training, punishment, and reward are all handled in the first instance by a sort of governess, and her assistants. Because of the demands placed on the resources of these women, children are attended to in more or less mechanical fashion, which introduces a discontinuity in the causal linkages between their needs and the response of the environment. Later, when they reach school age, the children are treated first and foremost as members of an integral group, and only secondarily as individuals. The group determines the nature of rewards and punishments, and serves as the principal mechanism for incentives and for establishing individual goals. Rewards and punishments are both used, and are mixed appropriately between physical and affection-oriented techniques. The essential difference in the Kibbutz style of child training is that the child is forced to adapt to a more demanding, more rigid, and less understandable social environment in seeking rewards for achievement.

The results of this training are striking, when Kibbutz children are compared with non-Kibbutz children also reared in Israel, under similar; that is, rural, agricultural circumstances. Uniformly, Kibbutz children tend to be of the low-risk type of personality, when measured against other Israeli children. They value positive achievement less, become more dejected when they fail, think of personal assaults (such as suicide) more when they confront failure, and generally regard the environment as a much less rewarding entity than do non-Kibbutz children. Their goals tend to be formulated either in terms of service and duty to the Kibbutz, or in terms of some personal chore or hobby (such as learning to play the violin), or, at the the other extreme, in terms of serving the country in wartime through some dangerous mission (sabotage, for example). The non-Kibbutz children formulated their goals in terms of acquiring and improving a farm of their own, earning more money, getting more utilitarian education, and so on.

The experience of the Israeli Kibbutz is cited for several reasons. We wish to make clear that child-rearing practices which produce failure-threatened personalities may be eufunctional given the cultural demands of the host social system. The requirements of the Kibbutzim for conformity and social orientation of individuals clearly makes such a personality formation essential for the integrity and smooth functioning of the group. By the same token, we also wish to bring out the fact that the child-rearing techniques available to a society are not a social "given" in the formulae of political modernization. These techniques are not beyond the control of man; as the Israeli experiment proves, child-training practices can, and indeed must, be adjusted to the social demands and requirements of the aggregate if the political development effort is to succeed.

DEVELOPMENT, CULTURE, AND RISK

So far, we have considered only the techniques and practices which have a tendency to yield higher than normal percentages of failure-threatened personalities in a given society. Once these personalities emerge as potential political actors, however, it is not at all certain that they will opt for high-risk, as opposed to low-risk, alternatives in the solution of their political problems. We shall want to turn our attention, then, to some factors which will deflect a failure-threatened personality toward either a high-risk or a low-risk solution to political stress.

To the extent that political development is accompanied by changes in values and attitudes on the part of political actors, the shift of such attitudes from fatalism to activism appears to be central to the shift from a low-risk to a high-risk modal personality. Many observers have pointed to such a transition in beliefs as of key importance in defining the change from traditional to modern societies. Traditional man is a fatalist. He is dependent upon insufficient material resources to try to eke out a marginal living, with little incentive or hope of improving his lot. When repressed or exploited by those with greater power or resources, he lacks the power to obtain redress. His response to a threatening environment is to seek to adjust to it with as small an amount of disorder as he can manage. Typically, when we encounter a failure-threatened personality in his life style, he would opt for low-risk solutions to problems. These low-risk options would include withdrawal, dependence on primitive drugs, such as the *coca* of the Andean Indians, or suicide.

The modernization of values, essential to the success of a political development effort, also threatens to bring in its wake an increase in high-risk behavior, simply because of the shift from fatalism to activism, or to a belief that man does indeed possess the capabilities to affect his environment.[30] Man need no longer subject himself to the deadening effects of *coca* when confronted with a stressful environment; he may act through revolutionary violence to bring about changes in his environment. Thus, in a social system characterized by a failure-threatened modal personality, the transition from fatalism to activism in value patterns brings with it a shift in emphasis from low-risk, escapist alternatives to high-risk solutions which promise to destabilize the broader political system.

Viewed through the prism of the motivational structure of the political actor in the above manner, the relationship between political development and political instability takes on a somewhat different character from that generally alleged. Many observers of political development feel that the very process of transition produces the stressful condtion which, in turn, drives men to the barricades for the rectification of newly discovered social injustices. The fragmentation of traditional social relationships heightens this psychological stress.[31] Our prior analysis suggests an alternate interpretation. Specifically, political instability may arise from the shift in attitudes about man's ability to alter his environment, which, in turn, impel the society's failure-threatened personalities to turn to high-risk solutions to problems of stress which have always been present. In other words, the process of political development, per se, is not necessarily productive of higher levels of psychological stress; rather, the process of value modernization gives men the idea that, at last, they may be able to do something to defend themselves from the stressful agent. If the modal personality of the society tends toward the failure threatened type, the stage is set for political instability and the possible interruption of the development process.

There is strong evidence that the cadres of the National Liberation Front (NLF) of South Vietnam understood well how to bring about this shift from low to high-risk revolutionary activity. The following statement, taken from a captured NLF document written in 1961, reveals the communists' conviction that rural, traditional villagers in South Vietnam were already highly stressed;

the goal of the Front in the South should be to direct this frustration into the struggle against imperialism and the Diem government. As the document outlines the problem:[32]

> Daily the masses are oppressed and exploited by the imperialists and feudalists and therefore are disposed to hate them and their crimes. But their hatred is not focused; it is diffuse. *The masses think their lot is determined by fate.* They do not see that they have been deprived of their rights. They do not understand the purpose and method of the Revolution. They do not have confidence in us. *They swallow their hatred and resentment or resign themselves to enduring oppression and terror, or, if they do so in a weak and sporadic manner.* For all these reasons, agit-prop work is necessary to stir up the masses, to make them hate the enemy to a high degree, to make them understand their rights and the purpose and method of the Revolution, and *to develop confidence in our capability.* It is necessary to change the attitude of the masses from a passive one to a desire to struggle strongly, to take part more and more violently to win their rights for survival.

In effect, then the objective of the NLF cadres was to modernize already stressed individuals, and to guide their stressful behavior into activist channels, away from self-defeating apathy.

In addition to the psychological factor of motivational structure, and the sociopsychological mechanism of values, at least three other variables present in developing countries may have an impact on the paths of potential political radicals. First, the political culture of a given state can facilitate or impede high-risk behavior by its rewarding or condemning of interpersonal violence. Lucian Pye, in discussing the guerrilla insurgency in Malaya in the early 1950's, points out that virtually every political system in Asia at that time had experienced high levels of civil disorder; nation-building was inevitably connected with the practice of political violence.[33] It was natural, then, that the Malayan guerrillas would tend to interpret their political truggle in terms of military operations.

The villages of the Tarascan area of Mexico offer still another example of cultural support for politically motivated violence and murder.[34] In the typical small village of Acan, for instance, with a population of no more than 1,500, there have been 77 homicides, over 100 woundings and countless exchanges of gunfire since 1920. Political murder has clearly become a well-entrenched feature of small-village Mexican politics. There is ample evidence that inhabitants of Tarascan villages regard political killings as a part of their cultural imperative. As the study by Friedrich points out, "The peasant who kills another in the course of . . . politics sees himself as performing a partly justified or even obligatory act, for the culture to which both killer and victim belong often justifies or enjoins political homicide." The actual cultural values which underpin this acceptance of murder for political gain are many and various:

the close kinship felt by all the townspeople, which tends to turn one isolated incident into the cause of a long blood feud; the traditional Latin American emphasis on personal valor and bravery; and a belief that all men possess a certain propensity for rage which simply cannot be contained under conditions of severe provocation. Whatever the exact mechanisms may be, the net result is that political violence receives the blessing of the dominant culture of the small Mexican village.

Bryant Wedge, in his comparison of the differences in student activism in Brazil and the Dominican Republic, points to cultural supports as being an important mediating variable.[35] Brazil, at the time of the overthrow of the leftist regime of President Goulart, was able to avert mass student uprisings, while the Domincan Republic, faced with a similar attempt to prevent the return of ousted President Bosch exploded in turmoil, with students carrying the brunt of the upheaval. While there were obviously many different factors which served to cause the difference, one of major importance was certainly the fact the Brazilian political culture condemns the resort to mob violence, and rewards the use of nonviolent methods to solve problems, while in the Dominican Republic tradition and the political culture support the use of violence for political ends. In Brazil, although there may be much discussion at the ideological level of resort to violence in politics, this proves to be generally rhetoric, and the family structure strongly discourages the use of force. In addition, Brazil's history, while not perfect in this regard, certainly suggests that Brazilians have, more often than not, sought nonviolent means of resolving their conflict. The Dominican Republic offers a sharp contrast, a system in which violence is prominent in their political tradition, and in which most political actors recognize the need, and perhaps the ultimate obligation to utilize force and coercion for what they consider legitimate aims. The weakened family structure reinforces this tendency. The result is the creation of a cultural environment in which those who use violence are not regarded as deviant; rather, on the contrary, they are apt to be greeted as heroes, in the best Dominican tradition.

A second contributing factor to the tendency of failure-threatened personalities to resort to high-risk acts is the degree to which imitative learning offers them examples of successful models of high-risk actors in other systems and other historical epochs. While this factor is sometimes referred to as the "contagion" of revolution, there is actually a much more substantial psychological principle at work.[36] According to the imitative learning principle, an individual learns how to perform a particular act by observing a model at work confronted with a similar task. The subject is able to avoid the laborious job of trial and error so often associated with more traditional and mechanistic forms of conditioning and learning; and imitative learning thus appears to be more useful in a social or interpersonal sphere.

In his detailed analysis of the Sarawak Communist Organization and guerrilla movement, Douglas Hyde reveals that the movement remained entirely at the theoretical level, marked by ideological and doctrinaire discussions without any overt action, until after the success of the Communists in the Chinese civil war and the beginning of the Communist uprising in Malaya.[37] In 1951, however, a Sarawak Chinese school teacher, one Teo Yong Jim, left Sarawak and traveled to Singapore, where he became involved in the study of the Chinese and Malayan Communist experiences. He paid especially close attention to their attempts to organize students and laboring groups into cells which could provide manpower for the Communist uprising which he dreamed of leading in Sarawak, which remained at that time in British hands. In 1954, Teo returned to Sarawak clandestinely and set to work organizing Communist cells. His labors were cut short by the pursuit of British police; and he fled to China, where he was never heard from again. But, he had done his work so well that the nucleus of his organization remained for more than a decade to plague first the British, and, subsequently the Malayasian government.

While much more subtle and difficult to uncover, there appeared to be similar learning processes at work during the rash of military interventions in small Latin American countries in 1963.[38] At issue were not only the domestic crises which prompted the armed forces of Guatemala, Ecuador, the Dominican Republic, and Honduras to consider the need to overturn the incumbent, civilian regimes. There was also the important question of how the United States government would react to such an usurpation of power. President Kennedy had gone to great lengths to impress upon Latin America's military leaders that democracies must be allowed to govern unmolested if U.S. aid, through the Alliance for Progress, were to continue. In spite of these warnings, the first two military coups, in Guatemala and Ecuador, were greeted with dismay from Washington, but the threatened severence of aid did not materialize. Kennedy's bluff had been called; and the social learning process, grinding out its message, led the military chiefs in the two remaining countries to conclude that Washington's insistence on democratic governments could not be enforced. When army leaders in the Dominican Republic and Honduras revolted against civilian governments, the response from the United States, at first, was harsh and pointed. In the Dominican Republic, Kennedy severed diplomatic relations and suspended aid; In Honduras, he did these things, and in addition, withdrew all aid personnel. Both Dominican and Honduran leaders were astonished for having been singled out for punishment when they had only behaved as their colleagues in Guatemala and Ecuador. The social learning process had led them astray. Or so it appeared. Soon after Kennedy's assassination, however, the United States restored relations and aid ties with both the Dominican Republic and Honduras, thereby confirming impressions of military leaders all over Latin America to the effect that military dictatorships would not be punished for overthrowing civilian governments.

A third factor which will influence the resort to high-risk solutions to political stress has to do with the availability of moderate-risk channels of access to the centers of power in the society. We presume that there are many political radicals who behave in a high-risk fashion simply because there are no meaningful moderate-risk options available to them. Our hypothesis here, a slight variation of one of the deprivation conditions described in Chapter Six, is that, as the political leaders of a system begin to close moderate-risk access channels which were previously opened to highly stressed political actors, these actors must either resort to low-risk, compensatory behavior (exile, withdrawal, psychosomatic discharge) or high-risk activities (violence and disorder).

Ghana under Kwame Nkrumah is frequently cited as an example of a political system brought under attack by the unjustified closure of moderate-risk approaches to political activism.[39] In reality, the closure had the dual effect of driving some of Nkrumah's supporters into low-risk noninvolvement, while the military and civilian bureaucracy was led into the high-risk coup attempt which eventually unseated Nkrumah in 1966. The better known of Nkrumah's repressive measures aimed at the restriction of formal political opposition. During the latter part of the 1950's, Ghana's parliament, under control of Nkrumah's Convention People's Party, passed several laws which served to intimidate political opponents with the threats of deportation, imprisonment, removal of political rights, and control over elections and voting. While Markowitz may be correct in asserting that no one ever died in prison as a result of these acts of suppression, they were effective in moving Ghana toward a one-party (and, eventually, a one-person) state, in which the legitimacy of organized opposition was denied. Within Nkrumah's own administration, however, these measures were paralleled with gradual closure of access to his two most important remaining sources of support: the army and the bureaucracy. The nation's large and (for a developing country) well trained civil service found itself bypassed and ignored in the course of the drive to development, with the dual result that the development effort foundered on bad advice, and the technocrats became restless when confronted with the failure of programs for which they were responsible, but for reasons that were beyond their control. The final act of closure, however, may have been Nkrumah's decision to arm a People's Militia, which was to serve as a counterweight to the professional army. This decision may have been the product of Nkrumah's growing sense of paranoia, due to repeated attempts on his life; it may have grown out of advice and recommendations from Russian military advisors. Whatever the source, the move was a clear signal to the army that they were about to be cut off from the decision-making centers in the government; the coup d'etat was their reply. As a consequence of the earlier repressive measures, political groups who could have been called upon to defend the constitutional regime had been cowed into a low-risk posture; and Nkrumah's government became an historical fact, rather than a promise of the future.

Admittedly, the decision about when, how, and to what extent an incumbent government should open moderate-risk channels to potentially high-risk actors is a difficult one to analyze. Very frequently, when violence breaks out, the incumbent government is expected to be able to make changes in public policy to conciliate the rebels and bring them back into the policy-making process. However, as Lucian Pye points out, this belief is usually the result of a lag in the government's response to the demands of the insurgents, since their ('the insurgents') decision to resort to force was probably made long before violence actually occurs.[40] Once the decision is made, furthermore, the rebels tend to shut themselves off from conciliation with the incumbents in order to maintain the momentum of their organization. Thus, it is somewhat problematic whether or not any reconciliation is possible, or whether or not the rebellious forces can be induced to resume moderate-risk political activity. Such openings apparently would have made no difference at all to the Malayan guerrilla forces in the days immediately prior to the outbreak of the insurgency, according to Pye. On the other hand, the guerrilla movement in Venezuela was defused to a large degree by the legalization of the Communist Party, and the granting of amnesty to former guerrilla fighters, both actions undertaken in the spring of 1969. In arriving at decisions of this sort, the leaders of developing states in the non-Western world must attempt to take into account, and balance, a wide range of variables, not the least of which is the personality structure of the forces of instability.

THE MANAGEMENT OF RISK-TAKING

Just as in the case of our analysis of stress and political instability, our task in this chapter will not be complete without a brief excursion into the realm of policy implications. Specifically, what can a development elite do to minimize the probability that a highly stressed political actor will turn to high-risk alternatives to resolve his stressful condition, and, in so doing, destabilize the entire political system?

As a general rule, the degree to which psychological stress contributes to "the making of a revolutionary," or high-risk actor, will vary inversely with the extent to which the personality structure of the actor is of the failure-threatened variety. That is, the greater the level of stress, the less a failure-threatened personality would be needed to propel an actor into high-risk avenues of political behavior. By the same token, the less the magnitude of stress in a given society, the more likely it is that the violent political actors possess personality structures which increase their propensity to engage in high-risk behavior. Therefore, if our development elites have been successful in managing stress, as we discussed in the previous chapter, they can be reasonably certain that individuals who engage in acts of political instability probably do so more from personality causes than from those of a systemic or environmental character. This constitutes a very real threat to rapid political development in many non-Western countries, however; for, as we have pointed out, there are several facets of non-Western cultures—child-rearing, social norms, and sexual role expectations—which seem prone to creating a failure-threatened modal personality. The managing of risk-taking propensities, then, may prove to be much more of a challenge to today's development elites than may have been the case in Western states a century ago.

The problem is complicated further by our realization that the propensity to take high risks arises from cultural features of a society imbedded deep in the family and other institutions which are bound to be highly resistant to change. Because the sources of the failure-threatened personality are so far beyond the normal reach of governmental power, it would appear that this aspect of a polity's modal personality will be one of the "givens" with which a development elite must learn to cope, but which it cannot alter to any great degree. We feel that this pessimistic attitude must not be allowed to obscure the examples—presented previously, and below—which contradict this notion. For we will find that the non-Western governments which have successfully resolved the stability problem of rapid change are precisely those which have addressed squarely the problem of educational and family training reform, with an eye to producing a modal personality more conducive to a modern, stable state within their own environmental conditions. Further, while we in the West regard state manipulation of family and educational training as being beyond the power of a properly limited government, we must realize that these same constraints do not—indeed, cannot—be applied to the countries in the process of political development today. As we tried to indicate in Chapter One, a Western insistence on limiting the powers of a constitutional government, in the style of James Madison, overlooks the fact that today's developing elites want to expand, not limit, their state's capabilities. For these reasons, we should not regard even the modal personality of a developing state as an untouchable variable, the alteration of which is beyond the purview of governmental authority. To the extent that the modal personality is failure-threatened—and, hence, high-risk—that personality structure must be altered if the development effort is to have a chance at success.

1. *The reduction of high-risk behavior by channeling failure-threatened personalities toward low-risk solutions to behavioral problems.* A developing political system faced with potential revolutionaries with failure-threatened personalities has a choice of two long-range alternatives. On the one hand, it can try to alter the modal personality so that it becomes achievement-oriented and moderate risk, rather than failure-oriented and high-risk. We shall discuss this rather more difficult alternative below. For those polities which have faced these long-range choices, however, a more feasible alternative would seem to be the channeling of the failure-threatened personality back into low-risk behavioral patterns. If this formula is successful, political violence and insurgency would be replaced by withdrawal, exile, apathy, and a return to a sort of postrevolutionary fatalism.

To be sure, the examples of a successful application of this policy are few in number; yet, by their very success they illustrate well the opportunities available to a developing country which chooses this route. We have already seen in some detail one example—that of the Israeli kibbutz—in which the learning of the child takes the form of complete subordination to the will, the needs, and the desires of the group. Achievement-orientation and moderate risk behavior are eschewed as being disruptive to the group's stability; and the early separation of the child from its mother, and the communal form of training seem to further this type of behavioral response to stress. In Cuba, under Fidel Castro, two separate kinds of low-risk behavior have been stimulated in an effort to establish balance to the system in the process of radical change. First, in the very short run, discontented Cubans were encouraged and allowed to go into exile, thereby turning a potential group of high-risk actors into a sector which had opted for low-risk alternatives of withdrawal and exile. Second, the Cuban educational system has undergone tremendous changes to instill in Cuban youth the feeling that patriotism requires the subjugation of the self to the group. In "Peasant-Worker Schools," such as those on the Isle of Pines, young men and women live as in a military commune, work in the fields by day, and study the lessons of the revolution by night. Separated from their families at the critical age of early adolescence, these Cubans are learning the virtues of adjusting to the needs of the group and of the state; their low-risk behavior may reward Castro with a more stable revolutionary environment in his second decade in power.[41]

A third example of the manipulation of the educational system to sustain a recently won revolution comes to us from the Soviet Union, in the 1920's and 1930's.[42] In the years immediately following the Bolshevik seizure of power, school rules were formulated in such a way as to force the student to accept the domination of the group of peers over his individualistic behavior. Student organizations called *kollektiv's,* were created to mobilize group sanctions against recalcitrant individual students who would bow to the disciplinary actions of the teacher. Children from a very early age were exposed to the social controls which have become fundamental parts of Soviet society: self-criticism, confession of sins, and recantation. Further, the *kollektiv* extended its authority beyond the walls of the school community to erode any private life of the students, as well as to turn any questions of state authority into matters of personal loyalty and emotion. The ultimate objective of the *kollektiv* method of social organization of schools was to produce children whose personal interests were identical with those of the social aggregate. In our terms, they sought to alter the personality structure of Russian youth to channel failure-threatened types into low-risk, socially nondisruptive behavior of a highly conformist variety. While the long-term success of this experiment cannot be evaluated even today, the idea of a consensually supported dictatorship certainly cannot be ruled out in light of the Soviet attempts at redirecting high-risk individuals to less disorderly pursuits.

2. *The reduction of high-risk behavior by changing the modal personality.* Since the option described above implies a solution built around a sizeable

amount of central governmental coercion and thought control, we must also explore the possibility (perhaps more congenial to the Western, liberal democratic tradition) of altering the modal personality of a non-Western society from the failure-threatened type to one more nearly approximating that described by McClelland as the achievement-motivated personality. Just as McClelland believed that a society must be of the achievement motivation variety in order to achieve significant economic or artistic progress, so also do we conclude that the achievement-motivated personality, or, in our terms, the moderate-risk actor, will also be conducive to stable political development. For even though this type of personality may be subjected to major stress levels, he will respond through moderate-risk alternatives, thereby contributing to incremental solutions to problems, rather than trying in vain to destroy the system through violence.

McClelland, in his study of achievement motivation, recognized the need to address the problem of how to increase the moderate-risk personality in a given society. In the final chapter of *The Achieving Society* he indicates several methods by which a government may try to increase a country's need for achievement, some of which may have utility for the political realm as well. Basically, our moderate-risk actor is built on a psychological base laid in his home life up to the age of about ten to fourteen. McClelland believes that this development is strongly connected to the child's relationship to his authority images, particularly his father. The ideal family life for a moderate-risk personality is one based on considerable psychological warmth, a concern for the child's independence, and a general slackening of restrictions beginning about the age of five. Since there appears to be little that a government can do to create this kind of home environment in a brief time, McClelland suggests alternate approaches. For example, the imagery contained in children's readers and the general approach toward fantasy and daydreaming in elementary school can be designed to contain many signs of achievement and moderate risk. Conversion of a state's religious orientation to promote more individualism and more direct identification of the individual with the deity may also help. In fact, the religious fervor associated with any kind of ideological conversion may bring in its wake a heightened sense of personal control over formerly threatening forces, and thereby foster an increase in achievement motivation. In addition to these steps, however, the development elite should undertake to utilize to the maximum whatever moderate-risk resources they have, and, in the short run, to minimize the impact of the high-risk actors in the system. This, in turn, leads us to our next conclusion.

3. *The reduction of the impact of high-risk actors.* The political economists Ilchman and Uphoff have cautioned about social science research which aims only at the very long-run solutions, when, in fact, the practicing politician is confronted with a series of uncompromising short-run problems. With many problems competing for scarce resources, a development elite simply cannot afford to put too much faith in solutions which promise great rewards a

generation hence.[43] Thus, we must turn our attention to several measures which our development leaders may use to reduce the adverse impact of high-risk actors over the first generation of the development program's life, while all the time working through the nation's education system to bring the modal personality structure more into line with the ultimate needs of the society.

In the first place, if, when faced with an insurgency, the development leadership seems fairly certain that the sources of instability are personality-specific, as opposed to being the result of psychological stress, then they must resist the temptation to acquiesce in the demands of the insurgents. If the rebels possess failure threatened personalities, then giving in to their demands will not alter their determination to continue to drive up the price, to raise their goals, and to seek the impossible. Repeated failure and repeated denial of an insurgent's claims may have a similar effect; but it may also turn the radicals toward low-risk behavior such as withdrawal or exile, which in turn will provide the leadership with valuable time. In any event, the government should not wish to provide moderate-risk actors in politics with examples of how high-risk behavior succeeds, since they may seek to imitate this successful model at some time in the future. It should almost go without saying that the leaders in this case must be very careful to determine whether a given act or insurgency is derived from real grievances, or whether it has a personality component which renders the grievance beyond the power of the government to satisfy. Only then will they know whether they should meet the insurgency with force or conciliation.

As a second step in the midst of defusing an insurgency, a government should seek to open alternate moderate-risk channels to potential rebels. We would suppose that the borderline between a moderate-risk and a high-risk revolutionary is so thin that the act of opening additional moderate-risk options could be sufficient to lead the former back into stable behavior. At the least, we presume that a development leader can never be absolutely certain that all of the insurgents are beyond his power of persuasion. As we shall show in the next chapter, in fact, leaders in non-Western developing systems have shown great ability to manipulate moderate-risk alternatives very adeptly in order to siphon off rank-and-rile insurgents, and thereby to break the back of the revolutionary movement.

CHAPTER NOTES

1. For a discussion of modal personality and national character studies, see Alex Inkeles, "National Character and Modern Political Systems," in Francis L. Hsu, ed., *Psychological Anthropology: Approaches to Culture and Personality* (Homewood, Ill.: Dorsey Press, 1961), pp. 172-202. Also reprinted in slightly abridged form in Roy C. Macridis and Bernard E. Brown, eds., *Comparative Politics: Notes and Readings,* 3rd ed. (Homewood, Ill.: Dorsey Press, 1968), pp. 36-44. See also

Normal M. Bradburn, "The Cultural Context of Personality Theory," in Joseph M. Wepman and Ralph W. Heine, eds., *Concepts of Personality* (Chicago: Aldine, 1963), pp. 333-60.

2. See especially John W. Atkinson, "Motivational Determinants of Risk-Taking Behavior," in Atkinson, Ed., *Motives in Fantasy, Action and Society: A Method of Assessment and Study* (Princeton, N.J.: D. Van Nostrand, 1958), pp. 322-39.

3. David C. McClelland, *The Achieving Society* (New York: Free Press, 1967), p. 211.

4. Sheldon J. Korchin and George E. Ruff, "Personality Characteristics of the Mercury Astronauts," in George H. Grosser, Henry Wechsler, and Milton Greenblatt, eds., *The Threat of Impending Disaster: Contributions to the Psychology of Stress* (Cambridge, Mass.: M.I.T. Press, 1964), pp. 197-207.

5. Lucian W. Pye, *Guerrilla Communism in Malaya: Its Social and Political Meaning* (Princeton, N.J.: Princeton University Press, 1956), esp. pp. 336-37.

6. Louis Fischer, *The Life of Lenin* (New York: Harper & Row, 1964), esp. pp. 149-50.

7. Kenneth Keniston, *Young Radicals: Notes on Committed Youth* (New York: Harcourt, Brace & World, Inc., 1968), esp. p. 5.

8. See for example, Abbie Hoffman (Free), *Revolution for the Hell of It* (New York: Simon and Schuster Inc., Pocket Books Edition, 1970), p. 173.

9. Keniston, pp. 140-42, 211.

10. Fred W. Grupp, Jr., "Personal Satisfaction Derived from Membership in the John Birch Society," *Western Political Quarterly,* XXIV, 1 (March, 1971): 79-83.

11. See particularly the article by Atkinson. Also, Robert C. Birney, Harvey Burdick and Richard C. Teevan, *Fear of Failure* (New York: Van Nostrand-Reinhold Co., 1969). Also, Nathan Kogan and Michael A. Wallach, *Risk Taking: A Study in Cognition and Personality* (New York: Holt, Rinehart and Winston, Inc., 1964). The latter two citations both contain extensive bibliographies on the fear-of-failure syndrome and risk-taking.

12. Birney, *et al.,* p. 14.

13. J. W. Atkinson and N. T. Feather, eds., *A Theory of Achievement Motivation* (New York: Wiley, 1966).

14. McClelland, p. 438.

15. J. Anthony Lukas, "The Making of a Yippie," *Esquire,* LXXII, 5 (November, 1969): 126-34, 220-41.

16. Walter H. Slote, "Case Analysis of a Revolutionary," in Frank Bonilla and Jose A. Silva Michelena, eds., *The Politics of Change in Venezuela: Vol. I, A Strategy for Research on Social Policy* (Cambridge, Mass.: M.I.T. Press, 1967), pp. 241-311.

17. Birney, *et al.,* Chap. Seven, esp. p. 138.

18. Justus M. van der Kroef, *Indonesian Social Evolution: Some Psychological Considerations* (Amsterdam: C.P.J. van der Peet, 1958), esp. pp. 37-41. In a less intense way, this formula of permissiveness followed by severe restrictions was followed by the parents of Keniston's young radicals. See Keniston, pp. 84-85.

19. A recent study of Indonesian foreign policy stresses the fact that Indonesians fear and distrust their external environment. See Franklin B. Weinstein, "The Uses of Foreign Policy in Indonesia: An Approach to the Analysis of Foreign Policy in the Less Developed Countries," *World Politics,* XXIV, 3 (April, 1972): 356-81.

20. Lucian W. Pye, *Politics, Personality, and Nation Building: Burma's Search for Identity* (New Haven: Yale University Press, 1968), esp. Chap. Thirteen.
21. McClelland, pp. 230-32, reports that individuals with a high need for achievement (the opposite of our failure-threatened personality) do best in situations where there is a clear link between performance and reward.
22. Similar child-rearing practices, and results, are reported from Vietnam. See Peter G. Bourne, *Men, Stress and Vietnam* (Boston: Little, Brown, 1970), Chap. Twelve. Also, David V. Forrest, "Vietnamese Maturation: The Lost Land of Bliss," *Psychiatry,* 34, 2 (May, 1971): 111-39.
23. Hamed Ammar, *Growing Up In An Egyptian Village* (London: Routledge & Kegan Paul Ltd., 1954), esp. Chaps. Four–Seven.
24. Sania Hamady, *Temperament and Character of the Arabs* (New York: Twayne Publishers, Inc. 1960), esp. pp. 28-48.
25. Hamady, pp. 33-34. A study of some years ago uncovered the fact that American political radicals were more likely to have been punished through nagging, ridicule, or reproach, than through physical punishment, such as spanking. See Maurice H. Krout and Ross Stagner, "Personality Development in Radicals: A Comparative Study," *Sociometry,* exact reference unavailable, pp. 31-46. Paper read at 45th annual meeting of the American Psychological Association, Minneapolis, Minn., September 1, 1937.
26. Carl E. Batt, "Mexican Character: An Adlerian Interpretation," *Journal of Individual Psychology,* 25, 2 (November, 1969): 183-201. Also, Rogelio Diaz-Guerrero, "Neurosis and the Mexican Family Structure," *American Journal of Psychiatry,* December, 1955, pp. 411-17.
27. Batt, p. 187.
28. Batt, p. 188.
29. The material for this analysis is drawn from A. I. Rabin, *Growing up in the Kibbutz* (New York: Springer Publishing Co., 1965).
30. See Joseph A. Kahl, *The Measurement of Modernism: A Study of Values in Brazil and Mexico* (Austin: University of Texas Press, Latin American Monograph Series No. 12, 1968), p. 18.
31. For example, see Lucian W. Pye, *Aspects of Political Development* (Boston: Little, Brown, 1966), esp. Chap. Seven.
32. Cited by Douglas Pike in *Viet Cong: The Organization and Techniques of the National Liberation Front of South Vietnam* (Cambridge, Mass.: MIT Press, 1966), pp. 122-23. Emphasis added.
33. Lucian W. Pye, *Guerrilla Communism in Malaya: Its Social and Political Meaning,* pp. 27-30.
34. Paul Friedrich, "Assumptions Underlying Tarascan Political Homicide," *Psychiatry,* 25, 4 (November, 1962): 315-27.
35. Bryant Wedge, "The Case Study of Student Political Violence: Brazil, 1964, and Dominican Republic, 1965," *World Politics,* XXI, 2 (January, 1969): 183-206.
36. For an example of an inquiry into the "contagion" theory, see Robert D. Putnam, "Toward Explaining Military Intervention in Latin American Politics," *World Politics,* XX, 1 (October, 1967): 83-110.
37. Douglas Hyde, *The Roots of Guerrilla Warfare,* (Chester Springs, Pa.: Dufour Editions, 1968), Chap. Seven.
38. Edwin Lieuwin, *Generals vs. Presidents: Neo-Militarism in Latin America* (New York: Praeger, 1964), esp. Chap. Seven.

39. W. Howard Wriggins, *The Ruler's Imperative: Strategies for Political Survival in Asia and Africa* (New York: Columbia University Press, 1969), pp. 161-65. Also, Aristide R. Zolberg, *Creating Political Order: The Party-States of West Africa* (Chicago: Rand McNally, 1966), Chap. Three. Also, Irving Leonard Markowitz, "Ghana Without Nkrumah: The Winter of Discontent," in Markowitz, ed., *African Politics and Society* (New York: Free Press, 1970), pp. 252-65.

40. Lucian W. Pye, *Aspects of Political Development,* pp. 148-49.

41. Jose Yglesias, "Cuban Report: Their Hippies, Their Squares," *New York Times,* January 12, 1969. Also, Richard R. Fagen, *Cuba: The Political Content of Adult Education* (Palo Alto, Calif.: Stanford University, Hoover Institution on War, Revolution and Peace, 1964).

42. Jeremy R. Azrael, "Soviet Union," in James S. Coleman, ed., *Education and Political Development* (Princeton, N.J.: Princeton University Press, 1965), pp. 233-71, esp. 244-47.

43. Warren F. Ilchman and Norman Thomas Uphoff, *The Political Economy of Change* (Berkeley: University of California Press, 1969), pp. 270-72.

Chapter 8

POLITICAL DEVELOPMENT AND THE MANAGEMENT OF INSTABILITY

Although in preceding pages we have pointed out several possible ways in which political development may be undertaken without excessive amounts of instability, we recognize that, in many cases, the alternatives we have described may be beyond the capabilities of development leaders in non-Western countries. More often than not, the development elites will lack either the time or the requisite resources to avoid engendering dissonance or deprivation stress in the course of the development process; this will be the case especially if the development effort is based on radical, searching social reform and is compressed into a brief span of time. At the same time, although moderate-risk channels of political activism may be opened widely for discontented citizens, a certain residue of failure-threatened personality structures may inject much more high-risk political behavior into the political system than can be tolerated. Therefore, while development is not inherently a destabilizing process, there may still be cases in which instability must be controlled if a development elite is to survive the opening phases of its process of change and reform.

With these facts in mind, we have endeavored in this chapter to present six case studies of development elites struggling against the forces of political instability—secession in Africa, rural insurgency in Southeast Asia, and military intervention in Latin America. We have attempted to summarize these cases, and to extract from them certain features which might be generalized to other, similar cases elsewhere. To the extent that the problems of secession, rural guerrilla war, and military *coups* are recurring throughout the non-Western world, we hope that these studies will prove helpful not only to political observers but to development elites bent on managing instability and preserving the gains of political modernization.

AFRICA: THE MANAGEMENT OF SECESSION

Secession, and the threat of regional separatism, is a source of instability often encountered by rapidly developing political systems. As we have noted before, the very notion of development of political capabilities implies the centralization of political authority, and the expansion of central government powers into previously neglected or inaccessible areas (defined either geographically or functionally). Thus, it is inevitable that a developing country with even a small residue of unassimilated, regionally based minorities will encounter resistance as the system's capabilities expand. By the same token, as the experience of the United States and the Soviet Union would suggest, a developing polity cannot really be assured of an unimpeded growth sequence until irredentist enclaves have been brought into the body politic, and acknowledge the authority and the expanded power of the central government.

In no corner of the non-Western world has this problem been more dramatically expressed than in the independent, black nations of sub-Saharan Africa. This brief analysis will focus on only the two most conflictual cases—those of the Congo and Nigeria. But, as we shall note below, virtually every nation in this area has had cause to fear the fragmentation and dispersal of their national territory, as irreconcilable ethnic and linguistic minorities have threatened to purchase their freedom through resort to violence.

Three special characteristics of the political order in Africa have converged to aggravate the general problem of regional separatism. First, the international boundaries of most African states were not the product of any internally generated political processes, but were, rather, the outcome of bargaining among the European colonial powers.[1] As has been pointed out repeatedly, then, the boundaries encompass some rather strange bed fellows, especially when they brought together tribes which had had a long history of warfare and hostility, and forced them to coexist under the same nation-state roof. Second, the destruction of the colonial system in Africa was hastened ideologically by the trumpeting of the doctrine of self-determination. Once the momentum of self-determination had begun to build, however, it was difficult to slow its movement; and leaders of ethnic minorities in neglected or oppressed regions began to ask why, if their central government could seek freedom from the metropole, they could not do likewise and sever their ties with the newly created central authority.[2] Finally, although most, if not all, states are sensitive to the problem of fragmentation, and no state can readily admit the legality of separatism, African states stand in a much more precarious position because of the tenuous nature of their national integration and unity. Observers in the

West have been so critical of the emphasis on unitary control in such African states as Ghana, that they may have overlooked the fact that a Madisonian insistence on pluralism simply does not provide satisfactory guidelines for development elites in Africa, confronted as they are with a need to expand, not contract the power of the central government.[3] How African states have responded to the challenge of separatist politics in the midst of political development can best be described by referring to the experiences of the Congo and Nigeria.

MANAGEMENT OF SEPARATISM IN THE CONGO

The entire tragic story of the first days of life of the Republic of the Congo is too lengthy and complicated to be compressed within a few lines here.[4] Our major concern must lie with the relations between the central authority of the newly created Congo state, in the capital of Leopoldville (now Kinshasa), and the rebellious province of Katanga, located in the mineral-rich southeast corner of the nation.[5]

The impetus for secession of Katanga from the broader Congolese state lay in two diverse, yet converging, lines of political action in the days prior to national independence, June 30, 1960. Representing the tribal interests of the "authentic Katangans" was the Conakat party (Confederation des Associations Tribales du Katanga), which was based on the Lunda and Bayeke tribes, the long-time residents of Katanga. Conakat was formed to protect the jobs and political influence of the Lunda and Bayeke tribes against encroachment from "strangers," in this case members of the Baluba tribe from neighboring Kasai province. The Kasai Baluba, who had tribal brothers on the Katanga side of the border, had migrated to prosperous Katanga in search of jobs, and had stayed to expand their political power. Their political influence was mobilized through their own party, the Balubakat, whose seat of power lay in northern Katanga province. Soon after King Baudouin of Belgium announced that the Congo would eventually be independent, the Conakat initiated its demands that Katanga remain "an autonomous and federated state" within the new republic, so that control of resources and power would continue to reside in the hands of the "authentic Katangans."

The demands of Conakat fit neatly into similar urgings from the European settlers of Katanga, most of whom owed their livelihood to the extensive Belgian mining interests in the province. While Conakat demanded autonomy to protect themselves from domination by the Baluba, the settlers made similar requests in order to perpetuate Belgian, and broader European control over the natural resources of the area. Rarely, if ever, had politics made stranger bed fellows. The result, however, was to taint the Conakat movement with accusations of being a pawn of the Europeans who wished to retain control over the Congo after independence.

Independence Day, June 30, 1960, dawned under the spell of great apprehension. Although Conakat leader Moise Tshombe declared himself satisfied with the degree of decentralization in the new constitutional framework of the republic, elections held immediately prior to independence placed Conakat in a difficult position nationwide. Although Tshombe's party manipulated effective control over Katanga's parliament, the Conakat demands for control over the key ministries of Defense, Finance, and Interior were denied by new Prime Minister Patrice Lumumba. Tshombe, now completely cut off from national power sources, laid plans to secede. An abortive plot was discovered on June 28 by Belgian authorities; Tshombe was forced to back away from this threat, but the potential dissolution of the Congo was not far over the horizon on the first day of the new republic.

With the mutiny of the Congolese *Force Publique* against its Belgian officers on July 5, Conakat leaders saw the opportunity they had been waiting for; on July 11, Tshombe, pressured by local Katangan politicians and encouraged by Belgian officers, formally declared independence of Katanga and requested aid from Belgium. With the rest of the Congo rapidly falling into disorder, Belgian troops entered Katanga, aided in the disarmament of Congolese forces, and placed themselves at the disposition of now-President Tshombe.

At this point, the United Nations Security Council entered the picture, as the central government of the Congo formally requested assistance from the Council to restore internal order.[6] Fully supported by the United States, which saw U.N. activity as a block to possible Soviet intervention, the U.N. Peace Force played a major role in defeating the Katangese secession. Although the international force was ostensibly prohibited from intervening in domestic politics, in reality this proved to be impossible; and the U.N. force was the spearhead of the central Congolese government's attempts to restore national integrity to the torn republic.

The secession attempt of Katanga reached its high point following the removal (and subsequent assassination) of Prime Minister Lumumba, in September, 1960. By March, 1961, Tshombe had reached such a position of power that a Round Table called to discuss a constitutional solution to the crisis resulted in a virtual emasculation of the Congolese state. Katanga's victory was short-lived, however; for in August, 1961, a new national government formally invested Prime Minister Cyrille Adoula with renewed power, and gave him a vote of confidence to restore order and unity to the Congo. With support of the U.N. forces, a second drive began to bring Tshombe's state back into the republic.

With U.N. troops occupying certain positions within Katanga, Adoula and Tshombe began a series of negotiations during the summer of 1962. When these broke down, the stage was set for a renewal of the U.N. probe into Katanga, marked by extensive fighting between Irish and Ethiopian troops on the U.N. side, and Tshombe's white mercenaries, on the other. By January, 1963, the U.N. forces had taken Tshombe's last stronghold; despite a last-minute warning that the mercenaries would resort to guerrilla warfare and terrorism, the end came peacefully as Tshombe and his cabinet capitulated on January 14, 1963. The secession of Katanga had come to an end after some 30 months of turmoil and upheaval.

MANAGEMENT OF SEPARATISM IN NIGERIA

When Nigeria obtained its independence from Great Britain on October 1, 1960, three months after the Congo, there were many signs which pointed to a more successful transition than the tragedy witnessed in Katanga and Leopoldville. Indeed, two years later, in 1962, the Nigerian Prime Minister, Sir Abubakar Tafawa Balewa, could write that "national unity has made great progress," and that Nigerians continued to be great advocates of the rule of law, and of the role of the judiciary as the arbiter of disputes.[7] Slightly more than three years after he penned those words, Tafawa Balewa lay dead at the hands of a military coup d'etat January 15, 1966; ironically, Balewa died defending the fragile Nigerian federal system, which he had accepted with great reluctance, and only as the least of many separate evils.[8]

An analysis of the dramatic fragmentation of the Nigerian Federation some seven years after its inception casts up some revealing parallels with the earlier case of the Congo. Nigeria possessed certain distinct advantages over the Congo: the British had spent more time and talent in preparing the Nigerian constitutional framework; and Nigeria lacked the extensive European financial interests which had funded and otherwise encouraged the abortive Katangan secession. The tribal animosities of Nigeria were severe nonetheless; as in the Congo, the departing colonial power had pulled together under one constitutional roof several disparate tribal, ethnic, and linguistic forces which simply could not be contained once the moderating force of the British colonial government was removed.[9]

Many, if not all, of Nigeria's constitutional problems at independence could be traced to the tight correlation between the regional and tribal divisions of the nation on the one hand, and the political party split on the other. The country was divided into three (later, four) regions, each with its own premier and considerable powers. In turn, each region was dominated by a single ethnic-based political party. In the relatively backward, Moslem Northern Region, the conservative Northern People's Congress (NPC), based on the Fulani and Hausa tribes, presided over the largest, and most powerful political force in the country. In the Eastern Region, the aggressive and upwardly mobile Ibos had formed their own National Council of Nigerian Citizens (NCNC) to advance the cause of their tribe; their leader, Dr. Nnamdi Azikiwe, was one of the champions of national independence and Nigeria's first President. From the Western Region came the Yoruba tribe, Nigeria's best educated and most progressive ethnic grouping, which had created the Action Group for their own political purposes.

The tribal schisms in Nigeria created a very precarious balance which, for all its defects, gave some promise of a successful beginning. For one thing, each of the major regions possessed about the same population; but the relatively greater constituency of the NPC insured that the Northern Region would dominate the first federal parliament, elected in 1959. Further, within each region there existed grave minority problems which arose from the dominance which the three major tribal groupings exercised internally within their respective region. The British had entertained the notion of further dividing the new nation into many smaller and weaker states, which would have been much more homogeneous ethnically and racially, but the idea was discarded as being a step away from national unity. Clearly, the entire federal division of powers required that each of the major tribes treat each other in a spirit of mutual trust and confidence; otherwise, the delicate machinery of the Federation would collapse at the first threat.

In broad outline, the drift of the Nigerian polity into secession has already been presented above (see Chapter Six). The constitutional processes had broken apart completely when, on January 15, 1966, a small group of younger officers in the Army, led by an Ibo major, instigated a coup d'etat which ousted the civilian governmental coalition and resulted in the deaths of the Prime Minister, Balewa, and many other important political figures.[10] Out of the turmoil emerged the Ibo-dominated government of Major General Johnson Aguyi-Ironsi, which embarked on a program which apparently had the purpose of changing Nigeria's federal system into a unitary one, under Ibo control. The response of the Northerners was to overthrow the government of Ironsi and replace it with another military junta under the control of Yakubu Gowon, a Northerner but not from one of the dominant tribes.

There was then unleashed a series of attacks against Ibos all over the nation, but particularly severe in the North.[11] First in May, then again in July, and for the third time in September and October, 1966, Ibos were assaulted and murdered by the thousands. An estimated 10,000 to 30,000 were killed in the September massacres alone. Over 600,000 refugees crowded back into the Eastern Region, where they could receive protection.

The new Federal Military Government attempted to initiate negtiations with the commander of the Eastern Region, Col. Odumegwu Ojukwu; but the colonel was hard pressed from his own tribesmen to move toward separation. At last, in May, 1967, events converged to produce the secession. A consultative assembly of distinguished Ibos directed Ojukwu to sever the ties between the Nigerian state and the Eastern Region "at an early practicable date." The military junta replied by decreeing the reorganization of Nigeria into 12 smaller and more coherent states, a move which would have cut the East into three racially compact units. While the Ibos were once supporters of a division of this sort, they now perceived such a move as being aimed at destroying their ability to survive as an autonomous entity, for the proposed manner of dividing the East would have cut the Ibos off from potentially large oil reserves and from the vital sea links of the ports at Port Harcourt and Calabar. The Ibo answer was the creation of the independent Republic of Biafra, later in May.

From May, 1967 to November, 1969, the corner of Nigeria occupied by Biafra was the scene of widespread bloodshed and death from starvation. The Nigerian government, with extensive aid and advisors from both Great Britain and the Soviet Union advanced rapidly at first; after September, 1968, however, the front tended to stabilize as Biafra received aid from France and Portugal, in the form of weapons and equipment.[12] The international charity organizations mounted a major airlift of food and medical supplies; but it was not sufficient to stave off death from starvation for some 6,000 Biafrans per day, at the height of the insurrection. Negotiations arranged by the Commonwealth, the Organization of African Unity, and Pope Paul VI all proved futile. The Ibos, recognizing that they were locked in a fight for survival, resisted all overtures from Lagos. The end came only after all capabilities for physical resistance had been exhausted, and the Ibos saw that continued fighting would only lead to an extinction of their ethnic group.

CONCLUSIONS

Three factors seem to be of major importance in enabling the governments of the Congo and Nigeria to manage the secessionist threats which faced them in the early days of their national development efforts. The first element had to do with the position taken by the international community. While in both cases the seceding party was not entirely alone, the central government authorities were able to secure support from the overwhelming majority of the members of the international security system. In the case of the Congo, the Katanga rebellion did receive some support from Angola and Northern Rhodesia, as well as arms from Belgian sources; but the United States and the Soviet Union cooperated, at least in the beginning, to grant the U.N. the required authority to put down the secession. In the Nigerian case, while the United Nations was not able to take any significant action to assist the central government, aid from Great Britain and Russia proved to be sufficient; Biafra was recognized by only a handful of African states—Tanzania, Zambia, Ivory Coast, and Gabon—and received military assistance in limited quantities from France, Portugal, and Spain. Most African political leaders were afraid to put their stamp of approval on separatism by recognizing either Katanga, or Biafra, for fear of encouraging their own separatists to take a similar route.[13] In the absence of large-scale international support, then, Katanga and Biafra were simply not physically capable of carrying off their separatist attempts.

Second, in both the Congo and Nigeria, the central government proved capable of forming a united front in the remainder of the nation for the purpose of restoring unity; the secessionist fever did not spread to other areas of unassimilated ethnic minorities. In the Congo, the Leopoldville group was able to reach a reconciliation with the Stanleyville forces to prevent the further fragmenting of the Republic. In Nigeria, the former enemies from the Yoruba and the Hausa-Fulani tribes managed to close ranks to bring the dissident Ibos back into the fold. In addition, the defeated separatists were not dealt with especially severely in the context of other civil wars, such as those of Spain or the United States. Katanga leader Moise Tshombe returned to become Prime Minister of a newly united Congo; the Biafran leader, Ojukwu, was forced to flee, but, from available press reports, it does at least appear that the defeated Ibos were not subjected to the genocide that their leaders had been predicting throughout the war. In October, 1970, at a celebration marking the tenth anniversary of Nigerian independence, held only nine months after the collapse of Biafra, Major-General Gowon announced a national development plan designed to repair war damage, revive the economy of war-affected areas, and provide for the full rehabilitation of the defeated Ibos. Free mobility of all citizens, regardless of ethnic origin, was to be guaranteed in order to permit Ibos to take jobs in other regions, and thereby relieve the unemployment crisis in the east. Although it would certainly be premature to announce the disappearance of ethnic strife in Nigeria, the military regime of Gowon was making efforts to reintegrate the vanquished Biafrans into a new Nigerian union.[14]

Finally, the position of both Katanga and Biafra was weakened greatly by the presence of their own unassimilated minorities who resisted local domination and wished to rejoin the larger nation-state. In northern Katanga, the Baluba tribe had to be repressed with force by Tshombe when it tried to reenter the Congolese republic. Nigerian leaders justified their move against Biafra on repeated occasions by saying that they had a duty to protect the 5,000,000 non-Ibos living in Biafra who had not wanted to be dominated by the Ibos, and who wanted the military government to regain control of the area to insure their personal freedoms. All these factors, plus the potential mineral wealth in both secessionist areas, combined to make separatism not only unattractive, but fully beyond the reach of dissatisfied ethnic minorities in two African states.

SOUTHEAST ASIA: THE MANAGEMENT OF RURAL INSURGENCY

While the new states of black Africa have been plagued by separatism and civil war, the emerging, fragmented societies of Southeast Asia have found themselves the scene of insurrections, acts of terrorism, assassinations, and prolonged guerrilla warfare in the numerous remote, rural areas of each country. A recent study by Jeffrey M. Paige suggests that an upsurge of rural violence may grow out of expanded contacts between the rural dweller and the new and frightening outside world.[15] The isolated, traditional peasant has nothing to gain or lose from the broader national or international markets; life for him is a dreary routine of low-risk withdrawal and resignation. Once exposed to the vagaries of the international market for his goods, and made dependent on the nation's urban areas for manufactured products, the peasant becomes sensitized to the uncertainties of modern life; and, lacking any institutional channels through which he can seek to regain his psychological balance, he becomes easy prey to the leaders of extremist movements. If this argument is correct, then the expansion of a central political "presence" into previously isolated areas—one of the concomitants of political development—should bring in its wake a heightened tendency toward rural insurrection and instability.

Such appears to have been the case, not only in Southeast Asia, but in other areas where major efforts at national political development have been observed in this century.[16] Whether in Mexico, Cuba, China, the Soviet Union, or the United States prior to 1800, states in the process of political development have often had to confront the challenge of insurrections initiated in their rural, interior regions.

Southeast Asia, however, seems to have been especially susceptible to rural insurgency. Since the withdrawal of the Japanese from the area at the end of World War II, and the beginning of the anticolonial movements, virtually every nation in Southeast Asia has been wracked by rural upheaval of one sort or another. The most dramatic of these—the complex struggle over control of Indo-China—has roots stretching back many hundreds of years, and the end will not come into sight even after the departure of American troops from the area. In two other cases—in Malaya and the Philippines—although some guerrillas remain at large, the conflict has been reduced to such a level that we may speak accurately of the "management" of the insurgency. In several other instances—Indonesia, Burma, Thailand, and Sarawak—sporadic fighting continues to be a constant factor in the country's political calculus, but not one which threatens to overcome the regulative capability of the incumbent regimes. In our detailed treatment below, we shall discuss the counter-insurgency efforts in Malaya and the Philippines.[17]

Several factors seem to have aggravated the unusually high propensity of states in Southeast Asia to suffer from rural insurgencies. For one thing, the topographic and climatic conditions *within* the region have combined with the strategic importance of the region in the broader struggle among the Great Powers of the nuclear age to produce a fertile breeding ground for guerrilla conflict. The extensive assistance to incumbent, pro-Western regimes from the United States, France, Great Britain, and other major states virtually guaranteed that the initial efforts by insurgents to gain power (such as Ho Chi Minh's attempted coup d'etat in Hanoi in August, 1945) would be blocked or defeated outright. The mountainous terrain, swamps, and tropical jungles of the region gave the defeated insurgents a much-needed sanctuary, where they could rebuild their forces and receive clandestine aid from major powers who viewed the insurgency with favor.[18] It is for this reason, incidentally, that we must examine carefully the origins of a rural insurgency, since, instead of stemming from grievances of an oppressed peasantry, it may simply reflect the tactical exigencies of a revolutionary force which finds that the short route to power, the urban coup d'etat, is closed due to the massing of superior power by the incumbents aided from abroad.

Most observers accept the age-old notion that rural unrest grows out of the inequality of land distribution, coupled with the oppressive manner in which land is exploited by those who own it. The unequal nature of land ownership has been accused of causing social unrest since the days of Alexis de Tocqueville. Recent statistical inquiries into the subject, while far from definitive, appear to confirm what social scientists have known intuitively—that social upheaval will be greatest in those societies in which there are few channels available for personal advancement, and in which access to these channels is distributed in a radically unequal manner.[19]

Douglas Hyde, an experienced observer of communist guerrilla movements in Southeast Asia, names land hunger as second only to anticolonialism as a driving force for rural insurgency.[20] To cite Paige again, in Burma, Thailand, the Philippines, and South Vietnam, the areas of greatest civil disorders have traditionally been those areas in which land is scarcest, where productive property is distributed in a most unequal manner, or where land ownership is most precarious.

There are two general ways in which the agrarian sector of a country can be turned toward revolutionary violence. In the first instance, the landless peasants or subsistence farmers of a particular region are persuaded to shield the guerrilla main force, to provide sustenance and shelter to the insurgents, and to deny intelligence to the incumbents. Only rarely do the peasants become the actual fighters in the guerrilla army; more commonly, they are simply the "sea" within which the fish of Mao Tse-tung's guerrillas must swim to survive. The treatment accorded to Fidel Castro by the peasants of the Sierra Maestra area of Cuba would be illustrative of this relationship. On the other hand, organized agricultural laborers who work for large, plantationlike farming concerns may constitute the shock troops for a rural rebellion. In Indo-China, the Viet-Minh gained its initial impetus in rural areas from the laborers of the French rubber plantations; in Malaya, the same function was performed by the Chinese workers on the large rubber estates, who supplied the local Communist guerrilla movement with many of its early recruits.

A third source of rural disorder in Southeast Asia can be found in the fragments of ethnic minorities who inhabit each country in the region, and who constitute a readily mobilized force to support a guerrilla government domination. Ethnic minorities are a potent factor in the politics or rural insurgency in Southeast Asia for various reasons. They are frequently more powerful than their limited numbers would indicate, since they occupy much strategic land in the interior of several key countries, especially in Laos and both halves of Vietnam. These ethnic groupings, moreover, occupy critical and ill-defined border areas, which makes them important ingredients in any insurgency which depends on sanctuaries in disputed frontier zones. Finally, the intense ethnic feeling on the part of many of these groups has facilitated the work of guerrilla bands who wish to obtain relative freedom of movement and operations within some remote, inaccessible sector of the country. By making vague promises of ethnic sovereignty to uneducated tribes, guerrillas are able to gain that foothold in a sanctuary region which is so crucial to their survival and eventual victory.[21] Whatever the source of discontent, rural insurrection has provided all the new states of Southeast Asia with an early test of their political capabilities; how they have responded will be discussed through reference to the Malayan and Philippine experiences.

MANAGEMENT OF RURAL INSURGENCY IN MALAYA

The insurrection which plagued Malayan politics for about a decade after 1948 can not be traced so much to the land hunger of peasants as it can to the struggle of Chinese laborers and their revolutionary leaders to gain power in a country where they constituted a distinct, though powerful, minority. Malayan mines and rubber plantations had been staffed primarily by resorting to the overpopulated areas of South India and South China, with the result that by 1938, the Chinese settlement amounted to the largest single ethnic group in all of British Malaya.[22] Throughout the insurrection, the Chinese were constantly hampered by their inability to obtain support from the bulk of the peasantry, who were Malays, and who had reason to fear and distrust the racially distinct Chinese.

With the arrival of Chinese immigrants to Malaya there came also in microcosm the ideological and political split which was raging at the same time in China, between the Communists and the Nationalists (the Kuomintang). Accordingly, the original Communist movement in Malaya grew out of the left wing of the Kuomintang organization in Singapore.[23] In 1930, the Malayan Communist Party was created with two organizational advantages: the heritage of the Chinese to operate through secret fraternities or societies, and the strength of the Malayan Chinese labor movement, which capitalized on the lower class Chinese who worked in the Singapore harbors, as well as in the tin mines and rubber plantations in the interior. The organizational strengths of the MCP were more than offset, however, by their ethnic distinctiveness and their inability to generalize the revolutionary struggle into a broader effort to oust the British and establish an independent Malayan state. The Malays appeared to prefer the British presence, feeling that the colonial regime was all that was protecting them from the more aggressive and better organized Chinese immigrants.

The occupation of Malaya by the Japanese during World War II provided the MCP with the opportunity they needed to appear as the champions of Malayan nationalism. Beginning in March, 1942, the Chinese created the Malayan People's Anti-Japanese Army (MPAJA), and its civilian counterpart, the Malayan People's Anti-Japanese Union, two groups which had the avowed purpose of driving the Japanese from Malaya. Although the actual impact of the MPAJA guerrilla activities on the Japanese forces was marginal, the occupation period ended with more than 10,000 Chinese guerrillas under arms. After the surrender of the Japanese, and before the arrival of the British, the MPAJA exercised quasi-governmental control over much of Malaya, and had established close ties with the more than 500,000 Chinese villagers who had fled the urban areas to live in small squatter towns along the edge of the jungle. Further, the MCP emerged as a powerful force in Chinese politics within Malaya, and as a group to be reckoned with by the returning British. Had they so desired, the Communists probably could have seized power from the Japanese in the closing days of the war, just as Ho Chi Minh did in Vietnam; as Pye notes, however, the MCP recognized that they were poorly equipped to attend to the enormous job of restoring Malaya after the devastation of the war, and they preferred to leave that task to the British. That decision was very likely the cause of their failure in the subsequent insurrection.

In the days immediately following the war, however, the MCP leaders had good reason to be confident of eventual victory. Thus, about 6,800 of the guerrillas—those who were already known to the British—were induced to turn in their arms, and their units were disbanded. About 4,000, whose identity remained secret, remained behind, along with great quantities of arms which had been supplied to them by the British during the war. For several years, the MCP attempted to work within the established Malayan political system to achieve the domination which they felt to be theirs. As the months passed, however, the leadership of the movement saw their chances for securing power become increasingly remote. Enlightened British policies regarding eventual independence robbed them of the nationalism argument; increasingly tough governmental policies to control labor agitation tended to undermine their support from the Chinese laborers. Internally, the party began to fragment over the question of militancy in the struggle to obtain power. Thus, in late 1947 and early 1948, the party leadership began to promote a series of strikes which they hoped would serve as the prelude to a general Chinese uprising which would lead to their gaining power. When the British moved decisively to control these acts, the MCP initiated a campaign of terrorist attacks, which resulted in the British declaration of a State of Emergency in June, 1948. The Communists then fled to the jungle, not, it should be noted, to lead an agrarian revolt, but because their bid for power in the urban areas had been defeated; although the MCP at times championed the cause of the landless Chinese squatter, the Malayan insurgency was a rural conflict for tactical, not ideological, reasons.

At the onset of hostilities, the Communist force, called the Malayan Races Liberation Army (MRLA) numbered about 4,000, and never reached above 6,000 active combatants. In support of this military unit was a civilian component called Min Yuen (Popular Movement) whose membership is estimated variously from 10,000 to 100,000, but probably was closer to about 40,000–

50,000.[24] To counteract this force, the British introduced about 50,000 regular troops, recruited some 75,000 special police and constables, and raised a home guard of 250,000, mostly Malay (a technique which was also proving successful against the Mau-Mau in Kenya at about the same time).

The counter-insurgency effort in Malaya may be described as the simultaneous closure militarily of the high-risk options available to the insurgents, while opening politically the moderate-risk alternatives. The British and Malay troops and police were aggressive in their operations in the jungle base areas; and, by agreement with the Thai government, they patrolled the Thai-Malayan border, often pursuing the guerrillas into Thai territory. At the same time, the Chinese squatters, upon whom the MRLA depended so much for material support, were relocated into New Villages, where they were protected from terrorism, and where they could be watched more closely by the incumbent authorities. Thus cut off from their main bases of support, the guerrillas began to resort to extensive terrorism, which had the effect of driving them even further away from not only the Malays and Indians, but also from their ethnic kind, the Chinese, whose allegiance they desperately needed.

Politically, both the British and the native government acted positvely to induce individual guerrillas to leave the armed struggle and return to peaceful political activity. The New Villages were given large amounts of assistance, especially in the areas of medical and educational programs; in this way, the lower class Chinese were brought to view the incumbents as the groups most capable of tending to their needs. The British, for their part, moved decisively toward freeing Malaya; the first national elections were held in July, 1955, and the first elected Prime Minister, Tengku Abdul Rahman, promptly offered amnesty for the guerrillas if they would return and lay down their arms. A cease-fire was negotiated at the end of 1955 on the basis of this amnesty. The cease-fire broke down over the issue of the legality of the MCP; but it is fair to assert that the Emergency was reduced to the state of a manageable nuisance at that time. By 1958, only a few guerrillas remained in the jungle areas of the border with Thailand.

MANAGEMENT OF RURAL INSURGENCY IN THE PHILIPPINES

On July 4, 1946, the Republic of the Philippines received its independence from the United States, thus removing what had been one of the most severe grievances of the Philippine radical left—the colonial relationship with America. There remained, however, two points of friction—maldistribution of land, and political corruption and electoral fraud—which would soon plunge the new Philippine government into a struggle with rural insurgents.

The Philippines, prior to World War II, was a classic example of inequality of land distribution, and other land tenure problems in Asia. The central part of Luzon Island was notorious for its bad social conditions among the rural population. In the Luzon province of Pampanga, for example, according to the 1939 census some 18 individuals controlled more than 22,000 hectares of land, out of the provincial total of 120,000 hectares; while 22,000 tenant farmers were left with 80,000 hectares.[25] Other provinces in the central Luzon area were equally bad. On top of the poor distribution of the land, life for the tenants was precarious, depending as it did on the good will of the landlord. The tenant farmer was usually constantly in debt to the owner, often to the point of having to sell one or more of his children to the landlord to pay off his note.

It is not hard to see, then, that there was ample reason for social unrest in the rural areas of Luzon. Jacoby reports that the provinces of Pampanga, Nueva Ecija, Tarlac, and Bulacan were the scenes of numerous bloody upris- ings against first the Spanish (who were the colonial power until 1898), and then later against the Americans and local Filipino administrators. The last such upheaval before World War II, the Sakdalist uprising, occurred in May, 1935, in the provinces surrounding Manila. Thus, in 1937, when the Philippine Communist Party finally gained legal status after five years of clandestine activity, one of their first moves was to effect an alliance with major leftwing peasant organizations to form a Popular Front.[26]

Just as was the case in Malaya, the local Communist party appeared to be effectively blocked from gaining power until the arrival of the Japanese occu- pation forces. With the collapse of American resistance, the Popular Front began to organize a counter-Japanese operation. In March, 1942, the Front created the People's Anti-Japanese Army (in Tagalog, Hukbong Bayan Laban Sa Hapon, or Hukbalahap, or Huk for short), and its civilian counterpart, the Barrio (Village) United Defense Corps. The Huks took advantage of the general confusion surrounding the war against the Japanese to wreak their vengeance against hated landlords, and eventually killed more Filipinos (20,- 000) than Japanese (about 5,000).[27] However, in a move parallel to what we have seen in Malaya, the Huks chose to return to constitutional activity at the end of the war, rather than try to seize power as the Japanese surrendered. This was to prove futile as the second great source of rebellion—electoral fraud and corruption—prevented the former Huks from reentering the peaceful political arena.

In the years immediately following World War II, the premature closure of moderate-risk, parliamentary channels to the former leaders of the communist, anti-Japanese guerrilla movement undoubtedly led to their decision to embark on a second rural insurgency, the famous Huk uprising of the late 1940's and the early 1950's. At the close of the war, the People's Anti-Japanese Army was disbanded, and the energies and resources of the leaders were channeled into the creation of a new political faction called Democratic Alliance, whose major political aims were to initiate land redistribution to landless peasants, and to oppose the reestablishment of what they termed colonial relations with the United States.[28] In the elections of 1946, this faction entered into a coalition with the Nacionalista Party, one of the nation's two traditional political organizations with broadly based support. The Democratic Alliance swept the congressional elections in the Central Luzon provinces. Nationwide, however, the pro-U.S. Liberal Party carried the elections; but the Liberals found themselves challenged in the congress without a sufficient margin to enact their proposals. Shortly before Independence Day in 1946, therefore, the Liberals launched a campaign of suppression against the former guerrilla leaders who had now been elected to congress, and the seats of these men were denied them. Simultaneously, government troops began to harrass former guerrilla organizations, including a newly established peasants union and the militant Congress of Labor Organizations, located in Manila. All in all, the incumbent regime set out to deny to the Communists and other anticolonial forces access to moderate-risk channels to the sources of political power. The result was the Huk rebellion of 1948–1954, which, at its height, claimed the active support of some 30,000 peasants in the Luzon area, and a hard core of 15,000 more trained guerrilla insurgents.[29]

The counter-insurgency program which finally defeated the Huks has been discussed in detail elsewhere;[30] our task here is to summarize the principal facets of the program in the context of the management of instability. Aided by considerable financial and material assistance and advice from the United States, Defense Minister (later President) Ramon Magsaysay, a hero of the guerrilla operations against the Japanese, launched a three-pronged operation designed to lure the insurgents back into the national political sector. First, the army itself had to be thoroughly reformed to eliminate corruption and incompetence which hampered its operations. In addition, the Filipino soldier was taught to respect and befriend the peasant, and to convince the peasant that the army could protect him from guerrilla terrorism. Second, electoral fraud had to be eliminated. To do this, Magsaysay organized NAMFREL, an association of former veterans of the war against the Japanese, and entrusted to them the task of watching the polls at election time for signs of fraud. The result was visibly free elections in both 1951 and 1953, something of a novelty for the Philippines. Third, in what Magsaysay termed his "Attraction Program," there was created the Economic Development Corps (EDCOR) which had as its task the reconstruction of rural life in certain key areas. Working closely with the army engineers, EDCOR undertook many badly needed public works measures to make rural agriculture prosperous. In addition, Magsaysay offered 15 acres of land to each Huk who surrendered, and helped them to settle and work the land. For those who preferred urban work, a Huk rehabilitation center was opened in Manila to teach the former rebels some useful, economically productive skills.

Magsaysay won brilliant success with his efforts. By 1954, according to Kennedy, the Huk movement had declined and was no longer considered a serious threat. To the extent that the Philippine government has failed to make much real progress in solving the problem of land maldistribution in central Luzon, however, the core of the Huk movement has never been completely destroyed; and the spark of resistance is still kindled from time to time.

CONCLUSIONS

Since we have already alluded to many of the factors which contributed to the defeat of the rural insurgents in Malaya and the Philippines, we may summarize these briefly in this concluding section. First, as in the case of the two African secessionist attempts, the aid of external powers proved to be crucial to insuring the success of the incumbent regime. In Malaya, obviously the British carried the brunt of the actual fighting since the country was a colony of the United Kingdom for most of the period of the insurgency; in the Philippines, the United States, through its military mission, provided most of the financial aid, military equipment, and advice necessary to carry on the counter-insurgency effort.[31] Equally important, because of the peculiar geographical situation of both countries, the insurgents could not count on similar assistance from Communist China or the Soviet Union. Thus, the international system formed an environment favorable for counter-guerrilla operations, and hostile to the guerrillas themselves.

Second, the incumbent regime in both cases managed to cut off the guerrillas from their contacts with their potential civilian supporters. In Malaya, this proved to be relatively easy as a result of the forced resettlement program which moved the Chinese squatters away from the edge of the jungle, and into compounds where they could be placed under surveillance by British troops. The loose attachment of the Chinese to the land made this relocation possible with a minimum of strife. Further, the ethnic separation between the Chinese guerrillas and the Malay peasants prevented the former from solidifying firm ties with the populace within which they were forced to fight. In the case of the Philippines, where these racial distinctions did not separate the peasants from the guerrillas, the government achieved the same purpose by moving vigorously to cut the rebels' lines of communication—couriers, for the most part—which created a great deal of disruption among the guerrillas.

Finally, both the Malayan and Philippine governments kept open the channels to entice the rebels to return to the peaceful political arena. Amnesty was granted, land was made available, some financial assistance was supplied for the purpose of facilitating relocation; in brief, the incumbents made it much more attractive to return to the society than to want to continue to destroy it. In the end, this factor, in judicious combination with governmental coercion, was successful in reducing the rural insurgency to the point of a minor annoyance.

LATIN AMERICA: THE MANAGEMENT OF MILITARY INTERVENTION

While we have not said so explicitly, it should be clear from only casual observation that an additional factor which enabled the governments of the Congo, Nigeria, Malaya, and the Philippines to manage their individual cases of instability was that they enjoyed the continued loyalty of the army and the internal security forces. Indeed, there has probably never been a successful secession or rural insurgency which has not been accompanied by major defections within the armed forces of the incumbent. As a recent study of political economy suggests, "Even if the anti-statesman can mobilize violence from his supporters, his efforts are usually not effective unless the statesman's ability to coerce is somehow reduced."[32]

For the leaders of developing states in Latin America, however, the loyalty of the army is a two-edged sword. Far from supporting the incumbent regime, the army in Latin America has maintained an allegedly higher loyalty—to the state, instead of to its civilian leadership—and has intervened repeatedly to overthrow constitutional governments by force. In so doing, they have interrupted and, in some cases, halted, the process of political development.

We do not mean to suggest that other developing states have been free of military rule; a brief glance at the histories of such disparate states as Ghana, Indonesia, Nigeria, and the Republic of Vietnam would quickly show us that military intervention is an oft-encountered phenomenon throughout the non-Western world.[33] It does seem to be the case, however, that Latin American political systems have been plagued by this form of instability for such a long time and in such chronic proportions that it has constituted a major stumbling block to the political development of that region. In the 36-year period from 1930 to 1965, there were 106 illegal and unscheduled changes in heads of state in the 20 Latin American republics; all but a tiny portion of these changes were initiated and carried out by the military, albeit often with civilian support and encouragement. The only state in the region which remained free from military intervention during this period was Mexico.[34] From 1962 to the present writing (1972), the military has overturned a constitutional regime or another military dictatorship on the average of once every six months.[35]

The origins of militarism in Latin America remain rather obscure in spite of several well founded attempts to unravel the tangle of its historical, economic, and social causes. Some students of the subject, such as Edwin Lieuwin, have reached back into the historical context of Latin America's wars of independence to analyze the *caudillo,* the man on horseback who used his proficiency at arms to propel himself and his followers into power in the period of upheaval throughout the nineteenth century.[36] In a now-classic article, Merle Kling attributed military intervention to the rigid social structure of most Latin American countries, a structure which restricts access to the sources of social and political power to a very few of the upper class, and thereby drives the poorer classes into the military, the only avenue available for personal advancement.[37]

Martin C. Needler, writing somewhat more recently, indicates that military intervention seems to be more likely when economic conditions are worsening; but he goes on to broaden this interpretation by linking economic depression with social unrest and agitation. What the armed forces of Latin America fear more than anything, apparently, is social upheaval, which, they feel, is brought on by incompetent civilian rule. Thus, in the face of a rapidly expanding political system, with many new members being mobilized into political activism, the military in the 1960's stood ready to terminate any constitutional regime which appeared to be losing control of internal order, or when an upcoming election gave promise of yielding a victory to a candidate patently unacceptable to the military. As a consequence, says Needler, military coup's are becoming more and more violent, as they are associated with growing political participation by the popular sectors of society.[38]

Finally, a recent article by Robert Putnam surveys the entire spectrum of possible causes for military intervention—social, political, economic, foreign, and historical—and yields some surprising conclusions.[39] According to Putnam, social mobilization appears to inhibit the resort to intervention by the military, by forcing them to control more diffused sources of social power. Economic development, on the other hand, has a positive effect on military rule, apparently because it promotes social unrest and agitation by the lower classes (a version of progressive deprivation, as discussed in Chapter Six, above). Further, the growth of a middle class also has the effect of reducing the armed forces' propensity to intervene. When Putnam turns to more political factors—elections, political party systems, and the like—he cannot be as convincing, inasmuch as many of the conclusions which he draws approach being tautologies, as he admits. For example, the strength and number of political parties correlate negatively with military intervention since the mere presence of a military dictatorship would probably mean that most political party activity had been banned. While high correlations may be obtained, the causal inferences to be drawn from them are far from clear.

Whatever may be the origins of military rule in Latin America, many observers seem to think that the long-run trend in the region is toward constitutional government, and away from the army's intervention in politics. Both Needler and Lieuwin agree that, while there may be cycles of increases in military governments, and while the achievement of constitutional government for the entire region may be many years away, the overall trend seems to be clearly downward for the proponents of military government. If this is the case (and much depends upon the year in which one is performing the analysis), the two examples which we are examining in detail—Mexico and Cuba— would certainly contribute to the downturn. For in both developing states, the experiences of the leadership furnish ample details of how two revolutionary elites succeeded in taming the armies which brought them to power.

MANAGEMENT OF MILITARY INTERVENTION IN MEXICO

Mexico in the nineteenth century offers us one of the best examples of military intervention as can be found in all of Latin America's history. The contribution of the Spanish colonial military forces, coupled with the ferocity and opportunism of the revolution of 1821, led newly independent Mexico into some 60 years of the most predatory form of militarism. Until the army was brought to heel in the 1880's, they intervened against the incumbent regimes on the average of more than once a year; for a great part of this time, the military share of the national budget exceeded total government revenues. Above all, the armed forces of Mexico felt themselves to occupy a position apart from Mexican society, a special caste with special privileges, which extended to a unique endowment with the right to make and unmake governments without regard to the needs or the will of the people.

The story of how Mexico's politicians brought the army under control is a long and complicated one (in contrast to the relatively short and straighforward account of the Cuban experience, related below). It is best to view the management of the Mexican army as taking place in three phases, covering almost 60 years, and engineered by three revolutionary generals who, at least in the beginning, were probably more concerned with the immediate problem of how to stay in power than with any more fundamental reform of Mexican political and social structure.[40]

The first Mexican leader to dominate the military sector was Porfirio Diaz, a revolutionary general who came to power after a generation of conflict between liberals and conservatives had brought Mexico to the verge of chaos. Beginning in 1876, Diaz launched a program of combined coercion and incentive which would have pleased even the most Machiavellian observer. Those rival generals who were too powerful to be challenged openly were bribed with opportunities for graft and exploitation of the lower classes. Others were sent abroad on ambassadorial or military missions. Totally unreliable senior officers were driven out of the service; and occasionally Diaz was forced to provoke them into outright rebellion, after which they were shot or sent into exile. For those officers who remained, Diaz created a confusing set of overlapping districts, units, and chains of command; and untrustworthy generals were shifted constantly from one command to another to prevent them from having too much influence with junior officers and enlisted men. By the early 1890's, Porfirio Diaz had completely sobordinated the military establishment to his domination. The structure was a fragile one, however, for when the Revolution began in 1910, over the issue of electoral fraud, the vaunted Mexican army virtually disintegrated in the face of the challenge from Francisco Madero. While Diaz had brought the army under his control, he had done so through the tactic of personalist domination; in the face of an assault, the armed forces proved neither loyal, militarily competent, nor able to transfer their institutional allegiance to the new incumbent regime. Future reformers were not to make the same mistakes.

Although the Revolution began in October, 1910, it was not until ten years later, 1920, that our second revolutionary general, Alvaro Obregon, was in a position to control the army. The liberal government of Madero tried to reconciliate the old Diaz army regulars (a mistake that Fidel Castro was to avoid 50 years later); and in return, the old generals overthrew him in February, 1913. There ensued a civil war which lasted until July, 1914; the result was a victory for the revolutionaries, and defeat and destruction for the regular army. Once in power, however, the radicals fell to quarreling among themselves, leading to another round of battles between the more moderate forces of Venustiano Carranza (backed by Obregon) and the agrarian radicals of Pancho Villa and Emiliano Zapata. Following Carranza's victory in the summer of 1916, a new wave of militarism swept Mexico, as the new revolutionary generals sought to achieve for themselves the same privileged place previously enjoyed by the Diaz army.

Obregon, who was Carranza's minister of war before becoming president in his own right in 1920, stood in opposition to this resurgence of militarism. His view was that the Revolution had been launched precisely in order to eliminate undue military intervention in Mexican politics. Indeed, he came to power in 1920 at the head of a popular military uprising to prevent Carranza from violating the constitution and imposing another general on the people as head of the government. Obregon began to enact a series of structural reforms designed to head off the power and influence of the revolutionary military leaders. He did this by building up the mass base of support for the central government, and then using this support to counteract the power of the army. In the early period of his regime, Obregon relied on organized labor for much of his support; labor had supplied him with troops during the struggle against the agrarian troops of Villa and Zapata five years earlier, and they were amply rewarded after Obregon came to power in 1920. When Obregon was forced to turn against the unions he had created in 1922 and 1923, and use troops to quell labor disturbances, he turned toward the peasants for support and began to distribute land in an accelerated program of land reform. To be sure, Obregon also wielded the tools of coercion and bribery employed by Diaz. Many opposition generals were shot or forced to go into exile; many others who had supported Obregon in his bid for power were rewarded from the public treasury, or with land or resource concessions from the public domain. Because he had built a more solid popular base from which to challenge the army, however, Obregon's opportunism was not so shallow, nor so ill-fated as had been that of Diaz. The army was never again to launch a successful rebellion against the incumbents, even though they were to try repeatedly until 1940.

Had Obregon lived longer, he probably would have seen his reforms bear much more fruit; as it was, an assassin's bullet ended his life in 1928, just as he was about to come back into the presidency after having been elected to a second term (his first lasted from 1920 to 1924). In his absence, the military surged back into prominence under the more conservative reign of Plutarco Elias Calles, and a succession of handpicked puppet presidents. In 1934, however, there rose to the presidency another revolutionary general—Lazaro Cardenas—who could not be controlled by the army; and it was under his administration that the final step to restrain the military in politics was taken.

In reality, most of the factors which contributed to Cardenas' control over the army were already established at least in rudimentary form by 1934. Thanks to Obregon's reforms, the precedent was already set for using peasant and labor militias to serve as a counter-force to the army. Cardenas, however, broadened and expanded the social reforms of the Revolution by distributing more land to the landless farmers, and by encouraging labor's right to strike. In so doing, he also created more effective mass support for his regime, which was to prove decisive in counteracting military threats to his power.

Cardenas also took advantage of incipient attempts to professionalize the army during the 1920's to undercut the control of untrustworthy generals. The Minister of War under Calles, Joaquin Amaro, had begun a series of vital reforms in the lives and working conditions of the enlisted men and junior officers in the mid-1920's in order to make them more loyal to the incumbent regime. Cardenas utilized these reforms to subvert the authority of any general who showed a tendency to intervene in political matters. The result of these changes was not only a more nearly apolitical army, but a military establishment better equipped and more competent to protect the national security interests of the state.

Finally, Cardenas delivered the ultimate blow to the army by integrating them into the organizational framework of his "revolutionary" political party, the Party of the Mexican Revolution (PRM), created in March, 1938. The PRM was the outgrowth of the old National Revolutionary Party (PNR) formed by Calles in 1928; and was to serve as the forerunner of the now-famous PRI, Mexico's principal contribution to political development experience. In 1938, however, when Cardenas reorganized the PNR into the PRM, and made explicit the status of the army as one of its four constituent sectors (along with labor, peasants, and the "popular" sector), he received considerable criticism for brining military intervention into politics. He replied by saying that the military already possessed such influence, and he was only seeking to reduce it to one vote out of four. Thus, he insured that, on any crucial issues involving military versus civilian matters, the army could always be outvoted three to one. This reform, when added to the other changes we have discussed above, spelled the end to military intervention in Mexican politics. In spite of a final struggle at the time of the 1940 elections, the army in Mexico was never again to threaten the stability of the constitutional regime.

MANAGEMENT OF MILITARY INTERVENTION IN CUBA

When Fidel Castro entered Havana as the triumphant leader of the rebel army, the FAR (Fuerzas Armadas Rebeldes), in January, 1959, he could not have been unaware that, militarily, his regime was indeed precarious. Incredible as it seemed at the time, a rough, ill-equipped guerrilla force of only about 1,500 at the height of its power had challenged and beaten the well supplied and seasoned 30,000 troops of former dictator Fulgencio Batista. Castro must have known, however, that the victory of his rebel army over Batista was the result of a rare case of complete demoralization and disintegration of the incumbent forces; toward the end of the conflict, in late 1958, generals of Batista's army were taking bribes from the guerrillas not to attack, and several had even begun to open negotiations with the rebels.[41] Instead of destroying the regular Cuban army during the insurgency, Castro's FAR had simply taken advantage of the self-destruction of a corrupt and shaky dictatorship, which, in the end, could not even defend itself.

As a consequence of this, Castro recognized in early 1959 that threats against his regime could be directed from two quarters—in the short run, from the regulars of the old Cuban armed forces, who probably still harbored "counter-revolutionary" feelings; and, in the longer run, from his comrades in the rebel army, who, becoming dissatisfied with the pace of the revolution, could begin to take on some of the attributes of a traditional Cuban army and wish to intervene in politics against Castro. Our analysis, then, must take into account his efforts to curb *both* armies—the old force of Bastistianos, and the newer rebel army which had carried him to success.

Castro's immediate concern was the regular Cuban army. Ever since the famous sergeants' coup d'etat which had brought Batista to power in September, 1933, the Cuban army had played a key role in internal politics. Led by Batista, the armed forces had managed to control the presidency and all other major offices of the political system, even during the period from 1940 to 1952 when Cuban politics operated ostensibly under a democratic constitution. Further, since 1952, when Batista launched his second coup, the army and security police had constituted the sole source of authority in the country. It seems as if they had acquiesced in Castro's victory confident that they could control his revolutionary fervor, and, in the final analysis, if necessary contribute to his defeat in much the same way that the Guatemalan army had destroyed the social reform government of Jacobo Arbenz in 1954.[42]

The army failed to recognize the extraordinary force of the revolution which they had unleashed, however; even before Castro reached Havana, in January, 1959, rebel groups had begun to execute former Batista officers who had become well known for their brutality. After his arrival in the capital, Castro set out to destroy the pro-Batista officer corps, through the mechanism of the "revolutionary tribunals," or courts-martial, presided over by majors in the FAR. In spite of an international cry of protest, Castro proceeded to sentence and execute by firing squad over 500 officers in Batista's army; in addition, between 1,000 and 4,500 soldiers and officers were imprisoned as a result of an alleged coup threat in August, 1959. Finally, those officers who were not pronounced completely trustworthy were discharged, and their positions were taken over by officers from the rebel army after the latter was integrated into the regular force. In sum, Castro managed to turn the force of the revolution to his advantage by decimating the regular officer corps of the Cuban army, and, in so doing, to buy precious time to consolidate his revolution.[43]

After having dealt a decisive blow to the regular Cuban military establishment, however, Castro realized that the rebel army constituted a much greater potential threat to his personal control of the Cuban state. To a larger extent than is normally recognized, the Cuban revolution was based almost solely on the 1,500 guerrilla troops and their military power. The Castro revolt was marked by the absence of support from any major popular sector, such as the peasants, the sugar workers, or other laboring classes. The guerrilla forces were composed primarily of the sons of middle class families, with only a very few recruits from the peasant or laboring sectors. These groups were mere onlookers during the process of the revolution; it fell to the rebel army to bear the entire burden of the struggle.[44]

This feature of the Cuban revolution placed the rebel army in a central position in the early days of the consolidation phase of the revolution. Most of the officials of the revolutionary institutions were drawn from the officer corps of the FAR. The land reform agency, INRA, for example was almost entirely staffed by former FAR officers and enlisted men. The FAR built most of the social infrastructure so badly needed by the agrarian reform office: schools, clinics, rural housing, farm-to-market roads, and the like.[45] In late 1960, when Castro created several local boards for coordinating local government activities (called JUCEI, for Junta de Coordinacion Ejecucion e Inspeccion) throughout the country, each of the boards was headed by the military commander for the province.[46] The power vacuum left by the revolution was filled convincingly by the FAR, to such an extent that Ernesto "Che" Guevara declared in January, 1959, that the rebel army should become the nucleus of the Cuban people, who would constitute an "armed democracy."[47]

The degree to which the rebel army threatened Castro is exemplified by the Hubert Matos affair. Matos was a former school teacher who had joined the FAR relatively late in the revolution, and thus was not motivated by personal loyalty to Castro, but rather, by a feeling that social reform was necessary for Cuba's benefit. He rose rapidly in the officer ranks to become a major, and after the war was over he became the military chief of Camaguey Province. From that position in June, 1959, Matos began to speak out against increased Communist infiltration into the revolutionary government. He apparently was also blocking some of the more extreme aspects of the agrarian reform law in Camaguey, as well as engaging in propaganda against the Cuban Communist party, the PSP. Matos was arrested personally by Castro in October, 1959, and sentenced to 20 years in prison. As late as autumn, 1960, however, one year after his arrest, Draper reports that the Rebel Army in Camaguey Province continued to harbor strong anti-Communist feelings. The rapid action by Castro against Matos illustrates well his dictum that no commander, no matter what his combat record or his loyalty, should ever be allowed to have troops under his control which might constitute an independent source of power.[48]

Fidel Castro's efforts to limit the strength of the rebel army may be summed up in three operating premises. First, he insisted on the personal loyalty of each major troop commander; those who were not loyal first and foremost to him were dismissed, sent into exile, or imprisoned. One of Castro's first moves was to name his brother, Raul, as his replacement as commander of the army in the event that Fidel was out of the country. Later, Raul became minister of the armed forces to tighten his control over all subordinate commanders. By the same token, however, any commander who threatened to become too strong found himself removed from command. In May, 1959, after his return from his famous trip to the United States, Castro dispatched "Che" Guevara on a long series of visits to Europe, Africa, and Asia. While Guevara was gone, Castro disbanded the forces which had fought under "Che," and the latter never commanded any troops again while he remained in Cuba. Castro's insistence on personal control of all the levers of power dictated that each commander be loyal as well as subservient to his authority.

Second, Castro created several organizations whose countervailing power he attempted to use to offset the strength of the Rebel Army. One of these groups, the Revolutionary Militia, was created in March, 1959, and paraded for the first time on May 1. Armed from the Soviet bloc, the militia reached the height of its power in the early 1960's. In the summer of 1962, however, the militia leaders grew restive under Cuba's economic hardships, and Castro purged the entire organization, forcing some to resign, reorganizing others, and incorporating the remainder into the Rebel Army. After the coup against Algerian leader Ben Bella in June, 1965, Castro, fearing a similar move against him, ordered the militia to turn in all their weapons, and the peasants' armed force began to dwindle into nonexistence.[49] In 1968, the Cuban revolutionary militia numbered about 200,000 men and women; by 1970, the order of battle for the Cuban armed forces did not even include a militia force of any size.[50] One could conclude, however, that the militia had served its limited purpose for the time it was in existence, since it did at least provide Castro with enough time to undertake his third step against the Rebel Army—its politicization through the revolutionary party.

In January, 1964, after Castro's second trip to Moscow, he began to organize cells of the revolutionary party, the PURS, within the ranks of the army. This process, substantially completed in eastern Cuba by autumn, saw the soldiers organized into cells, which then elected representatives to their higher level bureaus. These bureaus, in turn, were subordinated to the political department of the rebel army, which was controlled by the military department of the National Directorate of the PURS, Castro's personal weapon of control. Thus, Castro was assured that, if any commander seemed about to move against him, he, Castro, possessed an alternate chain of command to reach the enlisted men and deflect the threat.

In October, 1965, the Rebel Army was politicized even further as a consequence of Castro's change of the PURS to the Communist Party of Cuba. In a move reminiscent of the Mexican experience, the army was tied firmly into the revolutionary party in such a way that, although the military had more influence within the party, they were also bound more tightly into a mass-based political organization, controlled ultimately by Castro himself. In the National Directorate of the old PURS, for example, the rebel army had held 40 percent of the posts; their share of the Central Committee of the new PCC is 69 percent. At the same time, the power of organized labor and the old Communists has declined, while Castro's personal creation, the 26 of July Movement, has risen in control. The same thing seems to have happened in the party's politburo; out of the eight offices, six belong to rebel army representatives. Suarez suggests that the PCC was created especially to form a counterweight to the increasingly restless FAR; the inclusion of so many army representatives on the party's ruling councils was done precisely to provide Castro with a means of controlling the rebel army better.[51]

With only a decade of experience, it is hard to give Castro a final evaluation; in the short run, however, it appears as if he has performed an essential task for revolutionary development elites—he has brought under control the military forces which carried him to power. Only time will tell, however, whether his control over the power of the rebel army will continue to allow him to carry out one of history's most radical examples of political development.

CONCLUSIONS

While clearly different in many respects, the Mexican and Cuban development elites sought to control the major internal threat to their power—the revolutionary armed forces—in much the same ways. First, they were (or quickly became) utterly ruthless in dealing with insubordination and disloyalty among senior officials in the army. In Mexico, this process was delayed several years as Madero attempted to placate the old Diaz generals; eventually, however, Obregon and Cardenas were to recognize that only the most severe and rapid suppression of a military threat would make it possible for them to undertake more long-term social reforms. Castro apparently needed no such learning period, as the decimation of the Batista forces had begun even before he had entered Havana as the victor of the revolution. The ferocity with which Castro broke the structure of the old prerevolutionary Cuban army obviously provided him with more time in which to consolidate his regime without fearing a military coup.

The construction of countervailing forces—especially from organized labor and the peasants—was crucial for the success of the Mexican reformers; and the Revolutionary Militia in Cuba was of equal importance for a short period. Because of the more rapid change in Cuban society, however, and because of Castro's greater personal appeal, the Cuban leader did not have to depend on these counterforces for as long a time as did the Mexican presidents. In fact, once the militias began to threaten Castro, he lost no time in eliminating them as a force in Cuban politics.

In both cases, the final touch to the policy of controlling the armed forces was contained in the integration of the army into the decision-making structure of the revolutionary party. Although superficially giving the army a greater voice in politics, in both instances the development elites have used the integration to strengthen their personal control over the armed forces command structures. Once the army has found itself tied into a complex network of mass-based, revolutionary forces, they have ceased to be a source of instability, capable of independent actions, and have instead been brought much more under the effective direction of the revolutionary elite.

SOME COMMON DENOMINATORS

Based on the case studies presented, the following factors seem to have been of paramount importance to the six incumbent regimes in overcoming the violent threats to the stability and integrity of their systems.

First, the role of the international community is crucial. As if to echo the point made in Chapter Four, the regulative capability of a developing state can be sharply affected by the balance of favorable and unfavorable forces in the international system. The best the incumbent regime's leaders can hope for is that the bulk of Great Power and neighboring small power support will flow to them; this was the case in five of the studies we have presented. In the Congo, Nigeria, and Cuba, some foreign aid did flow to the insurgents, but not enough to offset assistance to the central government. In Malaya and the Philippines, external aid to the rebels was curtailed sharply, and Great Power aid to the incumbents was substantial. Only in the early days of the Mexican experience was the position of the international system ambiguous (particularly in the case of the United States and Germany during World War I). Even here, however, the incumbents received fairly neutral treatment from the international system as they proceeded to deal with insurgent army leaders.

Second, a successful incumbent regime must possess overwhelming (if not exclusive) control over the available military force in the country. Further, they must not be reluctant to use this force if need be to crush incipient rebellion. In our analysis of the role of military intervention in Latin America, we concluded that most successful insurgencies stem basically from a weakened will to fight in a deteriorating national military establishment. The fact that the governments in Nigeria, the Congo, Malaya, and the Philippines could count on their national armies to stand fast under pressure went far toward explaining the successful counter-insurgency effort in those countries. And, of course, the first objective of most developing states in Latin America has been to secure the loyalty of the military to the incumbent regime.

A mere resort to coercion and military control was not enough to stifle instability in our six cases, however. In each instance, a wise leadership coupled vigorous prosecution of regulatory measures with the opening up of moderate-risk channels to full participation in the political process to the rebels. At the same time, development elites have sought to deal positively with the tangible grievances of the insurgents—jobs, education, land ownership, respect for cultural differences. The ethnic minorities in the Congo and Nigeria were brought back into full participation in the economic and political life of the nation; the Huks were rewarded with land when they returned to peaceful pursuits; members of the MRLA were granted amnesty in Malaya for laying down their arms, and Chinese New Villages were made the targets of vigorous educational and health programs; and, of course, the armies in Mexico and Cuba were guaranteed a major voice in policy-making circles. While these measures may not have won over each and every one of the insurgents, they were successful in attracting the great majority of the rank-and-file rebels, thereby breaking the back of the opposition before long. The lesson seems clear: a rapidly developing country, threatened by instability, must combine military coercion with social reform in order to defuse the potentially explosive conditions which lead men to risk their lives in the cause of political change.

CHAPTER NOTES

1. Ravi L. Kapil, "On the Conflict Potential of Inherited Boundaries in Africa," *World Politics,* XVIII, 4 (July, 1966): 656-73.
2. Rupert Emerson, "The Problem of Identity, Selfhood, and the Image in the New Nations: The Situation in Africa," *Comparative Politics,* 1, 3 (April, 1969): 297-312.
3. William R. Bascom, "Tribalism, Nationalism, and Pan-Africanism," in Pierre L. Van Den Berghe, ed., *Africa: Social Problems of Change and Conflict* (San Francisco: Chandler Publishing Company, 1965), pp. 461-71.
4. For a full account of the Congo's drive to development, see Crawford Young, *Politics in the Congo: Decolonization and Independence* (Princeton, N.J.: Princeton University Press, 1965).
5. The best summary of the Katanga secession can be found in Crawford Young, "The Politics of Separatism: Katanga, 1960–63," in Gwendolen M. Carter, ed., *Politics in Africa: Seven Cases* (New York: Harcourt, 1966), pp. 167-208.

6. For a detailed discussion of the United Nations role in the Congo see Stanley Hoffman, "In Search of a Thread: The UN in the Congo Labyrinth," *International Organization,* XVI, 2 (Spring, 1962): 331-61.

7. "Nigeria Looks Ahead," *Foreign Affairs,* 41, 1 (October, 1962): 131-40.

8. Donald Rothchild, "The Limits of Federalism: An Examination of Political Institutional Transfer in Africa," in Marion E. Doro and Newell M. Stultz, eds., *Governing in Black Africa: Perspectives on New States* (Englewood Cliffs, N.J.: Prentice-Hall, 1970), pp. 206-21.

9. For an account of Nigeria's transition from a colony to an independent federation, see Frederick A. O. Schwarz, Jr., *Nigeria: The Tribes, the Nation, or the Race— The Politics of Independence* (Cambridge, Mass.: MIT Press, 1965).

10. A summary of the events leading up to the secession of the Ibos can be found in Joseph C. McKenna, "Elements of a Nigerian Peace," *Foreign Affairs,* 47, 4 (July, 1969): 668-80.

11. Colin Legum, "The Tragedy in Nigeria," in Irving Leonard Markowitz, ed., *African Politics and Society* (New York: Free Press, 1970), pp. 248-51.

12. For a discussion of arms supply patterns and their significance, see Neville Brown, "Arms Supply," *Venture* (Special issue on Nigeria), 21, 7 (July/August, 1969): 8-10.

13. Emerson, p. 302.

14. Pauline H. Baker, "The Politics of Nigerian Military Rule," *Africa Report,* 16, 2 (February, 1971): 18-21.

15. Jeffrey M. Paige, "Inequality and Insurgency in Vietnam: A Reanalysis," *World Politics,* XXIII, 1 (October, 1970): 24-37. Such is also the case in Latin America. See James Petras, *Politics and Social Forces in Chilean Development* (Berkeley: University of California Press, 1969), pp. 257-58.

16. Eric R. Wolf, *Peasant Wars of the Twentieth Century* (New York: Harper & Row, 1969).

17. For useful background on rural upheaval in the region generally, see Erich H. Jacoby, *Agrarian Unrest in Southeast Asia* (New York: Columbia University Press, 1949).

18. Robert W. McColl, "A Political Geography of Revolution: China, Vietnam and Thailand," *Journal of Conflict Resolution,* XI, 2 (June, 1967): 153-67.

19. For an on-going debate on this subject, see the following: Bruce Russett, "Inequality and Instability: The Relation of Land Tenure to Politics," *World Politics,* XVI, 3 (April, 1964): 442-54. Edward J. Mitchell, "Inequality and Insurgency: A Statistical Study of South Vietnam," *World Politics,* XX, 3 (April, 1968): 421-38. And Paige, "Inequality and Insurgency in Vietnam: A Reanalysis."

20. Douglas Hyde, *The Roots of Guerrilla Warfare* (Chester Springs, Pa.: Dufour Editions, 1968), esp. pp. 135-37.

21. For an excellent summary of ethnic aspects of rural insurgencies in Southeast Asia, see Walker Connor, "Ethnology and the Peace of South Asia," *World Politics,* XXII, 1 (October, 1969): 51-86. For a specific example of the impact of ethnic minorities on insurgency, see John T. McAlister, Jr., "Mountain Minorities and the Viet Minh: A Key to the Indochina War," in Peter Kunstadter, ed., *Southeast Asian Tribes, Minorities, and Nations* (Princeton, N.J.: Princeton University Press, 1967), Vol. II, pp. 771-844.

22. Jacoby, pp. 101-33, esp. p. 102.

23. See Ruth T. McVey, "The Southeast Asian Insurrectionary Movements," in Cyril E. Black and Thomas P. Thornton, eds., *Communism and Revolution: The Strategic Uses of Political Violence* (Princeton, N.J.: Princeton University Press, 1964), pp. 145-84, esp. pp. 150-51. See also Lucian W. Pye, *Guerrilla Communism in Malaya: Its Social and Political Meaning* (Princeton, N.J.: Princeton University Press, 1956), pp. 47-111.

24. D. E. Kennedy, *The Security of Southern Asia* (New York: Praeger, 1965), pp. 175-83.

25. Jacoby, p. 183.

26. McVey, p. 152.

27. Kennedy, p. 167.

28. Jorge Maravilla, "The Postwar Huk in the Philippines," in William J. Pomeroy, ed., *Guerrilla Warfare and Marxism* (New York: International Publishers, 1968), pp. 237-42.

29. Robert Shaplen, *Time Out of Hand: Revolution and Reaction in Southeast Asia* (New York: Harper & Row, 1968), pp. 230-65.

30. Napoleon D. Valeriano and Charles Bohannan, *Counter-Guerrilla Operations: The Philippine Experience* (New York: Praeger, 1962).

31. The extent of United States involvement in Philippines politics during the early 1950's is discussed in H. Bradford Westernfield, *The Instruments of America's Foreign Policy* (New York: Thomas Y. Crowell Company, 1963), pp. 404-21.

32. Warren F. Ilchman and Norman Thomas Uphoff, *The Political Economy of Change* (Berkeley: University of California Press, 1969), p. 185.

33. Among the vast literature on the role of the military in political development, see especially Wilson C. McWilliams, ed., *Garrisons and Government: Politics and the Military in New States* (San Francisco: Chandler Publishing Co., 1967).

34. U.S. Senate, *Nomination of Lincoln Gordon to be Assistant Secretary of State for Inter-American Affairs.* 89th Cong., 2nd Session, February 7, 1966. (Washington: U.S.G.P.O., 1966), pp. 68-71.

35. For the earlier portion of this period, see Edwin Lieuwin, *Generals vs. Presidents: Neo-Militarism in Latin America* (New York: Praeger, 1964).

36. Edwin Lieuwin, *Arms and Politics in Latin America,* rev. ed. (New York: Praeger, 1961).

37. "Toward a Theory of Power and Political Instability in Latin America," in John D. Martz, ed., *The Dynamics of Change in Latin American Politics* (Englewood Cliffs, N.J.: Prentice-Hall, 1965), pp. 130-39.

38. Martin Needler, "Political Development and Military Intervention in Latin America," *American Political Science Review,* LX, 3 (Sept., 1966): 616-26.

39. Robert Putnam, "Toward Explaining Military Intervention in Latin American Politics," *World Politics,* XX, 1 (October, 1967): 83-109.

40. Our account is drawn heavily from Edwin Lieuwin, *Mexican Militarism: The Political Rise and Fall of the Revolutionary Army* (Albuquerque, N.M.: University of New Mexico Press, 1968). See the same arguments presented in greatly abridged form in Lieuwin, *Arms and Politics in Latin America.*

41. Andres Suarez, *Cuba: Castroism and Communism, 1959–1966* (Cambridge, Mass.: MIT Press, 1967), p. 29.

42. See Richard N. Adams, *Crucifixion by Power: Essays on Guatemalan National Social Structure, 1944–1966* (Austin: University of Texas Press, 1970).

43. For details on the executions, see Lieuwin, *Arms and Politics in Latin America,* pp. 265-67. Also, see *New York Times,* January 8, February 24, March 20, and August 11, 1959.

44. James O'Connor, *The Origins of Socialism in Cuba* (Ithaca, N.Y.: Cornell University Press, 1970), p. 8, 43-44. Also Theodore Draper, *Castroism: Theory and Practice* (New York: Praeger, 1965), pp. 70-73.

45. O'Connor, pp. 130-31.

46. Suarez, pp. 117-18, 123-24.

47. Suarez, p. 41.

48. The entire Matos affair is told in Suarez, pp. 66 and 77. See also O'Connor, pp. 287-88; Draper, p. 242.

49. See Suarez, p. 165, 224-26.

50. Institute for Strategic Studies, *The Military Balance: 1968–1969* and *1970–1971* (London: ISS, 1968 and 1970), p. 12 and p. 76.

51. Suarez, pp. 228-30. See also the *New York Times,* March 11, 1969, for speech by Raul Castro explaining that 97 percent of the 1,200 young officers trained in 1969 were members of either the Communist Party of Cuba or the Communist Youth League.

Part 3

STRATEGIES OF DEVELOPMENT

Chapter 9

STRATEGIES OF DEVELOPMENT:

An Overview

James S. Coleman recently identified three alternate ways of looking at the issue of political development.[1] The first of these, which Coleman calls the historical perspective, seeks to place political development in the context of the broad, centuries-long process of modernization which began in Western Europe in the sixteenth century. The second approach, which he labels typological, describes development by means of postulating two ideal-types of political systems—one called traditional, and the other modern—with development indentified as the change from the former to the latter. While these two points of view have many advocates, Coleman criticizes them for envisioning development as (1) unilinear, and not reversible; and (2) having an identifiable historical point of departure and of termination. In any event, the focus of these two approaches is most definitely on the characteristics of the original and terminal political orders, on the traditional and the modern, on the underdeveloped and the developed.

The third perspective—which Coleman calls evolutionary—focuses instead on the *process* by which a system is changed and improved, rather than on the meaning of the end product. Coleman describes the political development process as ". . . that open-ended increase in the capacity of political man to initiate and institutionalize new structures, and supporting cultures, to cope with or resolve problems, to absorb and adapt to continuous change, and to strive purposely and creatively for the attainment of new societal goals."[2]

The evolutionary concept of development portrays the process of change as capable of reversal, as well as infinitely malleable into varying forms and directions. Further, there is no terminal point or stage according to this mode of looking at things, since—once begun—the process of development may go on endlessly, limited only by technology and the inventiveness of man. It is the evolutionary approach which we have modestly attempted to employ throughout this study.

Once we have opened up the Pandora's box of conceiving of development as process, we confront some obligation to address ourselves to the guidance of events to smooth the process, to accelerate it as much as possible, and to give it direction and meaning. These are the tasks of developmental statesmanship; and, with a few rare exceptions, they have been ignored by the world of academia. As a recent study points out, scholars and other observers of the developing world have been interested in system requisites or sociopsychological preconditions, while statesmen need to know how to stay in power, how to use resources, how to multiply resources that are scarce, and how to evaluate competing policy alternatives.[3] While these are concerns to politicians in industrialized, Western nations as well, in the developing world the lack of time and other resources, the pressure of events, and the inadequate conceptual and political tools create something of a crisis in the management of the development process.

This is not to indicate that there are no suggestions that statesmen might find useful which could be teased out of the available literature on political development; indeed, some studies have made some quite explicit recommendations about policy choices that development elites could find valuable. Some of the more insightful studies will be reviewed in this chapter and in Chapter Ten. The path of policy analysis in developing states is narrow and treacherous, however; and, while we may hope to shed some light on the issue in these chapters, we will consider our work well done if we manage to illuminate a few of the more relevant aspects of development strategy, and thus to build a little more onto the edifice of strategic theory in general.

A NOTE ON POLITICAL STRATEGIES

Howard Wriggins, one of the foremost students of political strategies, suggests that, in fact, the word "strategy" may not be entirely appropriate to describe what successful political actors actually do.[4] Although political leaders usually do distinguish between broad guiding principles and the particular exigencies of a given conflictual situation, still the term "strategy" may suggest to the reader more advance planning and rational choice than is in fact possible. The strategies adopted by political leaders, and by development-oriented political leaders especially, may undergo radical shifts as changes are perceived in goals, resources, the environment, the sectors involved, or the time available to act. As Robert Dahl puts it, "Adopting a strategy is a little bit like deciding how to look for a fuse box in a strange house on a dark night after all the lights have blown."[5]

In a political sense, then, strategy and tactics tend to merge into one overall approach to solving problems; whether or not one calls a series of acts "strategy" depends on the immediacy of the goal in question. As in the military usage, the term "strategy" is usually reserved for those maneuvers designed to position forces *before* the actual engagement, with long-range goals or objectives being uppermost in the perspective of the decision-maker. Tactical decisions typically involve the quest for more immediate, short-range objectives, sometimes called instrumental goals, in that their achievement facilitates the attainment of larger ends. To provide an example, a typical development *strategy* would be an initial decision by a statesman to divide the issue of modernization into several smaller problems, and a subsequent decision to arrange the smaller problems sequentially for attack. The *tactical* decisions, then, would focus on how to attack each of the smaller fragments of the larger issue of modernization.

Wriggins emphasizes the fact that each development leader will have to fashion his own peculiar strategic combination to suit his own environment. The relevant considerations will involve the ruler's personality, his organization, his power requirements, his goals, his opponents and supporters and their strengths and weaknesses, the "rules of the game" in his polity, and the costs of deviating from these, and perhaps others. In the face of these obstacles to a coherent treatment, we might be forgiven for backing away from the formidable task of codifying something as variegated as development strategies. Nevertheless, just as Wriggins thought he perceived some pattern to all these idiosyncracies, so might we be pardoned our attempt to impose some analytical order on what is really a very diverse collection of behavior patterns.[6]

In this chapter, we shall be examining two broad classes of writings on development strategies, those with a systemic bias, and those which focus on a much lower, tactical level. The first group of studies involve what we shall call "systemic strategies" after their obvious orientation to system-level behavior. These systemic approaches derive from a view of development that can best be described as "cosmic." The perspective of the advocates of this position stretches far back into history; and development patterns are perceived in a vast sweep of conflict between massive social forces, ideas, and larger-than-life personalities. The forte of this approach is the clear outline of ultimate goals toward which political actors must be striving; there is little, however, in the way of instrumental guidance for these actors. They are told at what point on the map they must end their journey, but are given little to help them pick the best route. Perhaps it is just as well, for these strategists also view development as being imposed upon political elites by such things as "events," "history," or "the system's imperatives." Development requirements are thrust upon political leaders who simply do what they can to avoid being overwhelmed by the faceless forces of change.

At the opposite end of the spectrum lie the development tacticians, the "reform-mongers" of Albert Hirschman, who perform best in an environment of small detail, unperturbed about the broader sweep of history. To the extent that these analysts are concerned about development per se at all, it is only by defining development as an increase in a system's ability to accept the changes they have proposed. That is, a reform politician attacking, say, the problem of unequal land distribution in his country tends either to discard the idea that what he is doing is "political development," or to identify political development as more nearly equal land distribution. Broader, more long-range goals of development, such as those described in Chapter One, are sought (if at all) in the context of a more immediate problem, and only rarely as the component part of a more inclusive strategy to increase the capability of the system as a whole.

The reader will have guessed by now that our proposed strategic approach will differ in some degree from both of the broad classes above described. In order to seek a better alternative, however, one that includes those elements of value found in both approaches—the cosmic and the tactical—we must first understand each in its fullest ramifications. Only then may we launch our own search for a useful set of suggestions to the practical politician.

SYSTEMIC STRATEGIES

THE SSRC MODEL

Certainly one of the most exciting research programs currently under way in political development has been the massive multi-volume study launched under the auspices of the Committee on Comparative Politics of the Social Science Research Council (SSRC). In volume number seven of their effort, entitled *Crises and Sequences in Political Development,*[7] the various threads of their previous works are pulled together to draw some preliminary conclusions about the nature of political development, and to attempt to formulate some new directions for future research. While the volume does not go so far as to offer a comprehensive "strategy" of development, the insights gained into development strategy via their notion of *sequences* of development crises do contribute greatly to our general understanding of the complexities facing development leaders. While we await future volumes of this study for more analysis of the sequential nature of development, we should attempt to put *Crises and Sequences* into our more general context of studies of development strategies.

Political development, as viewed by the SSRC authors, consists of structural, institutional, and attitudinal changes which lead to improvement in three key dimensions—equality, capacity, and differentiation. In the second essay of the volume,[8] James S. Coleman explores what he calls the development "syndrome," or a set of dimensions through which one can view the development of a political system. Equality, according to Coleman, refers to the drive for egalitarianism prominent in all aspects of modern life. This egalitarianism is best exemplified in politics through changes in the grounds for national citizenship, the universality of the legal order, and the adoption of achievement norms to reward members of the society. Capacity, Coleman's second dimension, refers to the ability of the political system to manage the tensions which arise from other changes, as well as from the environment (natural disaster, war, and so on). To be truly modern, however, a polity must have the capacity not only to adapt to a changing world, but to be creative, to seek out opportunities for improvement, and to take advantage of them. Finally, societal differentiation is a requirement of modernization, in that a modern society demands a specialization and separation of roles, institutional jurisdictions, and jobs. While a traditional society may get by with all the principal functions performed by only one person, for example, king or chieftain, a modern political order needs to assign specific roles to specific individuals or agencies to insure that bureaucratic rationality can be brought to bear on problems.

The problem of defining development as taking place along three separate dimensions is explicitly recognized in the SSRC work. How does one handle a system, for example, which is growing along two dimensions, but stagnating or actually regressing along a third? In the concluding essay in the book, Sidney Verba[9] argues that, were he forced to select only one dimension to plot the development of a state, it would have to be that of *capacity,* since the capacity of a political system must underpin all other changes—in equality and in structural differentiation—cited by the other authors. The implications of this conclusion for the present work are great, in that Verba seems to be arguing for an approach to development strikingly similar to that presented in Chapter One (this volume). Without in any way slighting the importance of equality or differentiation as important ingredients in overall societal development, one still comes away from the SSRC work strengthened in his belief that *development* of a political order means increasing the *capacity* or *capability* of that order to do things.

Given this orientation toward capacity, equality, and differentiation of a development elite, then, how do the SSRC authors propose to move the system along these dimensions? Specifically, through what phases, or in what stages, or in what sequences must decisions be made and problems solved in order for the development process to move smoothly? What development strategy do they fashion, based on their analysis of the requirements for development?

Unfortunately, the *Crises and Sequences* volume does not reach the level of a comprehensive review of possible development strategies. Each of the authors has put forward some tantalizing insights into the development process in a limited area, and some of the discussions, such as that of Joseph LaPalombara on educational investment strategies, are quite provocative.[10] The heart of the sequential concept of development offered by the SSRC team lies in the notion of certain crises through which all political systems must pass as they try to increase their own allocations to equality, capacity, and differentiation.

The discussion of these crises, full elaborations of their dimensions, causes, and attempted solutions, constitute the core of the book. Briefly, the five issue areas confronted by developing states consist of (1) the identity crisis, wherein the citizens of the polity search for a national identity, a renewed sense of the "we" and the "they" of political life; (2) the legitimacy crisis, which arises whenever there is conflict over the appropriate form which political decision-making takes in a society; (3) the penetration crisis, which grows out of a desire on the part of the central government leaders to extend their authority and jurisdiction into previously untouched areas of national political life; (4) the participation crisis, covering the multitude of ways in which citizens can demand access to and influence over the nodes of power; and (5) the distribution crisis, involving a dissatisfaction with the ways in which goods and values are allocated in the system.

There is obviously a considerable overlap between the SSRC set of crises, and the notion of capabilities which has underpinned the present work. The identity and legitimacy crises, based as they are on attitudinal data, seem more closely related to the symbolic capability of a state, as well as to the desired attitudinal changes we discussed in Chapter Two. The crises of participation, penetration, and distribution seem reminiscent of the issues raised in our discussion of the other capabilities in Chapter One. As a rough approximation, Chart 9.1 seems appropriate, in order to put the SSRC development theory into the context of the present work.

Chart 9.1 SSRC Crises Compared to Systemic Capabilities and Attitudinal Changes.

SSRC Crises	Capabilities	Attitudinal Changes
1. Identity	Symbolic	Orientation toward the nation, self as actor, others as actors
2. Legitimacy	Symbolic	Orientation toward policy inputs and outputs
3. Penetration	Regulative Extractive	
4. Participation	Responsive	
5. Distribution	Distributive	

The sequence in which the five crises occur apparently is a critical feature of a development effort. For one thing, there is a decided advantage for those states that can manage to avoid facing more than one crisis at once, as the multiplication of crises reduces the ability of development leaders to respond to any single crisis effectively. In addition, Verba offers some initial thoughts on certain sequences which appear to be easier to cope with than others. For instance, if a political system can meet and solve (at least temporarily) the identity crisis first, other crises are not quite so severe. Further, a resolution of the identity crisis makes it easier to move next to the legitimacy issue. With these two "psychological" crises successfully dealt with, the leaders can then move on to deal with the question of penetration (expand their ability to regulate, and extract resources from, the society); and, with this crisis out of the way, the participation and distribution problems fall into place rather agreeably.[11]

The reader will note that the "ideal" or "model" sequence of crises does not offer the development leader a great deal of leeway in which to operate to influence what his environment demands of him. If he has the good fortune to be the leader of a relatively inert society, he can mobilize the population and sensitize it to those issues which he feels ready to handle, at the time he desires. But then, if a development elite had that much control over the environment, there would be little call for concern, analysis, or indeed for books such as this one or the SSRC volumes. An inquiry into development strategies should address itself, on the contrary, to those environmental conditions which do not replicate the sequence of crises felt to be most advantageous by the SSRC, and to explicating a few ways in which a development elite might respond to, and survive in, such conditions.

THE ALMOND/POWELL MODEL

The work of Gabriel Almond and G. Bingham Powell provides us with another good illustration of the systemic approach to political development.[12] For the greater part of the book, Almond and Powell discuss development in totally systemic terms; in the final chapter, however, they begin to introduce certain strategic and tactical considerations in the selection and analysis of political investment opportunities. To this extent, they begin to move somewhat away from the SSRC model in explicating what a development elite must do in order to put their country on the path to modernity.

Almond and Powell develop their analytical framework based on the concept of the political system, its structures, and the functions that they must perform. Thus, they follow explicitly in the footsteps of the foremost systems theorists and functionalists in political science analysis—David Easton, Tallcot Parsons, and Karl Deutsch, among others. The Almond and Powell model posits the state as a processing organization whose main job it is to receive information from the society about social needs, and to convert this information into political output; that is, the acts of governance. The political process is thus seen to be a steady if sometimes erratic flow of inputs (supports and demands) into the political system's conversion facilities, where these resources are changed into government performance, such as laws, expenditures, and so on. The functions to be performed on the input side consist of interest aggregation, interest articulation, and communication; on the output side, the political system must engage in rule-making, rule enforcement and rule adjudication. In this formulation, the concept of political *development* seems to be the improvement of the process by which inputs are converted into outputs.

There are several ways in which this improvement may take place. For instance, more inputs (votes, demonstrations, and so on) may be generated and received; or the process for converting demands into responses may be made more efficient (less parliamentary immobilism, for example); or the rules which are finally made may be enforced more equitably and less arbitrarily (the paramountcy of the rule of law).

Almond and Powell argue that improvement in the ability of the political system to change inputs into outputs really means that the political order must undergo changes at three different levels of organizational behavior. First, the state's capabilities must be increased; the political system must experience an improvement in its capacity to do things. The capabilities suggested by Almond and Powell are regulative, extractive, symbolic, distributive, and responsive.[13] At the second level, the system should improve its internal conversion processes, as a separate and distinct capability. And finally, the political order should undergo changes in its ability to perform the tasks of system maintenance and adaptation. Without this additional capability to respond to a rapidly changing environment, the gains of development in one time frame may be lost during extreme crisis in a subsequent period.

The Almond and Powell model goes on to make explicit some of the auxiliary changes which must occur in the social and psychological realm of the developing state in order for the above-mentioned political changes to take place or to endure. Structural differentiation, or the increasing division of society into specialized groups with specific tasks, is a requirement if the society is to bring the best expertise that it can muster to bear on a problem. This implies something approaching the rational organization of bureaucracy, a point made by many other development analysts. Second, Almond and Powell call for subsystem autonomy, meaning that systems or institutions which support and feed into the political arena should retain a considerable amount of freedom from central direction. This is advocated apparently to insure that the solution of problems is made a community-wide concern, and thus buttresses the argument for structural differentiation made earlier. Finally, the model calls for cultural secularization, or the increasing reliance on science, technology, achievement norms, and rational choice, as opposed to mystical or religious grounds for making decisions.

Given the formidable nature of the development process, as described in the Almond and Powell thesis, it is easy to see why so few statesmen are willing to undertake the long road to modernity. Indeed, Almond and Powell interpret the initiation of a development sequence as being part of a challenge and response syndrome. According to them, development begins when a stagnant or traditional or underdeveloped state is challenged from one of three places: foreign threat; internal nonpolitical changes which have political implications, such as industrialization; or domestic counter-elites. Development then becomes the system's response to these stresses.

Along the road to modernization, however, the developing polity is fated to pass through four crises, or major issues. These crises are state-building, or the establishment of the forms and institutions of a modern political state; nation-building, which encompasses the growth of national consciousness and loyalty; participation, expressed in rising demands from new groups to be admitted to the political arena; and welfare, or distribution of resources in a more equitable fashion. The degree to which these crises parallel the SSRC crisis sequence described earlier is immediately apparent.

Several problems arise from the Almond and Powell usage of the crises approach. First, there is a definite implication that there is a preferred sequence or pattern to these crises. A political system is more fortunate if it can pass through these stages of development in the order we have listed them above, and if it can be challenged to solve the problems one at a time. There is a hint here of some kind of analogy to certain theories of human personality development, in which the individual personality proceeds through development stages. For Freudian psychologists, these stages involve varying kinds of psycho-sexual orientations, and if the problems specific to each phase are not solved in that phase, the entire growth pattern of the individual will be arrested. A failure of a developing nation to resolve its state-building issue first, for example, leaves behind a residue of national or cultural anxiety which contaminates the solution of subsequent problems. This idea is seen most clearly in the Almond and Powell discussion of national development of Germany in the late nineteenth and early twentieth centuries.[14]

Almond and Powell also believe that late arriving states are confronted with all four crises at once, which hampers or inhibits their ability to solve any single one with any degree of success. When we shift our focus from the systemic to the tactical level, however, we shall discover ways in which other analysts have described development elites coping with exactly that problem —the simultaniety of crises. Some reformers respond by breaking the problems up into little fragments, and solving them a little at a time. Others consider the "lumpiness" of political issues a blessing as it makes easier the formation of alliances and coalitions.

In this specific instance, then, both the Almond and Powell model, and the SSRC model, by focusing on systemic level crises, have introduced the notion of historical inevitability in development patterns, a notion sharply challenged by the authors to be considered in our next section.

Before we move away from the Almond and Powell effort, however, we should note their provocative discussion of political investment strategies with which they close their book, for it is here that they put aside their implications of historical inevitability and begin to discuss development as being the product of human intervention. The technique by which development elites should formulate their strategy is what Almond and Powell call a "rational choice" model of political growth.[15] The development leaders of a nation begin by analyzing the "starting point of a political system." Then they move on to elaborate their understanding of the structural, cultural, and conversion characteristics, and the capability levels of the system. Third, the leaders should make specific the properties of the political system they wish to strive for; that is, their goals. Finally, they should select that investment strategy which offers the highest probability of reaching the goal society, with the least risk and the lowest cost.

The reader is asked to keep the Almond and Powell rational choice model of development decision-making in mind as he proceeds through the remainder of this chapter, and especially Chapter Ten. The incremental style of making choices and decisions contrasts sharply with the rational choice model; in Chapter Ten, we shall examine the implications of both for development strategies. For now, let us simply note that the Almond and Powell formula places a great burden on the cognitive and information-gathering powers of both the individuals and the political system they administer. In addition, by requiring that the leaders specify the properties of the state they hope to create, it presupposes a degree of consensus on goals usually elusive in developing states today. Nevertheless, the formula does not tell development elites what to do in the meantime while they are gathering the reams of data and building the value consensus necessary to put the rational choice model into practice.

Almond and Powell do offer several guidelines for development strategists which should stimulate discussion and debate.[16] First, they say, a correct development strategy emphasizes "the scheduling of efforts at solution of . . . development problems." They go on to specify that this means that state- and nation-building should take priority over participation and welfare problems, a note sounded by other authors albeit in slightly different form. But most importantly, Almond and Powell recognize the need to fragment the development issues into manageable segments; in this respect, their approach resembles that of the incrementalists, as we shall show below. A second guideline offered by Almond and Powell specifies that "the pattern of investment in political growth will hold options open." This seems to mean that a state should not develop its coercive power to such an extent that newly mobilized groups are crushed before they ever have a chance to intervene in politics. The regulative and extractive capabilities should not grow until the state becomes totalitarian in form. Judging from our analysis of the present condition in non-Western political systems, few if any of them have generated enough power to run the risk of going this far. But the admonition is well made, all the same. Third, a good investment strategy should have a remedial element (another incrementalist note creeps in here) so that mistakes can be corrected, or, as Almond and Powell put it, the system can "cope with the disruptive consequences of modernizing processes." This recommendation is certainly in the best tradition of pluralistic, gradualist political theory, though, as Albert Hirschman points out below, many underdeveloped polities seem unable to respond to perceived mistakes in policy choices in time to do anything about them. Finally, our ideal development strategy should enable the decision-makers to cope with the impact of political change on extrapolitical sectors and institutions. Almond and Powell point to education, industrialization, the family, and the urban community as being especially sensitive to political investments, though the reader will of course be able to add others. A complete development strategy will be sensitive to these extrapolitical effects, and attempt to remedy any adverse consequences in the social or economic order, as they occur.

DEVELOPMENT TACTICIANS

ALBERT O. HIRSCHMAN

In contrast with some of the other observers of the development process we have considered, Albert O. Hirschman takes a decidedly narrow view of the nature of underdevelopment, and a clearly instrumental concept of what can be done to spur development. Since Hirschman's ideas are scattered throughout two works, we shall examine the two together, in the same sequence in which they appeared. The reader should note that Hirschman's ideas seem quite closely related to his experiences and field research in several Latin American countries, especially Colombia; his insights and propositions, however, have obvious application for development leaders around the world.

In his first work, *The Strategy of Economic Development,*[17] Hirschman presents us with his concept of the fundamental problem which causes a particular country to suffer from retarded development—the inability to make development decisions. While others may lament the lack of this resource or that advantage or the other psychocultural attribute as the principal obstacle blocking a nation's drive to development, Hirschman avers that the basic reason why nations do not develop is because they are unable to make decisions which induce development. This inability to make development decisions is, in turn, traced back to the predominant images of change—either group-related or ego-related—which inhibit the decision-making mechanisms of the country from bringing to bear the requisite amount of knowledge and commitment to make the proper judgments about the allocation of resources.

If the inability to make development decisions is the scarce resource in underdeveloped countries, then, the task of development is to find what Hirschman calls "inducement mechanisms" or "pacing devices" which will facilitate the making of such decisions. As he puts it, "Development theory and policy therefore face the task of examining under what conditions development decisions can be called forth in spite of these imperfections [in society and the political system], through pacing devices and inducement mechanisms."[18]

In approaching this problem, Hirschman makes use of the concept, familiar to economists, of "induced investment," or that investment which is called forth or stimulated or made easier as a result of the output of previous investment. In the same vein, then, Hirschman argues that ". . . the essence of development strategy consists in maximizing induced decision-making . . ."[19] The accumulated sequence of development decisions must have as their objective the facilitating of future decisions. In a sense, then, Hirschman is echoing a concern for decisional *capability*—albeit a capability much more broadly stated—which is contained in our opening chapters.

The remainder of *Strategy* demonstrates how Hirschman would implement such a development strategy. He concentrates on a search for those economic allocation decisions which make easier future choices about investment. For example, he is quite concerned with investing in those industries and sectors which maximize their *linkages* with other industries; that is, that either buy many products which are the output of other firms, or that sell many of their products to other firms in the country. Industries such as iron and steel, for example, have many such linkages (Hirschman labels them "backward" and "forward"), and therefore are good inducement mechanisms for calling forth more investment decisions.[20]

Several years later, in his second major analysis of economic decision-making, *Journeys toward Progress: Studies of Economic Policy-making in Latin America*,[21] Hirschman turned to a more general consideration of how development-oriented governments actually get around the obstacle of inadequate decision-making. In *Journeys,* Hirschman elaborates his theory of decisional underdevelopment by defining such underdevelopment in three areas: (1) an inability to select for immediate action those problems which are most severe; (2) an inability to learn from mistakes in policy, especially when the motivation to solve a problem outruns the knowledge needed to solve it; and (3) an inability to enact and implement needed reforms once they have been chosen.[22]

Appropriately, the first phase of a decision-making sequence where underdevelopment is made manifest is at the time when a political system's leaders select those problems which they are going to regard as critical, and demanding immediate attention. In contrast with more highly developed political systems, which enjoy many different avenues by which problems come to the attention of decision-makers, underdeveloped polities typically tend to be isolated from sources of information regarding which problems need attention and in what sequence. Frequently, then, the politics of problem selection in underdeveloped systems turns into a question of who, or which group, can threaten the system's stability most. Access to the weapons of violence, then, becomes the *sine qua non* of being recognized as a problem victim. And, as Hirschman continues, "Political development could . . . be described in terms of the emergence of a wide diversity of mechanisms and leverages, from elections to lobbying by pressure groups, through which individuals and groups can compel policymakers to pay attention to their problems."[23]

If political underdevelopment means a lack of channels available for decision-makers to recognize that problems exist, however, it makes little sense to urge these same policy-makers to work to create such channels. Rather, as Hirschman points out, the far more viable and useful strategy for development elites to adopt is acquiring indirect access for problem victims, through the clever use of several coping mechanisms.

One such coping device is the adept use of ideology to link two or more problems together, and thereby make possible the solution of a neglected problem by turning the political leaders' attention to it at the same time that they consider a favored problem. There is no clear need, Hirschman seems to be saying, for this linkage actually to exist; the only challenge confronting the policy-maker interested in reform is to create and make explicit the linkage. The neglected problem then rides into political prominence on the coattails of the obvious or already recognized problem.

Several other such adaptive mechanisms are discussed by Hirschman. Comprehensive planning, for instance, in the hands of a skillful reform-monger, becomes a device to obtain resources for one problem area, by linking the issue to a general set of economic or social projects described in a long-range planning document. In addition, the alert development leader will be quick to seize on a newly available policy tool, such as economic integration or central planning, to attack a problem which might actually be outside the purview of the new tool, but which had lain unsolved for a time, or which had actually resisted the attacks of more conventional political weapons. In these and other ways, Hirschman suggests methods by which the development elite might remedy (or at least offset) their country's inability to bring the right problems to the attention of the political system at the right time.

A second deficiency of politically underdeveloped countries is their inability to learn from their mistakes, and, consequently, their tendency to repeat the same mistaken policies in the face of their inability to resolve the issue in question. Here, the flaw in decision-making arises from the oft-encountered feature of politics in poor countries, that is, that motivation usually outruns understanding in problem-solving. Basically, problem-solving can begin in politics in one of two ways: either the solution can arise before the problem is recognized generally as being amenable to solution (understanding precedes motivation), or the sequence can be reversed (motivation coming before understanding). The latter sequence is more likely to be the case in developing countries as they seek to compress the development sequence of several generations into several decades (with a much less fortuitous environment).

When motivation precedes and exceeds understanding in problem-solving, the likely result is mistaken policy. Hirschman describes the decision-making sequence under these conditions as follows:

1. Recognition of problem under conditions of relatively great stress to "do something" to solve said problem.

2. Hasty, ill-considered, adaptive measure(s) taken.
3. Failure.
4. Call for comprehensive solution, coupled with criticism of previous efforts as being piecemeal or fragmented.
5. Borrowing of solution from abroad, which . . .
6. Removes the need for the country's own intellectuals to interact with the problem long enough to resolve it on the country's own terms.
7. All of the above steps lead the development elite to believe themselves to be "failure prone," to deprecate their own national style, and to escalate the ideological battle considerably.[24]

Hirschman argues, however, that this failure-prone style of problem-solving may not be such a hindrance to political development as it appears, if development elites know how to take advantage of such a style. For one thing, the wild swings in policy experiments may actually make sense in an underdeveloped country in the early stages of decision-making, especially when understanding of a problem is apt to be quite low or primitive. Further, if the policy-makers can depend on rapid and correct feedback on the results of their errors, then initially a failure-prone policy will at least provide them with valuable information about how to adjust for subsequent attacks against the problem. Finally, certain kinds of "utopian" policy-making, while not solving the problem at hand very effectively, can still leave behind their "marks" usually in the form of legislation or increased authority (at least "on paper") which can then be exploited by future reformers. The "failure-prone" decision-making style "becomes harmful," Hirschman adds,". . . only if it is persisted in after knowledge about the problem has accumulated and progress has been made in attacking it. The disregard of knowledge and the dismissal of progress implicit in the style then become wasteful. Naturally, it is not easy to tell when this stage is being reached.[25]

Hirschman's last point regarding an underdeveloped problem-solving style concerns the development elites' inability to enact and to implement needed reforms, after these reforms are perceived as necessary and beneficial. In this connection, Hirschman is quite concerned by the charge heard all over the developing world today that gradual, piecemeal reform will not accomplish anything; full, thorough revolution, with a consequent destruction of the old system, is the only way to accomplish the needed changes. Frequently, the grounds for these charges lie in the manifest inability of gradualists in developing countries to push through reforms in the face of entrenched, tradition-bound elites who refuse to divest themselves of long held power and wealth.

For these reforming elites, then, Hirschman has five recommendations, which will only be summarized here, due to lack of space:

1. Use violence productively. Hirschman argues that political violence, especially the kind which is not directed at overthrowing the government, but is only randomly directed (what he calls "decentralized violence") can actually serve a very valuable function in political reform. By signalling the decision-makers, violence can indicate where additional resources must be directed in order to alleviate problems. In addition, violence may reduce the magnitude of the problem, say, by redistributing resources like land, while at the same time putting pressure on elites to adjust more readily to demands for reform. Violence may also be used by astute development leaders to draw casual links between neglected and preferred problems, thereby facilitating attacks on the former.

2. Use crisis productively.   In the same vein, Hirschman calls on reform-mongers to take advantage of crisis periods to form, or to re-form, alliances, and thus to bring different combinations of power to bear on a problem. Crisis periods are noted for the increased fluidity of the political arena, when the perceptions of the actors are changed, often to remain uncertain about the future. The time is ripe, says Hirschman, to bring a new coalition of power sectors into action to achieve the solution to problems.

3. Use new problems productively.   The appearance of a new problem provides development elites with still another opportunity to change the constellation of political forces, by offering them the chance to negotiate with newly affected sectors previously not involved in a particular problem. Familiar techniques such as logrolling now become possible with the addition of a totally new problem to the political sphere; and the adept manipulation of the new issue may actually facilitate the solution of some old ones as well.

4. Mix antagonistic and nonantagonistic solutions to problems.   A nonantagonistic solution to a problem is one in which no single sector perceives a loss; an antagonistic solution, on the other hand, leaves some sector feeling injured. A good reform strategy will not depend on either one of these approaches exclusively, but will seek an appropriate "mix." Above all, if a proposed solution is apt to result in severe injury for one sector, the smart political leader will see to it that some other sector(s) accurately perceive major gains on their part.

5. Use alliances.   The best way to make alliances a good adjunct to policy reform strategy is to manipulate the issues with an eye to maximizing the alliance utility of each issue. This might mean breaking a big problem down into several small ones, to avoid alienating many people at once; it might mean consolidating problems into one general and comprehensive issue, to make the package attractive to many sectors. Flexibility in structuring the agenda of political action, however, is a key ingredient in reform-mongering, and, thus, in political development.

THE ILCHMAN/UPHOFF MODEL

As is the case with all the analysts we are examining in this section, Warren F. Ilchman and Norman Thomas Uphoff are vitally concerned with the inability of contemporary political science to address itself to the "real-world" problems of decision-makers in developing countries.[26] The two authors are, in fact, quite critical of just about every study of development problems which has appeared in recent years, primarily because they fail to provide much guidance for national leaders attempting to propel their states into modernity.

Systemic, or macro-analytical, studies, for instance, are inadequate, according to Ilchman and Uphoff, because they dictate the use of criteria which are not congruent with those of practicing politicians, and they fail to offer any convenient way to measure the cost or benefit of alternative policies. The analytical approach to development which centers on "stages" of growth similarly fails to tell the policy-maker when he has reached a certain stage, how to get from one to another, or how much of a certain capability is "enough." Still a third type of study, such as that by David McClelland,[27] misleads the policy-maker by focusing on solutions to development problems which can be undertaken only in a span of time measured by generations, when the real problems of development require immediate attention.

To remedy these, and other, defects in earlier social science analysis of development issues, Ilchman and Uphoff propose a framework for policy analysis which will include "some way of assessing the comparative efficiency of policy alternatives and some means of formulating priorities."[28] For the feature of realistic decision-making in a development setting is that of inadequacies—in time, resources, and information. As Hirschman pointed out, a useful development strategy is one which assumes these strict limitations, and builds in certain devices to facilitate the making of decisions.

Ilchman and Uphoff have reached rather deeply into the analytical kit of economics to come up with their proposed scheme. They begin their discussion with a description of the state (or political system) as essentially an organization designed to receive such inputs as demands and supports, to process these in some fashion, and to return these processed resources into the society by means of such output as controls, laws, expenditures, and so on. For Ilchman and Uphoff, politics is an exchange process, somewhat similar to that of the economic system, except for the obvious difference that the substances being exchanged are quite dissimilar. While the economic system exchanges scarce resources, goods, and services, the exchange patterns of the polity involve coercion, status, and access to power, as well as the more obvious resources such as wealth.

The exceptional political leader, for Ilchman and Uphoff, then, would be what they call a political entrepreneur, a person who manages to mobilize and invest political resources in order to maximize the capability of the state to perform the exchange function described above. In order to do this, these leaders must take into account the nature of the resources they possess, as well as those possessed by counter-elites, and the political propensities (or orientations to action) held by political sectors. Above all, the Ilchman and Uphoff model is one based on the ideas of conflict over scarce resources, and of rational choice among alternatives; and the bulk of their analysis is devoted to explicating how a statesman may make better choices. One advantage of the Ilchman and Uphoff approach is the variety of definitions of political development which it can encompass-definitions ranging from "an increased capacity to meet and induce changing and expanding demands" to "an increased number of political entrepreneurs."[29] Boiled down to its essentials, however, a politically developed state is defined by Ilchman and Uphoff as one in which political leaders are better able to make correct and intelligent choices as they go about expanding the resources of the state, and the state's capacity to act.

Along the road to this expanded capability, the political entrepreneur of Ilchman and Uphoff encounters a series of analytical and political difficulties which the authors hope to smooth over by means of their techniques of decision-making. First, our entrepreneur must master the intricacies of political resources management, including an understanding of such questions as what political resources are, how they can be spent, wasted, and recovered, and how they can be depreciated. The leader should also be concerned with weighing opportunity costs of certain investments (the value of alternative competing investments), as well as fiscal policy, taxation, budgeting, and planning, and other forms of monetary management which the authors apply to political resources.

A major difficulty surfaces at this point, a difficulty which the authors recognize, but which they admit is currently beyond their grasp. We are referring to the problem of valuation, or the lack of a political currency. Before one can propose a policy-making scheme based on economic techniques, he must first solve the central problem of how to weigh or evaluate competing plans, strategies, investments, resources, and so forth. In order to know whether or not a large army is a better investment than a dam, a leader must be able to calculate the relative values of political stability and flood control. In the absence of a technique for attaching values to such items, development elites fall back on intuition, guesswork, experience, and chance—exactly the traps from which Ilchman and Uphoff wish to extract them. But, as Hirschman quite correctly points out, one of the key measures of an underdeveloped country is its inability to muster the intelligence necessary to make the right choice. If leaders could make decisions with the precision required by the Ilchman and Uphoff model, then (according to Hirschman) the country would no longer be classified as underdeveloped.

Political resource management is only one of several analytical devices which Ilchman and Uphoff recommend for decision-makers. Development leaders must also be conscious of imbalances in the supply and demand of political resources, for these imbalances could lead to political inflation or deflation, with consequences even more grave than those which accompany the economic kind. Here, the concept of the exchange rate of various resources becomes very important. Since political resources cannot be valued; that is, they cannot be given a *price,* the only way we can estimate demand for a resource is by observing how much of other resources certain sectors (such as labor or university students) would be willing to exchange for the original item. In approaching the issue of political values in this manner, we think that Ilchman and Uphoff have helped clarify the way in which most resource acquisition and allocation decisions are actually made—through marginal comparisons and incremental decisions. We shall return to this point in Chapter Ten.

As they wind through their analytical scheme, however, it appears as if Ilchman and Uphoff are seeking something more than simply marginal comparisons of utility of resources; they are looking for ways to utilize cost-benefit analyses in political choice. Again the problem of paucity of information arises. If Ilchman and Uphoff aspire to precise cost-benefit calculations of ambiguously valued project comparisons (such as the army versus dam example cited above), this author feels that their reach has exceeded their grasp; and, although this justifies the positing of a political "heaven" sometime, development leaders must act in the here and now. Data to flesh out such an ambitious political feasibility study are simply not available, at least not at a cost acceptable to development elites who must act under the pressure of time.[30]

A final area of analysis which a political entrepreneur must master involves the all-important issue of political investment, or how to deploy those resources the state now has in order to maximize such resources at some future date. Here the Ilchman and Uphoff model begins to pay off with some valuable recommendations on beneficial investments. Essentially, there are four areas in which a state can make a productive investment: (1) stability (via coercion and regulation); (2) legitimacy (by means of education, ideological uses of the mass media, and so on); (3) solidarity (investments which seek to alter a strong sectional or parochial loyalty to one to the state); and (4) political and administrative infrastructure.

Inasmuch as Ilchman and Uphoff consider infrastructure investment as of prime importance, they devote more space to their discussion of this area; and their conclusions constitute one of the most valuable parts of the work. Institution-building, or the strengthening of political and administrative organizations, increases political efficiency by making it possible for the state to accomplish the same tasks with fewer resources, or by enabling it to accomplish more tasks with the same resources. Institution-building accomplishes this feat by increasing predictability (thereby facilitating compliance with the expenditure of fewer resources), and mobility (thereby making it easier to use the same resources for different tasks in different times and sites). The total effect is to weld the political infrastructure into a more efficient network of devices for assigning priorities and allocating resources. Such infrastructure as bureaucracies, political parties, auxiliary organizations like labor unions, local and regional government units, and economic development planning agencies are all examples of the best way in which a development elite can begin to invest in projects which *increase* the political capability of the state. The relative merits of each such project are displayed by Ilchman and Uphoff in an elaborate chart much too detailed to be summarized here; the interested reader is urged to consult the original work for further information.

In a closing chapter, Ilchman and Uphoff put forth a convincing argument for their brand of "reform-mongering," an argument based on gradualism, on fragmented solutions to problems in political reality, and on differences in available time. The authors are saying to the development leaders around the world that they should be concentrating their efforts in political investments which will begin to show a payoff in a relatively brief span of time, inasmuch as this is the best means of determining what adjustments and corrections there must be in policy. Confronted with a choice between two solutions to a problem—Solution A, which offers to resolve the problem completely but only after 20 years; and Solution B, which promises only to erode the problem, but to accomplish this erosion within five years—the development leader should adopt Solution B. Not only will he then be able to take full advantage of the insight gained during the first five years to move toward more erosion of the difficulty later; but the initial favorable results will buy valuable time politically with which to experiment later. The reader will note the similarity of this proposal with those of Hirschman discussed above.

Ilchman and Uphoff maintain that their system of applying economic concepts to politics offers the best means of evaluating competing development projects, and the most satisfactory technique for indicating to a development leader where he should be investing his resources. We have already offered some comment on the problems encountered by one who tried to put some real data into their analytical framework. This caveat aside, however, the authors of *The Political Economy of Change* have made great strides toward a more rational strategy for development.

HOWARD WRIGGINS

Perhaps the most instrumental or tactical analysis of political development to appear in recent years has been that written by W. Howard Wriggins.[31] As the subtitle of the book suggests, Wriggins is concerned with resolving the most crucial problem facing development elites today—how to survive in power.

After noting the ease and rapidity with which individuals lose power in developing states, Wriggins makes explicit his focus on political survival, the initial imperative confronted by development elites. Obviously, a reformist leader cannot begin to undertake any of the grandiose plans, or even the most minute incremental change, without occupying the pinnacle of power in his country.

It would appear at first glance that Wriggins' approach is excessively narrow, concerned as it is with simply the acquisition and continued enjoying of power. A careful reading of the study shows, however, that much more is implied by the approach. For Wriggins is clearly aware that, while the struggle for power goes on at the heart of the political arena, the ways in which the struggle is resolved, the strategies and tactics which politicians use to win their battles, are of prime importance to the development of other spheres of political life. Although the regulative capability (to use our terminology) is uppermost in the mind of a development leader, certainly other capabilities intrude into his calculus about how best to secure his position. As Wriggins puts it,

> How leaders tackle their problem of aggregating power in order to ensure their own political survival has an effect upon the way the polity develops. . . . The manner of their contention affects the political institutions and practices they leave behind. The more clearly leaders perceive the costs and advantages of the way they carry on their political competition, the more aware they may be of the possible side effects and the heritage they are preparing for their successors.[32]

The foremost chore facing any unsure development leader nowadays is what Wriggins calls "the aggregation of power." This task consists of identifying in society certain individuals who stand out as powerful because they influence others, and in drawing these individuals into coalitions, alliances, or power combinations around the government and its leadership, thereby adding to the latter's power. The more the coalition of alliance swells with powerful individuals from the nation's extrapolitical community (the "sectors" of Ilchman and Uphoff), the more power is added to that of the government.

Yet, as Wriggins correctly notes, in most developing states, these individuals who would be co-opted into the political elite usually retain a considerable amount of autonomy in the face of a (at first, at least) relatively weak governing coalition. The freshly created alliance, then, is apt to be rather shaky, and to fall apart with very little pressure. Political instability and political underdevelopment, then, tend to be coequal parts of the same vicious circle, as weak coalitions lead to disruption, and vice versa, in an endless agony of state inefficacy.

To this conflictual and uncertain enterprise then, successful political leaders have brought a series of strategies which have proven useful in aggregating power. Wriggins devotes the bulk of his book to a discussion of these strategies, which we shall summarize below.

1. Project the Personality.   The charismatic leader has frequently been considered an indispensable ingredient in successful statecraft, at least in the early days of political development. As Wriggins points out, the reason for this is often that there is nothing else so broad and all-encompassing in a new nation to rally disparate social forces in a more or less common effort. We might add that our earlier analysis of political culture in the non-Western world seems to offer a fertile ground for charisma to take root. In any case, charisma must eventually give way to other strategies for its long-range political potential is slight; and charismatic figures frequently find that they have created a monster that they cannot control after setting it in motion.

2. Build an Organization.   Many successful political reformers have based their long-range strength on a personal organization which they have built to channel the activity of their followers into a single force for acquiring and holding power. In many cases, this organization has been the personalist political party; in a few notable cases, the personality aspect has dwindled after the death of the founder, leaving a well entrenched institutionalized force for political action. In other instances, peasant leagues, student unions, military reform cliques or lodges, or bureaucracies have fulfilled this function. Wriggins notes that the organizing of politics is usually the base from which other reforming efforts are launched; but, personal, parochial, and tribal animosities and hostilities being what they are in much of Asia and Africa, organization-building proves to be quite a difficult task.[33]

3. Promote an Ideology.   Still another successful technique for wielding power in developing countries lies in the ideology formulated by the developing elite. As has been noted elsewhere, rapidly developing cultures are particularly vulnerable to ideological attractions because of the massive psychological uprooting which must occur during modernization. Thus, the promotion of a new ideology is often seen as a useful device to smooth the transition to modernity while, at the same time, drawing into the government coalition groups of divergent political actors who otherwise would have little in common. At the most simple level, the ideology of nationalism appears to be the most powerful of these ideas to employ in this regard; other, more complex ideologies appear to create as much havoc as order by aggravating old social wounds. We can see, then, that the principal disadvantage of ideology as a strategy lies in its offending so many potential supporters of a regime, unless it descends to the level of the least common denominator, at which time it usually becomes relatively useless.

4, 5. Reward the Faithful, and Intimidate the Opponent.   In the very broadest sense, this admonition from Wriggins seems to encompass virtually everything that a statesman does, or fails to do, for they all can be construed as either a reward or a punishment, for either compliance or disobedience. What Wriggins has in mind, however, are those acts taken by leaders to wield the more material weapons possessed by the state to aggregate power. What are at stake are wealth, personal liberty, and (in the extreme) life itself, as the state which has no other levers of power will inevitably fall back on these crudest of methods by which man manipulates man. It does seem to be the case, however, that certain development-minded individuals have been forced —either by circumstance, or by predisposition—to employ these techniques as the core of their strategy. Corruption and the unscrupulous buying of support, on the one hand, and police terror and concentration camps, on the other, have girded up more than one "reformer" in the non-Western world. It should be obvious, however, that the advantages of this sort of strategy are almost entirely short-run; no political system can call itself "developed" in any sense if it must rely on brute force or bribe to remain in power.

6. Develop the Economy. Economic development is often mentioned along with political development, as if the two were more or less the same phenomena. In Wriggins' treatment, economic development becomes simply another means by which leaders of political orders manipulate their slim resources to aggregate power. This may help to explain why so many economic development projects have such a fragile economic rationale—the road which connects the sea port with the plantation of the president's brother, for instance; or the housing development put in the precinct which gave the president his large majority in the last election. But other economic projects do have both a political and an economic component; roads, for example, open up the interior of the country not only to new goods but to new ideas; schools can be used not only to train industrial workers but to exalt the country's leadership. And, most important, a rising *per capita* income, a growing economic pie, makes it easier for the development leaders to make difficult extractive and distributive decisions.

7. Expand Political Participation. For many observers, the expansion of political participation, the mobilization of many new individuals into the political process, must go hand in hand with strategy number two, organization. For, it seems difficult to imagine the mobilization of new actors into politics without giving them an institutional home to go to when they arrive. The result of failing to do this would be street riots and mobs of angry citizens storming the capital. By the same token, some analysts of political change see an expansion of the political arena as a "given," a factor which will occur whether the leaders want it or not. The only thing they can do is provide the institutional channels through which the newly mobilized voices will find a response.[34]

8. Use Foreign Policy. We have discussed earlier (see Chapter Four) the complex interplay between political development and a nation's foreign adventures. Briefly, to recapitulate, a development elite may feel that it has to initiate some kind of foreign "confrontation" in order to divert the attention of their discontented populace away from the real problems of their society. Although this policy may also have its short-term appeal, over the long run it will almost always prove counter-productive. In fact, a more reliable prescription for development leaders seems to be to avoid foreign entanglements as much as possible in order to turn their scarce resources to more productive activities internally.

Having produced an impressive list of strategic requirements for an aspiring development elite, Wriggins proceeds in his final chapter to discuss some of the complexities of development strategies, again defined in the context of political survival. We are concerned here with, first, the linkages between certain strategies and coalition-building; second, linkages between and among strategies; third, the substitutability of strategies; and fourth, the linkages between strategies and both long- and short-range goals.

We have already seen a few of the advantages and disadvantages of some of the strategies Wriggins describes; a full listing would be beyond the scope of this brief summary. A few are included just to give the "flavor" of Wriggins' analysis. For instance, projecting the personality is a very popular approach at first, but difficult to sustain over time. Building an organization has more long-range validity, but the value depends greatly on the *type* of party organized, and on whether it can survive the demise of the founder. Economic development is hard to begin; but, once begun, it holds a little promise for everyone. Expanded participation offers increased strength in the rural sectors; but, unless organizational changes are made to absorb these individuals, the net result will be chaos. Ideologies are either mutually contradictory, or useless, unless they can bring disparate tribal or ethnic groups together under the banner of nationalism.

Wriggins goes on to discuss some of the interdependencies of various strategies, as if to indicate that no leader can depend on just one single strategy in isolation. Rewarding the faithful and punishing the opposition requires the building of an organization, at the least a police and military bureaucracy, and a "spoils"-type political party based on patronage. The building of an organization frequently needs a helping hand from a charismatic leader, especially in the early days. Economic development needs a bureaucracy to plan and implement projects and expenditures. The projection of a personality is often linked with the promotion of an ideology. In much the same vein, some strategies may be substituted for others, as, for example, the case of a charismatic leader substituting for a political party; but not much can be said about this until we confront the question of the goals of a political leader.

As Wriggins concludes, some strategies are definitely of greater value than others, depending on whether the development elite is thinking in terms of short-range or long-range goals. The defense of national independence against foreign threat, for instance, is probably going to be a rather short-term, crisis goal, demanding the employment of foreign policy and the projection of a charismatic personality to hold the country's loyalties while under attack. The problem of social tranformation, however, will require a much longer effort, stretching over decades; organization, economic development, and the expansion of political participation will all be important ingredients in this case. While Wriggins' analysis does not say much about goal selection, it is clear that he believes that, in the final analysis, how a leader goes about keeping himself in power depends on the goals he has set for himself beyond the simple aggregation of power.

While each of the five models of development described in this chapter is rich in its treatment of a very complex social phenomenon, and while each contributes significantly to an overall view of politics in developing states, we feel that some attempt at synthesis should be made. In the following chapter, we shall advance a view of development strategy which seeks to incorporate certain details and features of each of the polar approaches. From the cosmic perspective, we hope to draw a better understanding of how developing elites can fix their goals more accurately; from the tactician "school" of development, perhaps we can fashion techniques for guiding the process of developmental change along incremental lines. We reach this synthesis, however, only after first considering a somewhat less explicit, but nonetheless extremely valuable, approach to the engineering of development.

CHAPTER NOTES

1. James S. Coleman, "The Development Syndrome: Differentiation-Equality-Capacity," in Leonard Binder, *et al., Crises and Sequences in Political Development* (Princeton, N.J.: Princeton University Press, 1971), pp. 73-74.
2. Coleman, p. 73.
3. Warren F. Ilchman and Norman Thomas Uphoff, *The Political Economy of Change* (Berkeley: University of California Press, 1969), pp. 8-12.
4. W. Howard Wriggins, *The Ruler's Imperative: Strategies for Political Survival in Asia and Africa* (New York: Columbia University Press, 1969), pp. 91-93.
5. Robert Dahl, *Who Governs?* (New Haven: Yale University Press, 1961), p. 96. Quoted in Wriggins, p. 92.
6. Wriggins, pp. 92-93.
7. Binder, *et al., Crises and Sequences*
8. Coleman, pp. 73-100.
9. Sidney Verba, "Sequences and Development," in Binder, *et al.* pp. 283-316, esp. 292-94.
10. Joseph LaPalombara, "Distribution: A Crisis of Resource Management," in Binder, pp. 233-82, esp. 256-66.
11. For another detailed analysis of development sequences, see Eric A. Nordlinger, "Political Development: Time Sequences and Rates of Change," *World Politics,* XX, 3 (April, 1968): 494-520.
12. Gabriel Almond and G. Bingham Powell, *Comparative Politics: A Developmental Approach* (Boston: Little, Brown, paper ed., 1966).
13. Since we have made the capabilities concept the core of our definition of political development, and have dealt with it extensively in Part One, we will not dwell on this issue at length here. It should be noted, however, that our formulation is somewhat simpler than that of Almond and Powell, in that we have proceeded on the assumption that improvement in capabilities should encompass all other improvements, including those at the other two levels, to be discussed subsequently.
14. Almond and Powell, pp. 317-19.
15. This entire technique is described in Almond and Powell, pp. 328-29.
16. Almond and Powell, pp. 330-31.
17. Albert O. Hirschman, *The Strategy of Economic Development* (New Haven: Yale University Press, paper, 1961).
18. Hirschman, *Strategy,* p. 26.
19. Hirschman, *Strategy,* p. 44.
20. Hirschman, *Strategy,* p. 106.
21. Albert O. Hirschman, *Journeys toward Progress: Studies of Economic Policy-Making in Latin America* (New York: Twentieth Century Fund, 1963).

22. Most of these insights are contained in the final chapters of Hirschman's book, *Journeys,* pp. 227-97.

23. Hirschman, *Journeys,* p. 230.

24. The reader will be able to see certain similarities between Hirschman's description of a "failure-prone" decision-making system, and a failure-threatened political actor, as discussed in Chapter Seven.

25. Hirschman, *Journeys,* p. 242.

26. Ilchman and Uphoff, *The Political Economy of Change.* For a critique of the Ilchman/Uphoff book, as well as that of Wriggins, see Raymond F. Hopkins, "Securing Authority: The View from the Top," *World Politics,* XXIV, 2 (January, 1972): 271-92.

27. David McClelland, *The Achieving Society* (New York: Free Press, 1967).

28. Ilchman and Uphoff, *Political Economy,* p. 11.

29. Ilchman and Uphoff, p. 48.

30. The author had the pleasure a few years ago to work on an economic feasibility study of a road-port project in Honduras under contract to USAID. His major task was evaluating the impact of land tenure patterns and other nonmarket factors on the economic utilization of land in the area to be newly opened. Although the final analysis concluded with a "cost-benefit" ratio which was quite impressive, it did so by explicitly ignoring the author's input into the report. The experience left him with a healthy respect for the problems of conducting cost-benefit studies on politically related topics in developing countries. See Continental-Allied Co., Inc. *Northeastern Honduras Transportation Program* (Washington: Continental-Allied, 1965).

31. W. Howard Wriggins, *The Ruler's Imperative: Strategies for Political Survival in Asia and Africa.*

32. Wriggins, p. 5.

33. This strategy is dealt with extensively in Samuel P. Huntington's *Political Order in Changing Societies* (New Haven: Yale University Press, 1968).

34. This seems to be the argument made by Samuel P. Huntington, *Political Order.* See Chapter Ten, below.

Chapter 10

TOWARDS AN INCREMENTAL VIEW OF DEVELOPMENT

In this, the final, chapter of our excursion into developmental politics in the non-Western world, we shall present several features of an appropriate development "strategy," one which hopefully will avoid some of the difficulties described in Chapter Nine. As we saw there, one class of development techniques—the systemic—focuses on the ultimate directions of the development process, without much tactical assistance for the statesmen who must guide the process. On the other side of the coin are the development tacticians whose view of the long-range is often obscured by the minute details of political manipulation. Before we develop our own approach to development, which will build on the decision-making theory of incrementalism, we shall examine another effort at synthesis, that of Samuel P. Huntington, whose work differs slightly from those we have considered previously, but which yet makes valuable contributions to the science of development strategy and tactics.

SAMUEL P. HUNTINGTON

In explicating his primary thesis, which underlies the entire argument of *Political Order in Changing Societies,*[1] Huntington makes use of an observation of Alexis de Tocqueville to the effect that, "If men are to remain civilized or to become so, the art of associating together must grow and improve in the same ratio in which the equality of conditions is increased." This means for Huntington that a stable development policy depends upon the ability of the development elites to strengthen or create institutions so durable and so flexible that they can absorb the newly mobilized groups whose entrance into politics marks the beginning of modernization. Huntington equates modernization with a rapid expansion of the political arena, to bring into the process new faces and voices with new demands. As far as development itself is concerned, this is defined as an enhanced ability of the polity to respond to these demands. Further, none of these changes can be accomplished smoothly and peacefully without the growth of political institutions, particularly the political party.

Early in the study, Huntington attacks head-on the problem of goals by offering his version of that elusive concept, "the public interest." In keeping with his general approach, he defines the public interest as being "whatever strengthens governmental institutions." The public interest is best served when the nation enjoys a political organization which is capable of responding to demands, of making decisions, of formulating policies, and of enforcing laws once made. In other words, it is in the public interest for the government to be able to *govern;* with this capability entrenched, other definitions of the public will, such as popular sovereignty, flow naturally. Thus, development statesmen can best justify their developmental policies as aiming at a government with capability to perform such tasks as the society deems necessary.

For Huntington, the key political institution is, as we stated, the political party. The modern party, based on the expression of common interests and the sharing of efforts to have those interests accommodated in politics, has grown and flourished in a manner which parallels that of the modern political system itself. Whereas in 1800 the only political parties as such were found in the United States, by 1900 they had spread throughout the Western world. And, by 1970, many non-Western states could exhibit at least the rudimentary beginnings of a modern political party system.

In arriving at his conclusions about the critical role performed by the political party in modernization, Huntington first analyzes four separate approaches to political development, which we could label "strategies" for our purposes here. Each of these strategies is concerned with meeting and resolving three recurring problems which characterize all development processes.[2] First, power must be concentrated. Huntington has found that policy innovation varies more or less directly with the concentration of power; that government innovates best which has most power concentrated in central, nation-level institutions. Second, the system must develop the capability to assimilate the new social forces which are created and drawn into politics by modernization and industrialization. This issue involves the distribution of power. Third, the development statesmen must create or expand power, so that they not only change the relative distribution of power between sectors, but they also increase the total quantum of power available to competing political sectors. How four different types of political leaders have met and dealt with these three problems constitutes the bulk of Huntington's book.

Huntington first looks at the modernizing efforts of several traditional monarchs who have launched development processes in their countries even at the risk of losing power as a result. Traditional monarchies are somewhat scarce in the twentieth century, but the problems they have faced in attempting to modernize illustrate well the difficulties of any modernizing regime which seeks to preserve a major traditional sector of society. The few historical examples of this kind of regime would include those in Saudi Arabia, Iran, Afghanistan, Ethiopia, Morocco, and (perhaps) Greece, plus several smaller principalities.

Modernization typically begins for traditional monarchs when the monarchy finds itself under external attack, either by ideas, or by the armed forces of a foreign power. Confronted with this challenge, the traditional monarch determines that his regime cannot survive without improving its regulative capability, and stemming the foreign attempt to penetrate its society. In the course of this modernization, certain social forces are created and directed into the political sphere which render the monarch's position particularly precarious. The monarch responds to these challenges through the performance of certain tasks.

The first task involves the centralization of power in the regime, which the monarch accomplishes by mobilizing the army, the civil bureaucracy, or some organization loyal to him personally. The prior dispersion of power—whether feudal or bureaucratic—determines the ease or difficulty with which this first task is completed, and the directions in which the monarch must take his administration.

As a second task, and directly related to the first, the monarch discovers that he must organize the framework of the political system, or organize the state. This effort revolves around the building of a political and administrative infrastructure, the passing and enforcing of laws governing distribution of resources, and so on. This same stage has been considered central to the development effort by many other observers of the non-Western political process.[3]

Third, once the initial impetus of the drive to modernization has worn off, the ruler finds himself confronted with several dilemmas of power; the final satisfactory solution of the strategy of development hinges on a resolution of these dilemmas. First, the ruler faces the choice between liberty versus equality. If the monarch wishes to reform society and make it more nearly egalitarian, he finds that he must obtain and wield near-dictatorial power; if he chooses to act as a constitutional ruler, then he discovers that he lacks the authority necessary to deal with the social rigidities of his country. Naturally, the aristocracy of the country presses upon him to adopt a self-limiting role, for this insures a weak and halfhearted attempt at reform. The modernizing monarch can call upon support from certain reform-minded social classes, such as the bureaucracy and the army, or from foreign powers.

The other two dilemmas illustrate more or less the same approach to reform in developing monarchies. The monarch is pressed, for example, to open up the political process and admit new participants, on the grounds that this will lead to more thorough social change; yet, as Huntington argues, until the political institutions are built to accommodate these participants, their mobilization can only be disruptive. Here again, the feudal (dispersed) model of power distribution seems to offer a less destabilizing method of solving this problem than does the centralized or bureaucratic style, which may open up the system more quickly, but in a less institutionalized way. Finally, the ruler faces the ultimate choice—whether to succeed in modernizing the country to the point of eliminating his role and his power, or whether to try to survive in power. According to Huntington, this is the most difficult step of all, usually leading to some kind of constitutional monarchy or modified popular regime; but, the point is, very few modernizing monarchs have shown the ability to be able to ride the tiger of reform. The historical record of these regimes does not offer much confidence that this style of change is very productive of success.

The second style of political development which Huntington examines is engineered by a military dictator, recently come to power via a coup d'etat, who wishes to modernize his country as rapidly as possible. Huntington's argument can be summed up best by linking his notions of political mobilization to the question of military intervention in politics.

Radical military regimes, such as those of Juan Peron of Argentina, come into being in the midst of extremely rapid social and political mobilization. This mobilization produces such a massive influx of new participants into the political process that the country's political institutions are overwhelmed, order breaks down, and the army takes over in a coup to preserve the nation. Once in power, the army's leaders try to absorb the newly mobilized participants. At that point, the regime becomes radicalized, and sets off on a path of continued and, indeed, even accelerated social change. As mobilization increases, the army typically fails to provide new channels through which the new participants can move into the political process, while the former comrades of the military leadership become somewhat more conservative. The latter group now begins to see that the military has overstepped its bounds, and is trying to remake society in an authoritarian fashion. The result is a counter-coup launched by the more conservative forces in the military establishment. If steps are not taken at this point, or earlier, to construct some alternatives to a continuation of this vicious circle, radical and conservative military leaders will alternate in power through extra legal means, with the consequent disruption of society and failure of the government to address itself to the real problem—how to adapt to the newly aroused masses, and their shrill demands for state action.

As we might expect, the proper steps for a radical military regime to take once in power would aim at the reestablishment of a civil government bolstered by a well organized political party. The military leaders can easily take the lead in organizing such a party; indeed, the success of military regimes in Mexico and Turkey can be traced precisely to such organizing efforts. The extent to which the army can accomplish this feat seems directly related to the degree to which society is already mobilized when the radical militarists come to power. If they are dealing with a relatively inert social order, with mobilization still in its beginning stages, then a political party system can more readily be fashioned which will accommodate these new actors-to-be; if, on the other hand, social mobilization and political awareness are already at a fairly high level, then the military could well find that their tasks of party-building can be accomplished only over a very long time, and accompanied by a high degree of coercion.

The discussion of radical military regimes brings out one of the limitations of Huntington's analysis; namely, what produces a lack of social or political institutions in the first place. For instance, he makes the point that "For a society to escape from praetorianism requires both the coalescence of urban and rural interests and the creation of new political institutions."[4] Yet, we are not led into a discussion of why these institutions seem easier to build in some countries than in others, why the "urban and rural forces" find it easier to coalesce in some societies than in others. Answers to these questions can only be found beneath the systemic overlay of human behavior; and a focus on the party *qua* organization does little to help us understand why people find "the art of association" such a difficult objective to attain.

Huntington's third style of development is that which he calls the revolutionary modernizer. The revolutionary is usually a leader who knows how to take advantage of an especially volatile situation in the growth and expansion of the political arena. As the political system modernizes, there will be inevitably a certain degree of stress engendered in urban areas. Out of the disruption —both physical and psychological—of rapid urbanization come three emergent political forces which can supply the spark for revolution—slum dwellers, organized labor, and the intelligentsia (usually university students). Of these three groups, the students constitute the greatest potential threat to the established order, especially if their university is located in the capital city. Not even the students can bring about a true revolution, however, without the assistance of the peasants. Truly modernizing revolutions find strength in rural areas, as the peasants supply the manpower for the change—the guns, if violent; the votes, if nonviolent. Without the peasants, the students are doomed to failure; with the peasants, a revolution can be made.

But can the modernizing trend set in motion by the revolution last? Can revolutionary development be made durable? Only, according to Huntington, if two things are done. First, the new regime must institute a complete land tenure reform program which redistributes farm land to the peasants on whose backs they rode to power. This explains the central importance of land reform programs throughout the non-Western world, even in states which are not avowedly revolutionary. Second, in keeping with his general approach, Huntington calls on the revolutionary leadership to create a new mass party which will provide avenues of access for the newly mobilized peasants.

In this regard, the ideal type of revolutionary modernizer for Huntington was Lenin, who foresaw the need for organization of the political power he had unleashed through the Bolshevik revolution. The real genius of Communist politics, the real contribution of the Communist movement to national development, lies not in the way in which the Communist seize power, or in the manner in which they destroy the existing order. Any violent force can shatter a fragile and shaky edifice. The great revelation about Communist governments is that they can organize and channel popular participation so readily through their party apparatus. Thus, we see Lenin contradicting the famous Marxist dictum about the revolution arising spontaneously; instead, the purpose of the party was to create "an organization of revolutionaries" which would lead the rebellion, and organize the power of the new government once in control of the machinery of the state. If there is a difference between successful revolutionaries and modernizers, on the one hand, like Lenin, Castro, or Ho Chi Minh, and failures on the other, like Trotsky or Che Guevara, it is probably the relatively greater ability of the former to attend to the problems of statecraft in the wake of the revolution, and to build the organization which will enable them to extend the gains of the revolution throughout the nation.

The bulk of successful development elites are apparently found, however, among Huntington's fourth group—the moderate reformers. Although development via moderate reform is rather more difficult than the shattering of the old order by means of revolution, it is still quite a bit more productive of ultimate change. The problem is that moderate reform-mongering requires much greater political skill; and the reform statesman does not escape the imperative of development—organize a political party.

The reformer in a rapidly changing polity is frequently caught in a trap of opposing social forces which are brought into action precisely because of the reforms he had initiated. In the cities, slight reforms often serve as a catalyst to bring the students or the slum dwellers out into the streets to challenge the fragile development effort before it has really had a chance to blossom. As we noted before, if the intellectuals are able to rally the peasants and weld a coalition out of these disparate forces, then the development government is most certainly teetering on the brink of disaster. The only way to forestall this is through more reform—particularly reform in the area of land tenure. By means of an aggressive land reform program, the peasants can be swayed to support rather than attack the government, the intellectuals will be powerless to do more than disrupt the traffic patterns of the capital city, and the development reformers can remain in power to carry out their more substantial changes. What is involved, obviously, is a very delicate issue of the timing of reform.

Land reform, in any case, often becomes the central issue in moderate development politics. Huntington cites several preconditions which should smooth the land reform effort; the reader will note that many of these preconditions—structural or processual—have been discussed earlier in other contexts as being necessary for political development:

1. Concentrated power.
2. A modernizing elite.
3. A powerful executive, with no parliamentary intervention.
4. A break in the facade of unity maintained by the rural aristocracy.
5. A capable bureaucracy to administer the program.
6. An organization to bring the peasants into the political process.

As usual, Huntington manages to bring the discussion of development strategies back around to the question of political parties; in fact, this conscious focus on a single organizational approach to development makes his book a valuable contribution to the strategic literature of political change. At the close of the study, one is left with several good ideas about how to keep development from breaking apart in the face of multiple threat from newly mobilized masses of political actors. *Political Order in Changing Societies* does not say a great deal, however, about how to expand the ability of the state to accomplish other tasks apart from organizing participation. In fact, one has the distinct impression that Huntington feels that there *are* no other tasks beyond that of organization; a development elite with a good bureaucracy and a good political party is capable of meeting and resolving most if not all of the dilemmas of development strategy. This book has argued, however, that there are still an enormous number of choices to be evaluated, of problems to be resolved, of resource allocation decisions to be made, and so on. While Huntington offers some valuable ideas on how to maintain stability in the midst of a development process, his analysis does not contribute equally to a better understanding of the problem of development strategy per se. For a further consideration of that issue, in the light of the above-mentioned strategic analyses, we shall turn now to development seen as an incremental process.

AN INCREMENTAL VIEW OF DEVELOPMENT

In his discussion of the tactics and strategies of political development as moderate reform, Samuel Huntington describes with approval the approach of the great reform leader of Turkey, Mustafa Kemal (Ataturk).[5] Kemal employed what Huntington labels a judicious combination of Fabian gradualism in his strategy, and a sudden *blitzkrieg* in his tactics; the result was a relatively smooth, constant movement of political change which vaulted Turkey from a decadent monarchy to a liberal republic in the space of several decades.

As Huntington tells the story, Kemal came to power in full recognition of the monumental task that lay before him in order to modernize his nation. Rather than proclaim the gigantic goal of national modernization, Kemal preferred to slice the political issue into several smaller questions or sectors of activity, and to press forward with speed and insistence in each of these sectors in sequence. The sequence Kemal chose, apparently the result of conscious and rational calculation, according to Huntington, was unity-political authority-cultural modernization-economic growth. That is, Kemal decided to attack the question of definition of the national community first. Once finished, this struggle was followed by the establishment of the full authority of his political regime, which he accomplished with scant regard for the niceties of the democratic process. Then, cultural modernization was pressed, and the religious, educational and cultural framework of Turkish society was Westernized and secularized. When this had been accomplished, economic planning led to vigorous development.

In each case of reform, Kemal managed the issue in such a manner that the changes he desired were rammed through the national parliament with a minimum of debate, and, at times, under conditions of stress—either real or imagined. There was little public discussion of issues or suggested solutions, and the arena of consideration of policy alternatives was deliberately restricted. Kemal was the master of the political *blitz* once his decisions had been made. Through this technique, he was able to minimize opposition to his proposed policy choices.

Of much greater importance than the tactical *blitz,* however, was the incremental strategy adopted in the beginning: for it was only by dividing the problem of political development into several much smaller segments that Kemal was able to neutralize the broad opposition to such change. At each stage of the process of development, Kemal initiated his development plan while professing that he had no further intentions to make additional changes. Each small change was portrayed as independent of the others, and as marking the extent of governmental intervention in a particularly sensitive or controversial area. By means of this strategy, Kemal reduced opposition on each issue, and was able to fashion appropriate coalitions to support each major step.

It is important, however, that we try to keep in perspective the extent to which Kemal foresaw the direction of these developments, and planned consciously the exact strategy which carried the day for his view of a developed Turkey. Huntington argues that the Kemalist strategy was consciously planned in advance by farsighted leaders; and, indeed, Kemal attempts to leave that impression in his later speeches. We may be permitted some skepticism in the matter, however. In a recent analysis of Kemal as statesman, Dankwart Rustow shows how few of the proposed changes which Kemal steered through

Turkish politics were actually new with the leader; in fact, all of them—a centralized, secular political authority, Westernized dress and education, economic growth—had been widely discussed by Turkish intellectuals in the decade following 1908.[6] Moreover, Kemal tended to interpret all the changes involved in modernization as merely another facet of the struggle which brought him to power in the first place; that is, to drive foreigners out of Turkey, to restore Turkish boundaries, and to reestablish Turkey's place of prestige and power in the international system. Whatever changes he deemed necessary in the social, political, or economic spheres to accomplish this goal, Kemal pursued, albeit in an incremental and somewhat segmented style. As Rustow puts it,[7]

> Kemal's tactical secret was not . . . infallible foresight, but a sheer inexhaustible resourcefulness. No sooner had one plan run into difficulty than he came up with another that bypassed the obstacle. When unexpected opportunities offered, he stood ready to seize them. The long-range goal of independence was fixed, but to reach it Kemal was tacking with every changing wind.

Whatever the extent of Kemal's predictive capabilities, what Rustow and Huntington are describing is what we shall be calling in these pages the *incremental strategy of development.* The strategy itself is not new with us; it is found described in elaborate form in several recent works by one of its principal advocates, Charles Lindblom.[8] What we hope to do here is show how the strategy can be applied to problems of development decisions in modernizing states in the non-Western world.

Many of the characteristics of the incremental strategy stand out in bold relief when we compare the decision-making style of Kemal with the rational choice model of development planning described by Almond and Powell.[9] As the reader will remember from Chapter Nine, we listed the elements of a successful strategy for making political investments as (according to Almond and Powell):

1. ". . . an analysis of the starting point of a political system . . . its structural, cultural, and conversion characteristics and its capability profile."
2. ". . . we would need to specify the properties of the kind of political system we wish to introduce."
3. Select one investment strategy "among alternative strategies which will have a high probability of bringing us from the present to the given desired system characteristics with the least risk and cost."

Almond and Powell have provided us with a useful example of what Lindblom calls the "synoptic" style of decision-making. This style portrays rational decision-makers as, first, ordering all possible goals of public policy; second, collecting and sifting all data necessary to predict the outcomes of all possible strategic alternatives; and then, third, choosing that alternative which comes closest to yielding results which match the original ordering of priorities. Indeed, this style of rational choice is so well known, and so often portrayed as the best way of making difficult policy decisions, that many observers recognize no other way to proceed. In fact, according to Lindblom, very few if any decision sequences can be identified which even approximate the rational choice ideal, for many separate reasons.

In brief, the synoptic style of policy analysis does not accommodate itself to the real world of political decision-makers. The ideal of rational choice, for instance, does not adapt itself to the strict limitations on man's problem-solving capacities, to the high costs (in terms of time, resources, and political opportunities lost) of analysis. Further, the ideal model does not give decision-makers any clues about how to proceed with their policy analysis in the absence of any of the information required by the rational choice method; as we noted in Chapter Nine, the ultimate goals are spelled out, but few routes to these goals are specified. Finally, since the synoptic ideal posits a fairly static system during the time that policy evaluation is actually underway, it cannot cope with systems which are changing rapidly, especially with regard to the immense variety of problems which confront decision-makers, and the broad spectrum of values which development elites must take into account during their analysis.

The synoptic style of policy analysis seems to be strongly related to a particular type of decision, that is, one which results in a great deal of change, and which is bolstered by a high degree of understanding. Actually, as Lindblom makes clear, very few, if any, decisions really fit that pattern. More often, if decisions lead to great changes, they have been taken in spite of a lack of basic information about causes, effects, and so on. On the other hand, if a decision has been made on the basis of a relatively large degree of under-standing, it is probably of the type which produces little real change. Lindblom portrays these relationships in the following manner:[10]

	High Understanding	
Routine or bureaucratic decision-making		Revolutionary or utopian decision-making
Incremental Change		Large Change
Incremental decision-making		Wars, revolutions, crises and grand opportunities
	Low Understanding	

The reader will notice a good deal of similarity between Lindblom's formulation of decision styles and our discussion of risk-taking propensities in Chapter Seven. For instance, in the upper lefthand corner of the diagram we find well understood decisions which produce little change, characteristic of the low-risk behavior of bureaucratic administrators who have little impact on policy. The lower righthand quadrant, containing decisions which produce grand changes based on little understanding, seems reminiscent of our high-risk personalities. Finally, Lindblom's incremental style of decision-making, leading to marginal changes based on only partial understanding, approximates our moderate-risk actors. (The upper righthand corner, decisions which lead to great change, based on high understanding, has no empirical counterpart in the real world.) As we have argued in favor of a moderate-risk approach to decision-making, then, we find support for this thesis in Lindblom's formulation of incremental policy analysis and political change.

The incremental style of decision-making consists of eight separate, but closely interrelated, components. In the remainder of this section, we propose to list and discuss each of these in the specific context of development strategy.

MARGIN-DEPENDENT CHOICE

Choices between alternative policies are always choices at the margin. The synoptic method of problem-solving, as described in the passage from Almond and Powell above, would have us believe that alternate strategies are considered or evaluated by weighing every possible combination of factors, arranged in every conceivable pattern. Decision-makers, it might be thought, are asked to rank all relevant goals, all possible means of reaching each goal, and all the cost-benefit calculations which accompany each strategy. In fact, this superhuman job is not pressed upon policy analysts, for they resort to choices between marginal increments, and they restrict their analysis to only a few variables —typically only two or three. In this manner, decision-makers economize on available information and analysis capability, and thus convert an impossible task into a manageable one.

For this reason, it is not possible to specify any "correct" sequence of strategic steps for development elites. For questions of policy analysis are never presented to statesmen in the manner, "Do we want to expand first our regulative capabilities or our symbolic capabilities or some other combination?" Decision-makers are never asked, "Which do you prefer—liberty or equality?" The questions are always phrased in such a manner as to compare marginal increments of two desirable goals. Thus, the policy-maker is asked "How much regulative capability can we afford to risk in order to expand extractive capability by 'X' amount?", or "How much liberty should be sacrificed in order to secure 'Y' quantity of equality?" As Ilchman and Uphoff put the problem, decision-makers can assess the value of a particular objective only by measuring what they, and extragovernmental sectors, are willing to spend in order to achieve the objective.[11]

Sidney Verba, in his contribution to the SSRC volume discussed in Chapter Nine, laments the fact that the other contributors, in their analyses of the several crises, offer only fragmentary insights into the relationships between crises.[12] Instead of trying to link all five problem areas together, each analyst had focused on the way in which his issue-area interacted with other issues on a pairing basis. That is, the essays comment only on problems that arise when two crises coincide, and resource allocations to the two areas have to be balanced. Verba would like to have an analytical scheme which will accommodate all five crises. In reality, however, when using the incremental approach to decision-making, we see that decisions are made by weighing competing demands from two—or, at most, three—sectors or resource areas. Decision-makers rarely, if ever, confront the need to evaluate the need for the expansion of all five capabilities simultaneously; and, according to Lindblom, if they did confront such a challenge, their evaluative machinery could not begin to cope with the task. They would inevitably respond with certain kinds of coping mechanisms, many of which are described here and in Chapter Nine.

While it was tempting, then, in writing this chapter, to try to articulate certain capabilities development sequences which were faster or smoother or more stable than others, in fact, that task cannot be accomplished. In the great majority of cases in the developing world, decision-makers are aware of pressing needs in all five areas of system capabilities; they respond to this challenge by weighing incremental improvements in one sector against costs—either real or opportunity—in another sector.

A review of the historical examples of capability improvement offered the reader in Chapters One and Three does suggest that the ground is not quite so barren. While we cannot produce a complete sequence of capabilities expansion which is "best" for developing countries, some "rules of thumb" appear to have been seized upon by successful development elites acting intuitively. For instance, regulative and extractive capabilities are usually improved early in the sequence, to act as the base from which subsequent development efforts are launched. The only exceptions to this "rule" might be those systems in which a particularly charismatic figure attempted to depend on a heightened symbolic capability for support. Further, successful development statesmen have been careful not to allow their distributive capability to outreach their ability to extract the resources slated for reallocation. Following Huntington's thesis, these leaders should also be wary of building the machinery for stimulating popular participation until the system's responsive capabilities are sufficient to produce the answers to mass demands. These suggestions do no more than hint, however, that some kind of balance between certain pairs of capabilities is desirable at different levels of development; the precise weighing of alternatives cannot be undertaken in the absence of specific policy problems and available solutions.

RESTRICTED CONSIDERATION OF POLICY ALTERNATIVES AND CONSEQUENCES

We mentioned above that policy-makers, pressed for time, and lacking complete information on alternatives, tend to restrict their search to only those choices which offer incremental comparisons. Likewise, the same statesmen limit the burden on their evaluative skills by practicing similar self-restraint regarding, first, the evaluation of possible alternatives and, second, the possible consequences which will flow from these policies.

In the first instance, decision-makers practice the strategy of incrementalism by considering only those policy alternatives which differ incrementally from the status quo. Rather than try to evaluate each possible policy, they limit their consideration to only those choices which exhibit a slight or marginal difference with policies presently in effect. All other alternatives are discarded automatically. Second, the policy-maker deliberately restricts his scanning and analysis to certain selected consequences of the policies being debated; sequences of cause and effect relationships are not followed to their logical extremes; and, quite often, consequences which look important are left alone.

We have talked before about the problems underdeveloped countries face in making decisions regarding development. Albert O. Hirschman's works are devoted to analysis of exactly this condition. What one tends to overlook, however, is that even the most developed polities are confronted with burdens on decision-making capability due to lack of information and the cost of getting it. While the particular mechanisms at work in underdeveloped countries which create information gaps may differ from those in developed states, the same problem confronts statesmen in both kinds of systems; how to make policy in an environment of imperfect understanding. So, while the strategy of incremental decision-making seems most appropriate for highly developed polities, it has definite application to less developed states as well.

At this point, however, we should mention one aspect of the incremental strategy which may raise difficulties for rapidly developing political systems. The reason why a political leader feels that he can safely ignore many important policy alternatives and their consequences has to do with the fragmented arena within which the system's decision-making process takes place. Thus, we shall proceed to the next characteristic of the strategy to illustrate a flaw in the decision style of developing countries.

SOCIAL FRAGMENTATION OF ANALYSIS AND EVALUATION

Incremental decision-making typically occurs at many different locations around the political system. In a highly developed decision system, one is apt to find nodes of analysis scattered throughout the system, each one tackling a different aspect of the same problem. At one point in time, the executive authority may focus on the issue; somewhat later, the legislative branch will return to rectify some mistakes in the original solution; later still, a bureaucrat or a judge will intervene again to smooth out a rough part of the policy. What one group misses, another sector will catch. Even the so-called "private sector" will intervene actively to make sure that some mistake in policy-making or application does not work against their interests.

The incrementalist, then, can proceed with a less-than-complete analysis of policy consequences secure in the knowledge that, if he misses something, or makes an error in analysis, somewhere else in the system sits another policy analyst ready to catch the problem and act to resolve it. Unfortunately, one of the major difficulties which underdeveloped polities face is the limited number of policy analysis structures available to work on the evaluation of alternative policies and their consequences. Myron Weiner describes it this way:

> A modern political system has no single mechanism, no single proce-
> dure, no single institution for the resolution of conflict; indeed, it is pre-
> cisely the multiplicity of individuals, institutions and procedures for
> dispute settlement that characterizes the modern political system—both
> democratic and totalitarian. In contrast, developing societies with an in-
> creasing range of internal conflict, typically lack such individuals, institu-
> tions and procedures. It is as if mankind's capacity to generate conflict is
> greater than his capacity to find methods of resolving conflict; the lag is
> clearly greatest in societies in which fundamental economic and social
> relationships are rapidly changing.[13]

Weiner was addressing himself to the desirability of providing for multiple channels for the presentation of grievances as a technique for maintaining stability. But the incremental decision strategy also requires such multiplicity if decision-makers are to use the strategy with confidence. If the statesman feels that his nation may have to live with his errors for years to come because of a lack of alternate routes for policy consideration, he will undoubtedly try to make himself more synoptic, to try to take more and more alternatives into consideration. The result will be less policy action, rather than more; and caution and conservatism will yield to stagnation and immobilism.

ADJUSTMENT OF OBJECTIVES TO POLICIES

In Chapter Nine, it was noted that the complex relationship between ends and means, between goals and measures taken to reach them, was not handled at all adequately by the two classes of development strategies that were discussed. The systemic strategists focused principally on ends and goals and ultimate values, and neglected the tactical steps needed to reach a desired objective. The development tacticians envisioned development as essentially an improvement in their ability to make short-run decisions, and left very little in the way of suggestions about how to select the best objectives or how to evaluate the proper goals for development policy. Huntington's analysis moved somewhat closer to a careful blend of the two, but only by defining the goal—a stable, institutionalized polity—in such terms as to place it far beyond the reach of statesmen who live in the here and now.

The incremental strategy attempts to bridge the gap between ends and means by providing for a constant interplay of the evaluation processes for both factors. That is, instead of stabilizing one set of ingredients, such as the objectives of the state, and developing the strategies necessary to reach these objectives, the Lindblom thesis advocates a constant reevaluation of both ends and means, as new information about policy techniques becomes available. Although the synoptic ideal or the rational choice method of problem-solving would have us believe otherwise, in reality ends are very closely tied to the means available to accomplish them; and a perceptive policy of goal setting requires constant feedback about policy tools at the disposal of the statesman.

One very important variable which affects the availability of policy tools is the changing cost of undertaking a specific policy. In fact, what we usually mean when we say that policy X is "impossible" is simply that it is too expensive to implement to make it worthwhile. In a rapidly changing political and technological environment, one of the first visible effects of change may well be the reduced costs for accomplishing certain objectives. Unless the policy-makers are attuned to these cost reductions, and can insert the new calculations into their analysis, the old ends-means combinations will continue to govern resource allocation decisions long after they have become outdated. Lindblom describes the ways in which the policy-maker avoids this rigidity:

1. The analyst chooses as relevant objectives only those worth considering in view of the means actually at hand or likely to become available.
2. He automatically incorporates consideration of the costliness of achieving the objective into his marginal comparison, for an examination of incremental differences in value consequences of various means tells him at what price in terms of one value he is obtaining an increment of another.
3. While he contemplates means, he continues at the same time to contemplate objectives, unlike the synoptic analyst who ideally must at some point finally stabilize his objectives and then select the proper means.[14]

The implications of this approach for decision-making in non-Western countries become immediately apparent when we recall Albert Hirschman's description of the "failure-prone" strategies of Latin America. One of the major components of the policy debate was seen by Hirschman to be the call for comprehensiveness, the demand that all relevant variables be accounted for, and that the policy not be piecemeal and fragmented. Indeed, one of the most telling arguments against a policy decision was that it was not comprehensive, and it left some goals and objectives unmentioned.

If developing states in Asia, Africa, and Latin America are to put the incremental strategy to work for their development, they must be prepared to abandon the call for "once-and-for-all" solutions, master plans, and grand designs. The interplay between ends and means is far too complex to be encompassed within one single design for the future; an appropriate development strategy would allow for flexibility in selecting both objectives and tactics as long as new information continues to become available.

It should be noted in concluding this section that changes of this sort, while difficult to manipulate, possess both their costs and their benefits. The psychological costs of altering the political culture of a nation are obviously substantial; the interested reader may wish to return to Chapter Seven for a brief description of some ways in which modal personalities have been altered in the past. The benefits to be derived from such a change, however, are also substantial, for so long as the "grand design" approach to politics is allowed to dominate a developing country, the Hirschman "failure-prone" strategy will continue to be evident. Whenever goals are set impossibly high, failure is the only possible outcome; indeed, that is what sustains the failure-threatened personality. Thus, this approach to resolving problems constitutes a major obstacle to the efficient engineering of the development process.

RECONSTRUCTION OF DATA, SERIAL ANALYSIS, AND REMEDIAL TREATMENT

The last three components of the incremental strategy involve the ways in which policy analysts divide and combine issues to make them more amenable to attack. First, the strategy allows the policy-makers to rebuild an issue in an infinite variety of forms, depending on the information available, and the degree of success or failure encountered when the policy is implemented. By means of the strategy, decision-makers can restructure a policy issue, the goals which have been proposed, or the suggested solutions; and all of this can occur in the midst of the analysis and evaluation process. Second, the incrementalists are involved in a never-ending chain of policy steps, rather than a single blow designed to solve the problem immediately. Analysts know that they cannot solve a problem at one sitting; so they are content merely to reduce one aspect of it, to cope with it for a short time while they collect more information and try new policies. Thus, they are aware of their ability to return to the problem time and time again to attack either a particularly resistant part of the issue, or to deal with an entirely new and unforeseen difficulty which has arisen. Finally, the remedial orientation of the strategy allows the decision-makers to learn from their mistakes. As data pour in as a consequence of the evaluation of a policy decision, development leaders should be alert to the opportunities they enjoy to return to the issue, to remedy some additional problem, and to put into practice those lessons they have learned from the first experiment. The incremental strategy, by emphasizing the serial and open-ended nature of the policy analysis process, allows the development elites to do this in a manner not permitted by the synoptic ideal.

Again, the high-risk or failure-prone decision style of many non-Western countries intrudes to make these elements of the stragegy of incrementalism particularly difficult to obtain.[15] Virtually every one of the authors considered in Chapters Nine and Ten has mentioned the desirability of being able to break problems up into smaller fragments into issue-areas more amenable to solution. And, indeed, successful development leaders, such as Mustafa Kemal, have accomplished just that. Similarly, most would agree that the decision-making process is never ending, and that political leaders must not try to solve all the issue at once but merely be content to cope with part now, and return to deal with another part later, after evaluating policies for possible errors in fact or judgment. As we have noted repeatedly, however, non-Western political cultures generally do not reward incremental behavior. The insistence on comprehensive plans, immediate results, universal solutions, and an inability to admit and learn from mistakes all contribute to rigidities in decision-making in underdeveloped countries. And, while we may agree with a more systemic-oriented observer like Huntington that a greater degree of institutionalization in politics is desirable to limit instability, without some parallel changes in decision strategies, the advances in political change in many non-Western states are going to be transitory and fragile.

THE INCREMENTAL STRATEGY: A FINAL QUESTION

We have left to consider, then, only the question: Do successful development elites actually use the incremental strategy, even though they may not label it as such, or even recognize it for what it is? A definitive answer lies beyond the scope of the present inquiry, but the question certainly merits a place on some future research agenda. While the fragments of information about development decision-making and the logical force of Lindblom's arguments are powerful evidence in the affirmative, in the final analysis only detailed empirical study will confirm the hypotheses discussed above.

Nevertheless, the interested reader is invited to return to Chapters One and Three of this book to trace the development patterns described there. We think that the incremental nature of the development styles exhibited in those brief studies will strongly suggest that Lindblom's formulation has been employed more than occasionally by development elites.

For example, in Chapter One we were introduced to the modernizing elites of Japan as they sought to expand their country's regulative and extractive capabilities. In both cases, the stragegy followed exhibited a clear step-by-step, or incremental, character. The expansion of regulative capabilities lasted some 50 years, and progressed through a variety of different adjustments, including mechanical improvements in law enforcement techniques, reallocation of resources to the police force, changing concepts of the sphere of law enforcement jurisdiction, and many others. The incremental nature of the growth of the Japanese income tax as a technique for extracting resources is equally clearcut and obvious.

Even in the cases of avowedly revolutionary states attempting to increase their distributive capabilities—Cuban labor policy and Egyptian land reform—the incremental nature of the development process is still evident. The Castro government began its policy of labor reform by focusing first on job selection, transfer and hiring, and only later moved into the much more sensitive areas of work standards and remuneration. Between 1960 and 1962, the Ministry of Labor moved incrementally from a policy of stimulating work through propaganda and psychological rewards to a policy of setting standards and adjusting both positive and negative material incentives. In the Egyptian example, the revolutionary socialist government needed more than a decade, and a plethora of decrees and administrative decisions to make even a slight dent in the overwhelming land tenure problem in that country.

Finally, the growth of the revolutionary party, the PRI, in Mexico offers almost a textbook case of incremental adjustment in policy-making. Initially, the earlier version of the PRI was organized as a simple alliance of local chieftains who owed some allegiance to President Calles. From 1934 to 1938, more radical political leaders shaped and molded the party into a weapon to use to block the political intentions of the army; and only after significant electoral victories in the 1940's, and large-scale local precinct and village organizing, did the PRI emerge in its present role as one of the most successful mobilization parties in the non-Western world.

Quite significantly, the only example of capability expansion which differs even slightly from the incremental model was Kemal's decison to move the capital of Turkey from Istanbul to Ankara. While this decison may properly be viewed as merely a small part of a much larger sequence of incremental decisions, it is also quite possible that decisions regarding *symbolic* gestures do not lend themselves so readily to the incremental style. A high-risk attempt at large-scale change may be more appropriate here, even if we acknowledge that efforts to practice the synoptic method of decision-making are failure-prone by their very nature.

We must also point out that many of the development sequences we have examined here did not begin as conscious efforts to overcome underdevelopment. Calles' decision to create the PNR, Japan's levying of a tax to fight the Russo-Japanese War, or the launching of the Progressive Movement in the United States were not explicitly *development* steps. That they became the opening stage of a development sequence is due more to the opportunism and ingenuity of leaders who came later and sought to build on earlier steps, than to the wisdom and foresight of the original statesmen. To be sure, some decisions were consciously developmental—Cuban labor policy, Egyptian land reform, and the decision by Stalin to launch a policy of forced industrialization and farm collectivization. Even in these instances, however, the development elites made the decisions as much with an eye to breaking the power of an entrenched opposition as they did in order to initiate a long-range process of political development.

Some observers profess to find flaws in the incremental strategy of change because of its inherent conservative bias; when great problems are confronted, great changes and decisions are called for. Slight changes at the margin will not suffice.[16] The history of developmental politics suggests exactly the opposite, however. The rational choice decision style, and grand design politics have been used either by reactionaries to block real change by arguing that the system must "go slow" lest damage be done, or by romantics who think that the job of political renewal will be accomplished in a week, or a decade. The successful development elites have been those who recognized that the tasks of political change are not finished in a lifetime, and that the real challenge of political development lies in the maintenance of momentum in a never ending process of growth and learning.

CHAPTER NOTES

1. Samuel P. Huntington, *Political Order in Changing Societies* (New Haven: Yale University Press, 1968).
2. These common issues are dealt with by Huntington on pp. 140-47.
3. See especially above the analyses of the work by Ilchman and Uphoff, and by Almond and Powell.
4. Huntington, p. 240.
5. Huntington, pp. 347-357.
6. Dankwart A. Rustow, "Ataturk as Founder of a State," *Daedalus,* 97, 3 (Summer, 1968): 793-828, esp. 813-14.
7. Rustow, p. 803.
8. David Braybrooke and Charles E. Lindblom, *A Strategy of Decision: Policy Evaluation as a Social Process* (New York: Free Press, 1963). Elements of the strategy are also discussed in an earlier book by Robert A. Dahl and Charles E. Lindblom, *Politics Economics and Welfare: Planning and Politico-Economic Systems Resolved into Basic Social Processes* (New York: Harper & Row, paper ed., 1963). The strategy is further elaborated by Lindblom in *The Intelligence of Democracy: Decision Making through Mutual Adjustment* (New York: Free Press, 1965).
9. Gabriel A. Almond and G. Bingham Powell, Jr., *Comparative Politics: A Developmental Approach* (Boston: Little, Brown, paper ed., 1966), pp. 328-29.
10. Braybrooke and Lindblom, pp. 67 and 78.
11. Warren F. Ilchman and Normal Thomas Uphoff, *The Political Economy of Change* (Berkeley: University of California Press, 1969), p. 99.

12. Sidney Verba, "Sequences and Development," in Leonard Binder, *et al., Crises and Sequences in Political Development* (Princeton, N.J.: Princeton University Press, 1971), p. 309.
13. Myron Weiner, "Political Integration and Political Development," *The Annals,* Vol. 358 (March, 1965), pp. 52-64, esp. p. 60. Cited in Howard Wriggins, *The Ruler's Imperative: Strategies for Political Survival in Asia and Africa* (New York: Columbia University Press, 1969), p. 31.
14. Braybrooke and Lindblom, p. 94.
15. The author recalls leading a seminar discussion of the Lindblom thesis before a group of students and faculty of a public administration school in a Latin American country. At the end of the presentation, one of the faculty commented, "All those ideas are fine for an Anglo-Saxon; but we Latins need a more complete and well formulated way of thinking."
16. See, for example, Harrell R. Rodgers, Jr., and Charles S. Bullock, III, *Law and Social Change* (New York: McGraw-Hill, 1972), esp. Chap. Nine. See also the criticism by Ilchman and Uphoff, pp. 123-24.

APPENDIX

Political Development and Systemic Performance:

A Quantitative Examination of 48 Non-Western Countries

One of the principal aims of this book has been to interpret political development as the enhancement of the capability of the political system to perform certain tasks. In Chapter One, we presented data of a narrative, "case study" nature to illustrate this point. In recognition of the fact that some readers may desire a more empirical, precise, and quantitative statement of development and system performance, we present in this Appendix a set of statistical indicators which can be used to measure the progress of a state as it develops.

The data are arranged to reflect systemic performance in each of the five capabilities discussed in Chapter One. These capabilities are derived from the study by Gabriel Almond and G. Bingham Powell, *Comparative Politics: A Developmental Approach* (Boston: Little, Brown, 1966), Chapter Seven. For each capability, the Almond-Powell definition is supplied for the reader.

Data have been collected from a wide variety of sources covering 48 different political systems. As nearly as possible, the data were selected from the period 1955–1965. Of the 48 systems examined, 20 are located in Latin America, 13 are in Asia, 11 are in the Middle East and North Africa, and 4 are in Sub-Saharan Africa.

In each category of state performance, three quantitative indicators were selected for data collection. In the tables which follow, the raw data are presented on the lefthand side of the column. The data are then adjusted by granting the highest scoring country a maximum rating of 100, and all other countries some percentage of 100, according to their raw score. Thus, all scores are normalized to the same standard scale. Each set of three indicators is then summed to produce the total score for each capability. At the end of the Appendix, all five capabilities are summed to yield the cumulative score for each state. In addition, the 48 systems are grouped according to systemic performance to give the reader some idea of the relative level of development for each state in the sample. Full data sources are provided to assist the reader in replicating the study.

Before the reader moves on to examine the data, several comments about aggregate data analysis are in order.[1] First of all, the analysis of aggregate data (data emanating from units of observation which are larger than the individual actor; for example, the nation), offers us the opportunity to zero in on collective behavior which can be captured through collective analysis, but which would elude the observer of individuals. This technique may be especially appropriate in those instances where individuals are not accessible to the observer at the time of measurement; migration or riots come to mind as examples. In addition to helping smooth over the access problem, aggregate data measures often reflect conditions in the environment which simply do not have a counterpart in the behavior of individuals. For instance, the concept of "urbanization" is often taken to mean something more than, and conceptually distinct from, the clustering of many single individuals in close proximity in their living arrangements. Therefore, we must strive to find a measure of "urbanization" apart from the many separate measures of individual behavior required to produce the phenomenon of the growth of large cities. Thus, while aggregate data should not replace the analysis of individual cases (as used in Chapter One), they may usefully complement such a study, in that individual and aggregate analysis are appropriate for different kinds of social phenomena.

Many problems still exist for those who would seek to analyze aggregate data in developing or non-Western countries. We shall mention a few here simply to sensitize the reader to the pitfalls involved in this sort of study. First, in many of the nations we are examining, there exist substantial intranation differences in the data. The spread of modernization reaches into different parts of the country at differing rates; and a single indicator for the entire nation may mask sizeable differences within the nation on that variable. Second, we must be careful to assess both the reliability and the comparability of the data we are using. As we have mentioned in Chapter Nine, a politically underdeveloped state is one which finds difficulty in making development decisions, often for lack of credible data. This lack may be traced either to a lack of trained observers, or to an absence of adequate data gathering services. In some instances, data gathering is impeded because of the politically sensitive nature of the results. In a country divided precariously between two or more religious or ethnic groups, the population count becomes the source of great anxiety for fear that opposition groups may be gaining on one's own sect or tribe. The comparability problem is even more severe, as the same concept may be treated for definition purposes differently in different countries. The concept of "urban," for example, is defined in a unique way by virtually every country in Latin America.[2] Finally, the techniques by which we have formed our composite indices is subject to question. By the very nature of the study, we have had to assume that a given indicator reflected, or "stood for" the presence of the capability to which we had assigned it. For instance, we assumed that the extractive capability of a state would be reflected in the percentage of the total population serving in the armed forces of that state. This assumption obviously works against countries such as Costa Rica or Panama, which have no national army, not because they could not recruit troops for it, but because their leaders do not perceive a need to devote resources to this sector. More importantly, we have not *proved* the linkage between the indicator and the capability; we have simply assumed it as existing. There are statistical techniques, such as factor analysis, which would extract the underlying correlations among these factors, but such an exercise would go beyond the scope of this book. The interested reader is invited to test the data presented here using more sophisticated techniques to yield greater understanding of the empirical dimensions of political development.

A. Regulative Capability.
  1. Definition: "The political system's exercise of control over behavior of individuals and groups." (Almond and Powell, p. 196).
  2. Indicators:
    a. Coercive potential as of 1961. This is a figure designed to measure the size of the system's internal security force weighted for loyalty. The figure is taken from Ted Gurr, "A Causal Model of Civil Strife: A Comparative Analysis Using New Indices," *American Political Science Review*, LXII, 4 (December, 1968): 1104-24, Statistical Appendix.
    b. Political stability 1955–1961. This figure is derived from a study by Ivo and Rosalind Feierabend, "Aggressive Behavior Within Polities, 1948–1962: A Cross-National Study," *Journal of Conflict Resolution* (September, 1966), pp. 249-71. The Feierabend data are supposed to reflect *instability,* so their figures are subtracted from 1,000 to yield the converse, a stability score.
    c. Percentage of gross national product devoted to the central government budget, 1961–1965, or as close as possible. Derived principally from the *Yearbook of National Accounts Statistics,* Vols. I and II, 1969. For Afghanistan, the source was Donald N. Wilber, *Afghanistan: Its People, Its Society And Its Culture* (New Haven, Conn.: HRAF Press, 1962) Chaps. 14 and 15. For Laos, the source was T. D. Roberts, *et al., Area Handbook for Laos* (Washington, D.C.: U.S.G.P.O., 1967), pp. 277-78.

B. Extractive Capability.
  1. Definition: "The range of system performance in drawing material and human resources from the domestic and international environments." (Almond and Powell, p. 195.)
  2. Indicators:
     a. Percentage of government revenue derived from the direct tax on income, 1961–1965, or as close as possible. Source: United Nations *Statistical Yearbook,* 1964. Source for Saudi Arabia was *Economist* Intelligence Unit, *Quarterly Economic Review: The Arabian Peninsula and Jordan,* #4, 1970, p. 3. Source for Cuba was Cuban Economic Research Project, *A Study on Cuba* (Coral Gables, Fla.: University of Miami Press, 1965), p. 658. Source for Laos same as A, 2, c above.
     b. Percentage of total population serving in the armed forces, late 1960's. Soruces: Institute for Strategic Studies, *The Military Balance,* 1970–1971 (London: ISS, 1970). Richard Booth, *The Armed Forces of African States, 1970* (London: ISS, 1970) Adelphi Paper #67.
     c. Receipt of external resources from developed countries and multilateral agencies, 1962–1965, in U.S. $, *per capita.* Source: United Nations *Statistical Yearbook,* 1967.

C. Distributive Capability.
  1. Definition: "The capability of the system to allocate goods, services, honors, statuses and opportunities of various kinds from the political system to individuals and groups in the society." (Almond and Powell, p. 198.)
  2. Indicators:
     a. Hectares of arable land per capita of agricultural population, c. 1960. Sources: UN-FAO, *State of Food and Agriculture, 1970* (Rome: FAO, 1970). Also, UN-FAO, *Production Yearbook,* Vol. 23.
     b. Percentage of central government budget devoted to social welfare purposes (to include health, education, social services, etc.) expressed as an annual average for the period 1961–1965, or as close to that period as possible. Figures for Brazil and Pakistan represent both central and state expenditures. Figures for India represent only state expenditures, since central government expenditures not available. Major source: United Nations *Statistical Yearbook, 1964.* For Ethiopia, Libya, Tunisia, Taiwan, and Cambodia: *Yearbook of National Accounts Statistics, 1969, Vol. I.* For Cuba, Nicaragua, Paraguay, and Uruguay: Claudio Veliz, ed., *Latin America and the Caribbean: A Handbook* (New York: Praeger, 1968). Source for Laos same as A, 2, c above, p. 277. For Saudi Arabia: George A. Lipsky, *et al., Saudi Arabia, Its People, Its Society, Its Culture*

(New Haven: HRAF Press, 1959), p. 320. For Liberia: Russell U. McLaughlin, *Foreign Investment and Development in Liberia* (New York: Praeger, 1966), p. 35. For Afghanistan: Kurt Grunwald and Joachin O. Ronall, *Industrialization in the Middle East* (New York: Council for Middle Eastern Affairs Press, 1960), p. 172.

   c. Percentage of total population in nonprimary grades in school, c. 1958. Norton Ginsburg, *Atlas of Economic Development* (Chicago: University of Chicago Press, 1961), p. 44.

D. Symbolic Capability.

   1. Definition: "The rate of *effective* symbol flow from the political system into the society and the international environment." (Almond and Powell, p. 199).

   2. Indicators:

     a. Newspaper circulation per 1,000 population, c. 1958. Major Source: Norton Ginsburg, *Atlas of Economic Development* (Chicago: University of Chicago Press, 1961), p. 40. For Honduras: calculated from United States Information Agency Research and Reference Service, *Fact Book on Latin America: 1962* (Washington, D.C.: USIA, August 30, 1963), Tables 1 and 7. For South Korea: Calculated from Richard P. Stebbins and Alba Amoia, eds., *Political Handbook and Atlas of the World, 1970* (New York: Simon and Schuster, 1970), p. 186, 188-89.

     b. Percentage of adults who are literate, c. 1957. Source; Norton Ginsburg, *op. cit.,* p. 38.

     c. Km of road per 100 square kms, late 1950's. Major source: Norton Ginsburg, *op. cit.,* p. 70. For Afghanistan: calculated from Donald N. Wilber, *Afghanistan: Its People, Its Society, Its Culture* (New Haven: HRAF Press, 1962), p. 191, and *Statesman's Yearbook.* For Libya: calculated from International Bank for Reconstruction and Development, *The Economic Development of Libya* (Baltimore: Johns Hopkins Press, 1960), p. 231, and *Statesman's Yearbook.* For Sudan: calculated from a map in the frontispiece of K. M. Barbour, *The Republic of the Sudan* (London: University of London Press, Ltd., 1961), and *Statesman's Yearbook.*

E. Responsive Capability.

   1. Definition: "The ability of the system to respond to a set of internal and external pressures and demands." (Almond and Powell, p. 201.)

   2. Indicators:

     a. Stability and pervasiveness of the political party system, late 1960's. Definitions of two component scales—political party strength and strength of the *system* of parties—taken from Ted Robert Gurr, "A Causal Model of Civil Strife: A comparative Analysis Using New Indices," *American Political Science Review,* LXII, 4 (December, 1968): 1104-24. Data taken from Richard P. Stebbins and Alba

Amoia, eds., *Political Handbook and Atlas of the World, 1970* (New York: Simon and Schuster, 1970). The two indicators were multiplied to derive the overall index.

b. Urban-industrial access, c. 1965. This indicator is designed to reflect the degree to which the nation's population was found in urban centers (defined as cities of more than 20,000 population) and working under nonagricultural conditions. Nonagricultural population derived from UN-PAO, *The State of Food and Agriculture,* 1970 (Rome: FAO, 1970) and from UN-FAO, *Production Yearbook,* Vol. 23. Percent of population in cities of 20,000 or more from Norton Ginsburg, *Atlas of Economic Development* (Chicago: University of Chicago Press, 1961), p. 34, Table 11. Except Uruguay: UCLA Latin American Center, *Statistical Abstract of Latin America: 1967* (Los Angeles: UCLA-LAC, December, 1968), p. 68, Table 11. Also, Iran: *Echo of Iran: Iran Almanac and Book of Facts, 1969* (Tehran: *Echo,* 1969), p. 475.

c. Aggregate degree of political democracy. From Arthur K. Smith, Jr., "Socio-Economic Development and Political Democracy: A Causal Analysis," *Midwest Journal of Political Science,* VIII, 1 (Feb. 1969): pp. 95-125, esp. Table 1, pp. 104-5.

1. For a useful discussion of aggregate data analysis, see Ralph H. Retzlaff, "The Use of Aggregate Data in Comparative Political Analysis," *Journal of Politics,* 27, 4 (November, 1965): 797-817.

2. UCLA, Center of Latin American Studies, *Statistical Abstract of Latin America, 1962* (Los Angeles: UCLA, CLAS, 1962), pp. 14-15.

Table A.1   Regulative Capability of 48 Non-Western States

Country	(a) Raw	(a) Adj.	(b) Raw	(b) Adj.	(c) Raw	(c) Adj.	Total	Rank
Afghanistan	84	71.8	596	66.3	2.4	11.1	149.2	20
Argentina	17	14.5	401	44.6	10.4	48.0	107.1	43
Bolivia	18	15.4	444	49.4	9.8	45.3	110.1	42
Brazil	24	20.5	459	51.0	12.8	59.1	130.6	32
Burma	20	17.1	573	63.7	13.4	61.9	142.7	26
Cambodia	89	76.1	896	99.6	18.0	83.2	258.9	3
Ceylon	30	25.6	546	60.7	13.6	62.8	149.1	21
Chile	82	70.1	573	63.7	10.6	49.0	182.8	12
Colombia	23	19.7	319	35.5	7.0	32.3	87.5	46
Costa Rica	42	35.9	798	88.7	13.0	60.0	184.6	11
Cuba	35	29.9	301	33.5	12.6	58.2	121.6	36
Dominican Republic	30	25.6	537	59.7	15.4	71.1	156.4	17
Ecuador	23	19.7	578	64.3	13.8	63.8	147.8	23
Egypt	62	53.0	562	62.5	19.2	88.7	204.2	7
El Salvador	15	12.8	579	64.4	9.4	43.4	120.6	37
Ethiopia	24	20.5	693	77.1	8.0	37.0	134.6	29
Ghana	18	15.4	549	61.0	11.8	54.5	130.9	31
Guatemala	17	14.5	454	50.5	7.2	33.3	98.3	45
Haiti	22	18.8	522	58.0	6.5	30.0	106.8	44
Honduras	27	23.1	465	51.7	9.4	43.4	118.2	41
India	66	56.1	401	44.6	8.9	41.1*	142.1	27
Indonesia	12	10.2	301	33.5	7.8	36.0	79.7	47
Iran	55	47.0	541	60.2	11.6	53.6	160.8	16
Iraq	14	12.0	421	46.8	20.6	95.2	154.0	18
Jordan	117	100.0	552	61.4	21.6	100.0	261.4	1
Korea, Republic of	31	26.5	404	44.9	11.2	51.7	123.1	35
Laos	25*	21.4	348	38.7	2.0*	9.3	69.4	48
Lebanon	48	41.0	419	46.6	10.0	46.2	133.8	30
Liberia	47	40.2	585	65.1	8.8	40.6	145.9	24
Libya	96	82.0	691	76.8	14.6	67.4	226.2	5
Malaysia	73	62.4	587	65.3	16.4	75.8	203.5	8
Mexico	92	78.6	549	61.0	5.6	25.9	165.5	15
Morocco	75	64.1	557	61.9	14.2	65.6	191.6	10
Nicaragua	69	59.0	570	63.4	9.6	44.4	166.8	14
Pakistan	35	29.9	563	62.6	6.8	31.4	123.9	34
Panama	35	29.9	578	64.3	11.8	54.5	148.7	22
Paraguay	28	23.9	569	63.3	7.0	32.3	119.5	38
Peru	36	30.8	448	49.8	10.2	47.1	127.7	33
Philippines	63	53.8	899	100.0	9.8	45.3	199.1	9
Saudi Arabia	88	75.2	897	99.7	18.2	84.1	259.0	2
Sudan	10	8.6	555	61.7	10.4	48.0	118.3	40
Syria	17	14.5	446	49.6	17.4	80.4	144.5	25

Table A.1 (cont.)

Country	(a)		(b)		(c)			
	Raw	Adj.	Raw	Adj.	Raw	Adj.	Total	Rank
Taiwan	96	82.0	686	76.3	17.8	82.2	240.5	4
Thailand	58	49.6	549	61.0	9.0	41.6	152.2	19
Tunisia	77	65.8	672	74.7	16.8	77.6	218.1	6
Turkey	35	29.9	417	46.4	14.2	65.6	141.9	28
Uruguay	45	38.5	682	75.8	13.6	62.8	177.1	13
Venezuela	8	6.8	416	46.3	14.2	65.6	118.7	39

*Estimate

Table A.2 Rank Order of 48 Non-Western States in Regulative Capability

Perfect Score:	300.0	
1 Jordan	261.4	25 Syria — 144.5
2 Saudi Arabia	259.0	26 Burma — 142.7
3 Cambodia	258.9	27 India — 142.1
4 Taiwan	240.5	28 Turkey — 141.9
5 Libya	226.2	29 Ethiopia — 134.6
6 Tunisia	218.1	30 Lebanon — 133.8
7 Egypt	204.2	31 Ghana — 130.9
8 Malaysia	203.5	32 Brazil — 130.6
9 Philippines	199.1	33 Peru — 127.7
10 Morocco	191.6	34 Pakistan — 123.9
11 Costa Rica	184.6	35 Korea — 123.1
12 Chile	182.8	36 Cuba — 121.6
13 Uruguay	177.1	37 El Salvador — 120.6
14 Nicaragua	166.8	38 Paraguay — 119.5
15 Mexico	165.5	39 Venezuela — 118.7
16 Iran	160.8	40 Sudan — 118.3
17 Dominican Republic	156.4	41 Honduras — 118.2
18 Iraq	154.0	42 Bolivia — 110.1
— Average —	153.2	43 Argentina — 107.1
19 Thailand	152.2	44 Haiti — 106.8
20 Afghanistan	149.2	45 Guatemala — 98.3
21 Ceylon	149.1	46 Colombia — 87.5
22 Panama	148.7	47 Indonesia — 79.7
23 Ecuador	147.8	48 Laos — 69.4
24 Liberia	145.9	

Table A.3 Extractive Capability of 48 Non-Western States

Country	(a)		(b)		(c)			
	Raw	Adj.	Raw	Adj.	Raw	Adj.	Total	Rank
Afghanistan	12.0*	25.0	0.61	16.8	14.20	8.8	50.6	28
Argentina	15.5	32.2	0.56	15.5	6.52	4.0	51.7	27
Bolivia	4.1	8.5	0.44	12.2	37.87	23.4	44.1	39

Table A.3 (cont.)

Country	(a)		(b)		(c)			
	Raw	Adj.	Raw	Adj.	Raw	Adj.	Total	Rank
Brazil	30.0	62.4	0.20	5.5	11.79	7.3	75.2	18
Burma	28.8	59.9	0.51	14.1	5.64	3.5	77.5	15
Cambodia	12.8	26.6	1.80	49.7	13.92	8.6	84.9	13
Ceylon	21.0	43.7	0.10	2.8	11.90	7.4	53.9	26
Chile	28.6	59.5	0.62	17.1	62.06	38.4	115.0	7
Colombia	48.1	100.0	0.30	8.3	19.03	11.8	120.1	5
Costa Rica	19.1	39.7	0.00	0.0	46.97	29.0	68.7	21
Cuba	17.4	36.2	1.31	36.2	144.16	89.1	161.5	2
Dominican Republic	15.3	31.8	0.44	12.2	46.96	29.0	73.0	19
Ecuador	14.0	29.1	0.32	8.8	14.17	8.8	46.7	34
Egypt	9.0	18.7	0.86	23.8	56.44	34.9	77.4	16
El Salvador	15.6	32.4	0.16	4.4	1.74	1.1	37.9	42
Ethiopia	19.9	41.4	0.18	5.0	4.92	3.0	49.4	29
Ghana	12.0	25.0	0.18	5.0	28.10	17.4	47.4	31
Guatemala	10.7	22.2	0.17	4.7	9.46	5.8	32.7	45
Haiti	9.1	18.9	0.11	3.0	4.09	2.5	24.4	46
Honduras	14.0	29.1	0.18	5.0	20.58	12.8	46.9	33
India	5.6	11.6	1.86	51.4	11.07	6.8	69.8	20
Indonesia	9.1	18.9	2.00	55.2	4.64	2.9	77.0	17
Iran	9.1	18.9	0.56	15.5	17.80	11.0	45.4	36
Iraq	6.0	12.5	1.05	29.0	6.11	3.8	45.3	37
Jordan	10.0	20.8	2.70	74.6	161.78	100.0	195.4	1
Korea, Republic of	18.4	38.2	2.02	55.8	31.40	19.4	113.4	8
Laos	7.0	14.6	2.27	62.7	68.80	42.5	119.8	6
Lebanon	9.1	18.9	0.60	16.6	18.59	11.5	47.0	32
Liberia	15.0*	31.2	0.35	9.7	153.34	94.8	135.7	3
Libya	7.4	15.4	0.77	21.3	50.09	31.0	67.7	22
Malaysia	21.3	44.3	0.44	12.2	9.87	6.1	62.6	23
Mexico	34.9	72.6	0.13	3.6	5.74	3.6	79.8	14
Morocco	15.0*	31.2	0.32	8.8	29.80	18.4	58.4	24
Nicaragua	11.3	23.5	0.35	9.7	25.38	15.7	48.9	30
Pakistan	13.3	27.6	0.25	6.9	19.22	11.9	46.4	35
Panama	25.9	53.8	0.00	0.0	65.01	40.2	94.0	11
Paraguay	4.0	8.3	0.84	23.2	15.76	9.7	41.2	40
Peru	12.3	25.6	0.40	11.0	12.87	8.0	44.6	38
Philippines	23.4	48.6	0.08	2.2	7.98	4.9	55.7	25
Saudi Arabia	0.0	0.0	0.49	13.5	-4.87	-3.0	10.5	48
Sudan	3.5	7.3	0.17	4.7	8.40	5.2	17.2	47
Syria	9.9	20.6	1.43	39.5	52.57	32.5	92.6	12
Taiwan	4.8	10.0	3.62	100.0	22.02	13.6	123.6	4
Thailand	10.1	21.0	0.42	11.6	5.63	3.5	36.1	43
Tunisia	25.2	52.4	0.43	11.9	71.89	44.4	108.7	9

Table A.3 (cont.)

Country	(a)		(b)		(c)			
	Raw	Adj.	Raw	Adj.	Raw	Adj.	Total	Rank
Turkey	26.9	55.9	1.35	37.3	11.04	6.8	100.0	10
Uruguay	6.9	14.3	0.53	14.6	6.26	3.9	32.8	44
Venezuela	10.2	21.2	0.29	8.0	14.83	9.2	38.4	41

*Estimate

Table A.4 Rank Order of 48 Non-Western States in Extractive Capability

Perfect Score:		300.0			
1	Jordan	195.4	25	Philippines	55.7
2	Cuba	161.5	26	Ceylon	53.9
3	Liberia	135.7	27	Argentina	51.7
4	Taiwan	123.6	28	Afghanistan	50.6
5	Colombia	120.1	29	Ethiopia	49.4
6	Laos	119.8	30	Nicaragua	48.9
7	Chile	115.0	31	Ghana	47.4
8	Korea	113.4	32	Lebanon	47.0
9	Tunisia	108.7	33	Honduras	46.9
10	Turkey	100.0	34	Ecuador	46.7
11	Panama	94.0	35	Pakistan	46.4
12	Syria	92.6	36	Iran	45.4
13	Cambodia	84.9	37	Iraq	45.3
14	Mexico	79.8	38	Peru	44.6
15	Burma	77.5	39	Bolivia	44.1
16	Egypt	77.4	40	Paraguay	41.2
17	Indonesia	77.0	41	Venezuela	38.4
18	Brazil	75.2	42	El Salvador	37.9
19	Dominican Republic	73.0	43	Thailand	36.1
—	Average —	71.5	44	Uruguay	32.8
20	India	69.8	45	Guatemala	32.7
21	Costa Rica	68.7	46	Haiti	24.4
22	Libya	67.7	47	Sudan	17.2
23	Malaysia	62.6	48	Saudi Arabia	10.5
24	Morocco	58.4			

Table A.5 Distributive Capability of 48 Non-Western States

Country	(a)		(b)		(c)			
	Raw	Adj.	Raw	Adj.	Raw	Adj.	Total	Rank
Afghanistan	0.60	10.4	5	12.5	0.06	3.0	25.9	47
Argentina	4.95	85.8	20	50.0	2.86	71.8	207.6	2
Bolivia	1.13	19.6	40	100.0	1.00	25.1	144.7	8

258

Country	(a)		(b)		(c)			
	Raw	Adj.	Raw	Adj.	Raw	Adj.	Total	Rank
Brazil	0.82	14.2	33	82.5	1.40	35.1	131.8	11
Burma	1.04	18.0	22*	55.0	1.06	26.6	99.6	28
Cambodia	0.71	12.3	35	87.5	0.10	2.5	102.3	25
Ceylon	0.34	5.9	34	85.0	0.10	2.5	93.4	34
Chile	2.56	44.4	23	57.5	2.12	53.2	155.1	6
Colombia	0.77	13.3	17	42.5	1.00	25.1	80.9	39
Costa Rica	0.92	15.9	39	97.5	1.91	47.9	161.3	5
Cuba	0.76	13.2	27	67.5	1.16	29.1	109.8	17
Dominican Republic	0.58	10.0	16	40.0	0.93	23.3	73.3	41
Ecuador	0.98	17.0	21	52.5	1.19	29.9	99.4	29.5
Egypt	0.17	2.9	19	47.5	2.45	61.5	111.9	16
El Salvador	0.43	7.4	32	80.0	0.71	17.8	105.2	23
Ethiopia	0.61	10.6	2	5.0	0.02	0.5	16.1	48
Ghana	1.35	23.4	27	67.5	0.34	8.5	99.4	29.5
Guatemala	0.52	9.0	25	62.5	0.87	21.8	93.3	35
Haiti	0.10	1.7	17	42.5	0.34	8.5	52.7	44
Honduras	0.78	13.5	27	67.5	0.51	12.8	93.8	33
India	0.51	8.8	19	47.5	1.88	47.2	103.5	24
Indonesia	0.17	2.9	4	10.0	0.65	16.3	29.2	46
Iran	0.96	16.6	21*	52.5	0.63	15.8	84.9	38
Iraq	1.89	32.8	19	47.5	1.05	26.4	106.7	22
Jordan	1.70	29.5	11	27.5	2.50	62.8	119.8	14
Korea, Republic of	0.14	2.4	20	50.0	3.24	81.3	133.7	10
Laos	0.38	6.6	23	57.5	0.09	2.2	66.3	43
Lebanon	0.24	4.2	15	37.5	2.35	59.0	100.7	27
Liberia	4.77	82.7	25	62.5	0.11	2.8	148.0	7
Libya	3.88	67.2	10	25.0	0.59	14.8	107.0	21
Malaysia	0.50	8.7	22	55.0	1.42	35.6	99.3	31
Mexico	1.23	21.3	31	77.5	0.59	14.8	113.6	15
Morocco	1.32	22.9	25*	62.5	0.40	10.0	95.4	32
Nicaragua	0.90	15.6	23	57.5	0.69	17.3	90.4	36
Pakistan	0.42	7.3	12	30.0	1.51	37.9	75.2	40
Panama	1.11	19.2	34	85.0	2.88	72.3	176.5	4
Paraguay	1.96	34.0	18	45.0	1.12	28.1	107.1	20
Peru	0.39	6.8	25	62.5	1.29	32.4	101.7	26
Philippines	0.56	9.7	34	85.0	3.98	100.0	194.7	3
Saudi Arabia	0.12	2.1	11	27.5	0.05	1.2	30.8	45
Sudan	0.68	11.8	23	57.5	0.09	2.2	71.5	42
Syria	2.48	43.0	18	45.0	1.69	42.4	130.4	12.5
Taiwan	0.15	2.6	20	50.0	2.24	56.2	108.8	19

Table A.5 (cont.)

Country	(a)		(b)		(c)			
	Raw	Adj.	Raw	Adj.	Raw	Adj.	Total	Rank
Thailand	0.13	2.2	27	67.5	1.56	39.2	108.9	18
Tunisia	1.65	28.6	30	75.0	1.31	32.9	136.5	9
Turkey	1.22	21.0	18	45.0	0.77	19.3	85.4	37
Uruguay	5.77	100.0	25	62.5	2.88	72.3	234.8	1
Venezuela	2.23	38.6	29	72.5	0.77	19.3	130.4	12.5

*Estimate

Table A.6 Rank Order of 48 Non-Western States in Distributive Capability

Perfect Score: 300.0

1	Uruguay	234.8	25	Cambodia	102.3
2	Argentina	207.6	26	Peru	101.7
3	Philippines	194.7	27	Lebanon	100.7
4	Panama	176.5	28	Burma	99.6
5	Costa Rica	161.3	Tie (29.5	Ecuador	99.4
6	Chile	155.1	(29.5	Ghana	99.4
7	Liberia	148.0	31	Malaysia	99.3
8	Bolivia	144.7	32	Morocco	95.4
9	Tunisia	136.5	33	Honduras	93.8
10	Korea	133.7	34	Ceylon	93.4
11	Brazil	131.8	35	Guatemala	93.3
Tie (12.5	Syria	130.4	36	Nicaragua	90.4
(12.5	Venezuela	130.4	37	Turkey	85.4
14	Jordan	119.8	38	Iran	84.9
15	Mexico	113.6	39	Colombia	80.9
16	Egypt	111.9	40	Pakistan	75.2
17	Cuba	109.8	41	Dominican Republic	73.3
18	Thailand	108.9	42	Sudan	71.5
19	Taiwan	108.8	43	Laos	66.3
—	Average —	107.3	44	Haiti	52.7
20	Paraguay	107.1	45	Saudi Arabia	30.8
21	Libya	107.0	46	Indonesia	29.2
22	Iraq	106.7	47	Afghanistan	25.9
23	El Salvador	105.2	48	Ethiopia	16.1
24	India	103.5			

Table A.7 Symbolic Capability of 48 Non-Western States

Country	(a)		(b)		(c)			
	Raw	Adj.	Raw	Adj.	Raw	Adj.	Total	Rank
Afghanistan	1.0	0.4	5	5.6	0.9	1.9	7.9	47
Argentina	154.0	64.7	90	100.0	2.4	5.1	169.8	3
Bolivia	23.0	9.7	35	38.8	0.9	1.9	50.4	30

Country	(a)		(b)		(c)			
	Raw	Adj.	Raw	Adj.	Raw	Adj.	Total	Rank
Brazil	51.0	21.4	50	55.5	0.8	1.7	78.6	19
Burma	8.0	3.4	60	66.6	2.5	5.3	75.3	23
Cambodia	3.0	1.3	20	22.2	3.7	7.9	31.4	38
Ceylon	36.0	15.1	65	72.2	47.0	100.0	187.3	2
Chile	79.0	33.2	80	88.8	6.7	14.2	136.2	7
Colombia	59.0	24.8	55	61.0	2.3	4.9	90.7	15
Costa Rica	91.0	38.2	80	88.8	1.1	2.3	129.3	9
Cuba	101.0	42.4	80	88.8	4.0	8.5	139.7	6
Dominican Republic	24.0	10.1	45	50.0	8.0	17.0	77.1	20
Ecuador	50.0	21.0	60	66.6	1.0	2.1	89.7	16
Egypt	25.0	10.5	25	27.8	1.7	3.6	41.9	34
El Salvador	33.0	13.9	40	44.4	16.0	34.0	92.3	14
Ethiopia	0.3	0.1	5	5.6	1.5	3.2	8.9	46
Ghana	18.0	7.6	25	27.8	6.3	13.4	48.8	31
Guatemala	27.0	11.3	30	33.3	7.0	14.9	59.5	27
Haiti	4.0	1.7	15	16.6	11.0	23.4	41.7	35
Honduras	23.0	9.7	40	44.4	1.8	3.8	57.9	29
India	7.0	2.9	20	22.2	15.5	33.0	58.1	28
Indonesia	7.0	2.9	20	22.2	3.2	6.8	31.9	37
Iran	6.0	2.5	15	16.6	1.2	2.6	21.7	42
Iraq	21.0	8.8	15	16.6	1.6	3.4	28.8	40
Jordan	9.0	3.8	20	22.2	1.5	3.2	29.2	39
Korea, Republic of	55.0	23.1	40	44.4	13.0	27.6	95.1	12
Laos	1.0	0.4	20	22.2	1.1	2.3	24.9	41
Lebanon	77.0	32.3	50	55.5	27.9	59.3	147.1	5
Liberia	1.0	0.4	10	11.1	0.8	1.7	13.2	44
Libya	6.0	2.5	10	11.1	0.3	0.6	14.2	43
Malaysia	50.0	21.0	40	44.4	8.1	17.2	82.6	18
Mexico	48.0	20.2	65	72.2	3.0	6.4	98.8	11
Morocco	23.0	9.7	15	16.6	4.0	8.5	34.8	36
Nicaragua	51.0	21.4	40	44.4	5.1	10.8	76.6	21
Pakistan	9.0	3.8	20	22.2	10.3	21.9	47.9	33
Panama	111.0	46.6	70	77.7	3.0	6.4	130.7	8
Paraguay	12.0	5.0	70	77.7	1.4	3.0	85.7	17
Peru	40.0	16.8	50	55.5	1.9	4.0	76.3	22
Philippines	19.0	8.0	65	72.2	9.9	21.1	101.3	10
Saudi Arabia	2.0	0.8	5	5.6	0.1	0.2	6.6	48
Sudan	2.0	0.8	10	11.1	0.2	0.4	12.3	45
Syria	44.0	18.5	30	33.3	5.5	11.7	63.5	26
Taiwan	33.0	13.9	50	55.5	44.0	93.6	163.0	4
Thailand	4.0	1.7	55	61.0	1.4	3.0	65.7	24
Tunisia	33.0	13.9	20	22.2	5.7	12.1	48.2	32

Table A.7 (cont.)

Country	(a) Raw	Adj.	(b) Raw	Adj.	(c) Raw	Adj.	Total	Rank
Turkey	32.0	13.4	35	38.8	6.0	12.8	65.0	25
Uruguay	233.0	100.0	85	94.4	4.0	8.5	202.9	1
Venezuela	71.0	29.8	55	61.0	1.8	3.8	94.6	13

Table A.8 Rank Order of 48 Non-Western States in Symbolic Capability

Perfect Score:		300.0			
1	Uruguay	202.9	25	Turkey	65.0
2	Ceylon	187.3	26	Syria	63.5
3	Argentina	169.8	27	Guatemala	59.5
4	Taiwan	163.0	28	India	58.1
5	Lebanon	147.1	29	Honduras	57.9
6	Cuba	139.7	30	Bolivia	50.4
7	Chile	136.2	31	Ghana	48.8
8	Panama	130.7	32	Tunisia	48.2
9	Costa Rica	129.3	33	Pakistan	47.9
10	Philippines	101.3	34	Egypt	41.9
11	Mexico	98.8	35	Haiti	41.7
12	Korea	95.1	36	Morocco	34.8
13	Venezuela	94.6	37	Indonesia	31.9
14	El Salvador	92.3	38	Cambodia	31.4
15	Colombia	90.7	39	Jordan	29.2
16	Ecuador	89.7	40	Iraq	28.8
17	Paraguay	85.7	41	Laos	24.9
18	Malaysia	82.6	42	Iran	21.7
19	Brazil	78.6	43	Libya	14.2
20	Dominican Republic	77.1	44	Liberia	13.2
21	Nicaragua	76.6	45	Sudan	12.3
22	Peru	76.3	46	Ethiopia	8.9
23	Burma	75.3	47	Afghanistan	7.9
—	Average —	73.6	48	Saudi Arabia	6.6
24	Thailand	65.7			

Table A.9 Responsive Capability of 48 Non-Western States

Country	(a) Raw	Adj.	(b) Raw	Adj.	(c) Raw	Adj.	Total	Rank
Afghanistan	0	0	1.2	3.1	63.8	52.3	55.4	46
Argentina	0	0	39.1	100.0	105.9	86.8	186.8	9
Bolivia	10	62.5	7.2	18.4	107.8	88.4	169.3	13
Brazil	6	37.5	9.7	24.8	111.7	91.6	153.9	19
Burma	4	25.0	3.8	9.7	83.9	68.8	103.5	36
Cambodia	4	25.0	4.8	12.3	73.0	59.9	97.2	38

262

Country	(a)		(b)		(c)			
	Raw	Adj.	Raw	Adj.	Raw	Adj.	Total	Rank
Ceylon	12	75.0	5.7	14.6	108.0	88.6	178.2	10
Chile	15	93.8	29.5	75.5	119.5	98.0	267.3	2
Colombia	12	75.0	12.1	31.0	108.6	89.0	195.0	5
Costa Rica	15	93.8	7.6	19.5	111.9	91.8	205.1	4
Cuba	3	18.8	23.7	60.7	91.4	74.9	154.4	18
Dominican Republic	5	31.2	6.6	16.9	91.6	75.1	123.2	33
Ecuador	5	31.2	8.5	21.8	109.7	90.0	143.0	24
Egypt	4	25.0	12.5	32.0	86.4	70.8	127.8	29
El Salvador	6	37.5	5.2	13.3	101.7	83.4	134.2	28
Ethiopia	0	0	0.2	0.5	62.2	51.0	51.5	48
Ghana	0	0	2.7	6.9	91.0	74.6	81.5	41
Guatemala	5	31.2	4.0	10.2	104.1	85.4	126.8	31
Haiti	0	0	1.0	2.6	79.1	64.9	67.5	44
Honduras	12	75.0	2.2	5.6	105.1	86.2	166.8	14
India	9	56.2	3.2	8.2	107.1	87.8	152.2	20
Indonesia	5	31.2	3.0	7.7	95.0	77.9	116.8	34
Iran	3	18.8	15.2	38.9	80.8	66.2	123.9	32
Iraq	5	31.2	12.3	31.5	79.1	64.9	127.6	30
Jordan	0	0	16.8	43.0	72.8	59.7	102.7	37
Korea, Republic of	8	50.0	8.0	20.5	89.4	73.3	143.8	23
Laos	1	6.2	0.8	2.0	70.1	57.5	65.7	45
Lebanon	10	62.5	10.4	26.6	101.4	83.1	172.2	11
Liberia	9	56.2	0.0	0.0	101.0	82.8	139.0	25
Libya	0	0	5.2	13.3	75.7	62.1	75.4	42
Malaysia	9	56.2	11.7	29.9	103.8	85.1	171.2	12
Mexico	12	75.0	11.0	28.2	106.4	87.2	190.4	7
Morocco	5	31.2	10.6	27.1	96.2	78.9	137.2	27
Nicaragua	9	56.2	6.4	16.4	103.2	84.6	157.2	16
Pakistan	5	31.2	2.0	5.1	72.8	59.7	96.0	39
Panama	5	31.2	11.6	29.7	109.4	89.7	150.6	22
Paraguay	9	56.2	7.3	18.7	94.0	77.1	152.0	21
Peru	10	62.5	6.9	17.7	103.6	85.0	165.2	15
Philippines	12	75.0	7.1	18.2	118.0	96.8	190.0	8
Saudi Arabia	0	0	2.7	6.9	55.8	45.8	52.7	47
Sudan	5	31.2	1.2	3.1	69.4	56.9	91.2	40
Syria	3	18.8	17.1	43.8	91.7	75.2	137.8	26
Taiwan	2	12.5	12.7	32.5	81.7	67.0	112.0	35
Thailand	1	6.2	1.4	3.6	71.0	58.2	68.0	43
Tunisia	9	56.2	8.0	20.5	97.3	79.8	156.5	17
Turkey	15	93.8	3.6	9.2	110.7	90.8	193.8	6
Uruguay	16	100.0	30.8	78.8	120.9	100.0	278.8	1
Venezuela	15	93.8	22.2	56.8	109.8	90.0	240.6	3

Table A.10   Rank Order of 48 Non-Western States in Responsive Capability

	Perfect Score:	300.0			
1	Uruguay	278.8	25	Liberia	139.0
2	Chile	267.3	26	Syria	137.8
3	Venezuela	240.6	27	Morocco	137.2
4	Costa Rica	205.1	28	El Salvador	134.2
5	Colombia	195.0	29	Egypt	127.8
6	Turkey	193.8	30	Iraq	127.6
7	Mexico	190.4	31	Guatemala	126.8
8	Philippines	190.0	32	Iran	123.9
9	Argentina	186.8	33	Dominican Republic	123.2
10	Ceylon	178.2	34	Indonesia	116.8
11	Lebanon	172.2	35	Taiwan	112.0
12	Malaysia	171.2	36	Burma	103.5
13	Bolivia	169.3	37	Jordan	102.7
14	Honduras	166.8	38	Cambodia	97.2
15	Peru	165.2	39	Pakistan	96.0
16	Nicaragua	157.2	40	Sudan	91.2
17	Tunisia	156.5	41	Ghana	81.5
18	Cuba	154.4	42	Libya	75.4
19	Brazil	153.9	43	Thailand	68.0
20	India	152.2	44	Haiti	67.5
21	Paraguay	152.0	45	Laos	65.7
22	Panama	150.6	46	Afghanistan	55.4
23	Korea	143.8	47	Saudi Arabia	52.7
24	Ecuador	143.0	48	Ethiopia	51.5
—	Average —	140.6			

Table A.11 Total Record of System Performance of 48 Non-Western States

	Regulative Av.=153.2		Extractive Av.=71.5		Distributive Av.=107.3		Symbolic Av.=73.6		Responsive Av.=140.6		Total Av.=544.5	
	Score	Rank	Score	Rank	Score	Rank	Score	Rank	Score	Rank	Score	Rank
Afghanistan	149.2	20	50.6	28	25.9	47	7.9	47	55.4	46	289.0	47
Argentina	107.1	43	51.7	27	207.6	2	169.8	3	186.8	9	723.0	6
Bolivia	110.1	42	44.1	39	144.7	8	50.4	30	169.3	13	518.6	27
Brazil	130.6	32	75.2	18	131.8	11	78.6	19	153.9	19	570.1	21
Burma	142.7	26	77.5	15	99.6	28	75.3	23	103.5	36	498.6	32
Cambodia	258.9	3	84.9	13	102.3	25	31.4	38	97.2	38	574.7	19
Ceylon	149.1	21	53.9	26	93.4	34	187.3	2	178.2	10	661.9	11
Chile	182.8	12	115.0	7	155.1	6	136.2	7	267.3	2	856.4	2
Colombia	87.5	46	120.1	5	80.9	39	90.7	15	195.0	5	574.2	20
Costa Rica	184.6	11	68.7	21	161.3	5	129.3	9	205.1	4	749.0	3
Cuba	121.6	36	161.5	2	109.8	17	139.7	6	154.4	18	687.0	9
Dominican Republic	156.4	17	73.0	19	73.3	41	77.1	20	123.2	33	503.0	31
Ecuador	147.8	23	46.7	34	99.4	29.5	89.7	16	143.0	24	526.6	25
Egypt	204.2	7	77.4	16	111.9	16	41.9	34	127.8	29	563.2	23
El Salvador	120.6	37	37.9	42	105.2	23	92.3	14	134.2	28	490.2	34
Ethiopia	134.6	29	49.4	29	16.1	48	8.9	46	51.5	48	260.5	48
Ghana	130.9	31	47.4	31	99.4	29.5	48.8	31	81.5	41	408.0	40
Guatemala	98.3	45	32.7	45	93.3	35	59.5	27	126.8	31	410.6	39
Haiti	106.8	44	24.4	46	52.7	44	41.7	35	67.5	44	293.1	46
Honduras	118.2	41	46.9	33	93.8	33	57.9	29	166.8	14	483.6	35
India	142.1	27	69.8	20	103.5	24	58.1	28	152.2	20	525.7	26
Indonesia	79.7	47	77.0	17	29.2	46	31.9	37	116.8	34	334.6	44

Table A.11 (cont.)

	Regulative Av.=153.2		Extractive Av.=71.5		Distributive Av.=107.3		Symbolic Av.=73.6		Responsive Av.=140.6		Total Av.=544.5	
	Score	Rank	Score	Rank	Score	Rank	Score	Rank	Score	Rank	Score	Rank
Iran	160.8	16	45.4	36	84.9	38	21.7	42	123.9	32	436.7	37
Iraq	154.0	18	45.3	37	106.7	22	28.8	40	127.6	30	462.4	36
Jordan	261.4	1	195.4	1	119.8	14	29.2	39	102.7	37	708.5	7
Korea, Republic of	123.1	35	113.4	8	133.7	10	95.1	12	143.8	23	609.1	15
Laos	69.4	48	119.8	6	66.3	43	24.9	41	65.7	45	346.1	43
Lebanon	133.8	30	47.0	32	100.7	27	147.1	5	172.2	11	600.8	16
Liberia	145.9	24	135.7	3	148.0	7	13.2	44	139.0	25	581.8	18
Libya	226.2	5	67.7	22	107.0	21	14.2	43	75.4	42	490.5	33
Malaysia	203.5	8	62.6	23	99.3	31	82.6	18	171.2	12	619.2	14
Mexico	165.5	15	79.8	14	113.6	15	98.8	11	190.4	7	648.1	12
Morocco	191.6	10	58.4	24	95.4	32	34.8	36	137.2	27	517.4	28
Nicaragua	166.8	14	48.9	30	90.4	36	76.6	21	157.2	16	539.9	24
Pakistan	123.9	34	46.4	35	75.2	40	47.9	33	96.0	39	389.4	41
Panama	148.7	22	94.0	11	176.5	4	130.7	8	150.6	22	700.5	8
Paraguay	119.5	38	41.2	40	107.1	20	85.7	17	152.0	21	505.5	30
Peru	127.7	33	44.6	38	101.7	26	76.3	22	165.2	15	515.5	29
Philippines	199.1	9	55.7	25	194.7	3	101.3	10	190.0	8	740.8	5
Saudi Arabia	259.0	2	10.5	48	30.8	45	6.6	48	52.7	47	359.6	42
Sudan	118.3	40	17.2	47	71.5	42	12.3	45	91.2	40	310.5	45
Syria	144.5	25	92.6	12	130.4	12.5	63.5	26	137.8	26	568.8	22
Taiwan	240.5	4	123.6	4	108.8	19	163.0	4	112.0	35	747.9	14

Table A.11 (cont.)

	Regulative Av.=153.2		Extractive Av.=71.5		Distributive Av.=107.3		Symbolic Av.=73.6		Responsive Av.=140.6		Total Av.=544.5	
	Score	Rank	Score	Rank	Score	Rank	Score	Rank	Score	Rank	Score	Rank
Thailand	152.2	19	36.1	43	108.9	18	65.7	24	68.0	43	430.9	38
Tunisia	218.1	6	108.7	9	136.5	9	48.2	32	156.5	17	668.0	10
Turkey	141.9	28	100.0	10	85.4	37	65.0	25	193.8	6	586.1	17
Uruguay	177.1	13	32.8	44	234.8	1	202.9	1	278.8	1	926.4	1
Venezuela	118.7	39	38.4	41	130.4	12.5	94.6	13	240.6	3	622.7	13

Table A.12   Total Capabilities: Rank Order of 48 Non-Western States

Perfect Score:		1,500.0			
1	Uruguay	926.4	25	Ecuador	526.6
2	Chile	856.4	26	India	525.7
3	Costa Rica	749.0	27	Bolivia	518.6
4	Taiwan	747.9	28	Morocco	517.4
5	Philippines	740.8	29	Peru	515.5
6	Argentina	723.0	30	Paraguay	505.5
7	Jordan	708.5	31	Dominican Republic	503.0
8	Panama	700.5	32	Burma	498.6
9	Cuba	687.0	33	Libya	490.5
10	Tunisia	668.0	34	El Salvador	490.2
11	Ceylon	661.9	35	Honduras	483.6
12	Mexico	648.1	36	Iraq	462.4
13	Venezuela	622.7	37	Iran	436.7
14	Malaysia	619.2	38	Thailand	430.9
15	Korea, Republic of	609.1	39	Guatemala	410.6
16	Lebanon	600.8	40	Ghana	408.0
17	Turkey	586.1	41	Pakistan	389.4
18	Liberia	581.8	42	Saudi Arabia	359.6
19	Cambodia	574.7	43	Laos	346.1
20	Colombia	574.2	44	Indonesia	334.6
21	Brazil	570.1	45	Sudan	310.5
22	Syria	568.8	46	Haiti	293.1
23	Egypt	563.2	47	Afghanistan	289.0
—	Average —	544.5	48	Ethiopia	260.5
24	Nicaragua	539.9			

Table A.13 48 Non-Western States Distributed According to Upper, Middle, or Lower Thirds in 5 Capabilities

	Number of Capabilities in Which State Scored in Upper Third					
	0	1	2	3	4	5
Upper Third in All 5 Capabilities						Chile Mexico
Middle Third in All Remaining Capabilities	India	Syria Brazil	Malaysia Lebanon	Tunisia Panama	Costa Rica Philippines	
Middle Third in All Remaining Capabilities, Except Lowest Third in 1	Ecuador Ghana	Egypt Burma Morocco	Ceylon Cuba Liberia Nicaragua Turkey	Argentina Taiwan Korea	Uruguay	
Lowest Third in 2	Dominican Republic Thailand Iraq	Peru El Salvador Paraguay	Cambodia Libya Jordan Bolivia	Colombia Venezuela		
Lowest Third in 3	Guatemala Afghanistan Ethiopia	Honduras Iran	None			
Lowest Third in 4	Indonesia	Laos Saudi Arabia				
Lowest Third in 5	Haiti Sudan Pakistan					

INDEX